D0971569

High Noon on the Electronic Frontier

Digital Communication
Edward Barrett, editor

High Noon on the Electronic Frontier: Conceptual Issues in Cyberspace
Peter Ludlow, 1996

Technical Communication, Multimedia, and Information Systems
Edward Barrett, editor

The Nurnberg Funnel: Designing Minimalist Instruction for Practical Computer Skill, John M. Carroll, 1990

Hypermedia and Literary Studies, edited by Paul Delany and George P. Landow, 1991

Rhetoric, Innovation, Technology: Case Studies of Technical Communication in Technology Transfers, Stephen Doheny-Farina, 1992

Sociomedia: Multimedia, Hypermedia, and the Social Construction of Knowledge, edited by Edward Barrett, 1992

The Digital Word: Text-Based Computing in the Humanities, edited by George P. Landow and Paul Delany, 1993

Contextual Media: Multimedia and Interpretation, edited by Edward Barrett and Marie Redmond, 1995

High Noon on the Electronic Frontier
Conceptual Issues in Cyberspace

Peter Ludlow

The MIT Press
Cambridge, Massachusetts
London, England

This book was set in Sabon by Northeastern Graphic Services, Inc.
Printed and bound in the United States of America.

Library of Congress Cataloging-in-Publication Data

Ludlow, Peter, 1957–
High noon on the electronic frontier : conceptual issues in cyberspace / Peter Ludlow.
p. cm. — (Digital communication)
Includes bibliographical references and index.
ISBN 0-262-12196-4 (alk. paper). — ISBN 0-262-62103-7 (pbk. : alk. paper)
1. Computers—social aspects. 2. Information superhighway—Social aspects. 3. Computer networks—Security measures. 4. Sex—Computer network resources. I. Series.
QA76.9.C66L84 1996
302.23—dc20 96-3987
CIP

for lrepetti

Contents

Series Foreword

Digital Communication is one of the most exciting, rapidly expanding fields of study and practice throughout the world, as witnessed by the increasing number of Web sites and users of the Internet, as well as publication and use of multimedia CD-ROM titles in schools, homes, and corporate environments. In addition, Web and multimedia publications have created a vast secondary literature of scholarly analysis in a range of subject areas. Professional societies and degree-granting programs devoted to digital communication have steadily increased. And the language and concepts of digital life have become central in popular culture. In cyberspace the roles of writer and audience are no longer static but dynamic; the concept of text is no longer fixed but fluid. Computational technology has delivered us a powerful tool for the creation, presentation, exchange, and annotation of a text (in words, images, video, and audio) — so powerful that we speak in terms of transparent and seamless information environments that integrate all media.

We are witnessing a profound revolution in communication and learning in a post-Gutenberg world. The MIT Press series on Digital Communication will present advanced research into all aspects of this revolutionary change in our forms of expression, thought, and being. This research will be published in traditional book format or as Web sites or multimedia CD-ROM titles as demanded by content. As this series finds its expression in hardcopy or in digital format, it will seek to explore and define new genres of thought and expression offered by digital media.

Edward Barrett

Foreword

Mike Godwin

Thinking isn't tough—we're all born knowing how to do it. But thinking *rigorously,* with an eye for unexpected insights and conclusons, is hard work. So hard, in fact, that philosophers have been dedicating themselves for years to the task of learning (and relearning) how to think about the problems, old and new, that we have to face.

Nowhere has the challenge of thinking rigorously and clearly been greater than it has in cyberspace—what John Perry Barlow first called "the Electronic Frontier." Here we have a whole new mode of communications, of interaction, and of action itself—how are we to map our understandings of law, ethics, psychology, and the social order to this new arena of human behavior? In this book my friend Peter Ludlow takes an important first step by assembling a multitude of perspectives on this question and the many issues it raises.

These perspectives, from a range of observers of the emerging cyberculture (including yours truly), take the reader through what might be called the Standard Philosophical Journey, addressing basic questions like, Who am I? What am I? What do I know? How do I know what I know? What is my relationship to others? To the state? To the world at large? What are my abilities? What are my rights? How do I solve problems in this world?

This book suggests that when we enter cyberspace, we can't assume that we know the answers to these questions merely because we have some sense of what the answers are in nonvirtual reality. It's an attempt to plant the seeds of the kind of radical doubt that, like Descartes's, can lead to radical insights.

Among the issues Ludlow and his contributors address:

Property rights At what point does it make sense to say one has property rights on the Electronic Frontier? The ongoing tension between those with vested interests in so-called "intellectual property" and those who believe "information wants to be free" echoes the range wars between the cattlemen and the sheep men of nineteenth-century America. The questions being raised in this century are manifold: Can a copyright be "stolen"? Does it even make sense to focus on "the right to copy" when copying in cyberspace is both as easy and as necessary as breathing? Do authors have other kinds of rights in their digital works? Moral rights? Rights grounded in natural law? Answering these questions is central to thinking clearly about "property in cyberspace."

Hacking and computer intrusion Is the kid who hacks into a university mainframe a thief? A burglar? A trespasser? Should the courts throw the book at him? Should he be prosecuted at all? Are hackers threats to our privacy? Or are they the pillars of our future industrial competitiveness? Are they motivated by curiosity, love of technology, or something more sinister?

Privacy It has long been known that computers can be used to invade our privacy—thanks to the recent spread of encryption technology, however, it has become possible to use computers to *enhance* our privacy. This technology may be a boon to privacy, but it may come at a significant social cost: what if the ability of criminals to encode their communications erodes law enforcement's ability to protect the rest of us? What if terrorists use encryption to plot attacks like the World Trade Center bombing or the Oklahoma City bombing? What if *nuclear* terrorists use encryption to conceal the movements and placement of radioactive materials, or of a hydrogen bomb?

Nor is encryption the only aspect of privacy that's relevant in cyberspace. The federal government in the United States has increasingly sought guarantees of its ability to conduct wiretaps, and has been moving most recently in the direction of seeking greater access to commercial transactional data (how much could the government learn about you if it knew how you spent every dollar?). How do we balance the public goods of safety and security against the individual goods of privacy and autonomy? Can they be balanced? And are citizens willing to make the hard choices necessary to strike such a balance?

Freedom of speech and press The Electronic Frontier has spawned the greatest experiment in freedom of expression that the world has ever seen. No longer do you have to have ownership or access to millions of dollars of equipment to reach a mass audience—nowadays you can speak to tens or hundreds of thousands of other people for the cost of a terminal and a modem. But this revolution creates new legal problems as the laws of older media are applied to this new medium. Should system operators be held responsible for their users in the same way that newspaper publishers are held responsible for their reporters? Or is there something different about this medium that necessitates the crafting of new legal rules? Is there a way to adapt the law of libel so that people whose reputations are injured on the Net can be assured of redress? Or is libel law obsolete altogether, now that (potentially) everyone can correct the public record from a computer terminal? Are there classes of dangerous information (sexual materials, bomb-making instructions) that ought to be banned from the Net? Could the government even censor the Net if it wanted to?

Community In the course of a mere century, the American people have transmuted themselves from a primarily rural to a primarily urban population. With that change has come a sense of alienation and loss of community. Increasingly, though, it becomes possible to recreate that lost community in cyberspace, by forming communities of interest that are not bound by the accidents of geography. But are they really community? Can you really call someone a "neighbor" if you can't see her face or hear her voice? Is "the virtual community" something real, or is it "a consensual hallucination," like science-fiction author William Gibson's notion of cyberspace? If we give our allegiances to virtual communities, are we abandoning our geographic communities in a sort of "urban flight"? And to what extent should other communities, and the legal system itself, acknowledge and respect virtual communities?

Identity There's no subject touchier in late twentieth-century American culture than the subject of identity. It's a matter of course nowadays for citizens to define themselves by declaring their identities in various ways. We live in a world of labels: Democrat, Republican, African-American, Jew, heterosexual, lesbian, Catholic, New Yorker, Southerner, lawyer, teacher, male, female, child, adult, disabled. So what happens when you enter a world in which you can leave all the labels behind? A world in which Martin Luther King, Jr.'s dream is a necessary reality—we are judged not by the color of our skins, but by the content of our character?

Other than the fact that these issues are all raised by the existence of cyberspace, they have one element in common: They can be addressed only by critical, rigorous, and—most important—imaginative thinking, and there are no short cuts to the answers. You can't figure out the moral significance of changing gender online by looking at spreadsheet calculations. You can't balance public and private interests regarding privacy on any kind of physical scale. You can't tell whether information is property just by looking at it or holding it in your hand. In his preface, Peter comments that you don't need a professional philosopher to raise these issues. I think it's also true that, one way or another, the Electronic Frontier will require us all to become philosophers sooner or later.

I've been immersed in these issues for so long that I can only feel envious of readers who are encountering them for the first time here in Peter Ludlow's book. Prepare to have your minds expanded—you're about to become a new explorer on the Electronic Frontier.

Preface

The last time I edited a volume for the MIT Press, the contributors included writers like Plato, Aristotle, and Kant, and the readings came from works with titles like *Critique of Pure Reason*. This time the contributors have names like "The Mentor" and "humdog," and the sources include publications like the e-journal *Pirate*. Heads up, Toto, we're not in Kansas anymore!

In case you were wondering, I haven't gone pomo, and there is an explanation for all this. In the fall of 1994 I taught an undergraduate course entitled "Philosophical Issues on the Electronic Frontier." My plan was to lead with Julian Dibbell's *Village Voice* article "Rape in Cyberspace" and then move to more standard readings that might typically be taught in a course on computer ethics. Things began well enough, but the class slipped into a collective coma when we moved on to the standard academic readings in this area. Accordingly, I did what any reasonable person would do under the same circumstances—I sold out. I went back to assigning the more "in your face" rants and manifestos that are easy enough to find in cyberspace but virtually impossible to find in text books.

When I turned to the more gonzo readings, the class woke up (which always helps when you are trying to teach something) and it actually began to think seriously about some of the deeper issues underlying these assigned electronic rants. This shouldn't be surprising, really. Most of the academic writing on cyberspace is just awful. It either reeks of half-learned post-modern cant, or is a dense thicket of bad sociology. It puts me to sleep, so why shouldn't it put my students to sleep? Besides, even for students, it is sometimes more fun to do the thinking part yourself.

Sometimes we academics can analyze things to death, when maybe it would be better to set up the problem in an interesting way, and then just leave the room.

Basically, that's what this collection is all about—raising difficult conceptual issues and then leaving the room. As it turns out, you don't need professional philosophers or sociologists or psychologists or really professional anythings to accomplish this. What you need are people who see matters a little differently than the rest of us, and who also have the ability to explain their positions and maybe offer some sort of justification for their positions. Oh, there are flaws in some of these arguments, but these writings aren't here because they are paradigms of logical integrity. Rather they are here because they prompt debate on a deep conceptual level.

Starting any old debate is easy; one can just say "Abortion: pro or con?" But there are certain topics which do not lend themselves quite so readily to lively exchanges. Walk into a room of freshmen and ask them what they think a community is, or what they think the nature of the self is, and you are apt to get blank stares. But frame the question around the claim that a person can have a kind of embodiment in his or her MUD character, and you have a new way of thinking about these issues—crucially one that lends itself to discussion.

That explains why I selected the readings I have, but it doesn't exactly explain why I wanted to reprint them in a book (i.e., a book made of paper and ink). Since most of these readings are out there on the Internet, I could have set up a web site with pointers to most of these readings. Well, I probably will *still* do that, but to ask why the book is then necessary is to fail to understand what books are all about. They aren't *just* conveyers of information, but are vehicles that provide information in a particular format—a format that has a number of advantages. For me, at least, it is much easier to navigate around a paper book, and this ease of navigation is a feature of the paper book being a three-dimensional object. I know the location of certain passages in the book because I know how deep into the book the passage lies. I often remember whether the passage is on the right page or left, and so on.

Now I realize that contemporary text analysis software makes it possible to navigate around in electronic books, but these programs (while often useful) have their limitations. Maybe, within a few generations, everyone will be much better at navigating in a book with text analysis software and will be utterly unable to turn the pages of a paper book without serious injury. But that is some time off, and by then this book will be long out of print.

The key point to see is that by collecting these writings I am not attempting to "bottle" information that otherwise would be traveling freely on the Internet. Rather, this book is an attempt to provide that information in a certain format. What you are paying for is getting the information in that format, not the information itself.

I should hasten to add, however, that at least as I write this preface, not everything in this book is on the Internet (although it is perhaps being scanned and uploaded as you read this). Some of the essays were newly commissioned for this volume, and I have also supplied introductions to each of the five major sections of the book. Perhaps a few words are in order about my aim in writing these introductions.

Some of the readings in this book advocate what must seem like extreme positions to middle America (whoever, whatever, or wherever that is), as well as to my students (who may or may not be middle Americans). While these more "radical" writings do not generate blank stares, they sometimes generate rolled eyes and remarks to the effect that the author should "get a life." I attribute this reaction to our lifetime diet of information baby food—information strained and processed by the media to make it digestible by all, but utterly flavorless and utterly uninteresting. When nonprocessed ideas come along it is not surprising that we choke on them or spit them out; we simply aren't used to their texture or taste. It is true that some fringe ideas are nasty tasting, but if you approach them with an open mind, many are tasty and intellectually nourishing. The problem is getting people to try them.

As a first feeble attempt to solve this problem I have written section introductions that try to explain these unfamiliar ideas in ways that cast them in a reasonable light. Readers should take note that these introductions are therefore devices of pedagogy and not necessarily my position papers. If pressed to say whether I agreed or disagreed with any of these ideas, I would have to say that it is really too early to hold honest and informed opinions about most of these issues. In my view the debate has just begun, and it would be a shame if we took hard stands before the debate began rather than let our stands be informed by the course of the debate.

These coming debates about the Electronic Frontier will doubtless spawn their share of conferences, academic journals, and even academic departments—all to little profit, in my view. I'm all for academic discourse (I spend the better part of my life engaged in it), but it seems to me that the methods of the academy have evolved in response to questions of a different character, and I am doubtful that those methods really have anything useful to contribute to the issues being sorted out on the Electronic Frontier. Mind you, I don't object to people holding academic conferences on cyberspace (just so long as I don't have to go to them) and I don't even mind the inevitable new journals (so long as I don't have to read them).

None of this is to say that I won't be participating in discussions about conceptual issues on the Electronic Frontier, but it is to say I won't be doing it in the academy. Rather, I'll be discussing them with my friends in cyberspace. You're welcome to join us, of course. Just look us up out there, somewhere . . .

Peter Ludlow
ludlow@well.com
http://semlab2.sbs.sunysb.edu/users/pludlow/ludlow.html

Acknowledgments

I have learned an awful lot about these issues through interactions with my friends in various electronic communities, including Mindvox, the WELL, the Italian system Agora, and a number of bulletin boards found on the Italian Cybernet network—in particular the Decoder BBS (in Milano), the Senza Confine BBS (in Taranto), and the Trento based Bits Against the Empire (which was recently shut down by Italian authorities and remains off-line as this volume goes to press). I have learned the most, however, in my visits to the WELL, particularly in the eff, vc, and mondo conferences, and above all from my dialogues with wellperns (and sometimes wellperns) amicus, berny, bruces, dave, drude, gareth, humdog, jonl, jthomas, julian, prof, quit, roger, rusirius, steeler, and a legion of others. Special thanks are due to mnemonic (Mike Godwin) for many helpful discussions, and not least for writing the foreword to this work.

For comments on my piece "Hardware 1: The Italian Hacker Crackdown," special thanks are due to Bruce Sterling and Bernardo Parella, as well as to Andrea Sannucci from the Senza Confine BBS, Gomma from the Decoder BBS, and Luc Pac from Bits Against the Empire. None of them are responsible for mistakes that remain, nor should it be supposed that they agree with the conclusions I reached.

Although they may not realize it, my colleagues at Stony Brook also have had a profound influence on the choice of these materials and on the shape of the introductory sections. In particular, discussions with Mike Simon helped me to get clearer on issues of property and censorship, while discussions with Marshall Spector and Don Ihde helped me to get more clear on issues in the philosophy of technology generally. The introduction to section 5 has benefited from discussions with Donn

Welton on the philosophy of body, with Ken Baynes on the Frankfurt School ideas about community, and in particular from discussions with Norah Martin on social theories of the self and with Emily Zakin on the construction of gender.

In thanking Stony Brook colleagues, I would be remiss if I forgot to thank Patrick Heelan, whose actions as Dean of Humanities and Fine Arts back in 1991-92 first piqued my interest in the legal issues of cyberspace, and led me to make my initial contacts with the Electronic Frontier Foundation. I might have found the EFF in any case, but I doubt that I would have had the same empathy for its causes had I not myself been the target of extreme technophobia.

Even with all the help just mentioned, this project absolutely would not have happened were it not for the encouragement (i.e., arm twisting) by Teri Mendelsohn and Amy Pierce of the MIT Press. There were times (most of the times, in fact) when I didn't think I could afford to expend the effort necessary to complete this project. As it turns out, I was right. I couldn't afford it. Still, somehow I did it, and I'm glad I did.

Much credit is also due my students in phil 285, who were assigned an earlier incarnation of this material, and who helped me fine-tune the reading list. Although that course ended with the last class of Fall 1994, it lives on through the course e-list which continues to be active as of this writing. (School is never out in cyberspace.)

Finally, I want to thank Lori Repetti, who has discussed virtually every reading in this volume with me, and who has read and commented on all of the section introductions. Her contribution to the paper on the Italian crackdown was also invaluable, as she not only provided helpful comments, but also corrected errors in my translations from the Italian. I won't say the usual words here about how she was so understanding while I devoted my attention to this project. Rather, I want to thank her for taking time to help me, when those energies should have been devoted to her much more important research on the (rapidly dying) dialects of Northern Italy. For these, and many other reasons, this book is dedicated to her.

I

Property Rights, Piracy, etc.: Does Information "Want to Be Free"?

In the industrialized Western nations we have a fairly well developed notion of property and property rights. We are inclined to think, for example, that we can own pieces of land if we pay for them and that we can likewise own the minerals in that land. More generally, we are inclined to think that if we have legally purchased something like a car or a bicycle, it is ours. No one may take it from us without fair compensation. There are other views, or course. A Marxist might argue that all property belongs to the state (or the workers, after the state has withered away). Others might argue that no one (neither persons nor nations) has sole claim to land. This is a view often attributed to hunter-gatherer cultures, for example.

It would probably be useful for philosophers to give more serious consideration to the nature of property rights and how they are grounded, but, even if our assumptions about property rights are poorly grounded, in the case of physical property they at least have the virtue of being clear. The same cannot be said about our grasp of intellectual property rights.

To see the problem raised by intellectual property rights, simply contrast the case of the car that I own with the case of a program I have written. You can steal my car, and in doing so you deprive me of my property (at least until the insurance company pays up). But if you copy my computer program (in effect, if you pirate it) I still have the program. In a certain sense, intellectual property cannot be "stolen." Indeed, the law distinguishes "theft" (which applies to physical property), from "infringement" (which applies to intellectual property). You can infringe on my intellectual property rights by copying my program or song or patent, and in so doing you apparently deprive me of income, but it isn't exactly the same thing as stealing.

A number of individuals have gone so far as to question the very idea of intellectual property rights (see, for example, the readings in this section by Barlow and by Garfinkel, Stallman, and Kapor). It is one thing, they say, for someone to claim ownership of land or the means of production, but it is quite another for someone to claim ownership of ideas or information. Suppose, for example, that I discover a property of natural numbers that turns out to be useful in encryption technology. Is it really right that I should claim ownership of this idea? Isn't it the height of hubris for me to claim ownership of a mathematical law that, for all we know, some clever extraterrestrial programmer came up with centuries ago?

This issue has all the markings of a classical ethical dispute. On the one hand there are those who claim that it is a basic right to enjoy the fruits of one's labors, while on the other hand there are those who claim that no labors can entitle one to ownership of information. How are such disputes to be settled? A number of participants in the debate appear to make "consequentialist" arguments for their respective positions. In the great tradition of utilitarian philosophers like Jeremy Bentham and John Stuart Mill, they argue that protecting (or, contrarily, ignoring) intellectual property rights will contribute to the greatest good for the greatest number of people.

For example, some argue that if intellectual property rights are not protected no one will take the trouble to develop programs and patents and so forth (see, for example, the reading from Heckel). Perhaps potential programmers will go into law or accounting or (even worse) philosophy, and we shall all be poorer as a consequence. On the other hand there are those (e.g., Garfinkel, Stallman, and Kapor) who argue that eliminating software copyrights would actually contribute to the development and distribution of ideas and that it would benefit the programmer as well. Which side is right? For the utilitarian it may come down to a debate over the economic consequences of enforced property rights.

Of course, utilitarianism is not the only brand of ethics in town, and other folks might be inclined to argue for property rights on the basis of other considerations (e.g., natural law). Such arguments are difficult to find, or at least difficult to find in any sort of articulate form. Still, one can imagine arguments of this character, and I suppose they need to be considered. For example, one might think that quite apart from the economic consequences of protecting property there is the deeper ethical principle that one has the right to the fruits of one's labors. Of course, for the most part, principles of this nature tend to be defended on economic grounds (people produce more when they keep the fruits of their labors, etc.), but if this economic argument were somehow discredited it is likely that the general ethical principle would be retained—at least in some quarters. But why would it be retained? That is difficult to say.

It is one thing to ask, in the abstract, whether intellectual property rights are a good thing. It is quite another to ask whether, given our current laws, intellectual property rights should be flouted—that is, whether software piracy should be (illegally) practiced. The editorial from the electronic 'zine *Pirate* argues that it should. The stated justification is that pirate boards contribute to the widespread distribution of software, and that eventually corporations will want to buy that software for service, upgrades, and so forth.

Before we consider the merits of such a position we should perhaps get clear on what piracy is. For example, we need to distinguish software "piracy" from software "bootlegging." Roughly, the bootlegger copies software for profit (e.g., making multiple copies and selling them), while the pirate merely makes illicit copies for personal use, and perhaps for swapping pirated software with friends. A "pirate board," then, is a BBS set up to be a location where individuals can swap pirated software, and where money is not changing hands.

Strictly speaking, most of the readers of this book are software pirates. Nearly all of you have at least one piece of software that is unregistered or that was copied by a friend. Some of you may even have swapped software on a pirate board. Technically, this is copyright infringement and against the law; but just how wrong is it? For example, it is technically against the law to drive 56 miles an hour in a 55 mph zone, but we would hardly consider someone who drove over 55 a menace to society (in fact, we might reserve that opinion for those who obstruct traffic by puttering along at 55). Is software piracy like breaking the speed limit a little? Or is it even more justifiable, because in the long run it leads to good ends? Or is software piracy a form of civil disobedience? That may seem like a stretch, but if you really believed that information "wants to be free" (i.e., that it is wrong for individuals to hoard information), you might be tempted by this argument.

Even if we agree that software piracy is wrong, a number of conceptual issues surround that of how we should respond to piracy when we encounter it. First of all, what is the value of the pirated intellectual property? With normal property theft—for example, when someone steals my toaster—it is clear enough how to measure the loss. But how does one measure the loss of a piece of pirated software? By the retail value of the software? Such measures seem more apt for evaluating the loss from the theft of toasters. If someone steals a toaster from the store, the store will be unable to recoup its investment in that piece of inventory, but if someone downloads a program from a pirate board, no one's inventory is diminished. Nor is it reasonable to suppose that everyone who pulls free software off a pirate board would have otherwise purchased that piece of software. Precisely how do we quantify the losses (if, indeed, there are any)?

The situation becomes even more complex when the piece of intellectual property is not a program but a trade secret or a piece of proprietary information. The reading by Godwin discusses one of the most celebrated cases of such piracy (for background, see also the discussion in Barlow's "Crime and Puzzlement" in appendix 1). After a hacker downloaded a description of AT&T's 911 system, AT&T calculated the value of the loss at several hundred thousand dollars. The case was eventually dismissed when it turned out that another branch of AT&T was selling the same document for just a few dollars. Where did AT&T go wrong in evaluating its losses? That remains to be seen. This case, however, shows just how easy it is to be off by several orders of magnitude in evaluating such losses.

It is also worth keeping in mind that whatever the evils of pirated intellectual property, attempts to thwart such piracy can be disastrously counterproductive. Several recent "crackdowns" have highlighted the dangers. One example surrounded the case of the pilfered 911 document and subsequent events, such as the bust of Steve Jackson Games discussed by Barlow in appendix 1. Another example is the Italian crackdown code-named "Hardware 1" (see appendix 2) in which nearly one third of the electronic bulletin boards in Italy were busted because of the pretense of software piracy. In each case the rights of a number of innocent people were trampled by government zeal to crack down on alleged piracy of some form or another. The moral is that whatever the evils of piracy might be, it does not immediately follow that any arbitrary ham-handed governmental response is appropriate. To the contrary, responses will have to be measured, and government institutions will need to be cognizant of the rights of innocent bystanders. Is effective government action even possible within such constraints? That is very much an open question. It may well be that government institutions (American, Italian, or whatever) are just not the appropriate organizations for halting the activities of amateur pirates.

1

Selling Wine without Bottles: The Economy of Mind on the Global Net

John Perry Barlow

If nature has made any one thing less susceptible than all others of exclusive property, it is the action of the thinking power called an idea, which an individual may exclusively possess as long as he keeps it to himself; but the moment it is divulged, it forces itself into the possession of everyone, and the receiver cannot dispossess himself of it. Its peculiar character, too, is that no one possesses the less, because every other possesses the whole of it. He who receives an idea from me, receives instruction himself without lessening mine; as he who lights his taper at mine, receives light without darkening me. That ideas should freely spread from one to another over the globe, for the moral and mutual instruction of man, and improvement of his condition, seems to have been peculiarly and benevolently designed by nature, when she made them, like fire, expansible over all space, without lessening their density at any point, and like the air in which we breathe, move, and have our physical being, incapable of confinement or exclusive appropriation. Inventions then cannot, in nature, be a subject of property.
—Thomas Jefferson

Throughout the time I've been groping around Cyberspace, there has remained unsolved an immense conundrum that seems to be at the root of nearly every legal, ethical, governmental, and social vexation to be found in the Virtual World. I refer to the problem of digitized property.

The riddle is this: if our property can be infinitely reproduced and instantaneously distributed all over the planet without cost, without our knowledge, without its even leaving our possession, how can we protect it? How are we going to get paid for the work we do with our minds? And, if we can't get paid, what will assure the continued creation and distribution of such work?

Since we don't have a solution to what is a profoundly new kind of challenge, and are apparently unable to delay the galloping digitization of everything not obstinately physical, we are sailing into the future on a sinking ship.

This vessel, the accumulated canon of copyright and patent law, was developed to convey forms and methods of expression entirely different from the vaporous cargo it is now being asked to carry. It is leaking as much from within as without.

Legal efforts to keep the old boat floating are taking three forms: a frenzy of deck chair rearrangement, stern warnings to the passengers that if she goes down, they will face harsh criminal penalties, and serene, glassy-eyed denial.

Intellectual property law cannot be patched, retrofitted, or expanded to contain the gasses of digitized expression any more than real estate law might be revised to cover the allocation of broadcasting spectrum. (Which, in fact, rather resembles what is being attempted here.) We will need to develop an entirely new set of methods as befits this entirely new set of circumstances.

Most of the people who actually create soft property—the programmers, hackers, and Net surfers—already know this. Unfortunately, neither the companies they work for nor the lawyers these companies hire have enough direct experience with immaterial goods to understand why they are so problematic. They are proceeding as though the old laws can somehow be made to work, either by grotesque expansion or by force. They are wrong.

The source of this conundrum is as simple as its solution is complex. Digital technology is detaching information from the physical plane, where property law of all sorts has always found definition.

Throughout the history of copyrights and patents, the proprietary assertions of thinkers have been focused not on their ideas but on the expression of those ideas. The ideas themselves, as well as facts about the phenomena of the world, were considered to be the collective property of humanity. One could claim franchise, in the case of copyright, on the precise turn of phrase used to convey a particular idea or the order in which facts were presented.

The point at which this franchise was imposed was that moment when the "word became flesh" by departing the mind of its originator and entering some physical object, whether book or widget. The subsequent arrival of other commercial media besides books didn't alter the legal importance of this moment. Law protected expression and, with few (and recent) exceptions, to express was to make physical.

Protecting physical expression had the force of convenience on its side. Copyright worked well because, Gutenberg notwithstanding, it was hard to make a book. Furthermore, books froze their contents into a condition that was as challenging to alter as it was to reproduce. Counterfeiting or distributing counterfeit volumes were obvious and visible activities, easy enough to catch somebody in the act of doing. Finally, unlike unbounded words or images, books had material surfaces to which one could attach copyright notices, publisher's marques, and price tags.

Mental to physical conversion was even more central to patent. A patent, until recently, was either a description of the form into which materials were to be rendered in the service of some purpose or a description of the process by which rendition occurred. In either case, the conceptual heart of patent was the material result. If no purposeful object could be rendered due to some material limitation, the patent was rejected. Neither a Klein bottle nor a shovel made of silk could be patented. It had to be a thing and the thing had to work.

Thus the rights of invention and authorship adhered to activities in the physical world. One didn't get paid for ideas but for the ability to deliver them into reality. For all practical purposes, the value was in the conveyance and not the thought conveyed.

In other words, the bottle was protected, not the wine.

Now, as information enters Cyberspace, the native home of Mind, these bottles are vanishing. With the advent of digitization, it is now possible to replace all previous information storage forms with one meta-bottle: complex—and highly liquid—patterns of ones and zeros.

Even the physical/digital bottles to which we've become accustomed, floppy disks, CD-ROM's, and other discrete, shrink-wrappable bit-packages, will disappear as all computers jack in to the global Net. While the Internet may never include every single CPU on the planet, it is more than doubling every year and can be expected to become the principal medium of information conveyance, and perhaps eventually, the only one.

Once that has happened, all the goods of the Information Age—all of expressions once contained in books or film strips or records or newsletters—will exist either as pure thought or something very much like thought: voltage conditions darting around the Net at the speed of light, in conditions which one might behold in effect, as glowing pixels or transmitted sounds, but never touch or claim to "own" in the old sense of the word.

Some might argue that information will still require some physical manifestation, such as its magnetic existence on the titanic hard disks of distant servers, but these are bottles that have no macroscopically discrete or personally meaningful form.

Some will also argue that we have been dealing with unbottled expression since the advent of radio, and they would be right. But for most of the history of broadcast, there was no convenient way to capture soft goods from the electromagnetic ether and reproduce them in anything like the quality available in commercial packages. Only recently has this changed and little has been done legally or technically to address the change.

Generally, the issue of consumer payment for broadcast products was irrelevant. The consumers themselves were the product. Broadcast media were supported either by selling the attention of their audience to advertisers, using government to assess payment through taxes, or the whining mendicancy of annual donor drives.

All of broadcast support models are flawed. Support either by advertisers or government has almost invariably tainted the purity of the goods delivered. Besides, direct marketing is gradually killing the advertiser support model anyway.

Broadcast media gave us another payment method for a virtual product in the royalties which broadcasters pay songwriters through such organizations as ASCAP and BMI. But, as a member of ASCAP, I can assure you this is not a model that we should emulate. The monitoring methods are wildly approximate. There is no parallel system of accounting in the revenue stream. It doesn't really work. Honest.

In any case, without our old methods of physically defining the expression of ideas, and in the absence of successful new models for non-physical transaction, we simply don't know how to assure reliable payment for mental works. To make matters worse, this comes at a time when the human mind is replacing sunlight and mineral deposits as the principal source of new wealth.

Furthermore, the increasing difficulty of enforcing existing copyright and patent laws is already placing in peril the ultimate source of intellectual property, the free exchange of ideas.

That is, when the primary articles of commerce in a society look so much like speech as to be indistinguishable from it, and when the traditional methods of protecting their ownership have become ineffectual, attempting to fix the problem with broader and more vigorous enforcement will inevitably threaten freedom of speech.

The greatest constraint on your future liberties may come not from government but from corporate legal departments laboring to protect by force what can no longer be protected by practical efficiency or general social consent.

Furthermore, when Jefferson and his fellow creatures of The Enlightenment designed the system that became American copyright law, their primary objective was assuring the widespread distribution of thought, not profit. Profit was the fuel that would carry ideas into the libraries and minds of their new republic. Libraries would purchase books, thus rewarding the authors for their work in assembling ideas, which otherwise "incapable of confinement" would then become freely available to the public. But what is the role of libraries if there are no books? How does society now pay for the distribution of ideas if not by charging for the ideas themselves?

Additionally complicating the matter is the fact that along with the physical bottles in which intellectual property protection has resided, digital technology is also erasing the legal jurisdictions of the physical world, and replacing them with the unbounded and perhaps permanently lawless seas of Cyberspace.

In Cyberspace, there are not only no national or local boundaries to contain the scene of a crime and determine the method of its prosecution, there are no clear cultural agreements on what a crime might be. Unresolved and basic differences between European and Asian cultural assumptions about intellectual property can only be exacerbated in a region where many transactions are taking place in both hemispheres and yet, somehow, in neither.

Even in the most local of digital conditions, jurisdiction and responsibility are hard to assess. A group of music publishers filed suit against

Compuserve this fall for it having allowed its users to upload musical compositions into areas where other users might get them. But since Compuserve cannot practically exercise much control over the flood of bits that pass between its subscribers, it probably shouldn't be held responsible for unlawfully "publishing" these works.

Notions of property, value, ownership, and the nature of wealth itself are changing more fundamentally than at any time since the Sumerians first poked cuneiform into wet clay and called it stored grain. Only a very few people are aware of the enormity of this shift and fewer of them are lawyers or public officials.

Those who do see these changes must prepare responses for the legal and social confusion that will erupt as efforts to protect new forms of property with old methods become more obviously futile, and, as a consequence, more adamant.

From Swords to Writs to Bits

Humanity now seems bent on creating a world economy primarily based on goods that take no material form. In doing so, we may be eliminating any predictable connection between creators and a fair reward for the utility or pleasure others may find in their works.

Without that connection, and without a fundamental change in consciousness to accommodate its loss, we are building our future on furor, litigation, and institutionalized evasion of payment except in response to raw force. We may return to the Bad Old Days of property.

Throughout the darker parts of human history, the possession and distribution of property was a largely military matter. "Ownership" was assured those with the nastiest tools, whether fists or armies, and the most resolute will to use them. Property was the divine right of thugs.

By the turn of the first millennium AD, the emergence of merchant classes and landed gentry forced the development of ethical understandings for the resolution of property disputes. In the late Middle Ages, enlightened rulers like England's Henry II began to codify this unwritten "common law" into recorded canons. These laws were local, but this didn't matter much as they were primarily directed at real estate, a form of property that is local by definition. And which, as the name implied, was very real.

This continued to be the case as long as the origin of wealth was agricultural, but with the dawning of the Industrial Revolution, humanity began to focus as much on means as ends. Tools acquired a new social value and, thanks to their own development, it became possible to duplicate and distribute them in quantity.

To encourage their invention, copyright and patent law were developed in most western countries. These laws were devoted to the delicate task of getting mental creations into the world where they could be used—and enter the minds of others—while assuring their inventors compensation for the value of their use. And, as previously stated, the systems of both law and practice that grew up around that task were based on physical expression.

Since it is now possible to convey ideas from one mind to another without ever making them physical, we are now claiming to own ideas themselves and not merely their expression. And since it is likewise now possible to create useful tools that never take physical form, we have taken to patenting abstractions, sequences of virtual events, and mathematical formulae—the most un-real estate imaginable.

In certain areas, this leaves rights of ownership in such an ambiguous condition that once again property adheres to those who can muster the largest armies. The only difference is that this time the armies consist of lawyers.

Threatening their opponents with the endless Purgatory of litigation, over which some might prefer death itself, they assert claim to any thought that might have entered another cranium within the collective body of the corporations they serve. They act as though these ideas appeared in splendid detachment from all previous human thought. And they pretend that thinking about a product is somehow as good as manufacturing, distributing, and selling it.

What was previously considered a common human resource, distributed among the minds and libraries of the world, as well as the phenomena of nature herself, is now being fenced and deeded. It is as though a new class of enterprise had arisen which claimed to own air and water.

What is to be done? While there is a certain grim fun to be had in it, dancing on the grave of copyright and patent will solve little, especially when so few are willing to admit that the occupant of this grave is even deceased and are trying to uphold by force what can no longer be upheld by popular consent.

The legalists, desperate over their slipping grip, are vigorously trying to extend it. Indeed, the United States and other proponents of GATT are making adherence to our moribund systems of intellectual property protection a condition of membership in the marketplace of nations. For example, China will be denied Most Favored Nation trading status unless they agree to uphold a set of culturally alien principles that are no longer even sensibly applicable in their country of origin.

In a more perfect world, we'd be wise to declare a moratorium on litigation, legislation, and international treaties in this area until we had a clearer sense of the terms and conditions of enterprise in Cyberspace. Ideally, laws ratify already developed social consensus. They are less the Social Contract itself than a series of memoranda expressing a collective intent that has emerged out of many millions of human interactions.

Humans have not inhabited Cyberspace long enough or in sufficient diversity to have developed a Social Contract that conforms to the strange new conditions of that world. Laws developed prior to consensus usually serve the already established few who can get them passed and not society as a whole.

To the extent that either law or established social practice exists in this area, they are already in dangerous disagreement. The laws regarding unlicensed reproduction of commercial software are clear and stern—and rarely observed. Software piracy laws are so practically unenforceable and breaking them has become so socially acceptable that only a thin minority appears compelled, either by fear or conscience, to obey them.

I sometimes give speeches on this subject, and I always ask how many people in the audience can honestly claim to have no unauthorized software on their hard disks. I've never seen more than ten percent of the hands go up.

Whenever there is such profound divergence between the law and social practice, it is not society that adapts. And, against the swift tide of custom, the Software Publishers' current practice of hanging a few visible scapegoats is so obviously capricious as to only further diminish respect for the law.

Part of the widespread popular disregard for commercial software copyrights stems from a legislative failure to understand the conditions into which it was inserted. To assume that systems of law based in the physical world will serve in an environment that is as fundamentally different as Cyberspace is a folly for which everyone doing business in the future will pay.

As I will discuss in the next segment, unbounded intellectual property is very different from physical property and can no longer be protected as though these differences did not exist. For example, if we continue to assume that value is based on scarcity, as it is with regard to physical objects, we will create laws that are precisely contrary to the nature of information, which may, in many cases, increase in value with distribution.

The large, legally risk-averse institutions most likely to play by the old rules will suffer for their compliance. The more lawyers, guns, and money they invest in either protecting their rights or subverting those of their opponents, the more commercial competition will resemble the Kwakiutl Potlatch Ceremony, in which adversaries competed by destroying their own possessions. Their ability to produce new technology will simply grind to a halt as every move they make drives them deeper into a tar pit of courtroom warfare.

Faith in law will not be an effective strategy for high tech companies. Law adapts by continuous increments and at a pace second only to geology in its stateliness. Technology advances in the lunging jerks, like the punctuation of biological evolution grotesquely accelerated. Real world conditions will continue to change at a blinding pace, and the law will get further behind, more profoundly confused. This mismatch is permanent.

Promising economies based on purely digital products will either be born in a state of paralysis, as appears to be the case with multimedia, or continue in a brave and willful refusal by their owners to play the ownership game at all.

In the United States one can already see a parallel economy developing, mostly among small, fast-moving enterprises who protect their ideas by getting into the marketplace quicker than their larger competitors who base their protection on fear and litigation.

Perhaps those who are part of the problem will simply quarantine themselves in court while those who are part of the solution will create a new society based, at first, on piracy and freebooting. It may be that when the current system of intellectual property law has collapsed, as seems inevitable, that no new legal structure will arise in its place.

But something will happen. After all, people do business. When a currency becomes meaningless, business is done in barter. When societies develop outside the law, they develop their own unwritten codes, practices, and ethical systems. While technology may undo law, technology offers methods for restoring creative rights.

A Taxonomy of Information

It seems to me that the most productive thing to do now is to look hard into the true nature of what we're trying to protect. How much do we really know about information and its natural behaviors?

What are the essential characteristics of unbounded creation? How does it differ from previous forms of property? How many of our assumptions about it have actually been about its containers rather than their mysterious contents? What are its different species and how does each of them lend itself to control? What technologies will be useful in creating new virtual bottles to replace the old physical ones?

Of course, information is, by its nature, intangible and hard to define. Like other such deep phenomena as light or matter, it is a natural host to paradox. And as it is most helpful to understand light as being both a particle and a wave, an understanding of information may emerge in the abstract congruence of its several different properties that might be described by the following three statements:

- Information is an activity.
- Information is a life form.
- Information is a relationship.

In the following section, I will examine each of these.

Information Is an Activity

Information Is a Verb, Not a Noun

Freed of its containers, information is obviously not a thing. In fact, it is something that happens in the field of interaction between minds or objects or other pieces of information.

Gregory Bateson, expanding on the information theory of Claude Shannon, said, "Information is a difference which makes a difference." Thus, information only really exists in the Δ. The making of that difference is an activity within a relationship. Information is an action that occupies time rather than a state of being which occupies physical space, as is the case with hard goods. It is the pitch, not the baseball, the dance, not the dancer.

Information Is Experienced, Not Possessed

Even when it has been encapsulated in some static form like a book or a hard disk, information is still something that happens to you as you mentally decompress it from its storage code. But, whether it's running at gigabits per second or words per minute, the actual decoding is a process that must be performed by and upon a mind, a process that must take place in time.

There was a cartoon in the *Bulletin of Atomic Scientists* a few years ago which illustrated this point beautifully. In the drawing, a holdup man trains his gun on the sort of bespectacled fellow you'd figure might have a lot of information stored in his head. "Quick," orders the bandit, "Give me all your ideas."

Information Has to Move

Sharks are said to die of suffocation if they stop swimming, and the same is nearly true of information. Information that isn't moving ceases to exist as anything but potential—at least until it is allowed to move again. For this reason, the practice of information hoarding, common in bureaucracies, is an especially wrong-headed artifact of physically based value systems.

Information Is Conveyed by Propagation, Not Distribution

The way in which information spreads is also very different from the distribution of physical goods. It moves more like something from nature than from a factory. It can concatenate like falling dominos or grow in the usual fractal lattice, like frost spreading on a window, but it cannot be shipped around like widgets, except to the extent that it can be contained in them. It doesn't simply move on. It leaves a trail of itself everywhere it's been.

The central economic distinction between information and physical property is the ability of information to be transferred without leaving the possession of the original owner. If I sell you my horse, I can't ride him after that. If I sell you what I know, we both know it.

Information Is a Life Form

Information Wants to Be Free

Stewart Brand is generally credited with this elegant statement of the obvious, recognizing both the natural desire of secrets to be told and the fact that they might be capable of possessing something like a "desire" in the first place.

English biologist and philosopher Richard Dawkins proposed the idea of "memes," self-replicating patterns of information that propagate themselves across the ecologies of mind, saying they were like life forms.

I believe they are life forms in every respect but a basis in the carbon atom. They self-reproduce, they interact with their surroundings and adapt to them, they mutate, they persist. Like any other life form they evolve to fill the possibility spaces of their local environments, which are, in this case, the surrounding belief systems and cultures of their hosts, namely, us.

Indeed, the sociobiologists, like Dawkins, make a plausible case that carbon-based life forms are information as well, and that, as the chicken is an egg's way of making another egg, the entire biological spectacle is just the DNA molecule's means of copying out more information strings exactly like itself.

Information Replicates into the Cracks of Possibility

Like DNA helices, ideas are relentless expansionists, always seeking new opportunities for lebensraum. And, as in carbon-based nature, the more robust organisms are extremely adept at finding new places to live. Thus, just as the common housefly has insinuated itself into practically every ecosystem on the planet, so has the meme of "life after death" found a niche in most minds, or psycho-ecologies.

The more universally resonant an idea or image or song, the more minds it will enter and remain within. Trying to stop the spread of a really robust piece of information is about as easy as keeping killer bees south of the border. The stuff just leaks.

Information Wants to Change

If ideas and other interactive patterns of information are indeed life forms, they can be expected to evolve constantly into forms that will be more perfectly adapted to their surroundings. And, as we see, they are doing this all the time.

But for a long time, our static media, whether carvings in stone, ink on paper, or dye on celluloid, have strongly resisted the evolutionary impulse, exalting as a consequence the author's ability to determine the finished product. But, as in an oral tradition, digitized information has no "final cut."

Digital information, unconstrained by packaging, is a continuing process more like the metamorphosing tales of prehistory than anything that will fit in shrink wrap. From the Neolithic to Gutenberg, information was passed on, mouth to ear, changing with every re-telling (or re-singing). The stories that once shaped our sense of the world didn't have authoritative versions. They adapted to each culture in which they found themselves being told.

Because there was never a moment when the story was frozen in print, the so-called "moral" right of storytellers to keep the tale their own was neither protected nor recognized. The story simply passed through each of them on its way to the next, where it would assume a different form. As we return to continuous information, we can expect the importance of authorship to diminish. Creative people may have to renew their acquaintance with humility.

But our system of copyright makes no accommodation whatever for expressions that don't at some point become "fixed" nor for cultural expressions which lack a specific author or inventor.

Jazz improvisations, standup comedy routines, mime performances, developing monologues, and unrecorded broadcast transmissions all lack the Constitutional requirement of fixation as a "writing." Without being fixed by a point of publication the liquid works of the future will all look more like these continuously adapting and changing forms and will therefore exist beyond the reach of copyright.

Copyright expert Pamela Samuelson tells of having attended a conference last year convened around the fact that Western countries may legally appropriate the music, designs, and biomedical lore of aboriginal people without compensation to their tribe of origin since that tribe is not an "author" or "inventor."

But soon most information will be generated collaboratively by the cyber-tribal hunter-gatherers of Cyberspace. Our arrogant legal dismissal of the rights of "primitives" will be back to haunt us soon.

Information Is Perishable

With the exception of the rare classic, most information is like farm produce. Its quality degrades rapidly both over time and in distance from the source of production. But even here, value is highly subjective and conditional. Yesterday's papers are quite valuable to the historian. In fact, the older they are, the more valuable they become. On the other hand, a commodities broker might consider news of an event that is more than an hour old to have lost any relevance.

Information Is a Relationship

Meaning Has Value and Is Unique to Each Case

In most cases, we assign value to information based on its meaningfulness. The place where information dwells, the holy moment where transmission becomes reception, is a region that has many shifting characteristics and flavors depending on the relationship of sender and receiver, the depth of their interactivity.

Each such relationship is unique. Even in cases where the sender is a broadcast medium, and no response is returned, the receiver is hardly passive. Receiving information is often as creative an act as generating it.

The value of what is sent depends entirely on the extent to which each individual receiver has the receptors—shared terminology, attention, interest, language, paradigm—necessary to render what is received meaningful.

Understanding is a critical element increasingly overlooked in the effort to turn information into a commodity. Data may be any set of facts, useful or not, intelligible or inscrutable, germane or irrelevant. Computers can crank out new data all night long without human help, and the results may be offered for sale as information. They may or may not actually be so. Only a human being can recognize the meaning that separates information from data.

In fact, information, in the economic sense of the word, consists of data that have been passed through a particular human mind and found meaningful within that mental context. One fella's information is all just data to someone else. If you're an anthropologist, my detailed charts of Tasaday kinship patterns might be critical information to you. If you're a banker from Hong Kong, they might barely seem to be data.

Familiarity Has More Value Than Scarcity

With physical goods, there is a direct correlation between scarcity and value. Gold is more valuable than wheat, even though you can't eat it. While this is not always the case, the situation with information is usually precisely the reverse. Most soft goods increase in value as they become more common. Familiarity is an important asset in the world of information. It may often be the case that the best thing you can do to raise the demand for your product is to give it away.

While this has not always worked with shareware, it could be argued that there is a connection between the extent to which commercial software is pirated and the amount that gets sold. Broadly pirated software, such as Lotus 1-2-3 or WordPerfect, becomes a standard and benefits from the Law of Increasing Returns based on familiarity.

Regarding my own soft product, rock and roll songs, there is no question that the band I write them for, the Grateful Dead, has increased its popularity enormously by giving them away. We have been letting people tape our concerts since the early seventies, but instead of reducing the demand for our product, we are now the largest concert draw in America, a fact that is at least in part attributable to the popularity generated by those tapes.

True, I don't get any royalties on the millions of copies of my songs that have been extracted from concerts, but I see no reason to complain. The fact is, no one but the Grateful Dead can perform a Grateful Dead song, so if you want the experience and not its thin projection, you have to buy a ticket from us. In other words, our intellectual property protection derives from our being the only real-time source of it.

Exclusivity Has Value

The problem with a model that turns the physical scarcity/value ratio on its head is that sometimes the value of information is very much based on its scarcity. Exclusive possession of certain facts makes them more useful. If everyone knows about conditions that might drive a stock price up, the information is valueless.

But again, the critical factor is usually time. It doesn't matter if this kind of information eventually becomes ubiquitous. What matters is being among the first who possess it and act on it. While potent secrets usually don't stay secret, they may remain so long enough to advance the cause of their original holders.

Point of View and Authority Have Value

In a world of floating realities and contradictory maps, rewards will accrue to those commentators whose maps seem to fit their territory snugly, based on their ability to yield predictable results for those who use them.

In aesthetic information, whether poetry or rock 'n' roll, people are willing to buy the new product of an artist, sight-unseen, based on their having been delivered a pleasurable experience by previous work.

Reality is an edit. People are willing to pay for the authority of those editors whose filtering point of view seems to fit best. And again, point of view is an asset that cannot be stolen or duplicated. No one but Esther Dyson sees the world as she does and the handsome fee she charges for her newsletter is actually for the privilege of looking at the world through her unique eyes.

Time Replaces Space

In the physical world, value depends heavily on possession, or proximity in space. One owns that material that falls inside certain dimensional boundaries and the ability to act directly, exclusively, and as one wishes upon what falls inside those boundaries is the principal right of ownership. And of course there is the relationship between value and scarcity, a limitation in space.

In the virtual world, proximity in time is a value determinant. An informational product is generally more valuable the closer the purchaser can place himself to the moment of its expression, a limitation in time.

Many kinds of information degrade rapidly with either time or reproduction. Relevance fades as the territory they map changes. Noise is introduced and bandwidth lost with passage away from the point where the information is first produced.

Thus, listening to a Grateful Dead tape is hardly the same experience as attending a Grateful Dead concert. The closer one can get to the headwaters of an informational stream, the better his chances of finding an accurate picture of reality in it. In an era of easy reproduction, the informational abstractions of popular experiences will propagate out from their source moments to reach anyone who's interested. But it's easy enough to restrict the real experience of the desirable event, whether knock-out punch or guitar lick, to those willing to pay for being there.

The Protection of Execution

In the hick town I come from, they don't give you much credit for just having ideas. You are judged by what you can make of them. As things continue to speed up, I think we see that execution is the best protection for those designs that become physical products. Or, as Steve Jobs once put it, "Real artists ship." The big winner is usually the one who gets to the market first (and with enough organizational force to keep the lead).

But, as we become fixated upon information commerce, many of us seem to think that originality alone is sufficient to convey value, deserving, with the right legal assurances, of a steady wage. In fact, the best way to protect intellectual property is to act on it. It's not enough to invent and patent, one has to innovate as well. Someone claims to have patented the microprocessor before Intel. Maybe so. If he'd actually started shipping microprocessors before Intel, his claim would seem far less spurious.

Information as Its Own Reward

It is now a commonplace to say that money is information. With the exception of Krugerands, crumpled cab-fare, and the contents of those suit-cases which drug lords are reputed to carry, most of the money in the informatized world is in ones and zeros. The global money supply sloshes around the Net, as fluid as weather. It is also obvious, as I have discussed, that information has become as fundamental to the creation of modern wealth as land and sunlight once were.

What is less obvious is the extent to which information is acquiring intrinsic value, not as a means to acquisition but as the object to be acquired. I suppose this has always been less explicitly the case. In politics and academia, potency and information have always been closely related.

However, as we increasingly buy information with money, we begin to see that buying information with other information is simple economic exchange without the necessity of converting the product into and out of currency. This is somewhat challenging for those who like clean accounting, since, information theory aside, informational exchange rates are too squishy to quantify to the decimal point.

Nevertheless, most of what a middle class American purchases has little to do with survival. We buy beauty, prestige, experience, education, and all the obscure pleasures of owning. Many of these things can not only be expressed in non-material terms, they can be acquired by non-material means.

And then there are the inexplicable pleasures of information itself, the joys of learning, knowing, and teaching. The strange good feeling of information coming into and out of oneself. Playing with ideas is a recreation which people must be willing to pay a lot for, given the market for books and elective seminars. We'd likely spend even more money for such pleasures if there weren't so many opportunities to pay for ideas with other ideas.

This explains much of the collective "volunteer" work that fills the archives, newsgroups, and databases of the Internet. Its denizens are not working for nothing, as is widely believed. Rather they are getting paid in something besides money. It is an economy that consists almost entirely of information.

This may become the dominant form of human trade, and if we persist in modeling economics on a strictly monetary basis, we may be gravely misled.

Getting Paid in Cyberspace

How all the foregoing relates to solutions to the crisis in intellectual property is something I've barely started to wrap my mind around. It's fairly paradigm-warping to look at information through fresh eyes—to see how very little it is like pig iron or pork bellies, to imagine the tottering travesties of case law we will stack up if we go on treating it legally as though it were.

As I've said, I believe these towers of outmoded boilerplate will be a smoking heap sometime in the next decade and we mind miners will have no choice but to cast our lot with new systems that work.

I'm not really so gloomy about our prospects as readers of this jeremiad so far might conclude. Solutions will emerge. Nature abhors a vacuum and so does commerce.

Indeed, one of the aspects of the Electronic Frontier that I have always found most appealing—and the reason Mitch Kapor and I used that phrase in naming our foundation—is the degree to which it resembles the 19th century American West in its natural preference for social devices which emerge from it conditions rather than those which are imposed from the outside.

Until the West was fully settled and "civilized" in this century, order was established according to an unwritten Code of the West that had the fluidity of etiquette rather than the rigidity of law. Ethics were more important than rules. Understandings were preferred over laws, which were, in any event, largely unenforceable.

I believe that law, as we understand it, was developed to protect the interests that arose in the two economic "waves" which Alvin Toffler accurately identified in *The Third Wave*. The First Wave was agriculturally based and required law to order ownership of the principal source of production, land. In the Second Wave, manufacturing became the economic mainspring, and the structure of modern law grew around the centralized institutions that needed protection for their reserves of capital, manpower, and hardware.

Both of these economic systems required stability. Their laws were designed to resist change and to assure some equability of distribution within a fairly static social framework. The possibility spaces had to be constrained to preserve the predictability necessary to either land stewardship or capital formation.

In the Third Wave we have now entered, information to a large extent replaces land, capital, and hardware, and as I have detailed in the preceding section, information is most at home in a much more fluid and adaptable environment. The Third Wave is likely to bring a fundamental shift in the purposes and methods of law that will affect far more than simply those statutes that govern intellectual property.

The "terrain" itself—the architecture of the Net—may come to serve many of the purposes that could only be maintained in the past by legal imposition. For example, it may be unnecessary to constitutionally assure freedom of expression in an environment that, in the words of my fellow EFF co-founder John Gilmore, "treats censorship as a malfunction" and re-routes proscribed ideas around it.

Similar natural balancing mechanisms may arise to smooth over the social discontinuities that previously required legal intercession to set right. On the Net, these differences are more likely to be spanned by a continuous spectrum that connects as much as it separates.

And, despite their fierce grip on the old legal structure, companies which trade in information are likely to find that in their increasing inability to deal sensibly with technological issues, the courts will not produce results that are predictable enough to be supportive of long-term enterprise. Every litigation becomes like a game of Russian roulette, depending on the depth of the presiding judge's clue-impairment.

Uncodified or adaptive "law," while as "fast, loose, and out of control" as other emergent forms, is probably more likely to yield something like justice at this point. In fact, one can already see in development new practices to suit the conditions of virtual commerce. The life forms of information are evolving methods to protect their continued reproduction.

For example, while all the tiny print on a commercial diskette envelope punctiliously requires much of that who would open it, there are, as I say, few who read those provisos, let alone follow them to the letter. And yet, the software business remains a very healthy sector of the American economy.

Why is this? Because people seem to eventually buy the software they really use. Once a program becomes central to your work, you want the latest version of it, the best support, the actual manuals, all privileges that are attached to ownership. Such practical considerations will, in the absence of working law, become more and more important in getting paid for what might easily be obtained for nothing.

I do think that some software is being purchased in the service of ethics or the abstract awareness that the failure to buy it will result in its not being produced any longer, but I'm going to leave those motivators aside. While I believe that the failure of law will almost certainly result in a compensating re-emergence of ethics as the ordering template of society, this is a belief I don't have room to support here.

Instead, I think that, as in the case cited above, compensation for soft products will be driven primarily by practical considerations, all of them consistent with the true properties of digital information, where the value lies in it, and how it can be both manipulated and protected by technology.

While the conundrum remains a conundrum, I can begin to see the directions from which solutions may emerge, based in part on broadening those practical solutions that are already in practice.

Relationship and Its Tools

I believe one idea is central to understanding liquid commerce: Information economics, in the absence of objects, will be based more on relationship than possession.

One existing model for the future conveyance of intellectual property is real time performance, a medium currently used only in theater, music, lectures, stand-up comedy and pedagogy. I believe the concept of performance will expand to include most of the information economy from multi-casted soap operas to stock analysis. In these instances, commercial exchange will be more like ticket sales to a continuous show than the purchase of discrete bundles of that which is being shown.

The other model, of course, is service. The entire professional class—doctors, lawyers, consultants, architects, etc.—are already being paid directly for their intellectual property. Who needs copyright when you're on a retainer?

In fact, this model was applied to much of what is now copyrighted until the late 18th century. Before the industrialization of creation, writers, composers, artists, and the like produced their products in the private service of patrons. Without objects to distribute in a mass market, creative people will return to a condition somewhat like this, except that they will serve many patrons, rather than one.

We can already see the emergence of companies that base their existence on supporting and enhancing the soft property they create rather than selling it by the shrink-wrapped piece or embedding it in widgets.

Trip Hawkins' new company for creating and licensing multimedia tools, 3DO, is an example of what I'm talking about. 3DO doesn't intend to produce any commercial software or consumer devices. Instead, they will act as a kind of private standards setting body, mediating among software and device creators who will be their licensees. They will provide a point of commonality for relationships between a broad spectrum of entities.

In any case, whether you think of yourself as a service provider or a performer, the future protection of your intellectual property will depend on your ability to control your relationship to the market—a relationship that will most likely live and grow over time.

The value of that relationship will reside in the quality of performance, the uniqueness of your point of view, the validity of your expertise, its relevance to your market, and, underlying everything, the ability of that market to access your creative services swiftly, conveniently, and interactively.

Interaction and Protection

Direct interaction will provide a lot of intellectual property protection in the future, and, indeed, it already has. No one knows how many software pirates have bought legitimate copies of a program after calling its publisher for technical support and being asked for some proof of purchase, but I would guess the number is very high.

The same kind of controls will be applicable to "question and answer" relationships between authorities (or artists) and those who seek their expertise. Newsletters, magazines, and books will be supplemented by the ability of their subscribers to ask direct questions of authors.

Interactivity will be a billable commodity even without authorship. As people move into the Net and increasingly get their information directly from its point of production, unfiltered by centralized media, they will attempt to develop the same interactive ability to probe reality which only experience has provided them in the past. Live access to these distant "eyes and ears" will be much easier to cordon than access to static bundles of stored but easily reproducible information.

In most cases, control will be based on restricting access to the freshest, highest bandwidth information. It will be a matter of defining the ticket, the venue, the performer, and the identity of the ticket holder, definitions that I believe will take their forms from technology, not law.

In most cases, the defining technology will be cryptography.

Crypto Bottling

Cryptography, as I've said perhaps too many times, is the "material" from which the walls, boundaries—and bottles—of Cyberspace will be fashioned.

Of course there are problems with cryptography or any other purely technical method of property protection. It has always appeared to me that the more security you hide your goods behind, the more likely you are to turn your sanctuary into a target. Having come from a place where people leave their keys in their cars and don't even have keys to their houses, I remain convinced that the best obstacle to crime is a society with its ethics intact.

While I admit that this is not the kind of society most of us live in, I also believe that a social over-reliance on protection by barricades rather than conscience will eventually wither the latter by turning intrusion and theft into a sport, rather than a crime. This is already occurring in the digital domain as is evident in the activities of computer crackers.

Furthermore, I would argue that initial efforts to protect digital copyright by copy protection contributed to the current condition in which most otherwise ethical computer users seem morally untroubled by their possession of pirated software.

Instead of cultivating among the newly computerized a sense of respect for the work of their fellows, early reliance on copy protection led to the subliminal notion that cracking into a software package somehow "earned" one the right to use it. Limited not by conscience but by technical skill, many soon felt free to do whatever they could get away with. This will continue to be a potential liability of the encryption of digitized commerce.

Furthermore, it's cautionary to remember that copy protection was rejected by the market in most areas. Many of the upcoming efforts to use cryptography-based protection schemes will probably suffer the same fate. People are not going to tolerate much which makes computers harder to use than they already are without any benefit to the user.

Nevertheless, encryption has already demonstrated a certain blunt utility. New subscriptions to various commercial satellite TV services sky-rocketed recently after their deployment of more robust encryption of their feeds. This, despite a booming backwoods trade in black decoder chips conducted by folks who'd look more at home running moonshine than cracking code.

Another obvious problem with encryption as a global solution is that once something has been unscrambled by a legitimate licensee, it may be openly available to massive reproduction.

In some instances, reproduction following decryption may not be a problem. Many soft products degrade sharply in value with time. It may be that the only real interest in some such products will be among those who have purchased the keys to immediacy.

Furthermore, as software becomes more modular and distribution moves online, it will begin to metamorphose in direct interaction with its user base. Discontinuous upgrades will smooth into a constant process of incremental improvement and adaptation, some of it man-made and some of it arising through genetic algorithms. Pirated copies of software may become too static to have much value to anyone.

Even in cases such as images, where the information is expected to remain fixed, the unencrypted file could still be interwoven with code which could continue to protect it by a wide variety of means.

In most of the schemes I can project, the file would be "alive" with permanently embedded software that could "sense" the surrounding conditions and interact with them. For example, it might contain code that could detect the process of duplication and cause it to self-destruct.

Other methods might give the file the ability to "phone home" through the Net to its original owner. The continued integrity of some files might require periodic "feeding" with digital cash from their host, which they would then relay back to their authors.

Of course files that possess the independent ability to communicate upstream sound uncomfortably like the Morris Internet Worm. "Live" files do have a certain viral quality. And serious privacy issues would arise if everyone's computer were packed with digital spies.

The point is that cryptography will enable a lot of protection technologies that will develop rapidly in the obsessive competition that has always existed between lock-makers and lock-breakers.

But cryptography will not be used simply for making locks. It is also at the heart of both digital signatures and the aforementioned digital cash, both of which I believe will be central to the future protection of intellectual property.

I believe that the generally acknowledged failure of the shareware model in software had less to do with dishonesty than with the simple inconvenience of paying for shareware. If the payment process can be automated, as digital cash and signature will make possible, I believe that soft product creators will reap a much higher return from the bread they cast upon the waters of Cyberspace.

Moreover, they will be spared much of the overhead that presently adheres to the marketing, manufacture, sales, and distribution of information products, whether those products are computer programs, books, CD's, or motion pictures. This will reduce prices and further increase the likelihood of non-compulsory payment.

But of course there is a fundamental problem with a system that requires, through technology, payment for every access to a particular expression. It defeats the original Jeffersonian purpose of seeing that ideas were available to everyone regardless of their economic station. I am not comfortable with a model that will restrict inquiry to the wealthy.

An Economy of Verbs

The future forms and protections of intellectual property are densely obscured from the entrance to the Virtual Age. Nevertheless, I can make (or reiterate) a few flat statements that I earnestly believe won't look too silly in fifty years.

- In the absence of the old containers, almost everything we think we know about intellectual property is wrong. We are going to have to unlearn it. We are going to have to look at information as though we'd never seen the stuff before.
- The protections that we will develop will rely far more on ethics and technology than on law.

• Encryption will be the technical basis for most intellectual property protection. (And should, for this and other reasons, be made more widely available.)
• The economy of the future will be based on relationship rather than possession. It will be continuous rather than sequential.

And finally, in the years to come, most human exchange will be virtual rather than physical, consisting not of stuff but the stuff of which dreams are made. Our future business will be conducted in a world made more of verbs than nouns.

Ojo Caliente, New Mexico, October 1, 1992
New York, New York, November 6, 1992
Brookline, Massachusetts, November 8, 1992
New York, New York, November 15, 1993
San Francisco, California, November 20, 1993
Pinedale, Wyoming, November 24–30, 1993
New York, New York, December 13–14, 1993

This expression has lived and grown to this point over the time period and in the places detailed above. Despite its print publication here, I expect it will continue to evolve in liquid form, possibly for years.

The thoughts in it have not been "mine" alone but have assembled themselves in a field of interaction that has existed between myself and numerous others, to whom I am grateful. They particularly include: Pamela Samuelson, Kevin Kelly, Mitch Kapor, Mike Godwin, Stewart Brand, Mike Holderness, Miriam Barlow, Danny Hillis, Trip Hawkins, and Alvin Toffler.

2

Why Patents Are Bad for Software

Simson L. Garfinkel, Richard M. Stallman,
and Mitchell Kapor

In September 1990, users of the popular XyWrite word processing program got a disturbing letter in the mail from XyQuest, Inc., the program's publisher:

> In June of 1987, we introduced an automatic correction and abbreviation expansion feature in XyWrite III Plus. Unbeknownst to us, a patent application for a related capability had been filed in 1984 and was subsequently granted in 1988. The company holding the patent contacted us in late 1989 and apprised us of the existence of their patent.
>
> We have decided to modify XyWrite III Plus so that it cannot be construed as infringing. The newest version of XyWrite III Plus (3.56) incorporates two significant changes that address this issue: You will no longer be able to automatically correct common spelling errors by pressing the space bar after the misspelled word. In addition, to expand abbreviations stored in your personal dictionary, you will have to press control-R or another designated hot key.

XyQuest had been bitten by a software patent—one of the more than two thousand patents on computer algorithms and software techniques that have been granted by the U.S. Patent and Trademark Office since the mid-1980s. The owner of the patent, Productivity Software, had given XyQuest a choice: license the patent or take a popular feature out of XyWrite, XyQuest's flagship product. If XyQuest refused, a costly patent-infringement lawsuit was sure to follow.

Some choice.

XyQuest tried to license the patent, says Jim Adelson, vice president for marketing, but Productivity Software kept changing its terms. First Productivity said that XyQuest could keep the feature in some versions of XyWrite, but not in others. Then the company said that XyQuest could use one part of the "invention," but not other parts. And Productivity

Software kept increasing the amount of money it wanted. XyQuest finally gave up and took the feature out.

XyQuest was lucky it had that option. Other firms—including some of the nation's largest and most profitable software publishers—have been served with notice of patents that strike to the heart of their corporate vitality. In one of the most publicized cases, a company called Refac International—whose sole business is acquiring and litigating patents—sued Lotus, Microsoft, Ashton-Tate, and three other spreadsheet publishers, claiming they had all infringed on patent number 4,398,249, which spells out the order in which to recalculate the values in a complicated model when one parameter in the model changes. (Refac has since dropped its claims against all the companies except Lotus, but only because company lawyers anticipated a better chance of success if they faced just one opponent.)

Patent 4,398,249 does not have anything to do with spreadsheets in particular; the technique also appears in some graphics drawing and artificial intelligence programs. And the idea that values in a spreadsheet should be recalculated in the order specified by the patent is so obvious that it has probably occurred to nearly everyone who has written a spreadsheet program. But the Patent Office's standard for obviousness is extremely low; patents have been granted for ideas so elementary that they could have been answers to problems in a first-year programming course.

Practically once a month, the nation's computer networks are abuzz with news of another patent issued on a fundamental concept that is widely used. Although the Patent Office isn't supposed to grant patents on ideas, that's essentially what it's doing with software patents, carving up the intellectual domain of computer science and handing little pieces to virtually any company that files an application. And the practice is devastating America's software industry.

If Congress does not act quickly to redefine the applicability of patent law to computer programs, the legal minefield confronting the introduction of new computer programs will be so intimidating—and potentially so costly—that small companies will effectively be barred from the marketplace, while large, established firms will become embroiled in litigation that will have a stultifying effect on the entire industry.

What's Being Patented?

Software patents do not cover entire programs; instead, they cover algorithms and techniques—the instructions that tell a computer how to carry out a specific task in a program. Thousands of instructions make up any one computer program. But whereas the unique combination of algorithms and techniques in a program is considered an "expression" (like a book or a song) and is covered by copyright law, the algorithms and techniques themselves are treated as procedures eligible for patenting.

The judicial basis for this eligibility is tenuous at best. U.S. law does not allow inventors, no matter how brilliant they are, to patent the laws of nature, and in two Supreme Court cases (*Gottschalk v. Benson*, 1972, and *Parker v. Flook*, 1978) the Court extended this principle to computer algorithms and software techniques. But in the 1981 case *Diamond v. Diehr*, the Court said that a patent could be granted for an industrial process that was controlled by certain computer algorithms, and the Patent Office seems to have taken that decision as a green light on the patentability of algorithms and techniques in general.

Software patents are now being granted at an alarming rate—by some counts, more than a thousand are issued each year. Unfortunately, most of the patents have about as much cleverness and originality as a recipe for boiled rice—simple in itself but a vital part of many sophisticated dishes. Many cover very small and specific algorithms or techniques that are used in a wide variety of programs. Frequently the "inventions" mentioned in a patent application have been independently formulated and are already in use by other programmers when the application is filed.

When the Patent Office grants a patent on an algorithm or technique, it is telling programmers that they may not use a particular method for solving a problem without the permission of the idea's "owner." To them, patenting an algorithm or technique is like patenting a series of musical notes or a chord progression, then forcing composers to purchase a "musical sequence license."

Systems at Odds

The traditional rationale for patents is that protection of inventions will spur innovation and aid in the dissemination of information about technical advances. By prohibiting others from copying an invention, patents allow inventors to recoup their investment in development while at the same time revealing the workings of the new invention to the public.

But there's evidence that the patent system is backfiring in the computer industry; indeed, the system itself seems unsuited to the nature of software development. Today's computer programs are so complex that they contain literally thousands of algorithms and techniques, each considered patentable by the Patent Office's standards. Is it reasonable to expect a software company to license each of those patents, or even to bring such a legally risky product into the marketplace? To make things even more complicated, the Patent Office has also granted patents on combinations of algorithms and techniques that produce a particular feature. For example, Apple was sued because its Hypercard program allegedly violates patent number 4,736,308, which covers a specific technique that, in simplified terms, entails scrolling through a database displaying selected parts of each line of text. Separately, the scrolling and display functions are ubiquitous fixtures of computer programming, but combining them without a license from the holder of patent 4,736,308 is now apparently illegal.

Another problem with patenting software is the amount of time it takes to do so. The two to five years required to file for and obtain a patent are acceptable if a company is patenting, say, the formula for Valium, which hasn't changed in more than 20 years. But in the software industry, companies that don't continually bring out new versions of their programs go out of business. Success for them depends on spotting needs and developing solutions as quickly as possible.

Unfortunately, conducting a patent search is a slow, deliberative process that, when harnessed to software development, could stop innovation in its tracks. And because patent applications are confidential, there is simply no way for computer programmers to ensure that what they write will not violate some patent that is yet to be issued. Thus XyQuest "reinvented" its automatic spelling-error correction system and brought the product to market between the time that Productivity Software had filed for its application and been awarded the patent.

Such examples are becoming increasingly common. In another case, the journal *IEEE Computer* in June 1984 published a highly efficient algorithm for performing data compression; unbeknownst to the journal's editors or readers, the authors of the article had simultaneously applied for a patent on their invention. In the following year, numerous programs were written and widely distributed for performing the so-called "LZW data compression." The compression system was even adopted as a national standard and proposed as an international one. Then, in 1985, the Patent Office awarded patent number 4,558,302 to one of the authors of the article. Now Unisys, the holder of the patent, is demanding royalties for the use of the algorithm. Although programs incorporating the algorithm are still in the public domain, using these programs means risking a lawsuit.

Not only is the patent approval process slow, but the search for "prior art"—the criterion the Patent Office uses to determine whether an invention already exists at the time of a patent application—is all but impossible to conduct in the realm of computer software. After more than 25 years, the Patent Office has not developed a system for classifying patents on algorithms and techniques, and no such system may be workable. Just as mathematicians are sometimes unaware that essentially identical mental processes are being used in separate areas of mathematics under different terminology, different parts of computer science frequently reinvent the same algorithm to serve different purposes. It is unreasonable to expect that a patent examiner, pressed for time, would recognize all such duplication. For example, IBM was issued a patent on the same data-compression algorithm that Unisys supposedly owns. The Patent Office was probably not aware of granting two patents for the same algorithm because the descriptions in the patents themselves are quite different even though the formulas are mathematically equivalent.

The search for prior art is complicated by the fact that the literature of computer science is unbelievably large. It contains not only academic journals, but also users' manuals, published source code, and popular accounts in magazines for computer enthusiasts. Whereas a team of chemists working at a major university might produce 20 or 30 pages of published material per year, a single programmer might easily produce a hundred times that much. The situation becomes even more complex in the case of patented combinations of algorithms and techniques. Programmers often publish new algorithms and techniques, but they almost never publish new ways of combining old ones. Although individual algorithms and techniques have been combined in many different ways in the past, there's no good way to establish that history.

The inability to search the literature thoroughly for prior art is crucial, because unless an examiner can find prior art, he or she is all but obligated to issue the patent. As a result, many patents have been granted—and successfully defended in court—that are not "original," even by the Patent Office's definition. It was simply the case that neither the patent examiner nor the defendants in the lawsuit knew of the prior art's existence.

Some members of the commercial software community are now proposing the creation of a "Software Patent Institute" to identify software's prior art that existed before 1980. But even if such an institute could catalogue every discovery made by every programmer in the United States, it makes no sense to arbitrarily declare that only pre-1980 work is in the public domain. Besides, what would be the purpose? To allow the patenting of nature's mathematical laws?

Bad for Business

Even when patents *are* known in advance, software publishers have generally not licensed the algorithms or techniques; instead, they try to rewrite their programs to avoid using the particular procedure that the patent describes. Sometimes this isn't possible, in which case companies have often chosen to avoid implementing new features altogether. It seems clear from the evidence of the last few years that software patents are actually *preventing* the adoption of new technology, rather than encouraging it.

And they don't seem to be encouraging innovation, either. Software patents pose a special danger to small companies, which often form the vanguard of software development but can't afford the cost of patent searches or litigation. The programming of a new product can cost a few hundred thousand dollars; the cost of a patent search for each technique and combination of techniques that the new program uses could easily equal or even exceed that. And the cost of a single patent suit can be more than a million dollars.

"I'm not familiar with any type of litigation that is any more costly than patent litigation," says R. Duff Thompson, vice president and general counsel of the WordPerfect Corporation. But Thompson's greatest fear is that software patents will wipe out young, independent programmers, who until now have been the software industry's source of inspiration. Imagine what happens, says Thompson, when "some 23-year-old kid who has a terrific idea in a piece of software is hammered by a demand letter from someone holding a patent."

As for aiding the exchange of information, the expansion of software patents could mean instead the end of software developed at universities and distributed without charge—software that has been a mainstay of computer users in universities, corporations, and government for years. Many such programs—the X Window system, the EMACS text editor, the "compress" file-compression utility, and others—appear to be in violation of existing patents. Patents could also mean an end to public-domain software, which has played an important part in making computers affordable to public schools. There is obviously no way that an author who distributes a program for free could arrange to pay for royalties if one of the hundreds of techniques that were combined to create the program happens to be patented.

Few programmers and entrepreneurs believe that patents are necessary for their profession. Instead, the impetus for patents on algorithms and techniques comes from two outside sources: managers of large companies, who see patents as a means for triumphing over their competitors without having to develop superior products, and patent attorneys, who see the potential for greatly expanding their business.

Today, most patenting by companies is done to have something to trade or as a defense against other patent-infringement suits. Attorneys advise that patenting software may strengthen competitive position. Although this approach will work for large companies such as Microsoft, Apple, and IBM, small and even mid-sized companies can't play in their league. A future startup will be forced to pay whatever price the giants choose to impose.

Copyright and Trade Secrecy

The best argument against the wisdom of software patents may be history itself. Lotus, Microsoft, WordPerfect, and Novell all became world leaders in the software publishing industry on the strength of their products. None of these companies needed patents to secure funding or maintain their market position. Indeed, all made their fortunes before the current explosion of software patents began. Clearly patents are not necessary to ensure the development of computer programs. And for those who want more control over what they see as their property, the computer industry has already adopted two other systems: copyright and trade secrecy.

Today, nearly all programs are copyrighted. Copyright prohibits the users of a software program from making copies of it (for example, to give to their friends) without the permission of the individual or company that licenses the program. It prevents one company from appropriating another company's work and selling it as its own. But the existence of a copyright doesn't prevent other programmers from using algorithms or techniques contained in the program in their own work. A single software technique can be implemented in different ways to do totally different jobs; copyright only prohibits appropriating the actual code that a particular programmer wrote.

In general, copyrighting and patenting are thought to apply to very different kinds of material: the former to the expression of ideas, and the latter to a process that achieves a certain result. Until just a few years ago, computer algorithms and techniques were widely seen as unpatentable. And as Harvard University policy analyst Brian Kahin notes, this is the first time in history that an industry in which copyright was widely established was suddenly subjected to patenting.

Indeed, without conscious action by Congress or the Supreme Court, the most fundamental rule of software publishing—if you write a program, you own it—will change. The new rule will be that you might own what you write—if it is so revolutionary that it owes nothing to any previous work. No author in areas other than software is held to such an unrealistically high standard.

The U.S. patent system was created because the framers of the Constitution hoped that patents would discourage trade secrecy. When techniques are kept secret for commercial advantage, they may never become available for others to use and may even be lost. But although trade secrecy is a problem for software, as it is for other fields, it is not a problem that patents help to correct.

Many of the useful developments in the field of software consist of new features such as the automatic correction and abbreviation expansion feature in XyWrite III Plus. Since it is impossible to keep a program's features secret from the users of the program, there is no possibility of trade secrecy and thus no need for measures to discourage it. Techniques used internally in a software system can be kept secret; but in the past, the important ones rarely were. It was normal for computer scientists in the commercial as well as the academic world to publish their discoveries. Once again, since secrecy about techniques was not a significant problem, there is little to be gained by adopting the patent system to discourage it.

The place where trade secrecy *is* used extensively in software is in the "source code" for programs. In computer programming, trade secrets are kept by distributing programs in "machine code," the virtually indecipherable translation of programming languages that computers read. It is extremely difficult for another programmer to glean from a machine-code program the original steps written by the program's author. But software patents haven't done anything to limit this form of trade secrecy. By withholding the source code, companies keep secret not a particular technique, but the way that they have combined dozens of techniques to produce a design for a complete system. Patenting the whole design is impractical and ineffective. Even companies that have software patents still distribute programs in machine code only. Thus, in no area do software patents significantly reduce trade secrecy.

Reversing Direction

Many policymakers assume that any increase in intellectual property protection must be good for whoever works in the field. As we've tried to show, this is assuredly not the case in the field of computer programming. Nearly all programmers view patents as an unwelcome intrusion, limiting both their ability to do their work and their freedom of expression.

At this point, so many patents have been issued by the Patent and Trademark Office that the prospect of overturning them by finding prior art, one at a time, is almost unthinkable. Even if the Patent Office learns to understand software better in the future, the mistakes that are being made now will follow the industry into the next century unless there is a dramatic turnaround in policy.

The U.S. Patent and Trademark Office recently established an Advisory Commission on Patent Law Reform that is charged with examining a number of issues, including software patents—or what it prefers to call patents on "computer-program-related inventions." Unfortunately, the commission's subcommittee on software does not include any prominent software industry representatives who have expressed doubts about software patents. But the subcommittee is required to consider public comment.

Although influencing the Patent Office might produce some benefits, the really necessary reforms are likely to come only through intervention by the Supreme Court or Congress. Waiting for Court action is not the answer: No one can force the Supreme Court to rule on a relevant case, and there is no guarantee that the Court would decide to change Patent Office practice or to do anything about existing patents. The most effective course of action, therefore, is to encourage Congress to amend the patent law to disallow software patents and, if possible, invalidate those that have already been awarded. The House Subcommittee on Intellectual Property and the Administration of Justice should take the lead by scheduling hearings on the subject and calling for a congressionally sponsored economic analysis of the effect of software patents on the industry.

The computer industry grew to be vibrant and healthy without patents. Unless those who want software patents can demonstrate that they are necessary to the health of the industry, Congress should feel justified in eliminating this barrier to innovation.

Recommended Reading

Brian Kahin, "The Software Patent Crisis," *Technology Review* (April 1990): 53–58.

Mitchell Kapor, Testimony at Hearings before U.S. House of Representatives, Subcommittee on Courts, Intellectual Property and the Administration of Justice, of the Committee on the Judiciary (March 5, 1990).

Pamela Samuelson, "Benson Revisited: Should Patent Protection Be Available for Algorithms and Other Computer Program-Related Inventions?" *Emory Law Journal* (Fall 1990): 1025–1154.

Pamela Samuelson, "Should Program Algorithms Be Patented?" *Communications of the ACM* (August 1990): 23–27.

3

Against Software Patents

The League for Programming Freedom

Software patents threaten to devastate America's computer industry. Patents granted in the past decade are now being used to attack companies such as the Lotus Development Corporation for selling programs they have independently developed. Soon new companies will often be barred from the software arena—most major programs will require licenses for dozens of patents, making them infeasible. This problem has only one solution: software patents must be eliminated.

The Patent System and Computer Programs

The framers of the United States Constitution established the patent system to provide inventors with an incentive to share their inventions with the general public. In exchange for divulging an invention, the patent grants the inventor a 17-year monopoly on its use. The patent holder can license others to use the invention, but may also refuse to do so. Independent reinvention of the same technique by another person does not give that person the right to use it.

Patents do not cover systems. Instead, they cover particular techniques that can be used to build systems, or particular features that systems can offer. Once a technique or feature is patented, it may not be used in a system without the permission of the patent holder—even if it is implemented in a different way. Since a computer program typically uses many techniques and provides many features, it can infringe many patents at once.

Until recently, patents were not used in the software field. Software developers copyrighted individual programs or made them trade secrets.

Copyright was traditionally understood to cover the implementation details of a particular program. It did not cover the features of the program, or the general methods used. And trade secrecy, by definition, could not prohibit any development work by someone who did not know the secret.

On this basis, software development was extremely profitable, and received considerable investment, without any prohibition on independent software development. But it no longer works this way. A change in U.S. government policy in the early 1980s stimulated a flood of applications. Now many have been approved, and the rate is accelerating. Many programmers are unaware of the change and do not appreciate the magnitude of its effects. Today the lawsuits are just beginning.

Absurd Patents

The Patent Office and the courts have had a difficult time with computer software. Until recently the Patent Office refused to hire computer science graduates as examiners, and even now does not offer competitive salaries for the field. Patent examiners are often ill-prepared to evaluate software patent applications to determine if they represent techniques that are widely known or obvious—both of which are grounds for rejection.

Their task is made more difficult because many commonly used software techniques do not appear in the scientific literature of computer science. Some seemed too obvious to publish while others seemed insufficiently general; some were open secrets.

Computer scientists know many techniques that can be generalized to widely varying circumstances. But the Patent Office seems to believe each separate use of a technique is a candidate for a new patent. For example, Apple was sued because the Hypercard program allegedly violates patent number 4,736,308, a patent that covers displaying portions of two or more strings together on the screen—effectively, scrolling with multiple subwindows. Scrolling and subwindows are well-known techniques, but combining them is now apparently illegal.

The granting of a patent by the Patent Office carries a presumption in law that the patent is valid. Patents for well-known techniques that were in use many years before the patent application have been upheld by federal courts. It can be difficult to prove a technique was well known at the time in question.

For example, the technique of using exclusive-or to write a cursor onto a screen is both well known and obvious. (Its advantage is that another identical exclusive-or operation can be used to erase the cursor without damaging the other data on the screen.) This technique can be implemented in a few lines of a program, and a clever high school student might well reinvent it. But it is covered by patent number 4,197,590, which has been upheld twice in court even though the technique was used at least five years before the patent application. Cadtrak, the company that owns this patent, collects millions of dollars from large computer manufacturers.

English patents covering customary graphics techniques, including airbrushing, stenciling, and combining two images under control of a third one, were recently upheld in court, despite the testimony of the pioneers of the field that they had developed these techniques years before. (The corresponding U.S. patents, including 4,633,416 and 4,602,286, have not yet been tested in court, but they probably will be soon.)

All the major developers of spreadsheet programs have been threatened on the basis of patent 4,398,249, covering "natural order recalc"—the recalculation of all the spreadsheet entries that are affected by changes the user makes, rather than recalculation in a fixed order. Currently Lotus alone is being sued, but a victory for the plaintiff in this case would leave the other developers little hope. The League has found prior art that may defeat this patent, but this is not assured.

Nothing protects programmers from accidentally using a technique that is patented, and then being sued for it. Taking an existing program and making it run faster may also make it violate half a dozen patents that have been granted, or are about to be granted.

Even if the Patent Office learns to understand software better, the mistakes it is making now will follow us into the next century, unless Congress or the Supreme Court intervenes to declare these patents void.

However, this is not the entire problem. Computer programming is fundamentally different from the fields the patent system previously covered. Even if the patent system were to operate "as intended" for software, it would still obstruct the industry it is supposed to promote.

What Is Obvious?

The patent system will not grant or uphold patents that are judged to be obvious. However, the system interprets the word "obvious" in a way that might surprise computer programmers. The standard of obviousness developed in other fields is inappropriate for software.

Patent examiners and judges are accustomed to considering even small, incremental changes as deserving new patents. For example, the famous *Polaroid vs. Kodak* case hinged on differences in the number and order of layers of chemicals in a film—differences between the technique Kodak was using and those described by previous, expired patents. The court ruled that these differences were unobvious.

Computer scientists solve problems quickly because the medium of programming is tractable. They are trained to generalize solution principles from one problem to another. One such generalization is that a procedure can be repeated or subdivided. Programmers consider this obvious—but the Patent Office did not think it was obvious when it granted the patent on scrolling multiple strings, described earlier.

Cases such as this cannot be considered errors. The patent system is functioning as it was designed to—but with software, it produces outrageous results.

Patenting What Is Too Obvious to Publish

Sometimes it is possible to patent a technique that is not new precisely because it is obvious—so obvious that no one would have published a paper about it.

For example, computer companies distributing the free X Window System developed by MIT are now being threatened with lawsuits by AT&T over patent number 4,555,775, covering the use of "backing store" in a window system that lets multiple programs have windows. Backing store means that the contents of a window which is temporarily partly hidden are saved in off-screen memory, so they can be restored quickly if the obscuring window disappears.

Early window systems were developed on computers that could not run two programs at once. Since computers had small memories, saving window contents was obviously a waste of scarce memory space. Later, larger multiprocessing computers led to the use of backing store, and to permitting each program to have its own windows. The combination was inevitable.

The technique of backing store was used at MIT in the Lisp Machine System before AT&T applied for a patent. (By coincidence, the Lisp Machine also supported multiprocessing.) The Lisp Machine developers published nothing about backing store at the time, considering it too obvious. It was mentioned when a programmers' manual explained how to turn it on and off.

But this manual was published one week after the AT&T patent application—too late to count as prior art to defeat the patent. So the AT&T patent may stand, and MIT may be forbidden to continue using a method that MIT used before AT&T.

The result is that the dozens of companies and hundreds of thousands of users who accepted the software from MIT on the understanding that it was free are now faced with possible lawsuits. (They are also being threatened with Cadtrak's exclusive-or patent.) The X Window System project was intended to develop a window system that all developers could use freely. This public service goal seems to have been thwarted by patents.

Why Software Is Different

Software systems are much easier to design than hardware systems of the same number of components. For example, a program of 100,000 components might be 50,000 lines long and could be written by two good programmers in a year. The equipment needed for this costs less than $10,000; the only other cost would be the programmer's own living expenses while doing the job. The total investment would be less than $100,000. If done commercially in a large company, it might cost twice that amount. By contrast, an automobile typically contains under 100,000 components; it requires a large team and costs tens of millions of dollars to design.

And software is also much cheaper to manufacture: copies can be made easily on an ordinary workstation costing under $10,000. Producing a complex hardware system often requires a factory costing tens of millions of dollars.

What is the reason for these differences in cost? A hardware system must be designed using real components. They have varying costs; they have limits of operation; they may be sensitive to temperature, vibration or humidity; they may generate noise; they drain power; they may fail either momentarily or permanently. They must be physically assembled in their proper places, and they must be accessible for replacement in case they fail.

Moreover, each of the components in a hardware design is likely to affect the behavior of many others. This greatly complicates the task of determining what a hardware design will do: mathematical modeling may prove wrong when the design is built.

By contrast, a computer program is built from ideal mathematical objects whose behavior is defined, not modeled approximately, by abstract rules. When an if-statement follows a while-statement there is no need to study whether the if-statement will draw power from the while-statement and thereby distort its output, or whether it could overstress the while-statement and make it fail.

Despite being built from simple parts, computer programs are incredibly complex. The program with 100,000 parts is as complex as an automobile, though far easier to design.

While programs cost substantially less to write, market and sell than automobiles, the cost of dealing with the patent system will not be less. The same number of components will, on the average, involve the same number techniques that might be patented.

The Danger of a Lawsuit

Under the current patent system, a software developer who wishes to follow the law must determine which patents a program violates and negotiate with each patent holder a license to use that patent. Licensing may be prohibitively expensive, or even unavailable if the patent is held by a competitor. Even "reasonable" license fees for several patents can add up to make a project infeasible. Alternatively, the developer may wish to avoid using the patent altogether, but there may be no way around it.

License negotiations may be a problem in themselves, as the developers of XyWrite recently learned. This summer they sent the users of

XyWrite a "downgrade," removing a popular feature: the space bar served as a command to correct spelling errors and expand abbreviations. Threatened by the holder of a patent covering this feature, they tried to negotiate a license, but found that the patent holder kept increasing his demands. Eventually they felt compelled to remove the feature of the program.

The worst danger of the patent system is that a developer might find, after releasing a product, that it infringes one or many patents. The resulting lawsuit and legal fees could force even a medium-sized company out of business.

Worst of all, there is no practical way for a software developer to avoid this danger since there is no effective way to find out what patents a system will infringe. There is a way to try to find out—a patent search—but searches are unreliable and in any case too expensive to use for software projects.

Patent Searches Are Prohibitively Expensive

A system with a hundred thousand components can use hundreds of techniques that might already be patented. Since each patent search costs thousands of dollars, searching for all the possible points of danger could easily cost over a million. This is far more than the cost of writing the program.

The costs do not stop there. Patent applications are written by lawyers for lawyers. A programmer reading a patent may not believe that his or her program violates the patent, but a federal court may rule otherwise. It is thus now necessary to involve patent attorneys at every phase of program development.

Yet this only reduces the risk of being sued later—it does not eliminate the risk. Therefore, it is necessary to have a reserve of cash for the eventuality of a lawsuit.

When a company spends millions to design a hardware system, and plans to invest tens of millions to manufacture it, an extra million or two to pay for dealing with the patent system might be bearable. However, for the inexpensive programming project, the same extra cost is prohibitive. Individuals and small companies especially cannot afford these costs. Software patents will put an end to software entrepreneurs.

Patent Searches Are Unreliable

Even if developers could afford patent searches, these are not a reliable method of avoiding the use of patented techniques. This is because patent searches do not reveal pending patent applications (which are kept confidential by the Patent Office). Since it takes several years on the average for a software patent to be granted, this is a serious problem: A developer could begin designing a large program after a patent has been applied for, and release the program before the patent is approved. Only later will the developer learn that distribution of the program is prohibited.

For example, the implementors of the widely used public domain data compression program Compress followed an algorithm obtained from the journal *IEEE Computer*. (This algorithm is also used in several popular programs for microcomputers, including PKZIP.) They and the user community were surprised to learn later that patent number 4,558,302 had been issued to one of the authors of the article. Now Unisys is demanding royalties for using this algorithm. Although the program Compress is still in the public domain, using it means risking a lawsuit.

The Patent Office does not have a workable scheme for classifying software patents. Although patents are most frequently classified by end results, such as "converting iron to steel," many patents cover algorithms whose use in a program is entirely independent of the purpose of the program. For example, a program to analyze human speech might infringe the patent on a speedup in the Fast Fourier Transform; so might a program to perform symbolic algebra (in multiplying large numbers). But the category to search for such a patent would be difficult to predict.

You might think it would be easy to keep a list of the patented software techniques, or even simply remember them. However, managing such a list is nearly impossible. A list compiled in 1989 by lawyers specializing in the field omitted some of the patents mentioned in this column.

Obscure Patents

When you imagine an invention, you probably think of something that could be described in a few words, such as "a flying machine with fixed, curved wings" or "an electrical communicator with a microphone and a speaker." But most patents cover complex detailed processes that have no simple descriptions—often they are speedups or variants of well-known processes that are themselves complex.

Most of these patents are neither obvious nor brilliant; they are obscure. A capable software designer will "invent" several such improvements in the course of a project. However, there are many avenues for improving a technique, so no single project is likely to find any given one.

For example, IBM has several patents (including patent number 4,656,583) on workmanlike, albeit complex, speedups for well-known computations performed by optimizing compilers, such as register coloring and computing the available expressions.

Patents are also granted on combinations of techniques that are already widely used. One example is IBM patent 4,742,450, which covers "shared copy-on-write segments." This technique allows several programs to share the same piece of memory that represents information in a file. If any program writes a page in the file, that page is replaced by a copy in all of the programs, which continue to share that page with one another but no longer share with the file.

Shared segments and copy-on-write have been used since the 1960s; this particular combination may be new as a specific feature, but is hardly an invention. Nevertheless, the Patent Office thought it merited a patent, which must now be taken into account by the developer of any new operating system.

Obscure patents are like land mines: other developers are more likely to reinvent these techniques than to find out about the patents, and will then be sued. The chance of running into any one of these patents is small, but they are so numerous that you cannot go far without hitting one. Every basic technique has many variations, and a small set of basic techniques can be combined in many ways. The Patent Office has now granted at least 2,000 software patents—no less than 700 in 1989 alone, according to a list compiled by EDS. We can expect the pace to accelerate. In 10 years, programmers will have no choice but to march on blindly and hope they are lucky.

Problems of Patent Licensing

Most large software companies are trying to solve the problem of patents by getting patents of their own. Then they hope to cross-license with the other large companies that own most of the patents, freeing them to go on as before.

While this approach will allow companies like Microsoft, Apple and IBM to continue in business, it will shut new companies out of the field. A future start-up, with no patents of its own, will be forced to pay whatever price the giants choose to impose. That price might be high: established companies have an interest in excluding future competitors. The recent Lotus lawsuits against Borland and the Santa Cruz Operation (although involving an extended idea of copyright rather than patents) show how this can work.

Even the giants cannot protect themselves with cross-licensing from companies whose only business is to obtain exclusive rights to patents and then threaten to sue. For example, consider the New York-based Refac Technology Development Corporation, representing the owner of the "natural order recalc" patent. Contrary to its name, Refac does not develop anything except lawsuits—it has no business reason to join a cross-licensing compact. Cadtrak, the owner of the exclusive-or patent, is also a litigation company.

Refac is demanding 5% of sales of all major spreadsheet programs. If a future program infringes on 20 such patents—and this is not unlikely, given the complexity of computer programs and the broad applicability of many patents—the combined royalties could exceed 100% of the sales price. (In practice, just a few patents can make a program unprofitable.)

The Fundamental Question

According to the U.S. Constitution, the purpose of patents is to "promote the progress of science and the useful arts." Thus, the basic question at issue is whether software patents, supposedly a method of encouraging software progress, will truly do so, or will retard progress instead.

So far, we have explained the ways in which patents will make ordinary software development difficult. But what of the intended benefits of patents: more invention, and more public disclosure of inventions? To what extent will these actually occur in the field of software?

There will be little benefit to society from software patents because invention in software was already flourishing before such patents existed, and inventions were normally published in journals for everyone to use. Invention flourished so strongly, in fact, that the same inventions were often found again and again.

In Software, Independent Reinvention Is Commonplace

A patent is an absolute monopoly. Everyone is forbidden to use the patented process, even those who reinvent it independently. This policy implicitly assumes inventions are rare and precious, since only in those circumstances is it beneficial.

The software field is one of constant reinvention. It is sometimes said that programmers throw away more "inventions" each week than other people develop in a year. And the comparative ease of designing large software systems makes it easy for many people to do work in the field. A programmer solves many problems in developing each program. These solutions are likely to be reinvented frequently as other programmers tackle similar problems.

The prevalence of independent reinvention negates the usual purpose of patents. Patents are intended to encourage inventions and, above all, the disclosure of inventions. If a technique will be reinvented frequently, there is no need to encourage more people to invent it. Since some developers will choose to publish it (if publication is merited), there is no point in encouraging a particular inventor to publish it—at the cost of inhibiting use of the technique.

Overemphasis of Inventions

Many analysts of American and Japanese industry have attributed Japanese success in producing quality products to their emphasis on incremental improvements, convenient features and quality rather than noteworthy inventions.

It is especially true in software that success depends primarily on getting the details right. And that is most of the work in developing any useful software system. Inventions are a comparatively unimportant part of the job.

The idea of software patents is thus an example of the mistaken American preoccupation with inventions rather than products. And patents will encourage this mistaken focus, even as they impede the development work that actually produces better software.

Impeding Innovation

By reducing the number of programmers engaged in software development, software patents will actually impede innovation. Much software innovation comes from programmers solving problems while developing software, not from projects whose specific purpose is to make inventions and obtain patents. In other words, these innovations are byproducts of software development.

When patents make development more difficult, and cut down on development projects, they will also cut down on the byproducts of development—new techniques.

Could Patents Ever Be Beneficial?

Although software patents in general are harmful to society as a whole, we do not claim that every software patent is necessarily harmful. Careful study might show that under certain specific and narrow conditions (necessarily excluding the vast majority of cases) it is beneficial to grant software patents.

Nonetheless, the right thing to do now is to eliminate all software patents as soon as possible, before more damage is done. The careful study can come afterward.

Clearly, software patents are not urgently needed by anyone except patent lawyers. Patents did not solve any problems of the prepatent software industry. There was no shortage of invention, and no shortage of investment.

Complete elimination of software patents may not be the ideal solution, but it is close and is a great improvement. Its very simplicity helps avoid a long delay while people argue about details.

If it is ever shown that software patents are beneficial in certain exceptional cases, the law can be changed again at that time—if it is important enough. There is no reason to continue the present catastrophic situation until that day.

Software Patents Are Legally Questionable

It may come as a surprise that the extension of patent law to software is still legally questionable. It rests on an extreme interpretation of a particular 1981 Supreme Court decision, *Diamond vs. Diehr*.[1]

Traditionally, the only kinds of processes that could be patented were those for transforming matter (such as, for transforming iron into steel). Many other activities which we would consider processes were entirely excluded from patents, including business methods, data analysis, and "mental steps." This was called the "subject matter" doctrine.

Diamond vs. Diehr has been interpreted by the Patent Office as a reversal of this doctrine, but the Court did not explicitly reject it. The case concerned a process for curing rubber—a transformation of matter. The issue at hand was whether the use of a computer program in the process was enough to render it unpatentable, and the Court ruled that it was not. The Patent Office took this narrow decision as a green light for unlimited patenting of software techniques, and even for the use of software to perform specific well-known and customary activities.

Most patent lawyers have embraced the change, saying the new boundaries of patents should be defined over decades by a series of expensive court cases. Such a course of action will certainly be good for patent lawyers, but it is unlikely to be good for software developers and users.

One Way to Eliminate Software Patents

We recommend the passage of a law to exclude software from the domain of patents. No matter what patents might exist, they would not cover implementations in software; only implementations in the form of hard-to-design hardware would be covered. An advantage of this method is it would not be necessary to classify patent applications into hardware and software when examining them.

Many have asked how to define software for this purpose—where the line should be drawn. For the purpose of this legislation, software should be defined by the characteristics that make software patents especially harmful:

• Software is built from ideal infallible mathematical components, whose outputs are not affected by the components into which they feed.

• Ideal mathematical components are defined by abstract rules, so that failure of a component is by definition impossible. The behavior of any system built of these components is likewise defined by the consequences of applying the rules step by step to the components.

- Software can be easily and cheaply copied.

Following this criterion, a program to compute prime numbers is a piece of software. A mechanical device designed specifically to perform the same computation is not software, since mechanical components have friction, can interfere with one another's motion, can fail, and must be assembled physically to form a working machine.

Any piece of software needs a hardware platform in order to run. The software operates the features of the hardware in some combination, under a plan. We propose that combining the features in this way can never create infringement. If the hardware alone does not infringe a patent, then using it in a particular fashion under control of a program should not infringe either. In effect, a program is an extension of the programmer's mind, acting as a proxy for the programmer to control the hardware.

Usually the hardware is a general-purpose computer, which implies no particular application. Such hardware cannot infringe any patents except those covering the construction of computers. Our proposal means that, when a user runs such a program on a general-purpose computer, no patents other than those should apply.

The traditional distinction between hardware and software involves a complex of characteristics that used to go hand in hand. Some newer technologies, such as gate arrays and silicon compilers, blur the distinction because they combine characteristics associated with hardware with others associated with software. However, most of these technologies can be classified unambiguously for patent purposes, either as software or as hardware using the preceding criteria. A few gray areas may remain, but these are comparatively small, and need not be an obstacle to solving the problems patents pose for ordinary software development. They will eventually be treated as hardware, as software, or as something in between.

What You Can Do

One way to help eliminate software patents is to join the League for Programming Freedom. The League is a grass-roots organization of programmers and users opposing software patents and interface copyrights.

(The League is not opposed to copyright on individual programs.) Annual dues for individual members are $42.00 for employed professionals, $10.50 for students, and $21.00 for others. We appreciate activists, but members who cannot contribute their time are also welcome. Contact the League at:·

League for Programming Freedom
1 Kendall Square #143
PO Box 9171
Cambridge, MA 02139
or tel. (617) 243-4091;
Email: {league@prep.ai.mit.edu},

In the United States, you may also help by writing to Congress. You can write to your own representatives, but it may be even more effective to write to the subcommittees that consider such issues:·

House Subcommittee on Intellectual Property
2137 Rayburn Bldg.
Wash., DC 20515

Senate Subcommittee on Patents, Trademarks and Copyrights
United States Senate
Wash., DC 20510

You can phone your representatives at (202) 225-3121, or write to them using the following addresses:·

United States Senate
Wash., DC 20510

House of Representatives
Wash., DC 20510

Fighting Patents One by One

Until we succeed in eliminating all patenting of software, we must try to overturn individual software patents. This is very expensive and can solve only a small part of the problem, but that is better than nothing.

Overturning patents in court requires prior art, which may not be easy to find. The League for Programming Freedom will try to serve as a clearing house for this information, to assist the defendants in software patent suits. This depends on your help. If you know about prior art for any software patent, please send the information to the League.

If you work on software, you can help prevent software patents by refusing to cooperate in applying for them. The details of this may depend on the situation.

Conclusion

Exempting software from the scope of patents will protect software developers from the insupportable cost of patent searches, the wasteful struggle to find a way clear of known patents, and the unavoidable danger of lawsuits.

If nothing is changed, what is now an efficient creative activity will become prohibitively expensive. To picture the effects, imagine if each square of pavement on the sidewalk had an owner, and pedestrians required a license to step on it. Imagine the negotiations necessary to walk an entire block under this system. That is what writing a program will be like if software patents continue. The sparks of creativity and individualism that have driven the computer revolution will be snuffed out.—Prepared by Richard Stallman and Simson Garfinkle.

Note

1. See Samuelson, P. "Legally Speaking." *Commun. ACM* (Aug. 1990).

4

Debunking the Software Patent Myths

Paul Heckel

Jealousy and Envy deny the merit or the novelty of your invention; but vanity, when the novelty and merit are established, claims it for its own. . . . One would not therefore, of all faculties, or qualities of the mind, wish for a friend, or a child, that he should have that of invention. For his attempts to benefit mankind in that way, however well imagined, if they do not succeed, expose him, though very unjustly, to general ridicule and contempt; and if they do succeed, to envy, robbery, and abuse.

—Ben Franklin, 1775 [6]

The issue of software patentability is an important topic because it affects the environment in which programmers and designers work software innovation, the health of the software industry, and U.S. competitiveness. While the writing of this article was motivated by "Against Software Patents," by the League for Programming Freedom in the Jan. 1992 issue of *Communications* it is an overall defense of software patents.

An Absurd Patent

U.S. Patent 4,736,308, the first patent under the heading "Absurd Patents" in "Against Software Patents," is described: "For example, Apple was sued because the HyperCard program allegedly violates patent number 4,736,308, a patent that covers displaying portions of two or more strings together on the screen, effectively scrolling with multiple subwindows. Scrolling and subwindows are well-known techniques, but combining them is apparently illegal." The League calls this an "outrageous result." Based on this description alone, any reasonable person would have to agree.

But I am that inventor and Apple was actually sued on a prior related patent, 4,486,857. Because my patents were misrepresented, I researched the other patents described in the League's article and am reporting my results.

There is much the League did not say about my patent and the circumstances surrounding it. First, it did not describe my background. In 1963 I worked on the software for the first computer designed to be a timesharing computer. I was at Xerox PARC in its early days, wrote two articles for *Communications* [17,20] and a book on user interface design [16]. My patent covers a commercial product called Zoomracks [19], which introduced a new computer metaphor called the card and rack metaphor. Zoomracks was marketed primarily on the Atari ST. Zoomracks developed a strong base of users who used it for a very broad range of applications, but it was a financial struggle largely because Atari did poorly. In Aug. 1987, Apple Computer introduced HyperCard, which is based on a similar, but more limited card and stack version of the metaphor.

I was then faced with having invested six years of raising money, developing a product, marketing it, and proving its value in the market, only to find I was in debt, my customer base was on a dying computer and Apple was giving away *free* a more polished and featured, although less elegant, version of the metaphor. While Apple may not have set out to rip off Zoomracks, it was aware of Zoomracks (having seen it under nondisclosure), of HyperCard's similarity to Zoomracks, and that Zoomracks was protected by patents.

HyperCard created expectations that Zoomracks could not meet, and other companies began to develop HyperCard clones. Meanwhile, I asserted my rights, sued and settled with Apple, licensing the patents. Apple is to be applauded for respecting my patents.

IBM was less respectful: we had twice brought our patent to its attention with respect to products like HyperCard and we had visibly asserted our patents and sued and settled with Apple by the time IBM decided to bundle what many consider to be a HyperCard clone. If this article has an anti-IBM patina to it, it is because I spent six months patiently trying to deal with IBM. Finally, IBM representatives flew to San Francisco to show us prior art—earlier technology—invalidating our patents that they claimed to have. When they arrived, they refused to show us the prior art, "for fear the patent office would recertify our patents in error." Even if IBM had been straightforward with me during the six months, to accept such an assertion without evidence would have been naive.

Faced with a choice of accepting IBM's offer of 0.2% of the $5 million IBM is said to have paid to license the token ring patent, or to accept its challenge to "sue us" if we wanted to see the prior art, IBM left me no choice but to fight. But I have chosen to fight in the court of public opinion where possible, rather than the civil courts where, because of its financial strength, IBM has the detailed advantage. I added a description of my dealings with IBM to my book [16] and later sent copies of my book to the members of the Commission on Patent Reform when they asked for comments.

Based on my experience I formulated Heckel's Principle of Dealing with Big Companies: *There is no such thing as a free lunch; unless you're the lunch.*

With Apple and IBM, I did battle against large companies who were sophisticated about intellectual property, rather than small ones that were not. I felt it was in everyone's interest to force companies and the courts to make decisions about software patents so the rules and the marketplace realities can be clear to all, not just the sophisticated few. This article is written in that same spirit. While it is a personal issue, I write to clarify the software patent issues in general, to raise the level of discussion and because like most good inventors, I am curious about what the truth is.

One can only understand the need for patents in light of the competitive marketplace. We need a heavy to show what the innovator faces, just as Humphrey Bogart needed Sidney Greenstreet in *The Maltese Falcon*. IBM has already presented itself in that role; it will reappear as did Sidney Greenstreet.

The Informed Opinion

We will visit the other eight patents mentioned by the League in its article and show that the patents it selected, on examination, disprove its case. But first, we take the broader view.

Should software be patentable like other technologies? The primary issue is a policy one and so we have been influenced by Neustadt and May and their book on governmental decision-making [33]. We ask: "What analogies (to software) exist?" "What are the similarities and differences?" "What are the assumptions, explicit and hidden?" "What is known?" "What is the history of the issues?" "What are the interests of the various players?" We will follow the Goldberg rule and ask, not "What is the problem?" but "What is the story?" Most important, we should ask, "How did things turn out in the past?"

History and innovation economics, more than law and computer science, must be the foundation on which to make policy. We have framed 10 points which are, we believe, the consensus of informed opinion on software patents. We hope they help you crystallize your thoughts on patents and enable you to better articulate your differences, if any, with the informed opinion.

1. By creating property rights, patents promote innovation in non-software areas. They particularly promote innovation from small and mid-size companies.

Most of the arguments against software patents turn out to be arguments against patents *per se*. These arguments are advanced most credibly on the basis of established technologies where data and research already exist.

Patents have been accepted around the world as promoting innovation. Many giants of U.S. industry such as G.E., AT&T, Polaroid, Xerox and Hewlett-Packard, started as small companies that used patent protection to protect their inventions.

Yet, most of the articles on patents in the trade, business and even academic press read by the computer community [5, 13, 15, 26, 27, 28, 41, 42, 48] have an antisoftware patent bias. The reason is that for every patent there is one patentholder who is reluctant to speak because the issue is complex and what someone says could be used against him in litigation. And there are a dozen who might like to use the patented technology without paying for it and so are willing to malign the patent and patent system and pass on unsubstantiated rumors and misinformation.

Economists have researched innovation in other technologies [24, 30, 31, 41] and found the following: patents encourage innovation; and small entities—individual inventors and small companies—are a very important source of innovation. According to Jewkes et al. [24],

> It is almost impossible to conceive of any existing social institution so faulty in so many ways. It survives only because there seems to be nothing better. And yet for the individual inventor or the small producer struggling to market a new idea, the patent right is crucially important. It is the only resource he possesses and, fragile and precarious as his rights may be, without them he would have nothing by which to establish a claim to a reward for his work. The sale of his ideas directly or the raising of capital for exploiting the ideas would be hopeless without the patent.

While several articles discuss software patents and copyrights [8, 46, 47], few have been written for the software, as opposed to the legal, community [11, 16, 37]. Such studies have only rarely been linked to software [7], and we are unaware of any empirical studies of the effect of software patents on innovation other than this one.

If we are to reject patents in principle, we should argue that case. If we accept patents as promoting innovation elsewhere but not in software, then we should differentiate software from other technologies.

2. Patents have evolved to address concerns raised by those who suspect software patents.

The courts have developed a patent jurisprudence as a unifying mechanism to support many technologies and foster evolutionary improvement while balancing the rights of patentholders and potential infringers.

Patents have a long history (see a Brief History of Patents). Most of the concerns about patents raised by the League have been raised long ago in the context of other technologies and addressed in case law and legislation and have stood the test of time. The patent system, like MS/DOS, is not perfect. MS/DOS has a long history of evolutionary improvement: It is a derivative of CP/M, which is a derivative of TOPS-20, which is a derivative of the SDS-940 timesharing system, which evolved from the first timesharing system developed at BBN about 1960. Patent jurisprudence has a similar history of evolution.

Part of the value of patents is they are a proven, public domain *standard* of intellectual property protection having a history of improvement over 500 years, compared to the 30 or 40 years of experience developing operating systems. TopView and OS/2 demonstrate how developing a new operating system and crystallizing a new infrastructure around it are fraught

A Brief History of Patents

Until recently patents were thought to have originated in England and been used only there prior to America, an error propagated by Jefferson, Lincoln and as late as 1948 by the Supreme Court. Recent scholarship shows their Italian origin and their early use in France, Germany, the Netherlands as well as England. Venice granted 10-year monopolies to inventors of silk-making devices in the 1200s. These early patents were *ad hoc* grants. In 1474 Venice passed its first patent statute. It recognized patents as a matter of right, rather than royal favor, and provided for fines and the destruction of infringing devices. Gallileo was granted a patent [6]. In England, the queen granted so many monopolies to her friends that citizens protested; so England, in 1624, passed the Statute of Monopolies. This prevented the granting of monopolies, but gave people the right to obtain patents on inventions and imports new to the realm. This statute distinguished between monopolies, which it outlawed as taking from the public what it already had, and patents, which it permitted as giving to the public what it did not yet have.

These patent laws were enacted at the end of the dark ages just before the Renaissance in Italy and the Industrial Revolution in England, suggesting that they *stimulated* innovation.

The Founding Fathers also believed that inventions (and writings) belong to their creators inherently—rather than to the state to be granted at its pleasure. This principle was embodied in the Constitution [1, 6], where Article 1, Section 8 says,

The Congress shall have the power to promote the progress of science and the useful arts by securing for a limited time to authors and inventors the exclusive right to their respective writings and discoveries.

Congress has the power, not to grant rights but to secure inherent rights. This is the principle expressed in the Declaration of Independence that "all men are endowed by their creator with certain unalienable rights." In the Federalist Papers, James Madison, in describing the patent powers, observed that "The public good fully coincides . . . with the claims of individuals."

The creators of the Constitution knew history and understood the ways of men and women, and patents—9 of the 13 colonies granted patents. We should give weight to findings of fact embodied in the Constitution. Two concern patents: Patent rights are inherent rights like freedom of speech; and patents promote innovation.

with dangers—known and unknown. An infrastructure has crystallized around MS/DOS. It includes developers and consultants who know it, books explaining its use, and commercial products based on it. Similarly, an infrastructure has crystallized around the patent system. It includes patent lawyers, case law examples of valid and invalid, infringed and not infringed patents, and books and articles explaining patents to both lawyers and nonlawyers.

3. Patents are not perfect.

There are problems with the patent system. Only that which is not real is perfect. The patent community and the Patent and Trademark Office (PTO) are aware of the problems and have been working to address them. A Commission on Patent Reform is considering improvements such as better examination procedures and automatic publication of patent applications after 18 to 24 months.

If lack of perfection were a reason to get rid of something, no one would survive his or her teenage years. Other industries find patents useful in spite of these problems; software will too.

Patents, it is said, inhibit standards. They do not; they inhibit the expropriation of intellectual property without just compensation in violation of the Fifth Amendment. Where patents exist standards are created in two ways:·

• Where people want a standard that infringes a patent, the standards body usually negotiates an agreement whereby the patentholder in return for having his or her technology required as part of a standard, agrees to make a standard license and rate available to all.

• Often standards are agreed to which do not infringe any intellectual property. The QWERTY keyboard and the standard automobile controls (steering wheel, brake and accelerator) demonstrate that patents don't inhibit standards creation. Both public domain standards were developed during the working lifetime of Edison who received 1,100 patents.

4. Software is not inherently different from other technologies in the way innovation or patents work.

Arguments that software is different should be treated critically; you can be sure those same arguments will be used by those who do not believe that the protections of the Bill of Rights extend to areas where computers and software are used.

Fred Brooks, following Aristotle, suggested the distinction between essence and accident [3], and that distinction has guided our analysis in the issues raised by the League and the academics (see Obviousness: Polaroid vs. Kodak). The question is whether the differences between software are essential or accidental in their encouraging innovation. The League says software is different and so should be protected differently. They present two arguments.

A. Programs are complex.
Why, so they are; but so are airplanes, silicon chips, silicon chip fabrication plants, potato chip plants, oil refineries and many things. But people find the patent system beneficial in these other technologies.

B. Software is cheap to develop compared to other technologies because it is a cottage industry.
Other industries have cottage manufacturers and they deal with patents. Outside of software much invention is a cottage industry; about 5,000 independent inventors belong to the 37 organizations that are members

Obviousness: Polaroid vs. Kodak

As an example of how the patent system has evolved to address the concerns the League raises, consider the Polaroid patent which, they say, describes "differences in the number and order of layers of chemical in a film—differences between the technique Kodak was using and those described by previous expired patents." The League says such differences were obvious. The court held otherwise. Kodak could have avoided infringement by using the order described in the earlier, expired, patent the League refers to. Why would Kodak use the new order described in the later patent rather than the earlier one? Why would Polaroid patent it? Could it have been better? This demonstrates three things to those who must deal with patents. First, an active patent is a territorial warning. Second, technology described in expired patents is in the public domain. Third, patents protect the innovator. Polaroid was the innovator in instant photography. Kodak wanted a share of that market. The major obstacle was Polaroid patents. Kodak tried to get too near the fire. Kodak got burned and paid Polaroid over $900 million.

of the National Congress of Independent Inventors. And most cottage industries do not rely on invention.

We should no more optimize an intellectual property system for cottage developers than we should for Fortune 500 companies.

When one talks about marketing and maintaining commercial software products, the costs are much greater than the estimates made by the League. At the other extreme, IBM is reported to have spent 2.5 *billion* dollars to develop OS/2, including applications.

It is expensive to develop software if the task is to design it from scratch and make it a success in the market; it is cheap if the task is to clone something that already exists or is precisely specified.

Indeed, that clone software is so much cheaper to develop argues for the necessity of patent protection if one wants to stimulate the development of products worth cloning.

Making software nonpatentable or subjecting it to a different form of protection creates practical difficulties, rather like a state seceding from the Union and setting up check points on its border. And if one state secedes, they all can. If each technology has its own *sui generis* (unique) form of protection, we would have to set up boundaries between the different technologies and would need rules for what happens at the boundaries.

This situation occurs in software development. Should programmers be able to define their own conventions or should they conform to the system conventions even where they are not optimal? Do new programmers get to define their own conventions just because they were not involved in the original decision? Aren't programmers expected to abide by the conventions so the code will integrate better and others can maintain it later? Of course, as problems surface, it is foolish to resist all change in conventions just because changes have repercussions. Changes are made, but as part of a deliberative process in which the burden of proof is on those who advocate the changes.

The evolution of the law works the same way: computer law is just another subsystem to be integrated into the fabric of jurisprudence.

The problem of having different conventions in different areas is demonstrated by the Cadtrak patent. It is a hardware, rather than a software, patent. It requires a display device but no software to infringe it. A computer can be designed so it does not infringe, although a simple program running on it can. This demonstrates that simple software programs can infringe almost pure hardware patents and suggests the difficulty of drawing a legal distinction between hardware and software.

Pamela Samuelson laments that "patent lawyers [do not] claim software-related inventions in a straightforward manner" [39]. Patent lawyers are faced with a Catch 22 situation because of the line between what is patentable and what is not: Write a straightforward patent, and get it rejected as pure software because of *Benson*; write one that is patentable subject matter and it will not be straightforward. Attempting to make software unpatentable will no more prevent practical software patents from issuing and being enforced than prohibition will eliminate alcoholism.

The PTO and those patent lawyers who prosecute software patents have much more experience in the nitty-gritty of protecting software than academics. And the PTO and the courts have more experience weaving new technologies into the fabric of the patent system than the software community has in creating forms of intellectual property protection.

The debate in the academic world is described in The Academic Debate: Considered Opinion and Advocacy. The mainstream view taken by the practicing and academic patent bar and most computer lawyers on one side and the contrarians led by Samuelson, argue against software having the same breadth of protection as other technologies. The League for Programming Freedom has launched an offense in the debate. Like the Battle of the Bulge, it might appear formidable when seen up close. But while it must be treated seriously, it is the last gasp of a dying cause.

The pioneers in each new technology see that technology as new, different, and central, and expect the world to accommodate it. To some extent the world does. But each new technology slowly becomes woven into the tapestry of knowledge encompassing other technologies—each distinctive in its picture—but using the same threads and the same weave.

5. A nonprofit Marxist economic system is not optimal in promoting innovation in software.

This is the paradox one must confront if one argues software patents decrease innovation. The essential difference between Marxism and

The Academic Debate: Considered Opinion and Advocacy

The Mainstream View

Donald Chisum has written the standard reference on patent law [9] and is frequently quoted in judicial decisions. His expertise is in integrating patent decisions into a coherent view of the patent law across mechanical, electrical, chemical and other technologies as they are handed down. His reputation rests on the soundness of his analysis in predicting how courts will rule.

Chisum views software as one of many technologies and says software is almost as patentable as anything else and to the degree that it is not, it should be [8]. He has two concerns. First, the current decisions uphold most software as patentable in a way that forces patent lawyers and the technical community to focus on legal technicalities rather than the technical ones. Second, he questions whether lack of patentability will create underinvestment in software innovation as compared to other technologies.

His approach is similar to Judge Schwarzer's in determining how to calibrate the credibility of possible "junk science" in a courtroom. The question is not "Does this make sense in isolation?" but "How does it fit into an organized body of knowledge?" [44]

The Contrarian's View

The League provides no citations for its position in "Against Software Patents." But a similar article by the same authors [15] has four citations: Mitchell Kapor's congressional testimony and articles by lawyers Pamela Samuelson [39, 41] and Brian Kahin [26] let us see how the antisoftware patent position fits in with "an organized body of knowledge."

While patent lawyers conversant with software are in virtual unanimity that software should be patentable, neither of these lawyers is a patent lawyer.

As background we should consider the legal education most lawyers get. First, very few study patent law and thus are not exposed to the fundamental concept that patent rights are property rights. Second, most law students do take antitrust law where they learn that monopolies are illegal. Later, when they discover patents they often mistakenly see monopolies. Third, law students are taught to be advocates. Their job is not to make a considered opinion, but to present their case as best they can; someone else—the judge, Congress, the public—makes decisions.

This author's opinion is that those who took an antipatent point of view did it as a knee jerk intuitive reaction. Away from the mainline of software business and patent law, distrustful of monopolies and inexperienced with intellectual property, these lawyers and software developers found support in one another. This view gained respectability as a contrarian's view and is always welcome in legal journals and at conferences.

Samuelson argues that the basis of software patentability is weak and says the primary issue is a policy one [39]. She presents two arguments against software patentability and Kahin a third:

A. *The industry has flourished and innovated without patents.*

A more accurate statement would be: "The industry has flourished and innovated *with little realization in the software community* that patent protection was available."

The growth of the software industry was not due to differences between software and other technologies, but to its synergetic relationship with the computer industry and the new business opportunities created by the computer's rapidly decreasing costs. Until recently software has been seen by computer companies as a loss leader. Software created the demand for computers which was, and still is, the dominant industry: But software developers were to be kept fat, dumb and happy; salaries were high, patents were not mentioned, and there was lots of technology to play with.

Accidental Empires shows that the personal computer software successes were achieved by amateurs who were lucky enough to be in the right place at the right time [12]. The successful early PC software companies (a) marketed innovations *pioneered by others* and (b) aggressively pursued their own intellectual property rights: Microsoft's MS/DOS is a derivative of CP/M; and Lotus' 1-2-3 of VisiCalc. Had Digital Research, VisiCorp and Software Arts asserted intellectual property rights as aggressively as Microsoft and Lotus, they might not have been eclipsed by them.

In the early stage of the industrial life cycle, the first person in his garage who acts on the opportunity starts with the biggest and most established company in the business.

When there is no established competition, new companies can compete without patents. As the industry matures it becomes difficult for new companies to enter the market without a sustainable advantage such as patents. The free enterprise system rewarded entrepreneurs whose personal computer software companies were successful, as it should, but that success should not blind us to its nature—bringing the innovations of others to market. We expect that if patents had been more widely used by the software industry, the true innovators would have received a fairer share of the rewards, thus rewarding innovation as well as business savvy. Had patents been more widespread, the software industry would have been more profitable, it would have grown with less of a boom-and-bust cycle, albeit less rapidly and there would have been a greater diversity of software product categories and features. To base a software intellectual property system just on the experience of the last 10 years would be like raising teenagers in the expectation that their childhood will be repeated.

B. *Many in the software industry say software patents will discourage innovation.*

Samuelson says,

> . . . It is primarily from the widespread concerns about the effects of patents from within the industry and the technical community that she has pursued this study questioning the patent protection for computer program-related inventions. [39]

Samuelson addresses this perception by conducting a survey to see how widespread the perception is, at least in the related area of user interface copyrights [42], rather than attempting to determine if the perception reflects reality. In reporting the perception she gives it more credence, reinforcing any error, and creating more concern. It would seem to be more constructive to research the effect of patents on innovation and business formation in other industries to see how it might apply to software, and analyze software patents that exist for their effect on innovation and new business formation as we do.

It makes as much sense to devise theories of innovation by polling the software community as it does to devise laws of physics by polling people who walk. The intuitive answer is not necessarily the correct one. Ask people, "Assume you are walking at a steady pace holding a ball, and you drop the ball. Will the ball hit the ground in front of you, in back of you, or next to you?" most people will say "In back of me" [32]. A physicist will tell you that Newton's laws predict, "next to me," and can perform an experiment to prove it.

In contrast to Chisum and the mainstream of patent law where software is viewed from a broad perspective of many technologies, Samuelson views the law from inside the software community looking out. She has always advocated narrow protection—arguing as late as 1984 that CONTU's recommendation that software in machine readable form be copyrightable was ill considered [40].

Samuelson acknowledges that the conditions that promoted software innovation until now may be different from those that will promote it in the future.

Samuelson proposes to design a special *(sui generis)* form of protection for software, saying, "It is possible to design a law that is appropriate to the kind of subject matter that software is." How can one be certain of one's ability to build a skyscraper, if one is uncertain if one is building on bedrock or marshland?

Writing laws is like designing systems. They will have desired and undesired, intended and unintended consequences. The current law, especially *Benson,* forces patent lawyers into a Catch 22 dilemma: Write a straightforward patent and get it rejected as a mathematical algorithm; write one that is patentable subject matter and it will not be straightforward. Attempting to make only software unpatentable will no more prevent practical software patents from issuing and being enforced than prohibition will eliminate alcoholism. Samuelson laments that "patent lawyers [do not] claim software-related inventions in a straightforward manner" [39]; but this is like blaming a program's users or the market for not behaving as expected—a sure sign of an inexperienced designer. Law, software, and marketing strategies must be designed the same way the Constitution was: based not on how we would like people to behave, but on how self-interested people will actually behave.

Academics such as Samuelson, who pontificate on software patents and want to create a *sui generis* system of protection, seem ready to reinvent the wheel before they understand how a wagon works or the infrastructure of the highway system. Most show no knowledge or understanding of the processes of innovation over hundreds of years in a variety of technologies. Most have little, if any, experience prosecuting (filing), analyzing, or litigating patents. They argue that software is different from other technologies, not from the perspective of the history of innovation and patents over a range of technologies, but from the myopic view of the development of a single technology, largely in a single software marketplace in an atypical decade—the personal computer market in the 1980s.

Ben Franklin described a professor who was so learned he knew the word for horse in five languages: *equus* in Latin, *caballo* in Spanish, *cheval* in French, *cavallo* in Italian, and *Pferd* in German. He then went out to purchase one, and returned with a cow. Given your experience observing complex software systems develop and how the hype manifests itself in reality, when you hear *sui generis* protection systems being proposed as transport into the twenty-first century, ask yourself: "Will I ride a horse or a cow?"

Taking a contrary position and fighting for it, as Samuelson does, is in the highest tradition of the law. In part it is because truth emerges from the debate and if there is no one to debate with, a poor sort of truth will emerge. Yesterday's contrarian view may emerge as the mainstream view. It is like having advocates for a programming language like Forth. It forces identification and discussion of issues and influences the industry—PostScript is Forth-like. But software developers seriously consider programming in Forth only in unusual circumstances.

C. Software helps disseminate information

Brian Kahin, a research fellow in the Science, Technology and Public Policy Program at Harvard University's Kennedy School of Government offers a different reason software should not be patentable [25]:

> A deeper, more disturbing problem in patenting programs was barely evident before computers became ubiquitous personal tools. . . . The computer has developed into a medium for human expression and a mediator of human experience. Thus, what is increasingly at stake in software patents is the generation and flow of information.

The "barely evident" "problem" was addressed by Lincoln who, in his *Lecture on Discoveries* [23], said:

> certain inventions and discoveries occurred of particular value on account of their efficiency in facilitating all other inventions and discoveries. Of these were the arts of writing and of printing—the discovery of America and the introduction of Patent-laws.

Lincoln not only believed that the patent laws encouraged innovation, but he anticipated Kahin in realizing that inventions which promote dissemination of information are particularly important. Since Lincoln's speech, patents seem to have encouraged many inventions which engender the "generation and flow of information": the telephone (Bell), phonograph (Edison), movie camera (Edison), xerography (Carlson), radio (Armstrong and Marconi), phototypesetting (Scheffer), and TV (Philo T. Farnsworth).

Even at the birth of patenting, Aldus Manutius, the famous Venetian scholar-printer for whom the desktop publishing company is named, received two patents—one on a form of Greek type—and a ten year monopoly to use the Italic font which he invented.

Having discovered that he is treading in the footsteps of Lincoln, albeit in the opposite direction, Kahin might, in planning his future travel, consult the work of his colleagues at the Kennedy School of Government, which has guided our analysis [33].

capitalism is property rights. Patents and copyrights create intellectual property rights that can be bought, sold, rented and licensed like other property rights. Marxism may be better than capitalism in some areas—certainly not in Russia, but capitalism, with all its flaws, has outperformed Marxism.

The paradox of Marxism is not just a theoretical issue. Stallman, the founder of the *League for Programming Freedom*, heads the Free Software Foundation which is developing and planning to distribute a clone of the Unix™ operating system. AT&T has invested in Unix based on its ownership as manifest in patents and copyrights. AT&T cannot be pleased when Stallman gives away free copies of a clone of a product it invested millions in developing and marketing.

If AT&T had not used patents and user interface copyrights to protect its intellectual property rights, Stallman would have no trouble making and distributing a Unix clone. But AT&T must pay its bills with money it receives from customers and has asserted its rights. If it is acceptable to clone Unix or any program, will anyone invest in new ideas? Should we optimize an intellectual property jurisprudence for, not large entities, not small entities, but companies that distribute free clones of other people's software?

For all his talk about wanting to promote innovation, Stallman seems to get his ideas for technology from AT&T, 1969, and his ideas for intellectual property protection from IBM, 1965.

Many software developers do their work for the fun of it. But the distinction is based, not on the technology, but on amateurism: amateurs flourish in the early stages of a new technology. Professionals have accepted that others work for free, but they bristle if they are expected to work at the same rates.

6. Software, like every technology, has unique problems.

Software patents have unique problems: prior art libraries are limited, the search classification system was designed for hardware patents, few computer scientists are examiners. Still when it gets to specific cases, computer scientists and the PTO see invention similarly (see Document Comparison).

For the last two years the PTO has been improving the situation. It is improving its prior art search facilities in software, has published a new software classification system, and is actively recruiting computer scientists.

The PTO has still not been able to rid itself of the prejudice against software patents, as patent practitioners in the software area will tell you. It still is conservative in its interpretation of what constitutes patentable subject matter, and has rejected several applications that are being appealed.

Document Comparison: An Obvious Patent?

A criticism of the patent system is that computer scientists are qualified to judge invention in software while the PTO is not. In his article [26] Kahin says, the PTO is,

> awarding patents merely for automating familiar processes such as . . . comparing documents (Patent No. 4,807,182). But software developers have been routinely automating such [functions] for years.

In fact, the ACM published a refereed paper describing that (hashcoding) technique for comparing two text files albeit for source code, rather than document comparison [17]. It seems that the ACM and the PTO have similar standards of inventiveness.

It so happens I wrote that paper, and I brought it to the attention of the patentholder and (indirectly) to WordPerfect about 10 months before Kahin's article was published. Four companies put on notice about the patent brought the paper to the attention of the patentholder. This suggests that where prior art exists which narrows a patent's scope, it is likely to surface.

Advanced Software was founded to develop and market DocuComp which uses the patented technology. Its inventor, Cary Queen, a Ph.D. in mathematics, has filed over a dozen patents in genetic engineering where he is principle in a startup, Protein Design Labs. He also used the patented hashcoding technique to compare genes to identify similarities.

Cary Queen reports there is more prejudice against patents in software than in biotechnology, where hundreds of startups have been financed, as biotechnology patents are better respected.

7. Legally, software is patentable and it will remain so.

Prior to 1982, about 30 different software-related patent cases went through the Appellate Courts. The range of technologies—seismic, medical, petrochemical, telecommunications, firmware, and software—demonstrate that software is both well grounded in patent law, and basic to the advancement of American industry. Software has become pervasive in industry, which has been basing business decisions on software's being patentable for 10 to 20 years. This has created a sophisticated broad-based constituency for keeping software patentable. Congress has not given in to demands to make less pervasive technologies, such as biotechnology, unpatentable; it is less likely to do so with software. Software has been clearly patentable longer than it has been copyrightable (see Patents and Copyrights).

Chisum, the leading authority on patents, wrote an article on the patentability of software and concluded:

> The continuing confusion over the patentability of computer programming ideas can be laid on the doorsteps of a single Supreme Court decision, *Gottschalk vs. Benson*, which held that mathematical algorithms cannot be patented, no matter how new and useful. A careful analysis of that decision shows the holding is not supported by any of the authorities on which it relied, that the Court misunderstood the nature of the subject matter before it, and that the Court failed to offer any viable policy justification for excluding by judicial fiat mathematical algorithms from the patent system. The Benson decision is inconsistent with the later Supreme Court ruling in *Diamond vs. Chakabarty* that the patent system applies impartially to new technologies and that any policy issues for excluding new technologies should be addressed to Congress. Policy considerations indicate that patent protection is appropriate for mathematical algorithms that are useful for computer programming as for other technological innovations [8].

Chisum is in the mainstream in saying that the courts made a mistake by making software unpatentable. But courts are reluctant to overturn previous decisions directly, and then only after their scope has been eroded. A similar situation where prejudice had been part of the

Patents and Copyrights

Kahin says, "Never before has an industry in which copyright was widely established suddenly been subjected to patenting" [25].

In fact, patent protection for software was established before copyright protection. *Diamond vs. Diehr* (1981) preceded the two most important software copyright cases, *Apple Computer vs. Franklin Computer Company* (1982) and *SAS Institute Inc. vs. S&H Computer Systems Inc.* (1985). Even today the case law on user interface copyrights is sparse. Software, or "computer-related" patents, were obtained in the 1960s. Martin Goetz of Applied Data Research received U.S. patents 3,380,029 in 1968 on a Sorting System, and 3,533,086 in 1970 on AutoFlow, an automatic flow charting program. (When IBM started giving Roscoe, a flowcharting program, away free, Applied Data Research sued for antitrust and, in 1969, settled for about $2 million in damages.) The recalculation patent filed in 1970 was granted in 1983.

jurisprudence occurred earlier: *Plessy vs. Furgesson* [1896] held that "separate but equal" facilities for whites and blacks were lawful. The courts did not directly overturn it, but eroded its vitality on a case-by-case basis over a period of years in a number of decisions starting with *Murrey vs. Maryland* while appearing to show respect for *Plessy*. Finally, when faced with *Brown vs. Board of Education* [1954], ample precedent had been created for the Supreme Court to overrule *Plessy* directly.

Samuelson, having asked Chisum to write his article, now attempted to refute him, but after arguing for over 100 pages that the basis for software patentability is weak, was forced to conclude that:

> . . . the only principle which seems to have guided the court's decision is one of upholding the patentability of as many program-related inventions as possible while appearing to show respect for the Supreme Court's decisions. [39]

Samuelson's observation seems to be compelling evidence that while she has not been persuaded that *Benson*, like *Plessy*, is a fundamental error in giving prejudice the force of law, the Court has and will, in due course, reverse it and the original intent of Congress will again become law and statutory. Subject matter will "include anything under the sun that is made by man."

8. Whether or not one agrees that software patents are beneficial, patents are here to stay so we should plan to work with them.

The software community will be best served by articles about how to avoid infringement, how to deal with infringement notices, how to find prior art, how to use patents to protect new ideas, how to differentiate products, and how to make the patent system work better for software (based on experience rather than speculation). In brief, we should direct our energies toward making the system work in order to increase innovation and U.S. competitiveness, rather than fighting patents.

9. The practical effect of continuing to spread misinformation on software patents will be to hurt small developers and U.S. competitiveness in software.

Patents, like a cat's claws, function as weapons when necessary. A declawed cat will not survive in the wild; neither can a defenseless startup once it succeeds and attracts substantial competitors. Patents are not the only defense, but they are vital to innovative startups that must survive. In business, as in the jungle, respect is given only to those who can protect themselves.

Microsoft, IBM and others are applying for patents in quantity. Those who do not understand the situation are not. Many are happy to have software patents attacked. Why let your competitor in on a good thing? Why pioneer new product ideas when it is less risky to copy competing products and incorporate useful features once market success is proven.

From the perspective of large companies, a loud voice, such as the League, yelling against software patents can be useful as a means to destroy one's competition.

The Japanese are aggressively filing for U.S. patents on software. While our strength is innovation, Japan's is in adapting innovations and steady improvement. But if they have the improvement patents and we did not file for the basic patents, we lose. If we arrogantly dismiss the Japanese as incapable of creating good software or cavalierly dismiss patents as undesirable, then 20 years from now we will be trying to get back the software market from Japan just as today we are trying to get back the automobile and semiconductor markets. We are not even trying to get back the consumer electronics market.

Who is responsible for the misperception about the desirability and legality of software patents? In a certain sense, it is the League for Programming Freedom. But it knows not what it does. And its arguments are the ghosts of arguments for IBM's corporate self-interest of a bygone era. Is not the origin of the problem IBM's attempt in the 1960s to declaw a competing technology by depriving its practitioners of their constitutional rights as inventors? (See Software Patents: IBM's Role in History.)

If it were just a question of IBM outfoxing its competitors, we might learn our lesson and let it pass. But we think it useful to ask some questions: Is it in the interest of the United States to have a strong, competitive, innovative software industry? Is it in IBM's interest? Did IBM use its position on the 1966 Patent Commission to put its corporate self-interest ahead of that of the U.S.? Should IBM be held responsible for its role in creating the current software patent mess? Some have proposed making software patents unenforceable. Might a law making IBM pat-

Software Patents: IBM's Role in History

In the late 1960s when IBM's internal policy was that software should not be patentable, IBM vice president, J. W. Birkenstock, chaired a presidential commission on the patent system which recommended that software should not be patentable. We expect that the other commission members deferred to IBM's expertise on software, just as members of a commission designing an aviary would defer to its most knowledgeable member on birds: the cat.

Congress rejected this view, but three paragraphs of the Commission's recommendations, e.g., IBM's corporate policy, found their way into *Gottschalk vs. Benson,* the Supreme Court decision that limited the patentability of software. At this time IBM had 70% of the computer market, so it is not surprising that CBEMA, the Computer Business Equipment Manufacturers Association, filed an *amicus curie* brief against software patents in *Benson.*

From this historical perspective we can see that the conventional wisdom that "software has not been patentable," should be more accurately stated as "it was not in the interest of IBM or other computer manufacturers for people to think software is patentable." We have never seen it pointed out in the debate on software patents that the idea that software is not patentable subject matter was formed in the crucible of IBM's self-interest and corporate policies of an earlier time.

IBM and CBEMA have now rejected the Stallman-primal IBM view [7]. But the damage has been done. The PTO and the industry have not taken software patents seriously until recently, which explains the problems the PTO has had in examining patents and the prejudice against software inventors who assert their patent rights. Many in the software community have been suckered into believing software should not be patentable, while IBM has aggressively but quietly been getting software patents and become the company with the largest software sales.

ents unenforceable make more sense? Or a law that would prevent IBM from obtaining patents for a period of time, say 5 or 10 years? At a time when competitiveness with Japan is a major concern, what kind of a message should we send about what happens to those who use their positions on government commissions to sacrifice their country's interest to their corporate self-interest?

Similarly, should we eliminate patents to avoid patent litigation as the League suggests? Should we not eliminate all laws so as to avoid all litigation?

10. In considering the issues, we should deal with examples of real patents and, where possible, real infringement where facts for both sides are fairly stated.

If we are to have a meaningful debate on whether software should be patentable, I suggest we take our standards, both of debate and of where the burden of proof lies from Abraham Lincoln:

> I do not mean to say we are bound to follow implicitly in whatever our fathers did. To do so would be to discard all the lights of current experience—to reject all progress—all improvement . . . if we would supplant the opinions and policy of our fathers in any case, we should do so upon evidence so conclusive, and argument so clear, that even their great authority, fairly considered and weighed, cannot stand. . . .
>
> If any man [believes something], he is right to say so, and to enforce his position by all truthful evidence and fair argument which he can. But he has no right to mislead others, who have less access to history, and less leisure to study it, into [a] false belief . . . thus substituting falsehood and deception for truthful evidence and fair argument.

What I find most frustrating in this debate is that the mode of argument used against software patents by so many [15, 26, 27, 28] is to throw as much mud against the wall as possible and hope some of it will stick. I have expended some effort here removing some of the mud. I do not claim to have removed it all, but I hope I have wiped away enough to show you the rest will wash off too.

A Study of Nine Software Patents

In its article the League lists nine patents—mine and eight others to make its case. It is unlikely that the members of the League considered the positive side of any of the patents they cited. It is as if they went searching for quarters with heads showing, and finding several, reported their findings without turning any of them over. Here we turn over the other eight quarters in an attempt to produce some empirical results.

U.S. Patent 4,197,590

The inventor founded a company to develop and market what appears to be the first personal computer to write directly from memory to the display. This invention has been widely licensed to the personal computer industry by Cadtrak. The "XOR" is only part of the invention. Cadtrak filed and has won at least one lawsuit against a larger company. The idea behind the "XOR" claims of this patent is simple. A program XORs a cursor icon onto a display device; later a second XOR to the same place erases the cursor, restoring the original display. To move the cursor one XORs the cursor to its old location, then XORs it onto the new location. There are many ways to get around this patent. One can use an underline as a cursor or "logically or" the cursor onto the display, erasing later by rewriting the display with its original information. This approach is fast, lets you change cursor icons easily, accesses the minimum possible data, and requires no space be reserved on the screen for the cursor.

The League says this patent can be infringed in "a few lines of a program." It can be, *but not on a computer that was commercially available at the time the invention was made.* The invention is largely the invention of the frame buffer. As such, it requires hardware which has since become common, making it possible to infringe the XOR claims with a few lines of code. Many, if not most, computer manufacturers including Apple and IBM have taken out licenses which cover programs running on their computers.

This patent illustrates that it is usually easy to design around a patent one accidentally infringes. If this patent, a hardware patent, is a "bad" patent as some claim, it only demonstrates that the electronics industry tolerates "bad" patents because it finds patents beneficial on balance. Software should be able to tolerate "bad" patents similarly. To discard the patent system because some bad patents exist would be the same as suppressing free speech to stamp out lies.

U.S. Patent 4,398,249

This is what the League has mischaracterized as fact, in "Refrac recalculation patent." In 1970 Rene Pardo and Remy Landau invented the concept of an array of formulas that would enable businesspeople to write their own programs to create business applications. Although the word was not used, their invention is in essence the modern computer spreadsheet. The fact that the claims cover recalculation is an artifact of how the patent claims were written. Pardo and Landau marketed a commercial spreadsheetlike product based on this technology. This invention has been widely adapted in the personal computer industry—over 250 spreadsheets have been marketed.

This patent was originally rejected by the PTO as a mathematical algorithm and thus unpatentable subject matter. Pardo and Landau felt so strongly about their inventive contribution that they appealed their case *pro se*, which means they, not a lawyer, wrote the brief and argued it before the appeals court. The decision, *In re Pardo* [23], is a major legal precedent which establishes that an invention is patentable whether or not the invention involves software "novelty." If their experience was typical, they were stonewalled when they tried to enforce their patents. This would explain why they approached Refac—a white knight in the fight against the patent pirates. If Pardo and Landau have the same deal Refac offered others, then they can expect to collect royalties only as Refac does.

U.S. Patent 4,633,416

This patent is held by Quantel, a company that developed a line of commercial video editing products protected by its patents. Quantel filed for patents when it was small, and it has grown from being a small to a large company because it has used its patents to prevent competitors from using its technology. The first company Quantel sued was much larger than it was.

U.S. Patent 4,777,596

The League tells us XyQuest was notified that its product XyWrite infringed Productivity Software's patent, protecting the ability to accept an abbreviation or correct a spelling error by hitting a space bar. When licensing negotiations failed, XyQuest removed the feature from future releases.

Productivity Software was founded in 1984 to develop data input systems where minimal keystroke data input is important. Based on its patented technology, Productivity Software has grown to seven employees and markets 31 specialty products. It has found niches in the medical and legal transcription and the handicapped marketplaces.

Patent problems are generally minor compared to the other problems pioneering companies face. At about the same time XyQuest had

How Patents Work

Exclusive or territorial rights bestow on their owners a long-term outlook, and create a simple test for determining whether or not to fight. This leads to stable solutions and minimizes inefficient disputes. Such rights occur in many areas. A miner stakes a claim, salespeople have exclusive territories, and professors specialize in areas and are given tenure. Such territorial rights stimulate diversity by encouraging competitors to stake their territorial claims at a distance. Lee De Forest, for example, invented the triode, the amplifying vacuum tube, to avoid infringing Fessenden's spade detector patent [29].

Many mistakenly believe that the patent system protects only "flash of genius" insights. That is not true. In 1952, Congress overrode the "flash of genius" doctrine. Patents are designed, not to stimulate invention directly, but to stimulate their commercialization by giving exclusive rights for 17 years to anyone who invents something new and not obvious. Just as an author need meet a standard of creativity to get a copyright on an original work, a patentholder need meet a standard of nonobviousness to get a patent on something new.

The following discussion of patents is useful in providing an overall understanding of how patent infringement is determined, especially where an overly broad (e.g., "bad") patent may be involved.

Before the PTO will allow your patent application, it does a search (rather like a title search when you buy a house) to find prior art on your invention—what others have done earlier that is disclosed in publications or products. The PTO examines the prior art it finds along with any you send it. If what you did is sufficiently different, it issues claims that delimit the territory of your invention.

The process is rather like finding new territory. Suppose you suddenly landed in Left Fork, North Dakota, and found that no one lived there and wanted to claim it as yours. You might try to claim all the land west of the Mississippi. The PTO will likely find that people have lived in nearby states and may issue you a claim to say, North Dakota. Of course, the PTO could allow your claim in error. The too broad claim—all the land west of the Mississippi—will look impressive and could be useful as a source of cash from people impressed by surface rather than substance.

In practice, if you try to enforce the patent against, say, Californians who just discovered gold, they would show the court that people lived in California before you landed in Left Fork. The court will declare your broad claim invalid.

Practically speaking, you would not go to court once you realized that people lived in California earlier. You might go back to the PTO to get the patent reissued, showing them the prior art and claiming a smaller territory.

The PTO might only allow narrower claims that cover eastern North Dakota, or maybe only Left Fork, North Dakota.

A patent does not necessarily give you rights to what it says it does. Undiscovered prior art might considerably narrow its scope. The advantages of being issued a too broad patent are (a) potential infringers might keep a greater distance than they have to, and (b) you can wait to define the limits of your territory until you know the terrain better. The disadvantage is that you might make business decisions based on your belief that you had rights you did not possess.

There are two ways you can respect a patent: you can avoid infringement or you can take out a license. If you are infringing, the patentholder will usually forgive past infringement if you agree to remove infringing capability. Your show of respect for the patent gives its holder credibility with other infringers.

As a possible infringer you have several courses of action when you face an overly broad (or "bad") patent, or indeed any patent:

1. *Ignore the patent problem until confronted with it.*

Why look for trouble you might never have to face? When and if a patent is brought to your attention you can decide what to do. If you do a search and find a patent, you might spend effort designing around a patent that its owner would never have asserted against you. If you do not design around it, you might be liable for treble damages because you were aware of the patent. Of course if you are competing against products protected by patents, you might want to check into their patents before you design your product, as you can expect your competitor to examine your product for infringement, thus you will probably have to face the problem one way or another. Here, it is good accounting practice to set aside a reserve for infringement.

2. *Stay outside the claimed territory.*

If the patent claims all the land west of the Mississippi and you stay on the east of the Mississippi, you will not infringe.

3. *Go where people were.*

If you know people were in Bismark before the patentholder landed in Left Fork, settling in Bismark will protect you. Distrust rumors about earlier settlers. Make sure the prior art is documented in a published paper or was obviously used in a product. If you ask around the industry you are likely to find pointers to prior art. You might want to send the prior art to the patent owner, or the PTO for insertion in the file wrapper. The file wrapper is a file containing all the correspondence on the patent with the PTO. Your patent lawyer might consult it to find prior art which might help you design around a patent or understand its scope.

4. *Make a business deal with the patentholder.*

Generally you can license, or cross-license a patent or find some other way to get rights.

5. *Break the patent.*

You can attempt to get the patent invalidated by proving it is invalid over the prior art, the disclosure was inadequate or it was otherwise invalid. This is risky and expensive where the patent is good and the patentholder determined.

A patent must claim something new, lest its owner usurp others' rights; it also must be on something nonobvious to prevent giving protection to insignificant improvements.

As technical people, we often look at a patent differently from the way entrepreneurs and judges do. We see Left Fork, North Dakota, after it has become a thriving town, and are likely to say it is obvious—there are lots of places like Left Fork, and lots of them have similar buildings; thus constructing buildings in Left Fork seems obvious. It does not belong to the entrepreneur. Invite everyone!

The Left Fork patentholder, the entrepreneur, feels this is like arguing that it was obvious that land in Silicon Valley or Microsoft stock would appreciate in value. Given the advantage of hindsight, it is obvious, but the person who invested in the land, the stock, or the technology should benefit from its appreciation in value. The entrepreneur says, "I built the buildings based on my being granted rights to them and my having a vision of what I could make of it. And now you are looking for loopholes in my deed so others can move in! It may be a poor thing, but it is my own."

As technical people our immediate bias is to find inventions "obvious," because we focus on the technical sophistication, evaluated with the advantage of hindsight. The value of land, a patent or a copyright has to do with how the market evaluates it. If the land is in the Mohave desert, the copyrighted work banal, or the patent on technology people don't want, then it may be worthless. If the land is in downtown Manhattan, the copyright on Donald Duck, or the patent on technology others want, it can be very valuable. The important thing about an invention is not so much that it be inventive, but that it be new if it is to be patented, and that it be useful if people are to buy it.

postponed introduction of its latest version for about a year so it could upgrade to IBM standards as part of an agreement in which IBM would market XyWrite exclusively. At the last minute IBM reneged on the deal [25].

While the first five patents are held by small entities, the last four patents are held by large entities and they also protected commercial products.

U.S. Patent 4,558,302

UniSys licenses this, the LZW compression patent, for 1% of sales. It has threatened a large entity with a lawsuit, but no small ones.

U.S. Patent 4,555,775

The League describes AT&T's backup store patent as "Too Obvious to Publish." Yet, in a letter in this issue of *Communications*, Dennis Richie points out that this technology was published in the ACM [36] and was recently called "a seminal paper" whose ideas are seen in X Windows Macintosh and many other windows systems [14]. While AT&T has sent notification letters on this patent, it has put the patent into reexamination and has not threatened suit or sued anyone on this patent.

U.S. Patent 4,656,583

This is an IBM patent on compiler speedup.

U.S. Patent 4,742,450

This is an IBM-shared copy on write patent. These two patents are what IBM calls Group 1 patents whose royalty is 1% of sales. They have been licensed by IBM as part of general licensing agreements but have not been licensed individually. (About 50 of IBM patents are Group 2 patents. Group 2 patents can be licensed for 2% each; the entire Group 1 portfolio, for 2%; and the entire IBM patent portfolio for 5%.)

These two patents have not been litigated and I do not believe IBM has aggressively asserted these patents against anyone. IBM, like most companies, normally files for patents only to protect what they expect to become commercial products. We treat these patents as protecting commercial products.

Most patents are never asserted. Much of the value of patents, like that of the Swiss Army, is that they act as a deterrent. The patents described here are typical of the small number where the patentholder forces a resolution: the infringer may take a license, design around the patent, or produce prior art showing there was no infringement.

Many letters asserting patents are no trespassing signs, putting potential infringers on notice should they infringe or telling them not to. They require no action. The notified companies might send prior art back to the patentholder, who might send it to the PTO for reexamination. The "infringer" may ignore the notice, waiting to see the reexamined patent or for the patentholder to become more assertive. The resolution may be hidden, in that an infringer may design around the patent. Rarely, a product is withdrawn from the market. The statistics on the cited patents are summarized in Table 4.1.

Whether any patent including those described here, is valid and infringed is a complex legal and technical question. An advantage of the patent system is that the question is an objective one based on the patent, prior art, and the "infringing" device. Such a dispute is less acrimonious than one in which the task is to evaluate testimony where one person yells "thief," and another "liar." Whether infringement actually occurred in any of the cases is irrelevant. The relevant question is did the original patentholders bring commercial products to market based on the patented technology and motivated by the rights a patent bestows?

Trademarks: Apple Paid $30 Million to Use the Name "Apple"

Trademark law is like patent law in that the first one who claims it gets to own it. The Beatles recorded on their own label, Apple Records. When Apple Computer was founded it agreed not to use the *Apple* name in the music business. Later, when the Macintosh played music, the Beatles sued. Apple Computer settled, paying about $30 million dollars to use the name "Apple."

I have been publicly accused of extorting Apple. Did I extort Apple? Did the Beatles extort Apple? Should the computer business have its own *sui generis* trademark law?

Table 4.1.
Patents cited in "Against Software Patents"

Company Size	Large		Small		Total	
Patent Activity						
Patents granted	4	100%	5	100%	9	100%
Protected commercial products	4	100%	5	100%	9	100%
License appears to be available	4	100%	4	80%	8	89%
Firm founded to develop technology	0	0%	4	80%	4	44%
Sued large entities	0	0%	4	80%	4	44%
Sued small entities	0	0%	2	50%	2	22%
First suit against small entity	0	0%	0	0%	0	0%
Suits threatened	1	25%	5	100%	5	67%
Patent asserted (notice sent)	2	50%	5	100%	7	78%
Resolution (patent asserted)						
Infringement removed	0	0%	1	20%	1	11%
Product removed from market	0	0%	1	20%	1	11%
Licenses	1	25%	2	40%	3	33%
Unresolved	1	25%	1	20%	2	22%
Nothing to Resolve (No notice)	2	50%	0	0%	2	22%
Total	4	100%	5	100%	9	100%

Note: We treat multiple patents covering the same technology as a single patent. With the exception of Quantel, the small entities were less than a dozen people at the time the patent was filed, and the large entities were Fortune 1000 companies. We assume that if a lawsuit was threatened, a notice was sent and if a lawsuit was filed, a lawsuit was first threatened. We assume that if a patent has been asserted—people have been sent notices—there is a matter to be resolved. Even if one characterizes Cadtrak and Refac as being in the business of litigating patents as some do, the relevant fact is that the original patentholders were small entities introducing commercial products protected by patents.

Analysis Results

The nine patents cited by the League summarized in Table 4.1 lead us to these conclusions:

1. Software patents stimulate companies to bring commercial products to market.
All nine patents protected commercial products.

2. Software patents stimulate new business formation.
Four of the nine patents were from startups founded to exploit the patented technology. A fifth filed for its patent in its seventh year. All five companies struggled for years.

3. Software patents stimulate the commercial introduction of fundamental advances by small entities.
The technology pioneered by at least three of the small patentholders was significant in that it started new product categories or was widely adopted in the industry.

4. Licenses are usually available where companies enforce patents.
Only Quantel seems to be unwilling to license its patent.

5. Where similar-size companies had a dispute, they settled differences quickly without litigation.
The only patent dispute between similar-size companies (XyQuest) was settled readily. No small entities were faced with a lawsuit brought by a large entity without the advantage of the patentholder having settled earlier with a large infringer.

6. Small entities incurred little if any royalty and litigation costs for infringing patents.
The only disputes in which a small entity paid patent royalties or was sued were those in which the patentholder had previously settled disputes with larger companies. No case was cited in which a big company aggressively went after a small one over patents, unless a large company had respected the patents first. The only such instance the author knows of is IBM (see Big Companies Do Sue Small Ones).

Big Companies Do Sue Small Ones

While the League says that big companies will use patents against small ones, it cites no example. Two came to my attention. (I was contacted because I had arguably relevant prior art on the first patent.) In both, IBM sued former employees to get ownership of patents on technology developed on their own time, unrelated to their work and only *after* the technology proved to have value in the market.

IBM vs. Goldwasser Civil 5:91 00021 D. Conn.

IBM encouraged employees to develop software products on their own time and seek patent protection for them so IBM could evaluate them for marketing. Goldwasser developed such a software product, but IBM rejected it; he left IBM stating he intended to pursue his technology, as he did. Six years later, another company introduced a product that seemed to be infringing his patents and he sued them. That company claimed it was covered under its cross-license with IBM; IBM sued Goldwasser to get ownership of the patent.

IBM vs. Zachariades C-91 20419

Zachariades before and while working for IBM developed on his own time a plastic valuable to the medical industry. He kept IBM informed about what he was doing, applied for patents, started his own company, and licensed the technology to a medical prosthesis company. When he was not paid, he sued and a jury awarded him $99 million. IBM "suddenly" found out what was happening and fired, and sued, him for the patents, telling him they did it in part to "terrorize" other IBM employees.

Companies like to hire litigators who know what it is like from the other side. In both cases IBM is represented by the same firm that represented Edwin Armstrong, the great inventor of modern radio when David Sarnoff and RCA were refusing to respect Armstrong's rights. Ken Burns tells the story in his PBS documentary, *Empire of the Air:* On January 31, 1954, Edwin Armstrong, under the strain of RCA's tactics—well dressed as always, in a suit, overcoat, scarf and gloves—jumped from his 13th floor apartment onto the third story roof of the River Club below [29]. His widow won all the patent suits.

Having hired a firm that experienced firsthand the tactics that caused a great inventor to kill himself, IBM should be able to, by suing Goldwasser and Zachariades, "terrorize" its employees.

7. Patent piracy by large entities appears to be common and small entities have a tough time getting their rights respected.

Four of the five small entities had large entities use their technology without first licensing it. *All four were forced to sue.* This makes it unlikely that all the patent disputes were an honest difference of opinion, although some probably were. For this reason "piracy" seems a fair characterization. These same small entities have had their patents mischaracterized and their motives impugned in the academic, trade and business press read by the software community.

It can cost over a million dollars to litigate a patent through to trial. The data shows that large entities are quick to use their power to try to intimidate small ones into abandoning their rights or accepting nuisance settlements rather than address infringement issues on their merits. It appears that this high rate of patent piracy is caused in part by the *Federal Rules of Civil Procedure* which tilt the scales of justice against the weak.

Our results confirm the League's suggestion that big companies will readily bully small ones, but refutes its suggestion that a patentholder who asserts a patent will get showered with gold. The yellow matter is not gold.

8. U.S. companies are slow to accept software innovations from outside sources.

The Japanese adapt innovations from sources outside the company twice as fast as U.S. companies [31]. The technology protected by at least two of the patents (CadTrak and HyperRacks) was exposed to companies that later became the first infringers.

Japan's ability to accommodate outside [the firm] innovation may be one of the reasons it has been so successful in dominating markets. If the U.S. is to exploit its strengths in innovation, it must learn to adapt outside innovations without the inefficiency of legal confrontation. Fast and efficient patent enforcement should encourage U.S. companies to license outside technology early rather than wait until they have an infringing product in the market and face legal exposure.

If large companies are forced to deal with infringement issues early, they might see it is to their advantage to work with the inventors, using their knowledge. Now, the legal system keeps the patentholder and infringer at war until such time as the patentholder's knowledge is of little value to the "infringer," thus wasting one of our most valuable resources—the creativity and experience of innovators.

9. Developers do not seem to be infringing multiple patents on a single product.

The only example that was cited in which someone faced infringement issues from more than one patentholder seems to be X Windows facing the CadTrak and AT&T patents, but this has not been resolved and no lawsuits seem to have been filed or threatened.

10. The patent system seems to reject bad patents early in the patent assertion process.

We think the League is right in alleging that bad patents have been issued. The League, however, fails to identify a patent that was rejected by the courts. We think this is because issues of prior art and patent invalidity are considered early in the patent assertion process. Patentholders rarely continue to assert patents in the face of solid evidence of invalidity or noninfringement.

11. If software patents were more widely respected we would probably have had fewer variations on a theme, and more themes to vary on.

Product development effort seems to have focused on creating many versions of an invention once its value was proven. Over 250 different spreadsheets and at least four products generally considered to be HyperCard clones were marketed.

12. Big companies' patents do not seem to inhibit small developers.

The innovations protected by small entity patents listed here seem to have been more widely adopted than those of big companies in their industries. Big companies are better at commercializing and protecting their minor innovations, than their major ones.

That small entities seem to introduce the more fundamental innovations to the market is telling. Big companies are often unsuccessful in transforming innovations into commercial success: Xerox PARC pioneered much of modern-day personal computer and its software. Although IBM invented a predecessor to the spreadsheet (expired U.S. Patent 3,610,902), it did not market a commercial product based on it; it also did not assert the patent even though its claims seem to read on (i.e., be infringed by) modern spreadsheets. These technologies became major product categories primarily through the efforts of small entities

13. Small entities using patents are exceptionally cost-effective in encouraging innovation—especially compared to federal funding.
Table 4.2 shows a rough estimate of the efficacy of three major sources of innovation: federally funded, large entity, and small entity. Our results show that small entities are 7.5 times as cost-effective at stimulating innovation as large ones, and 200,000 times as cost-effective as federal funding. The U.S. grants patent rights to universities as part of its research contracts; thus patents are issued in all these areas and patents asserted is a reasonable measure of innovation. We believe a more scientific study would refine these results, but doubt it would change the basic conclusion.

As a software developer, you might review the patents discussed and put yourself in the place of each of the parties involved. If your product finds satisfied users, do you think better financed companies with stronger marketing organizations will market competitive products, using your

Table 4.2.
Cost effectiveness to taxpayers of innovation sources

Innovation source	Commercial products	Efficacy (Patents Asserted)	Cost (000,000/yr)	Cost-effectiveness
Large entity	4	2	0.03	67.
Small entity	5	5	0.01	500.
Commercial sector	9	7	0.04	175.
Federally funded	1	0	$487.00	0.0021

Note: None of the nine patents appears to result from federal funding. However, we arbitrarily allocate one patent to this category so as to prevent zero results. While the PTO is virtually self-funded, $1.8 million of its $419 million budget comes from taxpayers. Since about 25% of the patents are from small entities and 75% from large entities we distribute the $1.8 million accordingly. We assume that 2% of the patents are software related; it is probably less. Government R & D in computer science was $487 million in fiscal 1989 out of total federally funded research of $61 billion.

innovations? If so, will patents be useful to you? If a patent is enforced against you, do you think you will be able to design around it? If you have to license it, do you think your competitors will also have to license it, thus passing the cost on to the end customers? Which problem would you rather have: a big company entering a market you developed, or finding out you were accidentally infringing a patent? Do you think the effect of software patents might be more innovation, higher software prices and an industry with more long-term profitability?

If you are protected by patents, your success depends in part on your patented inventions as others must deal with them. If you accidentally infringe a patent, designing around it is within your expertise. If you do not have patents, success depends much more on the ability to finance and market products—capabilities outside of your expertise and control. If you are a software developer, don't patents benefit you by manifesting your contributions in rights you can bring to the bargaining table, while confining the problems largely to your area of expertise and control? *Issues in Science and Technology* (Winter 1992) contains a letter from Commissioner of Patents Harry F. Manbeck who said of another article by the same authors that they [15]:

> demonstrate they do not understand the current law. . . . Most of their statements . . . do not appear to be the result of a balanced and reasoned inquiry and do not appear to be supported by the facts. . . . They cavalierly dismiss the view of those who appear to have used the patent system successfully and impugn their motives. . . .

The PTO issued about 89,000 patents in 1990 from which the League, with the advantage of hindsight, can pick and choose the ones to attack. Consider the information presented here on patents the League selected to demonstrate the PTO's mistakes. Whose standards are higher, the League's or the PTO's?

Recommendations

After reviewing our results we can make some general recommendations.

1. Policy should be made on the assumption that innovation occurs in software as in other technologies until compelling evidence to the contrary is found.

This is consistent with the results described here. The operational implications are to continue to let the system operate as it is accepting evolutionary changes based on experience rather than speculation.

2. The PTO should be viewed as a source of innovation that competes for funding with other federally funded sources of innovation.
PTO fees should be reduced, especially for small entities, and the PTO should receive a higher level of funding to improve its ability to examine patents so it can issue better quality, more timely, patents in software and other technologies. European patent offices are much better equipped and much better funded. It seems that the PTO should compete with the NSF and other organizations for federal funding on the basis of their cost effectiveness in encouraging innovation.

In 1990 only $2 million of the PTO budget of $419 million came from federal funding; the remainder came from user fees. Superficially, it might seem that investing in the patent system will have a multiplier effect of 80,000 in creating innovation as compared to federally funded science. We suggest no such thing. We do, however, ask the question: If taxpayers were to spend an additional $160 million per year to support innovation, we could either increase the $64 billion federal funding on science by one fourth of one percent (0.25%) or increase PTO funding by 40%, enabling the PTO to issue better patents and restore reduced user fees for small entities. Which will likely produce more innovation? Which will achieve a greater multiplier effect by encouraging additional private investment?

An example of federally funded science is fusion power research, which has been going on for at least 25 years, has cost hundreds of millions of dollars and has produced little practical result. Pons and Fleishman developed (and filed for patents on) cold fusion without government funding yet they, having invested their own money and not being in the mainline of governmental funding, are heavily criticized. While it is not clear that Pons and Fleishman have produced cold fusion, respected people in the field believe that they have, even if no one yet understands what is happening. This is just an example of how the system is biased in favor of government funding of expensive conventional solutions, and against individuals and small companies who risk their own time and money to innovate.

Individuals taking a contrary view have been the major source of new ideas in both science [38] and engineering [24]. This is why small entities and the patent system are so important. Most will fail, but the successes more than make up for the failures.

It would be interesting to evaluate the results of federally funded science to see which projects are worth the cost. Some projects may have become like those welfare mothers who, generation after generation, are entrapped in a governmental support system.

3. The patent laws should be modified to make it possible for small entities to assert their patent rights more effectively.

The data show it is commonplace for large companies to pirate the technology of small entities. No case was cited where a large company licensed a small entities' technology without first being sued suggests the existing laws do not motivate large companies to resolve patent disputes with small companies quickly. The issue here is not just fairness to inventors and improved efficiency in settling disputes. Rather, it is concerned with avoiding the waste that occurs because U.S. companies are so much slower at adopting new innovations than Japanese companies.

Congress responded with antipiracy legislation where software copyrights were concerned; we would hope it would similarly pass legislation to prevent patent piracy. Remedies similar to the criminal penalties for copyright infringement and Rule 11 sanctions for attorneys who file frivolous suits are worth considering. We suggest the following as possible remedies for patent disputes to stimulate discussion:

- After being put on notice, an "infringer" would have six months to file any prior art to be used to defend the infringement suit with the PTO. (I find it difficult to believe it is well-known art if it cannot be found in six months.)
- If a patentholder prevails in a lawsuit, the remedies should include an extension of the period of exclusivity against that infringer equal to the length of time the suit was in progress.
- Discovery should be limited.

These suggestions, which should induce speedier resolution of patents disputes, are suggested for all patents disputes, not just software.

The patent system, an enormously productive system for inducing innovation, is being stymied by a cumbersome dispute resolution process. Is it in the public good to have a system of conflict resolution that discourages conflict resolution? Should innovators spend their time innovating or litigating? If the courts could resolve software patent and copyrights issues more quickly, it would clarify the law so everyone can make decisions with some predictability. The problems are not unique to patents but occur in all litigation. That the judicial and even the legal, community are beginning to address the inefficiency of dispute resolution and litigation is grounds for cautious optimism.

4. Further study of the role of patents and federal funding in software innovation is useful.

We are keenly aware that the sample is small and unscientific, and thus our results should be considered suggestive rather than definitive. A more definitive study should be useful in bringing out facts that would be useful in evaluating future changes to the patent law.

These recommendations can be summarized thus: Redress the balance of incentives so innovators will prefer to develop their ideas commercially, using patent protection rather than search for federal funding.

The Software Patent Confrontation

The software industry is getting more competitive. Almost every company that has hit products uses its cash flow to develop entries in other product categories. As a result, product categories are getting very competitive. Since most software companies have confined their intellectual property to source code copyrights, user interface copyright and trademarks, whenever they come up with a successful innovation, their competitors will often quickly replicate it. As a result, the impetus is toward similarly featured products competing on price, differing only in the mistakes which the originators must maintain to support their existing customers.

Now companies are recognizing that by using patents they can compete on features and function—not just tactically, but strategically. Even if competitors do replicate the features, they will likely make them different

ALPHA: Abraham Lincoln Patent Holders Association

This organization, founded in January 1992, supports the use of, and educates people about, software patents. Already, ALPHA's members include two software patentholders whose patents have been litigated, four patentholders whose patents are mentioned here, two former board members of the Software Publishers Association and lawyers from Merchant and Gould, Baker and McKenzie, Welch and Katz and the Franklin Pierce Law Center, and a former commissioner of patents and trademarks.

enough to avoid infringement. Companies following this approach will support standards, but their products will have a substantial proprietary component engendering products with more diverse feature sets. This will enable the industry to compete more on the profitable playing field of unique capabilities and market position and less on price. This is consistent with standard business school product marketing, where product differentiation and market segmentation are basic.

Intellectual property has already driven the market for those who got in early and established standards. Lotus owns the 1-2-3 standard. Novell owns a major network standard and WordPerfect, a major word processor standard. Apple owns the Macintosh user interface standard and Intel and Microsoft own the IBM compatibility standard. Patents give new companies the opportunity to establish and own something of value in the market based on their innovativeness rather than their marketing and financial capabilities.

While the problem of people accidentally infringing software patents has been greatly exaggerated, several patents will be successfully asserted against existing products. This will be primarily between those companies that focused on innovation and have patents, and those that focused on exploiting recognized business opportunities. This kind of confrontation occurred earlier in the aircraft and other industries [21].

During these confrontations, the businesses with a large volume of infringing products will understandably feel "extorted" since they did not anticipate patent infringement. Such businesspeople will take support for their position from those who argue against software patents and advocate or suggest invalidating existing software patents [15, 39].

The software innovators who advanced the technology and made business decisions based on their patent rights will similarly feel cheated especially where they pioneered commercial products based on their inventions. When depositors made decisions based on government guarantees of S&L deposits, no one suggested that the government default on its obligations to insured depositors, as people suggest the government invalidate existing software patents. No one vilifies the S&L depositors because the government has to pay them money; yet software innovators find themselves vilified with lies and half truths.

In this confrontation, both sides start out feeling cheated. Many "infringers" will react emotionally and view it as a problem to be gotten rid of and many will fight to the bitter end. This raises the stakes, since a company having been put on notice may be liable for treble damages and attorneys' fees. Patentholders will not likely pursue these cases for four or five years to let the infringers' liability build up. After a suit is filed these companies will be getting much of their advice from those who have most to profit from the litigation: their litigators. This seems to be what is happening to Lotus.

Some software developers on finding out that the rules were not what they thought, face the problems of infringing others' patents while not having patented their own successful innovations. Some will chalk it up as one of many risks and uncertainties of business. Those who react emotionally might find it useful to first ask: Which of the players have acted in good faith? Which have not? Which have been responsible for the patent mess? Which have been innocent victims? Having answered these questions, such developers can more effectively target their wrath.

Companies that act rationally will analyze the patents to ascertain their scope and validity, whether infringement is occurring, and how easy it is to remove the "infringing" capability. They will check with other licensees. They will consider the obvious options, such as taking out a license, removing the infringing capability, finding prior art and showing it to the patentholder, or fighting in court if that is the only possibility. They will probably try to address the problem early, before the liability builds and consider negotiating a license or using some form of alternative dispute resolution to resolve infringement and validity issues. If the problem is associated with purchased products, most companies will stand in back of their products and provide a license, warrant it against infringement, or provide guidelines on how to avoid infringement. It will put its "no problem" in writing.

Astute companies will view infringement as an opportunity in disguise. If the patent is good and competitors are, or soon will be, infringing it, the first licenses can generally get an inexpensive license forcing competitors to pay more if they want to use the technology. It may be possible to get an exclusive license on some feature which differentiates a product from the competitor's. It can be worthwhile to see if the patent covers useful capability which could be added to the product. The best time to

What You Can Do

Insist that the issues be debated. Don't let one side present its case unchallenged. If you need literature to distribute or a developer to join a debate on software, contact ALPHA.

One way to help correct the misinformation about software patents is to join ALPHA, The Abraham Lincoln Patent Holders Association. ALPHA is trying to correct the misinformation on software patents and to provide a forum for people to deal with issues of software patents, such as how to avoid infringement, setting licensing fees, finding prior art. Contact ALPHA at:

ALPHA
146 Main St.
Suite 404
Los Altos, CA 94022

You can help get the issue discussed intelligently in Congress.

Tell Congress it is important that the issues be discussed in open hearings where everybody gets to present his or her side, hear the issues debated and make up their own mind. Write:

House Subcommittee on Intellectual Property
2137 Rayburn Bldg.
Washington, DC 20515

Senate Subcommittee on Patents, Trademarks and Copyrights
U.S. Senate
Washington, DC 20510

negotiate for the license is when you do not have the liability of infringement but can offer to create a demand for that capability by incorporating it into a product. Invention being the mother of necessity, your competitors will be faced with the choice of paying a higher price to license the technology or leave it out, thus differentiating your product from theirs.

In brief, what superficially looks like another problem to be dealt with in the increasingly competitive, commodities-oriented software business, might prove to be what makes products less *price* competitive. Many industries have worked on this basis all along; patents make industries more diverse in their offerings, more profitable, more innovative, and ultimately will make the U.S. more competitive.

The essence of this article is simple: Software intellectual property issues are not inherently different in substance from other technologies; what motivates people is not inherently different; industry life cycle is not inherently different; marketing and business strategies and tactics are not inherently different; the law and policy issues are not inherently different; the technology is not inherently new. Software has been around for 40 years. The issues may be new to those who had no experience with them. But the only difference is that software is a mass market industry for the first time and real money is at stake.

Acknowledgments

I would like to thank Steve Lundberg, John P. Sumner, Susan Nycum, Lewis Gable, George Gates, David Pressman and Tom Hassing for their many useful comments.

References

1. American Bar Association, *Two Hundred Years of English and American Patent, Trademark and Copyright Law*, 1977.

2. Axelrod, R. *The Evolution of Cooperation.* Basic Books, 1985.

3. Brooks, F. No silver bullet: Essence and accidents of software engineering. *Computer* (Apr. 1987).

4. Bruce, R. *Lincoln and the Tools of War.* University of Illinois Press, 1989.

5. Bulkeley, W. Will software patents cramp creativity? *Wall Street J.* (Mar. 14, 1989).

6. Bugbee, B.W. *The Genesis of American Copyright Law.* Public Affairs Press, Wash., D.C., 1967.

7. CBEMA comments on computer-related invention patents. *Comput. Lawyer* (Oct. 1991).

8. Chisum, D. The patentability of algorithms. *U Pitt. L. Review 47*, 959-971, (1986).

9. Chisum, D. *A Treatise on the Law of Patentability, Validity and Infringement*, (7 volumes) M. Bender, 1978.

10. Choate, P. *Agents of Influence.* Touchstone, 1990.

11. Clapes, A. Software copyright, and competition. *Quorem* (1989).

12. Cringely, R.X. *Accidental Empires.* Addison Wesley, 1991.

13. Fisher, L.M. Software industry in uproar over recent rush of patents. *New York Times* (May 12), 1989.

14. Foley, et al. *Computer Graphics: Principles and Practice*, Second ed. Addison Wesley, 1990.

15. Garfinkel, S., Stallman, R. and Kapor, M. Why patents are bad for software. *Issues in Science and Tech.* (Fall 1991).

16. Heckel, P. The Wright Brothers and Software Innovation, in *The Elements of Friendly Software Design*, Second ed., Sybex, 1991 (First ed. Warner Books, 1984).

17. Heckel, P. Isolating differences between files. *Commun. ACM* (Apr. 1978).

18. Heckel, P. Software patents and competitiveness. Op Ed, *San Francisco Examiner*, (July 8, 1991), A13.

19. Heckel, P. Zoomracks, designing a new software metaphor. *Dr. Dobbs J.* (Nov. 1985).

20. Heckel, P. and Lampson, B. A terminal oriented communications system. *Commun. ACM* (July 1977).

21. Heckel, P. and Schroeppel, R. Software techniques cram functions and data into pocket sized microprocessor applications. *Elect. Des.* (Apr. 12, 1980).

22. Howard, F. *Wilbur and Orville.* Knopf, 1988.

23. *In re Pardo*, 684 F.2d 912 (C.C.P.A. 1982).

24. Jewkes, J., Sawers, D. and Stillerman, R. *The Sources of Invention*, Second ed., Norton, 1969.

25. Judas, J.B. Innovation, a casualty at IBM. *Wall Street J.* (Oct. 17, 1991), A23.

26. Kahin, B. The software patent crisis. *Tech. Rev.* (Apr. 1960), 543-558.

27. League for Programming Freedom. Against software patents. *Commun. ACM* (Jan. 1992).

28. League for Programming Freedom. Software patents. *Dr. Dobbs J.* (Nov. 1990).

29. Lewis, T. *Empire of the air*. HarperCollins, 1991.

30. Lincoln, A. *Selected Speeches and Writings*. Vintage, 1992.

31. Mansfield, E. Industrial innovation in Japan and the United States. *Science* (Sept. 30, 1988).

32. McCloskey, M. Intuitive physics. *Sci. Am.* (Apr. 1983), 123.

33. Neustadt, R.E. and May, E.R. *Thinking in time: The uses of history for decisionmakers*. The Free Press, 1986.

34. Nycum, S. Legal protection for computer programs. *Comput. Law J.* 1, 1 (1978).

35. Orwell, G. *Politics and the English Language*.

36. Pike, R. Graphics in overlapped bitmap layers. *ACM Trans. Graph.* 17, 3 (July 1983), 331.

37. Ritter, T. The politics of software patents. *Midnight Eng.* (May–June 1991).

38. Root-Bernstein, R. *Discovering*. Harvard University Press, 1989.

39. Samuelson, P. Benson revisited: The case against patent protection for algorithms and other computer program-related inventions. *Emory Law J.* 39, 1025 (1990).

40. Samuelson, P. CONTU revisited: The case against copyright protection for computer programs in machine readable form. *Duke Law J.* 663 (1984), 705–53.

41. Samuelson, P. Should program algorithms be patented? *Commun. ACM* (Aug. 1990).

42. Samuelson, P. and Glushko, R. Survey on the look and feel lawsuit. *Commun. ACM* (May 1990).

43. Schon, D. *Technology and Change*. Delacorte, 1967.

44. Schwarzer, W. Science in the Courtroom. 15th Annual Intellectual Property Law Institute, Intellectual Property Section of the California State Bar, Nov. 1990.

45. Schwartz, E. The coming showdown over software patents. *Bus. Week* (May 13, 1991).

46. Sumner, J. and Lundberg, S. The versatility of software patent protection: From subroutines to look and feel. *Comput. Lawyer* (June 1986).

47. Sumner, J. and Lundberg, S. Software patents: Are they here to stay? *Comput. Lawyer* (Oct. 1991).

48. Slutsker, G. and Churbuck, D. Whose invention is it anyway? *Forbes* (Aug. 19, 1991).

Unix is a registered trademark of Unix System Laboratories, Inc.

5

Pirate Editorial: "So You Want to Be a Pirate?"

What's a pirate? *Computer piracy* is copying and distribution of copyright software (warez). Pirates are hobbyists who enjoy collecting and playing with the latest programs. Most pirates enjoy collecting warez, getting them running, and then generally archive them, or store them away. *A pirate is not a bootlegger.* Bootleggers are to piracy what a chop-shop is to a home auto mechanic. Bootleggers are people who deal stolen merchandise for personal gain. Bootleggers are crooks. They sell stolen goods. Pirates are not crooks, and most pirates consider bootleggers to be lower life forms than child molesters.

Pirates *share* warez to learn, trade information, and have fun! But, being a pirate is more than swapping warez. It's a life-style and a passion. The office worker or classmate who brings in a disk with a few files is not necessarily a pirate any more than a friend laying a copy of the latest Depeche Mode album on you is a pirate. The *true* pirate is plugged into a larger group of people who share similar interests in warez. This is usually done through Bulletin Board Systems (BBSs), and the rule of thumb is "you gotta give a little to get a little; ya gets back what ya gives." Pirates are *not* freeloaders, and only lamerz think they get something for nothing.

A recent estimate in the *Chicago Tribune* (March 25, p. VII: 4) indicated that computer manufacturers estimate the cost of computer piracy at over $4 billion annually. This is absurd, of course. Businesses rarely pirate warez, because the penalties for discovery do not make it cost effective. Individuals who pirate are rarely going to spend several thousand dollars a year for warez they generally have little practical use for, and there's a lot of evidence that pirates spend more money on warez they probably don't need. In fact, pirates may be one of the best forms of advertising for quality products, because sharing allows a shop-around method for buying warez. Most of us buy a program for the documents and the support, but why invest in four or five similar programs if we aren't sure which best suits our needs? Nah, pirates aren't freeloaders.

Is piracy unethical? It may be illegal, although most states have laws providing a grey area between archiving (storing) and use. But, is it *unethical*? We think not. We challenge the claim that pirates cost software manufactures any lost revenue, and will argue that they spread the word for high quality products. The average person cannot afford the mega-bucks needed to buy Dbase-4 and Foxbase, and would do without either if forced to buy. But, by testing out both, we are able to inform those who *will* buy which is better. So, we spread computer literacy, indirectly encourage improvements, and keep the market alive. Pirates hurt no one, take money from nobody's pocket, and contribute far more to the computer industry than they are willing to acknowledge.

How many of us have had mega-fone bills in a month? The tele-comm folks must love pirates. No, pirates aren't cheapskates. The fun of finding an obscure program for somebody, the thrill of cracking a program, the race to see who can be the first to upload the latest version—these are the lure of piracy. We are collectors of information. Unlike those who would keep computer literacy to the affluent few, we make it more readily available to the masses.

So what's a pirate? A pirate is somebody who believes that information belongs to the people. Just as a book can be zeroxed or placed in a library to be shared, pirates provide a type of library service. The experienced pirate even acts as a tutor in helping those who may have purchased warez. We don't bitch about serving as unpaid consultants to the computer industry, and we wouldn't think to request payment for our services. By providing a user-friendly network of information sharers, we increase computer literacy which is in everybody's mutual interests.

The software industry is unlikely to acknowledge (or even recognize) the contributions of pirates to their enterprise, and continue to view us as "the enemy!" Pirates are not represented in legislation and have no strong constituency to challenge misrepresentation. *Pirate Newsletter* is intended to break down the power of media to define us as crooks and outcasts and bring us together. By keeping information open and flowing and not under the control of a privileged few, we are enhancing democracy and freedom of the market place.

Pirates are freedom fighters keeping the dream alive!

6

Some "Property" Problems in a Computer Crime Prosecution

Mike Godwin

The spread and pervasiveness of computer technology create the potential both for new kinds of crimes and for new variations of traditional crimes. Law enforcement, the judiciary, and the legislature can respond to these potentials in two ways: by seeking new laws to address new problems, or by attempting to apply old laws (and traditional notions of crime) in new and unforeseen situations. This article concerns what hazards may face prosecutors and judges when law enforcement chooses the latter tactic. In particular, it shows what can happen when prosecutors uncritically apply intellectual property notions in prosecuting a defendant under laws passed to protect tangible property.

The Government Stumbles in a "Hacker" Case

In the recent case of U.S. v. Riggs, the Chicago U.S. Attorney's office prosecuted two young men, Robert Riggs and Craig Neidorf, on counts of wire fraud (18 U.S.C. 1343), interstate transportation of stolen property (18 U.S.C. 2314) and computer fraud (18 U.S.C. 1030). Of these statutes, only the last was passed specifically to address the problems of unauthorized computer intrusion; the other two are "general purpose" federal criminal statutes that are used by the government in a wide range of criminal prosecutions. The wire fraud statute includes as an element the taking (by fraudulent means) of "money or property," while the interstate-transportation-of-stolen-property (ITSP) statute requires, naturally enough, the element of "goods, wares, merchandise, securities or money, of the value of $5,000 or more." (I do not address here the extent to which the notions of "property" differ between these two federal statutes. It is certain that they do differ to some extent, and the interests protected by the wire-fraud statute were expanded in the 1980s by Congress to include "the intangible right to honest services." (18 U.S.C. 1346.) Even so, the prosecution in the Riggs case relies not on 1346, but on intellectual-property notions, which are the focus of this article.) The 18 U.S.C. 1030 counts against Neidorf were dropped in the government's June 1990 superseding indictment, the indictment actually used at Neidorf's trial in July 1990.

The Riggs case is based on the following facts: Robert Riggs, a computer "hacker" in his early '20s, discovered that he could easily gain access to an account on a computer belonging to Bell South, one of the Regional Bell Operating Companies (RBOCs). The account was highly insecure—access to it did not require a password (a standard, if not always effective, security precaution). While exploring this account, Riggs discovered a word-processing document detailing procedures and definitions of terms relating the Emergency 911 system ("E911 system"). Like many hackers, Riggs had a deep curiosity about the workings of this country's telephone system. (This curiosity among young hackers is a social phenomenon that has been documented for more than 20 years. See, e.g., Rosenbaum, "Secrets of the Little Blue Box," *Esquire*, October 1971; and Barlow, "Crime and Puzzlement: In Advance of the Law on the Electronic Frontier" appendix 1 in this volume.)

Riggs knew that his discovery would be of interest to Craig Neidorf, a Missouri college student who, while not a hacker himself, was an amateur journalist whose electronically distributed publication, *Phrack*, was devoted to articles of interest to computer hackers. Riggs sent a copy of the E911 document to Neidorf over the telephone line—using computer and modem—and Neidorf edited the copy to conceal its origin. Among other things, Neidorf removed the statements that the information contained in the document was proprietary and not for distribution. Neidorf then sent the edited copy back to Riggs for the latter's review; following Riggs's approval of the edited copy, Neidorf published the E911 document in the February 24, 1989, issue of *Phrack*. Some months following publication of the document in *Phrack*, both Riggs and Neidorf were caught and questioned by the Secret Service, and all systems that might contain the E911 document were seized pursuant to evidentiary search warrants.

Riggs and Neidorf were indicted on the counts discussed supra; Riggs, whose unauthorized access to the BellSouth computer was difficult to dispute, later pled guilty to wire fraud for that conduct. Neidorf pled innocent on all counts, arguing, inter alia, that his conduct was protected by the First Amendment, and that he had not deprived BellSouth of property as that notion is defined for the purposes of the wire fraud and ITSP statutes.

The two defenses are closely related. Under the First Amendment, the presumption is that information is free, and that it can readily be published and republished. For this reason, information gives rise to a property interest only if it passes certain legal tests. Law enforcement cannot simply assume that whenever information has been copied from a private computer system a theft has taken place. In Neidorf's case, as it turns out, this is essentially what the Secret Service and the U.S. Attorney's office did assume. The assumption came back to haunt the government when it was revealed during trial that the information contained within the E911 document did not meet any of the relevant legal tests to be established as a property interest.

How Information Becomes Stealable Property

In order for information to be stolen property, it must first be property. There are only a few ways that information can qualify as a property interest, and two of these—patent law and copyright law—are creatures of federal statute, pursuant to an express Constitutional grant of legislative authority. (U.S. Constitution, Article I, Sec. 8, clause 8.) Patent protections were clearly inapplicable in the Neidorf case; the E911 document, a list of definitions and procedures, did not constitute an invention or otherwise patentable process or method. Copyright law might have looked more promising to Neidorf's prosecutors, since it is well established that copyrights qualify as property interests in some contexts (e.g., the law of inheritance).

Unfortunately for the government, the Supreme Court has explicitly stated that copyrighted material is not property for the purposes of the

ITSP statute. In Dowling v. United States, 473 U.S. 207 (1985), the Court held that interests in copyright are outside the scope of the ITSP statute. (Dowling involved a prosecution for interstate shipments of pirated Elvis Presley recordings.) In reaching its decision, the Court held, inter alia, that 18 U.S.C. 2314 contemplates "a physical identity between the items unlawfully obtained and those eventually transported, and hence some prior physical taking of the subject goods." Unauthorized copies of copyrighted material do not meet this "physical identity" requirement.

The Court also reasoned that intellectual property is different in character from property protected by generic theft statutes: "The copyright owner, however, holds no ordinary chattel. A copyright, like other intellectual property, comprises a series of carefully defined and carefully delimited interests to which the law affords correspondingly exact protections." The Court went on to note that a special term of art, "infringement," is used in reference to violations of copyright interests—thus undercutting any easy equation between unauthorized copying and "stealing" or "theft."

It is clear, then, that in order for the government to prosecute the unauthorized copying of computerized information as a theft, it must rely on other theories of information-as-property. Trade secret law is one well-established legal theory of this sort. Another is the breach-of-confidence theory articulated recently by the Supreme Court in Carpenter v. United States, 108 S.Ct. 316 (1987). I will discuss each theory in turn below.

Trade Secrets

Trade secrets are generally creatures of state law, and most jurisdictions have laws that criminalize the violations of a trade-secret holder's rights in the secret. There is no general federal definition of what a trade secret is, but there have been federal cases in which trade-secret information has been used to establish the property element of a federal property crime. See, e.g., United States v. Bottone, 365 F.2d 389 (2d Cir.), cert denied, 385 U.S. 974 (1966), affirming ITSP convictions in a case involving a conspiracy to steal drug-manufacturing bacterial cultures and related documents from a pharmaceutical company and sell them in foreign markets. (In Bottone, a pre-Dowling appellate court expressed a willingness to interpret 18 U.S.C. 2314 as encompassing the interstate transportation of copies of documents detailing the drug-manufacturing process, i.e., it did not require the "physical identity" element discussed supra. Recognizing possible problems with this approach, however, the appellate court reasoned in the alternative that the bacterial cultures themselves provided a sufficient nexus of a tangible property interest to justify application of the ITSP statute; this alternative analysis may render Bottone consistent with Dowling. It should be noted that the post-Dowling judge in Riggs expressed, in his denial of a motion to dismiss, 739 F.Supp. 414 (N.D.Ill, 1990), a similar willingness not to require actual physical identity as a predicate for ITSP. An appellate court later criticized this decision. U.S. v. Brown, 925 F.2d 1301 (1991)).

The problem in using a trade secret to establish the property element of a theft crime is that, unlike traditional property, information has to leap several hurdles in order to be established as a trade secret. Trade secret definitions vary somewhat from state to state, but the varying definitions typically have most elements in common. One good definition of "trade secret" is outlined by the Supreme Court in Kewanee Oil Co. v. Bicron Corp., 416 U.S. 470 (1974): "a trade secret may consist of any formula, pattern, device or compilation of information which is used in one's business, and which gives one an opportunity to obtain an advantage over competitors who do not know or use it. It may be a formula for a chemical compound, a process of manufacturing, treating or preserving materials, a pattern for a machine or other device, or a list of customers." The Court went further and listed the particular attributes of a trade secret:

• The information must, in fact, be secret—"not of public knowledge or of general knowledge in the trade or business."

• A trade secret remains a secret if it is revealed in confidence to someone who is under a contractual or fiduciary obligation, express or implied, not to reveal it.

• A trade secret is protected against those who acquire via unauthorized disclosure, violation of contractual duty of confidentiality, or through "improper means." ("Improper means" includes such things as theft, bribery, burglary, or trespass. The Restatement of Torts at 757 defines such means as follows: "In general they are means which fall below the generally accepted standards of commercial morality and reasonable conduct.")

• A court will allow a trade secret to be used by someone who discovered or developed the trade secret independently (that is, without taking it in some way from the holder), or if the holder does not take adequate precautions to protect the secret.

• An employee or contractor who, while working for a company, develops or discovers a trade secret, generally creates trade secret rights in the company.

The holder of a trade secret may take a number of steps to meet its obligation to keep the trade secret a secret. These may include:

a) Labelling documents containing the trade secret "proprietary" or "confidential" or "trade secret" or "not for distribution to the public";

b) Requiring employees and contractors to sign agreements not to disclose whatever trade secrets they come in contact with;

c) Destroying or rendering illegible discarded documents containing parts or all of the secret, and;

d) Restricting access to areas in the company where a nonemployee, or an employee without a clear obligation to keep the information secret, might encounter the secret. Dan Greenwood's *Information Protection Advisor,* April 1992, page 5.

Breach-of-Confidence

Even if information is not protected under the federal patent and copyright schemes, or under state-law trade-secret provisions, it is possible, according to the Supreme Court in Carpenter, for such information to give rise to a property interest when its unauthorized disclosure occurs via the breach of confidential or fiduciary relationship. In Carpenter, R. Foster Winans, a *Wall Street Journal* reporter who contributed to the *Journal*'s "Heard on the Street" column, conspired with Carpenter and others to reveal the contents of the column before it was printed in the *Journal,* thus allowing the conspirators to buy and sell stock with the foreknowledge that stock prices would be affected by publication of the column. Winans and others were convicted of wire fraud; they appealed the wire-fraud convictions on the grounds that they had not deprived the *Journal* of any money or property.

It should be noted that this is not an "insider trading" case, since Winans was no corporate insider, nor was it alleged that he had received illegal insider tips. The "Heard on the Street" column published information about companies and stocks that would be available to anyone who did the requisite research into publicly available materials. Since the information reported in the columns did not itself belong to the *Journal*, and since the *Journal* planned to publish the information for a general readership, traditional trade secret notions did not apply. Where was the property interest necessary for a wire-fraud conviction?

The Supreme Court reasoned that although the facts being reported in the column were not exclusive to the *Journal*, the *Journal*'s right—presumably based in contract—to Winans' keeping the information confidential gave rise to a property interest adequate to support a wire-fraud conviction. Once the Court reached this conclusion, upholding the convictions of the other defendants followed: even if one does not have a direct fiduciary duty to protect a trade secret or confidential information, one can become civilly or criminally liable if one conspires with, solicits, or aids and abets a fiduciary to disclose such information in violation of that person's duty. The Court's decision in Carpenter has received significant criticism in the academic community for its expansion of the contours of "intangible property," but it remains good law today.

How the Theories Didn't Fit

With these two legal approaches—trade secrets and breach of confidence—in mind, we can turn back to the facts of the Riggs case and see how well, or how poorly, the theories applied in the case of Craig Neidorf.

With regard to any trade-secret theory, it is worth noting first of all that the alleged victim, BellSouth, is a Regional Bell Operating Company—a monopoly telephone-service provider for a geographic region in the United States. Recall the observation in Kewanee Oil, supra, that a trade secret "gives one an opportunity to obtain an advantage over competitors who do not know or use it." There are strong arguments that—at least so far as the provision of Emergency 911 service goes—BellSouth has no "competitors" within any normal meaning of the term. And even if BellSouth did have competitors, it is likely that they would both know and use the E911 information, since the specifications of this particular phone service are standardized among the regional Bells.

Moreover, as became clear in the course of the Neidorf trial, the information contained in the E911 document was available to the general public as well, for a nominal fee. (One of the dramatic developments at trial occurred during the cross-examination of a BellSouth witness who had testified that the E911 document was worth nearly $80,000. Neidorf's counsel showed her a publication containing substantially the same information that was available from a regional Bell or from Bellcore, the Bells' research arm, for $13 to any member of the public that ordered it over an 800 number.) Under the circumstances, if the Bells wanted to maintain the E911 information as a trade secret, they hadn't taken the kind of steps one might normally think a keeper of a secret would take.

BellSouth had, however, taken the step of labelling the E911 document as "NOT TO BE DISCLOSED OUTSIDE OF BELLSOUTH OR ITS SUBSIDIARIES" (it was this kind of labelling that Neidorf attempted to remove as he edited the document for publication in *Phrack*). This fact may have been responsible for the federal prosecutors' oversight in not determining prior to trial whether the E911 document met the tests of trade-secret law. It is possible that prosecutors, unfamiliar with the nuances of trade-secret law, read the "proprietary" warnings and, reasoning backwards, concluded that the information thus labelled must be trade-secret information. If so, this was a fatal error on the government's part. In the face of strong evidence that the E911 document was neither secret nor competitively or financially very valuable, any hope the government had of proving the document to be a trade secret evaporated. (Alternatively, the government may have reasoned that the E911 information could be used by malicious hackers to damage the telephone system in some way. The trial transcript shows instances in which the government attempted to elicit information of this sort. It should be noted, however, that even if the information did lend itself to abuse and vandalism, this fact alone does not bring it within the scope of trade-secret law.)

Nor did the facts lend themselves to a Carpenter-like theory based on breach of confidence; Neidorf had no duties to BellSouth not to disclose its information. Neither did Riggs, from whom Neidorf acquired a copy of the document. The Riggs case lacks the linchpin necessary for a conviction based on Carpenter—in order for nonfiduciaries to be convicted, there must be a breaching fiduciary involved in the scheme in some way. There can be no breach of a duty of confidence when there is no duty to be breached.

Thus, when its trade-secret theory of the E911 document was demolished in mid-trial, the government had no fall-back theory to rely on with regard to its property-crime counts, and the prosecution quickly sought a settlement on terms favorable to Neidorf, dropping prosecution of the case in return for Neidorf's agreement to a pre-trial diversion on one minor count.

The lesson to be learned from Riggs is that it is no easy task to establish the elements of a theft crime when the property in question is information. There are good reasons, in a free society, that this should be so—the proper functioning of free speech and a free press require that information be presumptively protected from regulation by government or by private entities invoking the civil or criminal law property protections. The government in Riggs failed in its duty to recognize this presumption by failing to make the necessary effort to understand the intellectual property issues of the case. Had it done so, Neidorf might have been spared an expensive and painful trial, and the government might have been spared a black eye.[1]

Note

1. See, e.g., "Score One for the Hackers of America," *Newsweek*, Aug. 6, 1990, p. 48, and "Dial 1-800 . . . for BellSouth 'Secrets,'" *Computerworld*, Aug. 6, 1990, p. 8.

II

How Should We Respond to Exploratory Hacking/Cracking/Phreaking?

Hacker is a term that has two uses on the electronic frontier. Originally, a hacker was someone who liked to hack computer code (i.e., write programs) or, in some cases, hack electronic hardware (i.e., design and build hardware). Thanks to the news media, "hacker" has also come to have a negative connotation, usually meaning those who illicitly hack their way into other people's computer systems. Some folks have tried to preserve the original (good) sense of "hacker" by introducing the term *cracker* to cover the cases of electronic trespassers, but like all attempts to fight lexical drift, their efforts have failed. In any case, the idea that there are certain kinds of hacking that are illicit begs the central question of this section, namely, whether there is anything wrong with hacking (or cracking) your way into someone else's system.

The knee-jerk reaction is to say that trespassing is trespassing whether it is real-world trespassing or the electronic kind, but this reaction needs to be defended. There are lots of reasons real-world trespassing laws might be justified. Trespassers might hurt themselves on our property, thus exposing us to legal liability, or trespassers might pose a potential physical threat to us, or they might pose a threat to our property. These considerations do not carry over neatly to electronic trespassing. Hackers certainly aren't going to hurt themselves as they browse our system, and they do not pose an immediate threat to us, although they may try to crash the system, which can certainly ruin your entire day!

But even the system-crashing justification for electronic trespassing laws at best answers a policy question, not the central conceptual question. The policy question is whether sysops have a right to try and keep exploratory hackers out. The conceptual question is whether there is anything wrong with the hackers trying to get in (assuming that they intend no harm). Is there some sense in which (nondestructive) exploratory hacking is just plain wrong?

One possible argument against exploratory hacking is that it involves a kind of invasion of privacy. Isn't it an invasion of my privacy for you to poke around in my system and read my files? To some, however, this argument gets privacy considerations completely backward. The real invasion of privacy, they argue, occurs when corporations like TRW keep records of our personal financial transactions in a centralized data base, and sell those records to other corporations (and individuals) for a price.

In fact, according to this line of thinking, exploratory hackers have actually exposed cases of privacy invasion by uncovering files that were (illicitly) kept on their friends. Perhaps exploratory hackers help ensure that our privacy is not violated by centralized data bases.

Still, there remains the issue of the hacker who takes an interest in my system when there is no reason to suppose that my system contains detailed files on anyone except for me. Whatever the merits of hacking into a large data base, isn't the hacker invading my privacy by hacking into my system? The answer is far from clear. Consider, for example, my garbage, which I put out on the street twice a week. Legally, anyone can pick it up and go through it looking for clues and information about my life. Legally, it is not an invasion of my privacy because I have no reasonable expectation that what I place on the street in a garbage can will not be compromised. If I am concerned about my privacy I had best shred my documents or incinerate my trash. Analogously, it can be argued that if I am concerned about the security of my Internet site I had best encrypt my sensitive documents, or perhaps keep sensitive documents off Internet sites altogether.

It might be argued that exploratory hacking is wrong because it amounts to theft of proprietary information. In the previous section we saw that the very notion of theft of information is a matter of debate. If no one can own information, then how can someone steal it? Even if we agreed that it was wrong to steal information from a remote system, it would not follow that hacking into that system was wrong. One motivation for hacking in the early days was to gain access to a system such as UNIX so that one could learn how the operating system worked. Some have claimed that these considerations no longer apply because a UNIX box can be acquired for a few hundred dollars, but in the abstract the point needs to be taken seriously. Would it be wrong to hack into a system with no intention of damaging the system or even reading files, but merely to try and understand how the system works?

The above question can be sharpened with the help of an analogy. We can distinguish between car theft and joy-riding, where someone merely "borrows" my car (without permission) in order to take a spin. Ordinarily, we consider theft much more serious than joy-riding, and would deal with the perpetrators in different ways. But now consider a hypothetical "car-hacker" who borrows cars without permission to open them up and study how they work. Let's suppose further that this car-hacker was not studying these cars for financial gain, but merely to satisfy his or her curiosity about internal combustion engines. Would we really want to treat this car-hacker on a par with a genuine car thief or even a joy-rider? Surely there seems to be something much more redeeming about the motives of the hypothetical car-hacker, even if his or her actions became something of a nuisance. Likewise, it might be argued that the electronic system hacker should not be treated as a common thief or trespasser, because the motives are, by hypothesis, simply to learn.

Of course, apprehended hackers are often treated much worse than common thieves or trespassers. In his essay on Phiber Optik, Julian Dibbell speculates that the sentencing of Phiber was not due to the moral content of the crime, but rather to the fact that hackers in general and Phiber in particular represent anarchy at a time when corporate robber barons are trying to seize control of the electronic frontier. Dibbell might also have added that hackers represent an embarrassment to these interests as well, for hackers show that one individual, armed only with a laptop computer can out-maneuver corporations with security budgets in the tens of millions of dollars. The key word here is embarrassment, and if The Mentor is right, the crux of the problem is that the true crime of the hacker is being too smart. As he says in his "Conscience of a Hacker": "My crime is that of outsmarting you, something that you will never forgive me for."

So far my remarks have suggested that hackers are only interested in exploring computer systems, but this, of course, is too narrow a view. As a brief perusal of the magazine *2600* ("The Hacker Quarterly") suggests, hacking might involve any sort of activity from building a cable-TV descrambler to constructing a red box (for simulating the tone made by a pay phone). Can these activities be part of a learning exercise? In his congressional testimony, Emmanuel Goldstein (editor of *2600*) suggests that they can. Of course, as Congressman Markey points out in his questioning, such devices can also be used to break the law, and the question arises as to how appropriate it is for Goldstein to publish information on how to build such systems. In Goldstein's view, the fact that the information might be misused is no reason to keep that information bottled up. He also stresses that one needs to distinguish between hackers and those who use hacker-like methods to break the law. Consider the following remarkable exchange between Goldstein and Markey.

Mr. Markey . . . Let's go to the other side of the problem, the joy rider or the criminal that is using this information. What penalties would you suggest to deal with the bad hacker? Are there bad hackers?

Mr. Goldstein There are a few bad hackers. I don't know any myself, but I'm sure there are.

Mr. Markey I assume if you knew any, you would make sure we did something about them. But let's just assume there are bad people subscribing. What do we do about the bad hacker?

Mr. Goldstein Well, I just would like to clarify something. We have heard here in testimony that there are gang members and drug members who are using this technology. Now, are we going to define them as hackers because they are using the technology?

Mr. Markey Yes. Well, if you want to give them another name, fine. We will call them hackers and crackers, all right?

Mr. Goldstein I think we should call them criminals.

Mr. Markey So the crackers are bad hackers, all right? If you want another word for them, that is fine, but you have got the security of individuals decreasing with the sophistication of each one of these technologies, and the crackers are out there. What do we do with the crackers who buy your book?

Mr. Goldstein I would not call them crackers. They are criminals. If they are out there doing something for their own benefit, selling information—

Mr. Markey Criminal hackers. What do we do with them?

Mr. Goldstein There are existing laws. Stealing is still stealing.

One of the themes of Goldstein's testimony, the idea of hacking as a kind of quest for knowledge has been elevated to something of a "hacker ethic" in some quarters—an ethic in which the hacker construes his or her role as the liberator of information or as a disseminator of knowledge. To this end Dorothy Denning, in her study of hackers, has envisioned a coming ethical conflict between the bureaucratic tendency to hoard information and the hacker ethic of acquiring and sharing information. In Denning's words:

> Hackers say that it is our social responsibility to share information, and that it is information hoarding and disinformation that are the crimes. This ethic of resource and information sharing contrasts sharply with computer security policies that are based on authorization and "need to know." This discrepancy raises an interesting question: Does the hacker ethic reflect a growing force in society that stands for greater sharing of resources and information—a reaffirmation of basic values in our constitution and laws?

This nicely frames what I view as the central conceptual question of this section, whether the underlying ethic of hacking is one that we ought to encourage and indeed nurture. Can we, for example, learn something from hackers and their curiosity, or do they represent a dangerous challenge to our extant conceptions of property and information control? Again from Denning:

> What conflict in society do hackers stand at the battle lines of? Is it owning or restricting information vs. sharing information—a tension between an age-old tradition of controlling information as property and the Enlightenment tradition of sharing and disseminating information? Is it controlling access based on "need to know," as determined by the information provider, vs. "want to know," as determined by the person desiring access? Is it law enforcement vs. freedoms granted under the First and Fourth Amendments? . . . The issue is not simply hackers vs. system managers or law enforcers; it is a much larger question about values and practices in an information society.

7

The Conscience of a Hacker

The Mentor

Another one got caught today, it's all over the papers. "Teenager Arrested in Computer Crime Scandal," "Hacker Arrested after Bank Tampering"...

Damn kids. They're all alike.

But did you, in your three-piece psychology and 1950's technobrain, ever take a look behind the eyes of the hacker? Did you ever wonder what made him tick, what forces shaped him, what may have molded him?

I am a hacker, enter my world . . .

Mine is a world that begins with school . . . I'm smarter than most of the other kids, this crap they teach us bores me . . .

Damn underachievers. They're all alike.

I'm in junior high or high school. I've listened to teachers explain for the fifteenth time how to reduce a fraction. I understand it. "No, Ms. Smith, I didn't show my work. I did it in my head . . ."

Damn kid. Probably copied it. They're all alike.

I made a discovery today. I found a computer. Wait a second, this is cool. It does what I want it to. If it makes a mistake, it's because I screwed it up. Not because it doesn't like me . . .

Or feels threatened by me . . .

Or thinks I'm a smart ass . . .

Or doesn't like teaching and shouldn't be here . . .

Damn kid. All he does is play games. They're all alike.

And then it happened . . . a door opened to a world . . . rushing through the phone line like heroin through an addict's veins, an electronic pulse is sent out, a refuge from the day-to-day incompetencies is sought . . . a board is found.

"This is it . . . this is where I belong . . ."

I know everyone here . . . even if I've never met them, never talked to them, may never hear from them again . . . I know you all . . .

Damn kid. Tying up the phone line again. They're all alike . . .

You bet your ass we're all alike . . . we've been spoon-fed baby food at school when we hungered for steak . . . the bits of meat that you did let slip through were pre-chewed and tasteless. We've been dominated by sadists, or ignored by the apathetic. The few that had something to teach found us willing pupils, but those few are like drops of water in the desert.

This is our world now . . . the world of the electron and the switch, the beauty of the baud. We make use of a service already existing without paying for what could be dirt-cheap if it wasn't run by profiteering gluttons, and you call us criminals. We explore . . . and you call us criminals. We seek after knowledge . . . and you call us criminals. We exist without skin color, without nationality, without religious bias . . . and you call us criminals. You build atomic bombs, you wage wars, you murder, cheat, and lie to us and try to make us believe it's for our own good, yet we're the criminals.

Yes, I am a criminal. My crime is that of curiosity. My crime is that of judging people by what they say and think, not what they look like. My crime is that of outsmarting you, something that you will never forgive me for.

I am a hacker, and this is my manifesto. You may stop this individual, but you can't stop us all . . . after all, we're all alike.

8

The Prisoner: Phiber Optik Goes Directly to Jail

Julian Dibbell

Phiber Optik is going to prison this week and if you ask me and a whole lot of other people, that's just a goddamn shame.

To some folks, of course, it's just deserts. Talk to phone-company executives, most computer-security experts, any number of U.S. attorneys and law-enforcement agents, or Justice Louis Stanton of the Southern District of New York (who handed Phiber his year-and-a-day in the federal joint at Minorsville, Pennsylvania), and they'll tell you the sentence is nothing more than what the young hacker had coming to him. They'll tell you Phiber Optik is a remorseless, malicious invader of other people's computers, a drain on the economic lifeblood of our national telecommunications infrastructure, and/or a dangerous role model for the technoliterate youth of today.

The rest of us will tell you he's some kind of hero. Just ask. Ask the journalists like me who have come to know this 21-year-old high-school dropout from Queens over the course of his legal travails. We'll describe a principled and gruffly plain-talking spokesdude whose bravado, street-smart style, and remarkably unmanipulative accessibility have made him the object of more media attention than any hacker since Robert Morris nearly brought down the Internet. Or ask the on-line civil libertarians who felt that Phiber's commitment to nondestructive hacking and to dialogue with the straight world made him an ideal poster boy for their campaign against the repressive excesses of the government's war on hackers. You might even ask the small subset of government warriors who have arrived at a grudging respect for Phiber's expertise and the purity of his obsession with the workings of the modern computerized phone system (a respect that has at times bordered on parental concern as it grew clear that a 1991 conviction on state charges of computer trespass had failed to curb Phiber's reckless explorations of the system).

But for a truly convincing glimpse of the high regard in which Phiber Optik is held in some quarters, you'd have to pay an on-line visit to ECHO, the liberal-minded but hardly cyberpunk New York bulletin-board system where Phiber has worked as resident technical maven since last spring. Forsaking the glories of phonephreaking for the workaday pleasures of hooking the system up to the Internet and helping users navigate its intricacies, he moved swiftly into the heart of ECHO's virtual community (which took to referring to him by the name his mother gave him—Mark—as often as by his nom de hack). So that when he was indicted again, this time on federal charges of unauthorized access to phone-company computers and conspiracy to commit further computer crimes, ECHO too was drawn into the nerve-racking drama of his case.

As the "coconspirators" named in the indictment (a group of Phiber's friends and government-friendly ex-friends) pleaded guilty one by one, there remained brave smiles and high hopes for Phiber's jury trial in July. By the time the trial date arrived, however, Phiber had made an agonizing calculus of risks and decided to plead guilty to one count each of computer intrusion and conspiracy. ECHO was left on tenterhooks waiting for the day of the sentencing. Given Mark's newfound enthusiasm for more legitimate means of working with computers and his undisputed insistence at the time of his plea that he had never damaged or intended to damage any of the systems he broke into, it seemed reasonable to wish for something lenient. A long probation, maybe, or at worst a couple months' jail time. After all, the infamous Morris had done considerably greater harm, and he got off with no jail time at all.

When the news arrived, therefore, of Phiber's 12-month prison sentence (plus three years' probation and 600 hours of service), it hit like a slap in the face, and ECHO responded with a massive outburst of dismay and sympathy. ECHO's director, Stacy Horn, posted the information at 3 PM on November 3 in the system's main conference area, and within 24 hours the place was flooded with over 100 messages offering condolences, advice on penitentiary life, and curses on Judge Stanton. Not all the messages were what you'd want to call articulate ("shit," read the first one in its entirety; quoth another: "fuckfuckfuckfuckfuckfuckfuckfuck-fuckfuckfuckfuckfuckfuckfuckfuckfuckfuck"), nor was all the advice exactly comforting ("Try not to get killed," a sincere and apparently quite prison-savvy Echoid suggested; "Skip the country," proposed one user who connects from abroad, inviting Phiber to join him in sunny South Africa). But the sentiment throughout was unmistakably heartfelt, and when Phiber Optik finally checked in, his brief response was even more so:

"I just finished reading all this and . . . I'm speechless. I couldn't say enough to thank all of you."

He didn't have to thank anybody, of course. Motivated by genuine fellow feeling as this electronic lovefest was, it was also the last step in the long-running canonization of Phiber Optik as the digital age's first full-fledged outlaw hero, and making somebody else a hero is not necessarily the most generous of acts. For one thing, we tend to get more from our heroes than they get from us, and for another, we tend to be heedless of (when not morbidly fascinated by) the very high psychic overhead often involved in becoming a hero—especially the outlaw kind. To their credit, though, the Echoids proved themselves sensitive to the weight of the burden Phiber had been asked to take on. As one of them put it: "Sorry Mark. You've obviously been made a martyr for our generation."

There was some melodrama in that statement, to be sure, but not too much exaggeration. For ironically enough, Judge Stanton himself seemed to have endorsed its basic premise in his remarks upon passing sentence. Not unmoved by the stacks of letters sent him in support of Phiber Optik's character and motivations, the judge allowed as how a less celebrated Phiber Optik convicted of the same crimes might not deserve the severity of the discipline he was about to prescribe (and in Phiber's case it could be argued that 12 months locked up without a computer is severe enough to rate as cruel and unusual). But since Phiber had made of himself a very public advertisement for the ethic of the digital underground, the judge insisted he would have to make of the sentence an equally public countermessage. "The defendant . . . stands as a symbol here today," said Stanton, making it clear that the defendant would therefore be punished as one too.

The judge did not make it clear when exactly it was that the judicial system had abandoned the principle that the punishment fits the crime and not the status of the criminal, though I suppose that happened too long ago to be of much interest. More frustratingly, he also didn't go into much detail as to what it was that Phiber Optik was to stand as a symbol *of*. In at least one of his remarks, however, he did provide an ample enough clue:

"Hacking crimes," said Judge Stanton, "constitute a real threat to the expanding information highway."

That "real threat" bit was a nice dramatic touch, but anyone well-versed in the issues of the case could see that at this point the judge was speaking symbolically. For one thing, even as practiced by the least scrupulous joyriders among Phiber Optik's subcultural peers, hacking represents about as much of a threat to the newly rampant telecommunications juggernaut as shoplifting does to the future of world capitalism. But more to the point, everybody recognizes by now that all references to information highways, super or otherwise, are increasingly just code for the corporate wet dream of a pay-as-you-go telecom turnpike, owned by the same megabusinesses that own our phone and cable systems today and off-limits to anyone with a slender wallet or a bad credit rating. And *that*, symbolically speaking, is what Phiber Optik's transgressions threaten.

For what did his crimes consist of after all? He picked the locks on computers owned by large corporations, and he shared the knowledge of how to do it with his friends (they had given themselves the meaningless name MOD, more for the thrill of sounding like a conspiracy than for the purpose of actually acting like one). In themselves the offenses are trivial, but raised to the level of a social principle, they do spell doom for the locks some people want to put on our cyberspatial future. And I'm tempted, therefore, to close with a rousing celebration of Phiber Optik as the symbol of a spirit of anarchic resistance to the corporate Haussmannization of our increasingly information-based lives, and to cheer Phiber's hero status in places like ECHO as a sign that that spirit is thriving.

But I think I'll pass for now. Phiber Optik has suffered enough for having become a symbol, and in any case his symbolic power will always be available to us, no matter where he is. Right now, though, the man himself is going away for far too long, and like I said, that's nothing but a goddamn shame.

9

Concerning Hackers Who Break into Computer Systems

Dorothy E. Denning

1 Introduction

The world is crisscrossed with many different networks that are used to deliver essential services and basic necessities—electric power, water, fuel, food, goods, to name a few. These networks are all publicly accessible and hence vulnerable to attacks, and yet virtually no attacks or disruptions actually occur.

The world of computer networking seems to be an anomaly in the firmament of networks. Stories about attacks, breakins, disruptions, theft of information, modification of files, and the like appear frequently in the newspapers. A diffuse group called "hackers" is often the target of scorn and blame for these actions. Why are computer networks any different from other vulnerable public networks? Is the difference the result of growing pains in a young field? Or is it the reflection of deeper tensions in our emerging information society?

There are no easy or immediate answers to these questions. Yet it is important to our future in a networked, information-dependent world that we come to grips with them. I am deeply interested in them. This paper is my report of what I have discovered in the early stages of what promises to be a longer investigation. I have concentrated my attention in these early stages on the hackers themselves. Who are they? What do they say? What motivates them? What are their values? What do they have to say about public policies regarding information and computers? What do they have to say about computer security?

From such a profile I expect to be able to construct a picture of the discourses in which hacking takes place. By a discourse I mean the invisible background of assumptions that transcends individuals and governs our ways of thinking, speaking, and acting. My initial findings lead me to conclude that this discourse belongs at the very least to the gray areas between larger conflicts that we are experiencing at every level of society and business, the conflict between the idea that information cannot be owned and the idea that it can, and the conflict between law enforcement and the First and Fourth Amendments.

But, enough of the philosophy. On with the story!

2 Opening Moves

In late fall of 1989, Frank Drake (not his real name), editor of the now defunct cyberpunk magazine *W.O.R.M.*, invited me to be interviewed for the magazine. In accepting the invitation, I hoped that something I might say would discourage hackers from breaking into systems. I was also curious about the hacker culture. This seemed like a good opportunity to learn about it.

The interview was conducted electronically. I quickly discovered that I had much more to learn from Drake's questions than to teach. For example, he asked: "Is providing computer security for large databases that collect information on us a real service? How do you balance the individual's privacy vs. the corporations?" This question surprised me. Nothing that I had read about hackers ever suggested that they might care about privacy. He also asked: "What has (the DES) taught us about what the government's (especially NSA's) role in cryptography should be?" Again, I was surprised to discover a concern for the role of the government in computer security. I did not know at the time that I would later discover considerable overlap in the issues discussed by hackers and those of other computer professionals.

I met with Drake to discuss his questions and views. After our meeting, we continued our dialog electronically with me interviewing him. This gave me the opportunity to explore his views in greater depth. Both interviews appear in "Computers Under Attack," edited by Peter Denning (DenningP90).

My dialog with Drake increased my curiosity about hackers. I read articles and books by or about hackers. In addition, I had discussions with nine hackers whom I will not mention by name. Their ages ranged from 17 to 28.

The word "hacker" has taken on many different meanings ranging from 1) "a person who enjoys learning the details of computer systems and how to stretch their capabilities" to 2) "a malicious or inquisitive meddler who tries to discover information by poking around . . . possibly by deceptive or illegal means . . ." (Steele83). The hackers described in this paper are both learners and explorers who sometimes perform illegal actions. However, all of the hackers I spoke with said they did not engage in or approve of malicious acts that damage systems or files. Thus, this paper is not about malicious hackers. Indeed, my research so far suggests that there are very few malicious hackers. Neither is this paper about career criminals who, for example, defraud businesses, or about people who use stolen credit cards to purchase goods. The characteristics of many of the hackers I am writing about are summed up in the words of one of the hackers: "A hacker is someone who experiments with systems. . . . [Hacking] is playing with systems and making them do what they were never intended to do. Breaking in and making free calls is just a small part of that. Hacking is also about freedom of speech and free access to information—being able to find out anything. There is also the David and Goliath side of it, the underdog vs. the system, and the ethic of being a folk hero, albeit a minor one."

Richard Stallman, founder of the Free Software Foundation who calls himself a hacker according to the first sense of the word above, recommends calling security-breaking hackers "crackers" (Stallman84). While this description may be more accurate, I shall use the term "hacker" since the people I am writing about call themselves hackers and all are interested in learning about computer and communication systems. However, there are many people like Stallman who call themselves hackers and do not engage in illegal or deceptive practices; this paper is also not about those hackers.

In what follows I will report on what I have learned about hackers from hackers. I will organize the discussion around the principal domains of concerns I observed. I recommend Meyer's thesis (Meyer89) for a more detailed treatment of the hackers' social culture and networks, and Meyer and Thomas (MeyerThomas90) for an interesting interpretation of the computer underground as a postmodernist rejection of conventional culture that substitutes "rational technological control of the present for an anarchic and playful future."

I do not pretend to know all the concerns that hackers have, nor do I claim to have conducted a scientific study. Rather, I hope that my own informal study motivates others to explore the area further. It is essential that we as computer security professionals take into account hackers' concerns in the design of our policies, procedures, laws regulating computer and information access, and educational programs. Although I speak about security-breaking hackers as a group, their competencies, actions, and views are not all the same. Thus, it is equally important that our policies and programs take into account individual differences.

In focusing on what hackers say and do, I do not mean for a moment to set aside the concerns of the owners and users of systems that hackers break into, the concerns of law enforcement personnel, or our own concerns as computer security professionals. But I do recommend that we work closely with hackers as well as these other groups to design new approaches and programs for addressing the concerns of all. Like ham radio operators, hackers exist, and it is in our best interest that we learn to communicate and work with them rather than against them.

I will suggest some actions that we might consider taking, and I invite others to reflect on these and suggest their own. Many of these suggestions are from the hackers themselves; others came from the recommendations of the ACM Panel on Hacking (Lee86) and from colleagues.

I grouped the hackers' concerns into five categories: access to computers and information for learning; thrill, excitement and challenge; ethics and avoiding damage; public image and treatment; and privacy and first amendment rights. These are discussed in the next five subsections. I have made an effort to present my findings as uncritical observations. The reader should not infer that I either approve or disapprove of actions hackers take.

3 Access to Computers and Information for Learning

Although Levy's book *Hackers* (Levy84) is not about today's security-breaking hackers, it articulates and interprets a "hacker ethic" that is shared by many of these hackers. The ethic includes two key principles that were formulated in the early days of the AI Lab at MIT: "Access to computers—and anything which might teach you something about the way the world works—should be unlimited and total," and "All information should be free." In the context in which these principles were formulated, the computers of interest were research machines and the information was software and systems information.

Since Stallman is a leading advocate of open systems and freedom of information, especially software, I asked him what he means by this. He said: "I believe that all generally useful information should be free. By 'free' I am not referring to price, but rather to the freedom to copy the information and to adapt it to one's own uses." By "generally useful" he does not include confidential information about individuals or credit card information, for example. He further writes: "When information is generally useful, redistributing it makes humanity wealthier no matter who is distributing and no matter who is receiving." Stallman has argued strongly against user interface copyright, claiming that it does not serve the users or promote the evolutionary process (Stallman90).

I asked hackers whether all systems should be accessible and all information should be free. They said that it is OK if some systems are closed and some information, mainly confidential information about individuals, is not accessible. They make a distinction between information about security technology, e.g., the DES, and confidential information protected by that technology, arguing that it is the former that should be accessible. They said that information hoarding is inefficient and slows down evolution of technology. They also said that more systems should be open so that idle resources are not wasted. One hacker said that the high costs of communication hurts the growth of the information economy.

These views of information sharing seem to go back at least as far as the 17th and 18th centuries. Samuelson (Samuelson89) notes that "The drafters of the Constitution, educated in the Enlightenment tradition, shared that era's legacy of faith in the enabling powers of knowledge for society as well as the individual." She writes that our current copyright laws, which protect the expression of information, but not the information itself, are based on the belief that unfettered and widespread dissemination of information promotes technological progress. (Similarly for patent laws which protect devices and processes, not the information about them.) She cites two recent court cases where courts reversed the historical trend and treated information as ownable property. She raises questions about whether in entering the Information Age where information is the source of greatest wealth, we have outgrown the Enlightenment tradition and are coming to treat information as property.

In a society where knowledge is said to be power, Drake expressed particular concern about what he sees as a growing information gap between the rich and poor. He would like to see information that is not about individuals be made public, although it could still be owned. He likes to think that companies would actually find it to their advantage to share information. He noted how IBM's disclosure of the PC allowed developers to make more products for the computers, and how Adobe's disclosure of their fonts helped them compete against the Apple-Microsoft deal. He recognizes that in our current political framework, it is difficult to make all information public, because complicated structures have been built on top of an assumption that certain information will be kept secret. He cites our defense policy, which is founded on secrecy for military information, as an example.

Hackers say they want access to information and computing and network resources in order to learn. Both Levy (Levy84) and Landreth (Landreth89) note that hackers have an intense, compelling interest in computers and learning, and many go into computers as a profession. Some hackers break into systems in order to learn more about how the systems work. Landreth says these hackers want to remain undiscovered so that they can stay on the system as long as possible. Some of them devote most of their time to learning how to break the locks and other security mechanisms on systems; their background in systems and programming varies considerably. One hacker wrote: "A hacker sees a security hole and takes advantage of it because it is there, not to destroy information or steal. I think our activities would be analogous to someone discovering methods of acquiring information in a library and becoming excited and perhaps engrossed."

We should not underestimate the effectiveness of the networks in which hackers learn their craft. They do research, learn about systems, work in groups, write, and teach others. One hacker said that he belongs to a study group with the mission of churning out files of information and learning as much as possible. Within the group, people specialize, collaborate on research projects, share information and news, write articles, and teach others about their areas of specialization. Hackers have set up a private system of education that engages them, teaches them to think, and allows them to apply their knowledge in purposeful, if not always legal, activity. Ironically, many of our nation's classrooms have been criticized for providing a poor learning environment that seems to emphasize memorization rather than thinking and reasoning. One hacker reported that through volunteer work with a local high school, he was trying to get students turned on to learning.

Many hackers say that the legitimate computer access they have through their home and school computers do not meet their needs. One student told me that his high school did not offer anything beyond elementary courses in BASIC and PASCAL, and that he was bored by these. Hans Huebner, a hacker in Germany who goes by the name Pengo, wrote in a note to the RISKS Forum (Huebner89) : "I was just interested in computers, not in the data which has been kept on their disks. As I was going to school at that time, I didn't even have the money to buy my own computer. Since CP/M (which was the most sophisticated OS I could use on machines which I had legal access to) didn't turn me on anymore, I enjoyed the lax security of the systems I had access to by using X.25 networks. You might point out that I should have been patient and waited until I could go to the university and use their machines. Some of you might understand that waiting was just not the thing I was keen on in those days."

Brian Harvey, in his position paper (Harvey86) for the ACM Panel on Hacking, claims that the computer medium available to students, e.g., BASIC and floppy disks, is inadequate for challenging intellectual work. His recommendation is that students be given access to real computing power, and that they be taught how to use that power responsibly. He describes a program he created at a public high school in Massachusetts during the period 1979-1982. They installed a PDP-11/70 and let students and teachers carry out the administration of the system. Harvey assessed that putting the burden of dealing with the problems of malicious users on the students themselves was a powerful educational force.

He also noted that the students who had the skill and interest to be password hackers were discouraged from this activity because they also wanted to keep the trust of their colleagues in order that they could acquire "superuser" status on the system.

Harvey also makes an interesting analogy between teaching computing and teaching karate. In karate instruction, students are introduced to the real, adult community. They are given access to a powerful, deadly weapon, and at the same time are taught discipline and responsibility. Harvey speculates that the reason that students do not misuse their power is that they know they are being trusted with something important, and they want to live up to that trust. Harvey applied this principle when he set up the school system.

The ACM panel endorsed Harvey's recommendation, proposing a three-tiered computing environment with local, district-wide, and nation-wide networks. They recommended that computer professionals participate in this effort as mentors and role models. They also recommended that government and industry be encouraged to establish regional computing centers using donated or re-cycled equipment; that students be apprenticed to local companies either part-time on a continuing basis or on a periodic basis; and, following a suggestion from Felsenstein (Felsenstein86) for a "Hacker's League," that a league analogous to the Amateur Radio Relay League be established to make contributed resources available for educational purposes.

Drake said he liked these recommendations. He said that if hackers were given access to powerful systems through a public account system, they would supervise themselves. He also suggested that Computer Resource Centers be established in low-income areas in order to help the poor get access to information. Perhaps hackers could help run the centers and teach the members of the community how to use the facilities. One of my colleagues suggested cynically that the hackers would only use this to teach the poor how to hack rich people's systems. A hacker responded by saying this was ridiculous; hackers would not teach people how to break into systems, but rather how to use computers effectively and not be afraid of them. In addition, the hackers I spoke with who had given up illegal activities said they stopped doing so when they got engaged in other work.

Geoff Goodfellow and Richard Stallman have reported that they have given hackers accounts on systems that they manage, and that the hackers have not misused the trust granted to them. Perhaps universities could consider providing accounts to pre-college students on the basis of recommendations from their teachers or parents. The students might be challenged to work on the same homework problems assigned in courses or to explore their own interests. Students who strongly dislike the inflexibility of classroom learning might excel in an environment that allows them to learn on their own, in much the way that hackers have done.

4 Thrill, Excitement, and Challenge

One hacker wrote that "Hackers understand something basic about computers, and that is that they can be enjoyed. I know none who hack for money, or hack to frighten the company, or hack for anything but fun."

In the words of another hacker, "Hacking was the ultimate cerebral buzz for me. I would come home from another dull day at school, turn my computer on, and become a member of the hacker elite. It was a whole different world where there were no condescending adults and you were judged only by your talent. I would first check in to the private Bulletin Boards where other people who were like me would hang out, see what the news was in the community, and trade some info with people across the country. Then I would start actually hacking. My brain would be going a million miles an hour and I'd basically completely forget about my body as I would jump from one computer to another trying to find a path into my target. It was the rush of working on a puzzle coupled with the high of discovery many magnitudes intensified. To go along with the adrenaline rush was the illicit thrill of doing something illegal. Every step I made could be the one that would bring the authorities crashing down on me. I was on the edge of technology and exploring past it, spelunking into electronic caves where I wasn't supposed to be."

The other hackers I spoke with made similar statements about the fun and challenge of hacking. In *SPIN* magazine (Dibbell90), reporter Julian Dibbell speculated that much of the thrill comes from the dangers associated with the activity, writing that "the technology just lends itself to cloak-and-dagger drama," and that "hackers were already living in a world in which covert action was nothing more than a game children played."

Eric Corley (Corley89) characterizes hacking as an evolved form of mountain climbing. In describing an effort to construct a list of active mailboxes on a Voice Messaging System, he writes, "I suppose the main reason I'm wasting my time pushing all these buttons is simply so that I can make a list of something that I'm not supposed to have and be the first person to accomplish this." He said that he was not interested in obtaining an account of his own on the system. Gordon Meyer says he found this to be a recurring theme: "We aren't supposed to be able to do this, but we can"—so they do.

One hacker said he was now working on anti-viral programming. He said it was almost as much fun as breaking into systems, and that it was an intellectual battle against the virus author.

5 Ethics and Avoiding Damage

All of the hackers I spoke with said that malicious hacking was morally wrong. They said that most hackers are not intentionally malicious, and that they themselves are concerned about causing accidental damage. When I asked Drake about the responsibility of a person with a PC and modem, his reply included not erasing or modifying anyone else's data, and not causing a legitimate user on a system any problems. Hackers say they are outraged when other hackers cause damage or use resources that would be missed, even if the results are unintentional and due to incompetence. One hacker wrote: "I have *always* strived to do *no* damage, and to inconvenience as few people as possible. *I never, ever, ever delete a file.* One of the first commands I do on a new system is disable the delete file command." Some hackers say that it is unethical to give passwords and similar security-related information to persons who might do damage. In the recent incident where a hacker broke into BellSouth and downloaded a text file on the emergency 911 service, hackers say that there was no intention to use this knowledge to break into or sabotage the 911 system. According to Emmanuel

Goldstein (Goldstein90), the file did not even contain information about how to break into the 911 system.

The hackers also said that some break-ins were unethical, e.g., breaking into hospital systems, and that it is wrong to read confidential information about individuals or steal classified information. All said it was wrong to commit fraud for personal profit.

Although we as computer security professionals often disagree with hackers about what constitutes damage, the ethical standards listed here sound much like our own. Where the hackers' ethics differ from the standards adopted by most in the computer security community is that hackers say it is not unethical to break into many systems, use idle computer and communications resources, and download system files in order to learn. Goldstein says that hacking is not wrong: it is not the same as stealing, and uncovers design flaws and security deficiencies (Goldstein89).

Brian Reid, a colleague at Digital who has spoken with many hackers, speculates that a hacker's ethics may come from not being raised properly as a civilized member of society, and not appreciating the rules of living in society. One hacker responded to this with "What does 'being brought up properly' mean? Some would say that it is 'good' to keep to yourself, mind your own business. Others might argue that it is healthy to explore, take risks, be curious and discover." Brian Harvey (Harvey86) notes that many hackers are adolescents, and that adolescents are at a less advanced stage of moral development than adults, where they might not see how the effects of their actions hurt others. Larry Martin (Martin89) claims that parents, teachers, the press, and others in society are not aware of their responsibility to contribute to instilling ethical values associated with computer use. This could be the consequence of the youth of the computing field; many people are still computer illiterate and cultural norms may be lagging behind advances in technology and the growing dependency on that technology by businesses and society. Hollinger and Lanza-Kaduce (HollingerLanza-Kaduce88) speculate that the cultural normative messages about the use and abuse of computer technology have been driven by the adoption of criminal laws in the last decade. They also speculate that hacking may be encouraged during the process of becoming computer literate. Some of my colleagues say that hackers are irresponsible. One hacker responded, "I think it's a strong indication of the amount of responsibility shown that so *few* actually *damaging* incidents are known."

But we must not overlook that the differences in ethics also reflect a difference in philosophy about information and information handling resources; whereas hackers advocate sharing, we seem to be advocating ownership as property. The differences also represent an opportunity to examine our own ethical behavior and our practices for information sharing and protection. For example, one hacker wrote, "I will accept that it is morally wrong to copy some proprietary software, however, I think that it is morally wrong to charge $6,000 for a program that is only around 25K long." Hence, I shall go into a few of the ethical points raised by hackers more closely. It is not a simple case of good or mature (us) against bad or immature (hackers), or of teaching hackers a list of rules.

Many computer professionals such as Martin (Martin89) argue the moral questions by analogy. The analogies are then used to justify their judgment of a hacker's actions as unethical. Breaking into a system is compared with breaking into a house, and downloading information and using computer and telecommunications services is compared with stealing tangible goods. But, say hackers, the situations are not the same. When someone breaks into a house, the objective is to steal goods, which are often irreplaceable, and property is often damaged in the process. By contrast, when a hacker breaks into a system, the objective is to learn and avoid causing damage. Downloaded information is copied, not stolen, and still exists on the original system. Moreover, as noted earlier, information has not been traditionally regarded as property. Dibbell (Dibbell90) says that when the software industries and phone companies claim losses of billions of dollars to piracy, they are not talking about goods that disappear from the shelves and could have been sold.

We often say that breaking into a system implies a lack of caring for the system's owner and authorized users. But, one hacker says that the ease of breaking into a system reveals a lack of caring on the part of the system manager to protect user and company assets, or failure on the part of vendors to warn managers about the vulnerabilities of their systems. He estimated his success rate of getting in at 10–15%, and that is without spending more than an hour on any one target system. Another hacker says that he sees messages from vendors notifying the managers, but that the managers fail to take action.

Richard Pethia of CERT (Computer Emergency Response Team) reports that they seldom see cases of malicious damage caused by hackers, but that the break-ins are nevertheless disruptive because system users and administrators want to be sure that nothing was damaged. (CERT suggests that sites reload system software from secure backups and change all user passwords in order to protect against possible back doors and Trojan Horses that might have been planted by the hacker. Pethia also noted that prosecutors are generally called for government sites, and are being called for non-government sites with increasing frequency.) Pethia says that break-ins also generate a loss of trust in the computing environment, and may lead to adoption of new policies that are formulated in a panic or management edicts that severely restrict connectivity to outside systems. Brian Harvey says that hackers cause damage by increasing the amount of paranoia, which in turn leads to tighter security controls that diminish the quality of life for the users. Hackers respond to these points by saying they are the scapegoats for systems that are not adequately protected. They say that the paranoia is generated by ill-founded fears and media distortions (I will return to this point later), and that security need not be oppressive to keep hackers out; it is mainly making sure that passwords and system defaults are well chosen.

Pethia says that some intruders seem to be disruptive to prove a point, such as that the systems are vulnerable, the security personnel are incompetent, or "it's not nice to say bad things about hackers." In the *New York Times,* John Markoff (Markoff90) wrote that the hacker who claimed to have broken into Cliff Stoll's system said he was upset by Stoll's portrayal of hackers in "The Cuckoo's Egg" (Stoll90). Markoff reported that the caller said: "He (Stoll) was going on about how he hates all hackers, and he gave pretty much of a one-sided view of who hackers are."

"The Cuckoo's Egg" captures many of the popular stereotypes of hackers. Criminologist Jim Thomas criticizes it for presenting a simplified view of the world, one where everything springs from the forces of light (us) or of darkness (hackers) (Thomas90). He claims that Stoll fails to see the similarities between his own activities (e.g., monitoring communications, "borrowing" monitors without authorization, shutting off network access without warning, and lying to get information he wants) and those of hackers. He points out Stoll's use of pejorative words such as "varmint" to describe hackers, and Stoll's quote of a colleague: "They're technically skilled but ethically bankrupt programmers without any respect for others' work—or privacy. They're not destroying one or two programs. They're trying to wreck the cooperation that builds our networks," (Stoll90, p. 159). Thomas writes: "At an intellectual level, it (Stoll's book) provides a persuasive, but simplistic, moral imagery of the nature of right and wrong, and provides what—to a lay reader—would seem a compelling justification for more statutes and severe penalties against the computer underground. This is troublesome for two reasons. First, it leads to a mentality of social control by law enforcement during a social phase when some would argue we are already over-controlled. Second, it invokes a punishment model that assumes we can stamp out behaviors to which we object if only we apprehend and convict a sufficient number of violators. . . . There is little evidence that punishment will in the long run reduce any given offense, and the research of Gordon Meyer and I suggests that criminalization may, in fact, contribute to the growth of the computer underground."

6 Public Image and Treatment

Hackers express concern about their negative public image and identity. As noted earlier, hackers are often portrayed as being irresponsible and immoral. One hacker said that "government propaganda is spreading an image of our being at best, sub-human, depraved, criminally inclined, morally corrupt, low life. We need to prove that the activities that we are accused of (crashing systems, interfering with life support equipment, robbing banks, and jamming 911 lines) are as morally abhorrent to us as they are to the general public."

The public identity of an individual or group is generated in part by the actions of the group interacting with the standards of the community observing those actions. What then accounts for the difference between the hacker's public image and what they say about themselves? One explanation may be the different standards. Outside the hacking community, the simple act of breaking into systems is regarded as unethical by many. The use of pejorative words like "vandal" and "varmint" reflect this discrepency in ethics. Even the word "criminal" carries with it connotations of someone evil; hackers say they are not criminal in this sense. Katie Hafner notes that Robert Morris, Jr., who was convicted of launching the Internet worm, was likened to a terrorist even though the worm did not destroy data (Hafner90).

Distortions of events and references to potential threats also create an image of persons who are dangerous. Regarding the 911 incident where a hacker downloaded a file from BellSouth, Goldstein reported "Quickly, headlines screamed that hackers had broken into the 911 system and were interfering with emergency telephone calls to the police. One newspaper report said there were no indications that anyone had died or been injured as a result of the intrusions. What a relief. Too bad it wasn't true" (Goldstein90). In fact, the hackers involved with the 911 text file had not broken into the 911 system. The dollar losses attributed to hacking incidents also are often highly inflated.

Thomas and Meyer (ThomasMeyer90) say that the rhetoric depicting hackers as a dangerous evil contributes to a "witch hunt" mentality, wherein a group is first labeled as dangerous, and then enforcement agents are mobilized to exorcise the alleged social evil. They see the current sweeps against hackers as part of a reaction to a broader fear of change, rather than to the actual crimes committed.

Hackers say they are particularly concerned that computer security professionals and system managers do not appear to understand hackers or be interested in their concerns. Hackers say that system managers treat them like enemies and criminals, rather than as potential helpers in their task of making their systems secure. This may reflect managers' fears about hackers, as well as their responsibilities to protect the information on their systems. Stallman says that the strangers he encounters using his account are more likely to have a chip on their shoulder than in the past; he attributes this to a harsh enforcer mentality adopted by the establishment. He says that network system managers start out with too little trust and a hostile attitude toward strangers that few of the strangers deserve. One hacker said that system managers show a lack of openness to those who want to learn.

Stallman also says that the laws make the hacker scared to communicate with anyone even slightly "official," because that person might try to track the hacker down and have him or her arrested. Drake raised the issue of whether the laws could differentiate between malicious and nonmalicious hacking, in support of a "kinder, gentler" relationship between hackers and computer security people. In fact, many states such as California initially passed computer crime laws that excluded malicious hacking; it was only later that these laws were amended to include nonmalicious actions (HollingerLanza-Kaduce88). Hollinger and Lanza-Kaduce speculate that these amendments and other new laws were catalyzed mainly by media events, especially the reports on the "414 hackers" and the movie *War Games*, which created a perception of hacking as extremely dangerous, even if that perception was not based on facts.

Hackers say they want to help system managers make their systems more secure. They would like managers to recognize and use their knowledge about system vulnerabilities. Landreth (Landreth89) suggests ways in which system managers can approach hackers in order to turn them into colleagues, and Goodfellow also suggests befriending hackers (Goodfellow83). John Draper (Cap'n Crunch) says it would help if system managers and the operators of phone companies and switches could cooperate in tracing a hacker without bringing in law enforcement authorities.

Drake suggests giving hackers free access in exchange for helping with security, a suggestion that I also heard from several hackers. Drake says that the current attitude of treating hackers as enemies is not very conducive to a solution, and by belittling them, we only cause ourselves problems.

I asked some of the hackers whether they'd be interested in breaking into systems if the rules of the "game" were changed so that instead of being threatened by prosecution, they were invited to leave a "calling card" giving their name, phone number, and method of breaking in. In exchange, they would get recognition and points for each vulnerability they discovered. Most were interested in playing; one hacker said he would prefer monetary reward since he was supporting himself. Any system manager interested in trying this out could post a welcome message inviting hackers to leave their cards. This approach could have the advantage of not only letting the hackers contribute to the security of the system, but of allowing the managers to quickly recognize the potentially malicious hackers, since they are unlikely to leave their cards. Perhaps if hackers are given the opportunity to make contributions outside the underground, this will dampen their desire to pursue illegal activities.

Several hackers said that they would like to be able to pursue their activities legally and for income. They like breaking into systems, doing research on computer security, and figuring out how to protect against vulnerabilities. They say they would like to be in a position where they have permission to hack systems. Goodfellow suggests hiring hackers to work on tiger teams that are commissioned to locate vulnerabilities in systems through penetration testing. Baird Info-Systems Safeguards, Inc., a security consulting firm, reports that they have employed hackers on several assignments (Baird87). They say the hackers did not violate their trust or the trust of their clients, and performed in an outstanding manner. Baird believes that system vulnerabilities can be better identified by employing people who have exploited systems.

One hacker suggested setting up a clearinghouse that would match hackers with companies that could use their expertise, while maintaining anonymity of the hackers and ensuring confidentiality of all records. Another hacker, in describing an incident where he discovered a privileged account without a password, said, "What I (and others) wish for is a way that hackers can give information like this to a responsible source, *and have hackers given credit for helping!* As it is, if someone told them that 'I'm a hacker, and I *really* think you should know . . .' they would freak out, and run screaming to the SS (Secret Service) or the FBI. Eventually, the person who found it would be caught, and hauled away on some crazy charge. If they could only just *accept* that the hacker was trying to help!" The clearinghouse could also provide this type of service.

Hackers are also interested in security policy issues. Drake expressed concern over how we handle information about computer security vulnerabilities. He argues that it is better to make this information public than cover it up and pretend that it does not exist, and cites the CERT to illustrate how this approach can be workable. Other hackers, however, argue for restricting initial dissemination of flaws to customers and users. Drake also expressed concern about the role of the government, particularly the military, in cryptography. He argues that NSA's opinion on a cryptographic standard should be taken with a large grain of salt because of their code breaking role.

Some security specialists are opposed to hiring hackers for security work, and Eugene Spafford has urged people not to do business with any company that hires a convicted hacker to work in the security area (ACM90). He says that "This is like having a known arsonist install a fire alarm." But, the laws are such that a person can be convicted for having done nothing other than break into a system; no serious damage (i.e., no "computer arson") is necessary. Many of our colleagues, including Geoff Goodfellow (Goodfellow83) and Brian Reid (Frenkel87), admit to having broken into systems in the past. Reid is quoted as saying that because of the knowledge he gained breaking into systems as a kid, he was frequently called in to help catch people who break in. Spafford says that times have changed, and that this method of entering the field is no longer socially acceptable, and fails to provide adequate training in computer science and computer engineering (Spafford89). However, from what I have observed, many hackers do have considerable knowledge about telecommunications, data security, operating systems, programming languages, networks, and cryptography. But, I am not challenging a policy to hire competent people of sound character. Rather, I am challenging a strict policy that uses economic pressure to close a field of activity to all persons convicted of breaking into systems. It is enough that a company is responsible for the behavior of its employees. Each hacker can be considered for employment based on his or her own competency and character.

Some people have called for stricter penalties for hackers, including prison terms, in order to send a strong deterrent message to hackers. John Draper, who was incarcerated for his activities in the 1970s, argues that in practice this will only make the problem worse. He told me that he was forced under threat to teach other inmates his knowledge of communications systems. He believes that prison sentences will serve only to spread hacker's knowledge to career criminals. He said he was never approached by criminals outside the prison, but that inside the prison they had control over him.

One hacker said that by clamping down on the hobbyist underground, we will only be left with the criminal underground. He said that without hackers to uncover system vulnerabilities, the holes will be left undiscovered, to be utilized by those likely to cause real damage.

Goldstein argues that the existing penalties are already way out of proportion to the acts committed, and that the reason is because of computers (Goldstein89). He says that if Kevin Mitnick had committed crimes similar to those he committed but without a computer, he would have been classified as a mischief maker and maybe fined $100 for trespassing; instead, he was put in jail without bail (Goldstein89). Craig Neidorf, a publisher and editor of the electronic newsletter *Phrack,* faces up to 31 years and a fine of $122,000 for receiving, editing, and transmitting the downloaded text file on the 911 system (Goldstein90). (Since the time I wrote this, a new indictment was issued with penalties of up to 65 years in prison. Neidorf went on trial beginning July 23. The trial ended July 27 when the government dropped all charges. DED)

7 Privacy and the First and Fourth Amendments

The hackers I spoke with advocated privacy protection for sensitive information about individuals. They said they are not interested in invading people's privacy, and that they limited their hacking activities to acquiring information about computer systems or how to break into them. There are, of course, hackers who break into systems such as the TRW credit database. Emanuel Goldstein argues that such invasions of privacy took place before the hacker arrived (Harpers90). Referring to credit reports, government files, motor vehicle records, and the "megabytes of data piling up about each of us," he says that thousands of people legally can see and use this data, much of it erroneous. He claims that the public has been misinformed about the databases, and that hackers have become scapegoats for the holes in the systems. One hacker questioned the practice of storing sensitive personal information on open systems with dial-up access, the accrual of the information, the methods used to acquire it, and the purposes to which it is put. Another hacker questioned the inclusion of religion and race in credit records. Drake told me that he was concerned about the increasing amount of information about individuals that is stored in large data banks, and the inability of the individual to have much control over the use of that information. He suggests that the individual might be co-owner of information collected about him or her, with control over the use of that information. He also says that an individual should be free to withhold personal information, of course paying the consequences of doing so (e.g., not getting a drivers license or credit card). In fact, all Federal Government forms are required to contain a Privacy Act Statement that states how the information being collected will be used and, in some cases, giving the option of withholding the information.

Goldstein has also challenged the practices of law enforcement agencies in their attempt to crack down on hackers (Goldstein90). He said that all incoming and outgoing electronic mail used by *Phrack* was monitored before the newsletter was shutdown by authorities: "Had a printed magazine been shut down in this fashion after having all of their mail opened and read, even the most thick-headed sensationalist media types would have caught on: hey, isn't that a violation of the First Amendment?" He also cites the shutdown of several bulletin boards as part of Operation Sun Devil, and quotes the administrator of the bulletin board Zygot as saying "Should I start reading my users' mail to make sure they aren't saying anything naughty? Should I snoop through all the files to make sure everyone is being good? This whole affair is rather chilling." The administrator for the public system The Point wrote, "Today, there is no law or precedent which affords me . . . the same legal rights that other common carriers have against prosecution should some other party (you) use my property (The Point) for illegal activities. That worries me. . . ."

About 40 personal computer systems and 23,000 data disks were seized under Operation Sun Devil, a two-year investigation involving the FBI, Secret Service, and other federal and local law enforcement officials. In addition, the Secret Service acknowledges that its agents, acting as legitimate users, had secretly monitored computer bulletin boards (Markoff90a). Markoff reports that California Representative Don Edwards, industry leader Mitchell Kapor, and civil liberties advocates are alarmed by these government actions, saying that they challenge freedom of speech under the First Amendment and protection against searches and seizures under the Fourth Amendment. Markoff asks: "Will fear of hackers bring oppression?"

John Barlow writes: "The Secret Service may actually have done a service for those of us who love liberty. They have provided us with a devil. And devils, among their other galvanizing virtues, are just great for clarifying the issues and putting iron in your spine" (Barlow90). Some of the questions that Barlow says need to be addressed include: "What are data and what is free speech? How does one treat property which has no physical form and can be infinitely reproduced? Is a computer the same as a printing press?" Barlow urges those of us who understand the technology to address these questions, lest the answers be given to us by law makers and law enforcers who do not. Barlow and Kapor are constituting a foundation to "raise and disburse funds for education, lobbying, and litigation in the areas relating to digital speech and the extension of the Constitution into Cyberspace."

8 Conclusions

Hackers say that it is our social responsibility to share information, and that it is information hoarding and disinformation that are the crimes. This ethic of resource and information sharing contrasts sharply with computer security policies that are based on authorization and "need to know." This discrepancy raises an interesting question: Does the hacker ethic reflect a growing force in society that stands for greater sharing of resources and information—a reaffirmation of basic values in our constitution and laws? It is important that we examine the differences between the standards of hackers, systems managers, users, and the public. These differences may represent breakdowns in current practices, and may present new opportunities to design better policies and mechanisms for making computer resources and information more widely available.

The sentiment for greater information sharing is not restricted to hackers. In the best seller, *Thriving on Chaos,* Tom Peters (Peters87) writes about sharing within organizations: "Information hoarding, especially by politically motivated, power-seeking staffs, has been commonplace throughout American industry, service and manufacturing alike. It will be an impossible millstone around the neck of tomorrow's organizations. Sharing is a must." Peters argues that information flow and sharing is fundamental to innovation and competitiveness. On a broader scale, Peter Drucker (Drucker89) says that the "control of information by government is no longer possible. Indeed, information is now transnational. Like money, it has no 'fatherland.'"

Nor is the sentiment restricted to people outside the computer security field. Harry DeMaio (DeMaio89) says that our natural urge is to share information, and that we are suspicious of organizations and individuals who are secretive. He says that information is exchanged out of "want to know" and mutual accommodation rather than "need to know." If this is so, then some of our security policies are out of step with the way people work. Peter Denning (DenningP89) says that information sharing will be widespread in the emerging worldwide networks of computers and that we need to focus on "immune systems" that protect against mistakes in our designs and recover from damage.

I began my investigation of hackers with the question, who are they and what is their culture and discourse? My investigation uncovered some of their concerns, which provided the organizational structure to this paper, and several suggestions for new actions that might be taken. My investigation also opened up a broader question: What conflict in society do hackers stand at the battle lines of? Is it owning or restricting information vs. sharing information—a tension between an age-old tradition of controlling information as property and the Englightenment tradition of sharing and disseminating information? Is it controlling access based on "need to know," as determined by the information provider, vs. "want to know," as determined by the person desiring access? Is it law enforcement vs. freedoms granted under the First and Fourth Amendments? The answers to these questions, as well as those raised by Barlow on the nature of information and free speech, are important because they tell us whether our policies and practices serve us as well as they might. The issue is not simply hackers vs. system managers or law enforcers; it is a much larger question about values and practices in an information society.

Acknowledgments

I am deeply grateful to Peter Denning, Frank Drake, Nathan Estey, Katie Hafner, Brian Harvey, Steve Lipner, Teresa Lunt, Larry Martin, Gordon Meyer, Donn Parker, Morgan Schweers, Richard Stallman, and Alex for their comments on earlier versions of this paper and helpful discussions; to Richard Stallman for putting me in contact with hackers; John Draper, Geoff Goodfellow, Brian Reid, Eugene Spafford, Dave, Marcel, Mike, RGB, and the hackers for helpful discussions; and Richard Pethia for a summary of some of his experiences at CERT. The opinions expressed here, however, are my own and do not necessarily represent those of the people mentioned above or of Digital Equipment Corporation.

References

ACM90 "Just Say No," *Comm. ACM* 33, no. 5, May 1990, p. 477.

Baird87 Bruce J. Baird, Lindsay L. Baird, Jr., and Ronald P. Ranauro, "The Moral Cracker?" *Computers and Security* 6, no. 6, December 1987, pp. 471–478.

Barlow90 John Barlow, "Crime and Puzzlement," June 1990, to appear in *Whole Earth Review*. [Appendix 1 in this volume.]

Corley89 Eric Corley, "The Hacking Fever," in Pamela Kane, *V.I.R.U.S. Protection,* Bantam Books, New York, 1989, pp. 67–72.

DeMaio89 Harry B. DeMaio, "Information Ethics, a Practical Approach," *Proc. of the 12th National Computer Security Conference, 1989,* pp. 630–633.

DenningP89 Peter J. Denning, "Worldnet," *American Scientist* 77, no. 5, Sept.-Oct. 1989.

DenningP90 Peter J. Denning, *Computers Under Attack,* ACM Press, 1990.

Dibbell90 Julian Dibbell, "Cyber Thrash," *SPIN* 5, no. 12, March 1990.

Drucker89 Peter F. Drucker, *The New Realities,* Harper and Row, New York, 1989.

Felsenstein86 Lee Felsenstein, "Real Hackers Don't Rob Banks," in full report on ACM Panel on Hacking (Lee86).

Frenkel87 Karen A. Frenkel, "Brian Reid, A Graphics Tale of a Hacker Tracker," *Comm. ACM* 30, no. 10, October 1987, pp. 820–823.

Goldstein89 Emmanuel Goldstein, "Hackers in Jail," *2600 Magazine* 6, no. 1, Spring 1989.

Goldstein90 Emmanuel Goldstein, "For Your Protection," *2600 Magazine* 7, no. 1, Spring 1990.

Goodfellow83 Geoffrey S. Goodfellow, "Testimony Before the Subcommittee on Transportation, Aviation, and Materials on the Subject of Telecommunications Security and Privacy," Sept. 26, 1983.

Hafner90 Katie Hafner, "Morris Code," *New Republic,* February 16, 1990, pp. 15–16.

Harpers90 "Is Computer Hacking a Crime?" *Harper's,* March 1990, pp. 45–57.

Harvey86 Brian Harvey, "Computer Hacking and Ethics," in full report on ACM Panel on Hacking (Lee86).

HollingerLanza-Kaduce88 Richard C. Hollinger and Lonn Lanza-Kaduce, "The Process of Criminalization: The Case of Computer Crime Laws," *Criminology* 26, no. 1, 1988, pp. 101–126.

Huebner89 Hans Huebner, "Re: News from the KGB/Wiley Hackers," *RISKS Digest* 8, no. 37, 1989.

Landreth89 Bill Landreth, *Out of the Inner Circle,* Tempus, Redmond, WA, 1989.

Lee86 John A. N. Lee, Gerald Segal, and Rosalie Stier, "Positive Alternatives: A Report on an ACM Panel on Hacking," *Comm. ACM* 29, no. 4, April 1986, pp. 297–299; full report available from ACM Headquarters, New York.

Levy84 Steven Levy, *Hackers,* Dell, New York, 1984.

Markoff90 John Markoff, "Self-Proclaimed 'Hacker' Sends Message to Critics," *New York Times,* March 19, 1990.

Markoff90a John Markoff, "Drive to Counter Computer Crime Aims at Invaders," *New York Times,* June 3, 1990.

Martin89 Larry Martin, "Unethical 'Computer' Behavior: Who Is Responsible?" *Proc. of the 12th National Computer Security Conference, 1989.*

Meyer89 Gordon R. Meyer, The Social Organization of the Computer Underground, Master's thesis, Dept. of Sociology, Northern Illinois Univ., Aug. 1989.

MeyerThomas90 Gordon Meyer and Jim Thomas, "The Baudy World of the Byte Bandit: A Postmodernist Interpretation of the Computer Underground," Dept. of Sociology, Northern Illinois Univ., DeKalb, IL, March 1990.

Peters87 Tom Peters, *Thriving on Chaos,* Harper & Row, New York, Chapter VI, S-3, p. 610, 1987.

Spafford89 Eugene H. Spafford, "The Internet Worm, Crisis and Aftermath," *Comm. ACM* 32, no. 6, June 1989, pp. 678–687.

Stallman84 Richard M. Stallman, Letter to ACM Forum, *Comm. ACM* 27, no. 1, January 1984, pp. 8–9.

Stallman90 Richard M. Stallman, "Against User Interface Copyright" to appear in *Comm. ACM.*

Steele83 Guy L. Steele, Jr., Donald R. Woods, Raphael A. Finkel, Mark R. Crispin, Richard M. Stallman, and Geoffrey S. Goodfellow, *The Hacker's Dictionary,* Harper & Row, New York, 1983.

Stoll90 Clifford Stoll, *The Cuckoo's Egg,* Doubleday, 1990.

Thomas90 Jim Thomas, "Review of *The Cuckoo's Egg,*" *Computer Underground Digest* 1, no. 6, April 27, 1990.

ThomasMeyer90 Jim Thomas and Gordon Meyer, "Joe McCarthy in a Leisure Suit: (Witch)Hunting for the Computer Underground," Unpublished manuscript, Department of Sociology, Northern Illinois University, DeKalb, IL, 1990; see also the *Computer Underground Digest* 1, no. 11, June 16, 1990.

Postscript, June 11, 1995

After completing the article five years ago, I interviewed people in law enforcement and industry who investigated cases of system intrusion. I found that many of the claims made by hackers were not substantiated by the evidence collected and that with few exceptions, the cases were handled competently and professionally. First and Fourth Amendment rights were not being trampled, and the issue was not law enforcement vs. civil liberties. As a result of my continued research, I developed a better understanding of all sides of the hacker issue, and came to disagree with some of my earlier interpretations and conclusions. The purpose of this postscript is to summarize some of my current thoughts on hackers.

Hacking is a serious and costly problem. Even when there is no malicious intent, intrusions can be extremely disruptive if not outright damaging. A system administrator must assess whether passwords or sensitive information might have been compromised, check for altered files and Trojan horses, and, when necessary, restore the system to a previous "safe" state or change passwords. A system might be down for hours or more than a day while these activities take place. At one university I know, a full-time person is needed just to respond to intruders. Hackers either do not appreciate the consequences of their "non-malicious" hacking on system administrators and users, or else they deny these negative effects in order to justify their actions.

Hackers place responsibility for their intrusions on system developers and administrators for not making their systems secure. They do not seem to appreciate that security is only one factor that must be considered in the design and operation of a system. Real-world requirements, constraints, and budgets can lead to tradeoffs with other factors such as ease of use, network access, development time, and system or administration overhead. One system administrator I know spends about a third of his time keeping up with and responding to security threats. That is time that otherwise could be spent installing new software or making other improvement to the system. Even when security is of high priority, it is difficult to fully achieve since new designs and protocols can introduce new vulnerabilities. In one recent case, a network security tool (SATAN) that had been developed by security experts to detect vulnerabilities was found to introduce one of its own. I do not mean to suggest that system developers, administrators, and users have no responsibility for making their systems secure, but rather that those who carry out an attack are responsible for the attack itself in the same way that robbers and other criminals are responsible for their deeds. It is unrealistic to expect or demand that all systems will be fully secure.

In placing the blame for their intrusions on their victims, hackers fail to acknowledge how their own actions have contributed to the security problem. They spread knowledge about how to penetrate systems through electronic publications and bulletin board systems, and by teaching novices. The current issue of *Phrack* (vol. 6, no. 47), for example, contains articles on how to crack Unix and VMS passwords, gain root access, erase one's tracks from system logs, send fake mail, and defeat copy protection. Many articles contain code for implementing an attack or point the reader to sites where penetration software can be downloaded and run. Many attacks have been sufficiently automated that novices can perform them with little effort or understanding of the systems they are attacking.

Hackers justify their illegal or unethical actions by appealing to the First Amendment and by claiming that the vulnerabilities they find need to be widely exposed lest they be exploited by "real criminals" or "malicious hackers." In fact, information disseminated through hacker publications and bulletin boards has frequently been used to commit serious crimes, with losses sometimes reaching millions of dollars. Hackers do not acknowledge the value of information to those that produce it (even while jealously guarding access to some of their own files), using the hacker ethic that "all information should be free" as a convenient rationale for disseminating whatever they please. They do not distinguish between the dissemination of information about system vulnerabilities and attacks for the purpose of preventing attacks vs. performing them, a distinction that leads to considerably different articles and publications (e.g., CERT advisories vs. *Phrack*'s hacker tutorials). Hackers do not see that in many cases, they are the biggest threat. Were it not for hackers, many systems might never be attacked despite their weaknesses, just as many of us are never robbed even though we are vulnerable.

I do not have a solution to the hacker problem, but I no longer recommend working closely with hackers towards one. I doubt that many hackers have any serious interest in seeing their attacks successfully thwarted, as it would destroy a "game" they enjoy. Moreover, working with people who flagrantly violate the law sends the wrong message and rewards the wrong behavior. Computer ethics education might deter some potential hackers, but it will not deter those hackers who are determined to pursue their trade and take advantage of computer networks to spread their knowledge far and wide. Better security and law enforcement are the best approaches, so that the chances of penetration are reduced while those for detection and prosecution are increased. However, neither will solve the problem completely. There is no "silver bullet" that will stop hacking.

10

Congressional Testimony by Emmanuel Goldstein

Mr. Markey [...] We will take questions now from the subcommittee members. Let me begin, Mr. Delaney. I would like you and Mr. Goldstein to engage in a conversation, if we could. This is Mr. Goldstein's magazine, *The Hacker Quarterly: 2600,* and for $4 we could go out to Tower Records here in the District of Columbia and purchase this. It has information in it that, from my perspective, is very troubling in terms of people's cellular phone numbers and information on how to crack through into people's private information. Now you have got some problems with *The Hacker Quarterly,* Mr. Delaney.

Mr. Delaney Yes, sir.

Mr. Markey And your problem is, among other things, that teenagers can get access to this and go joy riding into people's private records.

Mr. Delaney Yes, sir. In fact, they do.

Mr. Markey Could you elaborate on what that problem is? And then, Mr. Goldstein, I would like for you to deal with the ethical implications of the problem as Mr. Delaney would outline them.

Mr. Delaney Well, the problem is that teenagers do read the *2600* magazine. I have witnessed teenagers being given free copies of the magazine by the editor-in-chief. I have looked at a historical perspective of the articles published in *2600* on how to engage in different types of telecommunications fraud, and I have arrested teenagers that have read that magazine. The publisher, or the editor-in-chief, does so with impunity under the cloak of protection of the First Amendment. However, as I indicated earlier, in that the First Amendment has been abridged for the protection of juveniles from pornography, I also feel that it could be abridged for juveniles being protected from manuals on how to commit crime—children, especially teenagers, who are hackers, and who, whether they be mischievous or intentionally reckless, don't have the wherewithal that an adult does to understand the impact of what he is doing when he gets involved in this and ends up being arrested for it.

Mr. Markey Mr. Goldstein, how do we deal with this problem?

Mr. Goldstein First of all, *2600* is not a manual for computer crime. What we do is, we explain how computers work. Very often knowledge can lead to people committing crimes, we don't deny that, but I don't believe that is an excuse for withholding the knowledge. The article on cellular phones that was printed in that particular issue pretty much goes into detail as to how people can track a cellular phone call, how people can listen in, how exactly the technology works. These are all things that people should know, and perhaps if people had known this at the beginning they would have seen the security problems that are now prevalent, and perhaps something could have been done about it at that point.

Mr. Markey Well, I don't know. You are being a little bit disingenuous here, Mr. Goldstein. Here, on page 17 of your spring edition of 1993, "How to Build a Pay TV Descrambler." Now that is illegal.

Mr. Goldstein Not building. Building one is not illegal.

Mr. Markey Oh, using one is illegal?

Mr. Goldstein Exactly.

Mr. Markey I see. So showing a teenager, or anyone, how to build a pay TV descrambler is not illegal. But what would they do then, use it as an example of their technological prowess that they know how to build one? Would there not be a temptation to use it, Mr. Goldstein?

Mr. Goldstein It is a two-way street, because we have been derided by hackers for printing that information and showing the cable companies exactly what the hackers are doing.

Mr. Markey I appreciate it from that perspective, but let's go over to the other one. If I am down in my basement building a pay TV descrambler for a week, am I not going to be tempted to see if it works, Mr. Goldstein? Or how is it that I then prove to myself and my friends that I have actually got something here which does work in the real world?

Mr. Goldstein It is quite possible you will be tempted to try it out. We don't recommend people being fraudulent—

Mr. Markey How do you know that it works, by the way?

Mr. Goldstein Actually, I have been told by most people that is an old version that most cable companies have gotten beyond.

Mr. Markey So this wouldn't work then?

Mr. Goldstein It will work in some places, it won't work in all places.

Mr. Markey Oh, it would work? It would work in some places?

Mr. Goldstein Most likely, yes. But the thing is, we don't believe that because something could be used in a bad way, that is a reason to stifle the knowledge that goes into it.

Mr. Markey That is the only way this could be used. Is there a good way in which a pay TV descrambler could be used that is a legal way?

Mr. Goldstein Certainly, to understand how the technology works in the first place, to design a way of defeating such devices in the future or to build other electronic devices based on that technology.

Mr. Markey I appreciate that, but it doesn't seem to me that most of the subscribers to *2600* magazine—

Mr. Goldstein That is interesting that you are pointing to that. That is our first foray into cable TV. We have never even testified on the subject before.

Mr. Markey I appreciate that. Well, let's move on to some of your other forays here. What you have got here, it seems to me, is a manual where you go down Maple Street and you just kind of try the door on every home on Maple Street. Then you hit 216 Maple Street, and the door is open. What you then do is, you take that information, and you go down to the corner grocery store, and you post it: "The door of 216 Maple is open." Now, of course, you are not telling anyone to steal, and you are not telling anyone that they should go into 216 Maple. You are assuming that everyone is going to be ethical who is going to use this information, that the house at 216 Maple is open. But the truth of the matter is, you have got no control at this point over who uses that information. Isn't that true, Mr. Goldstein?

Mr. Goldstein The difference is that a hacker will never target an individual person as a house or a personal computer or something like that. What a hacker is interested in is wide open, huge data bases that contain information about people, such as TRW. A better example, I feel, would be one that we tried to do 2 years ago where we pointed out that the Simplex Lock Corporation had a very limited number of combinations on their hardware locks that they were trying to push homeowners to put on their homes, and we tried to alert everybody as to how insecure these are, how easy it is to get into them, and people were not interested. Hackers are constantly trying to show people how easy it is to do certain things.

Mr. Markey I appreciate what you are saying. From one perspective, you are saying that hackers are good people out there, almost like—what are they called?—the Angels that patrol the subways of New York City.

Mr. Goldstein Guardian Angels. I wouldn't say that though.

Mr. Markey Yes, the Guardian Angels, just trying to protect people. But then Mr. Delaney here has the joy riders with the very same information they have taken off the grocery store bulletin board about the fact that 216 Maple is wide open, and he says we have got to have some laws on the books here to protect against it. So would you mind if we passed, Mr. Goldstein, trespassing laws that if people did, in fact, go into 216 and did do something wrong, that we would be able to punish them legally? Would you have a problem with that?

Mr. Goldstein I would be thrilled if computer trespassing laws were enforced to the same degree as physical trespassing laws, because then you would not have teenage kids having their doors kicked in by Federal marshals and being threatened with $250,000 fines, having all their computer equipment taken and having guns pointed at them. You would have a warning, which is what you get for criminal trespass in the real world, and I think we need to balance out the real world—

Mr. Markey All right. So you are saying, on the one hand, you have a problem that you feel that hackers are harassed by law enforcement officials and are unduly punished. We will put that on one side of the equation. But how about the other side? How about where hackers are violating people's privacy? What should we do there, Mr. Goldstein?

Mr. Goldstein When a hacker is violating a law, they should be charged with violating a particular law, but that is not what I see today. I see law enforcement not having a full grasp of the technology. A good example of this was raids on people's houses a couple of years ago where in virtually every instance a Secret Service agent would say, "Your son is responsible for the AT&T crash on Martin Luther King Day," something that AT&T said from the beginning was not possible.

Mr. Markey Again, Mr. Goldstein, I appreciate that. Let's go to the other side of the problem, the joy rider or the criminal that is using this information. What penalties would you suggest to deal with the bad hacker? Are there bad hackers?

Mr. Goldstein There are a few bad hackers. I don't know any myself, but I'm sure there are.

Mr. Markey I assume if you knew any, you would make sure we did something about them. But let's just assume there are bad people subscribing. What do we do about the bad hacker?

Mr. Goldstein Well, I just would like to clarify something. We have heard here in testimony that there are gang members and drug members who are using this technology. Now, are we going to define them as hackers because they are using the technology?

Mr. Markey Yes. Well, if you want to give them another name, fine. We will call them hackers and crackers, all right?

Mr. Goldstein I think we should call them criminals.

Mr. Markey So the crackers are bad hackers, all right? If you want another word for them, that is fine, but you have got the security of individuals decreasing with the sophistication of each one of these technologies, and the crackers are out there. What do we do with the crackers who buy your book?

Mr. Goldstein I would not call them crackers. They are criminals. If they are out there doing something for their own benefit, selling information—

Mr. Markey Criminal hackers. What do we do with them?

Mr. Goldstein There are existing laws. Stealing is still stealing.

Mr. Markey OK. Fine. Dr. Tippett.

Mr. Tippett I think that the information age has brought on an interesting dilemma that I alluded to earlier. The dilemma is that the people who use computers don't have parents who used computers, and therefore they didn't get the sandbox training on proper etiquette. They didn't learn you are not supposed to spit in other people's faces or contaminate the water that we drink, and we have a whole generation now of 100 million in the United States computer users, many of whom can think this through themselves, but, as we know, there is a range of people in any group, and we need to point out the obvious to some people. It may be the bottom 10 percent.

Mr. Markey What the problem is, of course, is that the computer hacker of today doesn't have a computer hacker parent, so parents aren't teaching their children how to use their computers because parents don't know how to use computers. So what do we do?

Mr. Tippett It is incumbent upon us to do the same kind of thing we did in the sixties to explain that littering wasn't right. It is incumbent upon us to take an educational stance and for Congress to credit organizations, maybe through a tax credit or through tax deductions, for taking those educational opportunities and educating the world of people who didn't have sandbox training what is good and what is bad about computing. So at least the educational part needs to get started, because I, for one, think that probably 90 percent of the kids—most of the kids who do most of the damage that we have all described up here, in fact, don't really believe they are doing any damage and don't have the concept of the broadness of the problem that they are doing. The 10 percent of people who are criminal we could go after potentially from the criminal aspect, but the rest we need to get after from a plain, straight ahead educational aspect.

Mr. Markey I appreciate that. I will just say in conclusion—and this is for your benefit, Mr. Goldstein. When you pass laws, you don't pass laws for the good people. What we assume is that there are a certain percent of people—5 percent, 10 percent; you pick it—who really don't have a good relationship with society as a whole, and every law that we pass, for the most part, deals with those people. Now, as you can imagine, when we pass death penalty statutes, we are not aiming it at your mother and my mother. It is highly unlikely they are going to be committing a murder in this lifetime. But we do think there is a certain percentage that will. It is a pretty tough penalty to have, but we have to have some penalty that fits the crime. Similarly here, we assume that there is a certain percentage of pathologically damaged people out there. The cerebral mechanism doesn't quite work in parallel with the rest of society. We have to pass laws to protect the rest of us against them. We will call them criminal hackers. What do we do to deal with them is the question that we are going to be confronted with in the course of our hearings. Let me recognize the gentleman from Texas, Mr. Fields.

Mr. Fields Thank you, Mr. Chairman. Just for my own edification, Mr. Goldstein, you appear to be intelligent; you have your magazine, so obviously you are entrepreneurial. For me personally, I would like to know, why don't you channel the curiosity that you talk about into something that is positive for society? And, I'm going to have to say to you, I don't think it is positive when you invade someone else's privacy.

Mr. Goldstein I agree.

Mr. Fields Whether it is an individual or a corporation.

Mr. Goldstein Well, I would like to ask a question in return then. If I discover that a corporation is keeping a file on me and I access that corporation's computer and find out or tell someone else, whose privacy am I invading? Or is the corporation invading my privacy? You see, corporations are notorious for not volunteering such information: "By the way, we are keeping files on most Americans and keeping track of their eating habits and their sexual habits and all kinds of other things." Occasionally, hackers stumble on to information like that, and you are much more likely to get the truth out of them because they don't have any interest to protect.

Mr. Fields Are you saying with this book that is what you are trying to promote? Because when I look through this book, I find the same thing that the Chairman finds, some things that could actually lead to criminal behavior, and when I see all of these codes regarding cellular telephones, how you penetrate and listen to someone's private conversation, I don't see where you are doing anything for the person, the person who is actually doing the hacking. I see that as an invasion of privacy.

Mr. Goldstein All right. I need to explain something then. Those are not codes, those are frequencies. Those are frequencies that anybody can listen to, and by printing those frequencies we are demonstrating how easy it is for anybody to listen to them. Now if I say that by tuning to 871 megahertz you can listen to a cellular phone call, I don't think I am committing a crime, I think I am explaining to somebody. What I have done at previous conferences is hold up this scanner and press a button and show people how easy it is to listen, and those people, when they get into their cars later on in the day, they do not use their cellular telephones to make private calls of a personal nature because they have learned something, and that is what we are trying to do, we are trying to show people how easy it is. Now, yes, that information can be used in a bad way, but to use that as an excuse not to give out the information at all is even worse, and I think it is much more likely that things may be fixed, the cellular industry may finally get its act together and start protecting phone calls. The phone companies might make red boxes harder to use or might make it easier for people to afford phone calls, but we will never know if we don't make it public.

Mr. Fields I want to be honest with you, Mr. Goldstein. I think it is frightening that someone like you thinks there is a protected right in invading someone else's privacy.

III

Encryption, Privacy, and Crypto-Anarchism

This section begins with the question of whether individuals should be allowed to use military-grade encryption technology to encrypt their electronic communications. It should be obvious why good encryption technology is attractive to many people. Current encryption programs like PGP (Pretty Good Privacy; see the readings by Zimmermann) make it possible to communicate with friends and business partners without allowing inquisitive enemies to "eavesdrop" on our communications. On the other hand, it should also be obvious why certain government agencies are cool to the idea of widespread encryption technology. If encryption is so good that government security forces cannot break the code, then in principle criminals can communicate freely over the Internet without fear of having their plans compromised. The question is, which set of concerns should weigh more heavily, those of individuals, or those of government security forces?

Some have argued that the dilemma just posed is a false one—that there is a solution that allows individuals to have military-grade encryption while at the same time giving the government a "back door" which allows it to decipher the encrypted communications of potential terrorists, for example. In current versions of this proposal a chip (called the "Clipper Chip"), designed to encrypt and decipher digital communications, could be installed in all phones and computers and would provide standardized, military-grade encryption to users (see, for example, the reading by Denning). Yet the government would have a "key" that would be held in escrow by a government agency (or agencies) and that could only be used when a court order was issued. Thus, if the FBI had evidence that potential terrorists were exchanging encrypted plans, the government could apply for a court order, retrieve the "key," and begin monitoring the communications of the terrorists. So everyone should be happy, right? Wrong.

A number of commentators (see for example, the reading by Barlow) are highly suspicious of any plan that gives the government a "built-in" way of tapping into our communications. In the view of these commentators, our government has given us little reason to trust it with control over our secret encryption keys. When corporations, for example, can exchange business information worth millions of dollars, is it not plausible that someone would try to acquire these keys from poorly paid government bureaucrats through bribery? Or why suppose that our government might not exploit its key ownership to gather information on political foes? This is not a wildly implausible scenario. Government officials are notorious for mistaking their political well-being with the well-being of the nation. In recent years the Nixon administration was famous for blurring this distinction, but the problem goes back much further.

For example, according to Dorothy Fowler (in her book *Unmailable*), in 1785 at the request of the secretary for the Department of Foreign Affairs, a resolution was passed authorizing that office to inspect any mail when it thought the safety and interest of the United States required such inspection. Congress was exempted from this ruling; it appears, however, that their mail was opened and read. For example, George Washington complained that his mail that went through the post office was opened and its content made known to everyone. Supposedly the problem was so bad that Madison, Jefferson, and Monroe took to using a cipher to communicate.

In 1792 an act was passed officially prohibiting this letter opening, but it didn't seem to help. Most of the postmasters were Federalists and had little problem with opening the mail. For example, in 1798 Jefferson wrote to John Taylor that he owed him a "political letter" but that "the infidelities of the post office and the circumstances of the times are against my writing fully and freely." Jefferson anonymously wrote another letter to a colleague saying "you will know from whom this comes without a signature; the omission of which has rendered almost habitual with me by the curiosity of the post offices." Who says only criminals have need of encryption and anonymous remailers?

Advocates of the Clipper chip maintain that the proposed safeguards should be adequate to prevent most abuses, and add that the potential consequences of unrestrained encryption could be devastating. Suppose terrorists used PGP encryption software to plot the construction and planting of a nuclear bomb. Of course, one might ask why terrorists smart enough to build such a device would be dumb enough to communicate their plans using an encryption devise for which the United States government has a key.

Clipper-type strategies also reflect a certain peculiar view about the nature of communications in the global marketplace. It is one thing to allow the United States government to be free to intercept all communications between its citizens, but what happens when those citizens work for corporations based in other countries, or when U.S. corporations communicate with corporations in other countries? For example, suppose that Smith works for a Japanese auto manufacturer here in the United States. Is it appropriate that the U.S. government be able to spy on the communications between Smith and Smith's employer, particularly if the information being exchanged includes valuable trade secrets that might be of value to U.S. auto makers? Or what if the sales office of a German auto maker wants to communicate sales info to its home office in Stuttgart. Is it appropriate that the U.S. Government be able to eavesdrop on those communications? The questions need to be seriously considered, lest we lapse into a sort of myopic thinking about our own interests in a global marketplace filled with competing interests.

The discussion thus far has merely taken up some of the obvious benefits and problems attributed to the use of encryption technologies, but it is arguable that there are some more far-reaching consequences to consider. Technologically it is possible not only to encrypt simple messages, but to effectively digitize and encrypt our financial transactions as well (see the reading from Chaum). So, for example, it is possible to set up an electronic bank somewhere on the Internet (the exact location could be protected by an anonymous remailer), which could pay "info credits" to other accounts upon receiving an encrypted order from the payer's account. In effect, we could have a network of financial transactions taking place entirely in encrypted communications with a bank of unknown location.

It is interesting to speculate on the consequences of such a banking arrangement. One immediate consequence might be the emergence of underground black-market economies engaged in the swapping of proprietary information (see the Timothy May readings on one such hypothetical network, "blacknet"). Are such scenarios utopian or antiutopian? That issue is apparently subject to debate (May himself seems to take the utopian view).

But there are even more far-reaching possibilities than the mere emergence of black-market economies (which will always be with us to some degree in any case). Some of the cypherpunks have hypothesized that the emergence of encrypted banking may eventually lead to the death of the nation-state. According to this line of thinking, as more transactions take place in the underground banking networks, more money will escape traditional attempts at taxation. As this happens the nation-states will lose more power or be forced to impose higher taxes, forcing even more corporations into the underground economy.

Are predictions about the death of the nation-state just speculative science fiction? Not necessarily. If my business is information intensive, there is no reason I cannot conduct my business from an underground computer account, trade with underground partners, and use underground banks (all via encrypted communications). At times, I will need to buy tangible goods, and these transactions will certainly be visible to the government; but why would the government need to know about the rest of my transactions? It is inevitable that there will be future information barons who amass billion-dollar fortunes, and who conduct their business using underground banks on the Internet. This does not make for a mere billion-dollar underground economy, however. The underground electronic bank will potentially invest in other ventures, thus expanding the monetary supply in the underground economy. At a certain crucial threshold, enough money could escape the taxation net of the nation-state so that its abilities to operate effectively will erode. If the nation-state chooses to raise taxes, more businesses will slip into the electronic underground, further eroding the viability of the national government.

Taxes, contrary to what some of the cypherpunks think, are still inevitable. New underground trading confederations would probably require new security arrangements (such as hacker defense), and those will, of course, have to be paid for. The future does not promise to be tax free. Nevertheless, taxation authority will be radically restructured without reference to traditional nation-state boundaries. The significance? The cypherpunks may not be too far off base when they prophesize the end of the nation-state.

So far this is just an observation, not a judgment, and we might well recoil in horror at such scenarios. In any case it is time to take such possibilities seriously and ask ourselves the following questions: Will encryption technologies hasten the demise of national governments as we know them? Is this a bad thing, or a good thing? If it is a bad thing, is there anything that can prevent it? If it is a good thing, what can be done to speed matters along?

11

How PGP Works/Why Do You Need PGP?

Philip R. Zimmermann

How It Works

It would help if you were already familiar with the concept of cryptography in general and public key cryptography in particular. Nonetheless, here are a few introductory remarks about public key cryptography.

First, some elementary terminology. Suppose I want to send you a message, but I don't want anyone but you to be able to read it. I can "encrypt," or "encipher" the message, which means I scramble it up in a hopelessly complicated way, rendering it unreadable to anyone except you, the intended recipient of the message. I supply a cryptographic "key" to encrypt the message, and you have to use the same key to decipher or "decrypt" it. At least that's how it works in conventional "single-key" cryptosystems.

In conventional cryptosystems, such as the U.S. Federal Data Encryption Standard (DES), a single key is used for both encryption and decryption. This means that a key must be initially transmitted via secure channels so that both parties can know it before encrypted messages can be sent over insecure channels. This may be inconvenient. If you have a secure channel for exchanging keys, then why do you need cryptography in the first place?

In public key cryptosystems, everyone has two related complementary keys, a publicly revealed key and a secret key. Each key unlocks the code that the other key makes. Knowing the public key does not help you deduce the corresponding secret key. The public key can be published and widely disseminated across a communications network. This protocol provides privacy without the need for the same kind of secure channels that a conventional cryptosystem requires.

Anyone can use a recipient's public key to encrypt a message to that person, and that recipient uses her own corresponding secret key to decrypt that message. No one but the recipient can decrypt it, because no one else has access to that secret key. Not even the person who encrypted the message can decrypt it.

Message authentication is also provided. The sender's own secret key can be used to encrypt a message, thereby "signing" it. This creates a digital signature of a message, which the recipient (or anyone else) can check by using the sender's public key to decrypt it. This proves that the sender was the true originator of the message, and that the message has not been subsequently altered by anyone else, because the sender alone possesses the secret key that made that signature. Forgery of a signed message is infeasible, and the sender cannot later disavow his signature.

These two processes can be combined to provide both privacy and authentication by first signing a message with your own secret key, then encrypting the signed message with the recipient's public key. The recipient reverses these steps by first decrypting the message with her own secret key, then checking the enclosed signature with your public key. These steps are done automatically by the recipient's software.

Because the public key encryption algorithm is much slower than conventional single-key encryption, encryption is better accomplished by using a high-quality fast conventional single-key encryption algorithm to encipher the message. This original unenciphered message is called "plaintext." In a process invisible to the user, a temporary random key, created just for this one "session," is used to conventionally encipher the plaintext file. Then the recipient's public key is used to encipher this temporary random conventional key. This public-key-enciphered conventional "session" key is sent along with the enciphered text (called "ciphertext") to the recipient. The recipient uses her own secret key to recover this temporary session key, and then uses that key to run the fast conventional single-key algorithm to decipher the large ciphertext message.

Public keys are kept in individual "key certificates" that include the key owner's user ID (which is that person's name), a timestamp of when the key pair was generated, and the actual key material. Public key certificates contain the public key material, while secret key certificates contain the secret key material. Each secret key is also encrypted with its own password, in case it gets stolen. A key file, or "key ring" contains one or more of these key certificates. Public key rings contain public key certificates, and secret key rings contain secret key certificates.

The keys are also internally referenced by a "key ID," which is an "abbreviation" of the public key (the least significant 64 bits of the large public key). When this key ID is displayed, only the lower 24 bits are shown for further brevity. While many keys may share the same user ID, for all practical purposes no two keys share the same key ID.

PGP uses "message digests" to form signatures. A message digest is a 128-bit cryptographically strong one-way hash function of the message. It is somewhat analogous to a "checksum" or CRC error checking code, in that it compactly "represents" the message and is used to detect changes in the message. Unlike a CRC, however, it is computationally infeasible for an attacker to devise a substitute message that would produce an identical message digest. The message digest gets encrypted by the secret key to form a signature.

Documents are signed by prefixing them with signature certificates, which contain the key ID of the key that was used to sign it, a secret-key-signed message digest of the document, and a timestamp of when the signature was made. The key ID is used by the receiver to look up the sender's public key to check the signature. The receiver's software automatically looks up the sender's public key and user ID in the receiver's public key ring.

Encrypted files are prefixed by the key ID of the public key used to encrypt them. The receiver uses this key ID message prefix to look up the secret key needed to decrypt the message. The receiver's software automatically looks up the necessary secret decryption key in the receiver's secret key ring.

These two types of key rings are the principal method of storing and managing public and secret keys. Rather than keep individual keys in separate key files, they are collected in key rings to facilitate the automatic lookup of keys either by key ID or by user ID. Each user keeps his own pair of key rings. An individual public key is temporarily kept in a separate file long enough to send to your friend who will then add it to her key ring.

Why Do You Need PGP?

It's personal. It's private. And it's no one's business but yours. You may be planning a political campaign, discussing your taxes, or having an illicit affair. Or you may be doing something that you feel shouldn't be illegal, but is. Whatever it is, you don't want your private electronic mail (e-mail) or confidential documents read by anyone else. There's nothing wrong with asserting your privacy. Privacy is as apple-pie as the Constitution.

Perhaps you think your e-mail is legitimate enough that encryption is unwarranted. If you really are a law-abiding citizen with nothing to hide, then why don't you always send your paper mail on postcards? Why not submit to drug testing on demand? Why require a warrant for police searches of your house? Are you trying to hide something? You must be a subversive or a drug dealer if you hide your mail inside envelopes. Or maybe a paranoid nut. Do law-abiding citizens have any need to encrypt their e-mail?

What if everyone believed that law-abiding citizens should use postcards for their mail? If some brave soul tried to assert his privacy by using an envelope for his mail, it would draw suspicion. Perhaps the authorities would open his mail to see what he's hiding. Fortunately, we don't live in that kind of world, because everyone protects most of their mail with envelopes. So no one draws suspicion by asserting their privacy with an envelope. There's safety in numbers. Analogously, it would be nice if everyone routinely used encryption for all their e-mail, innocent or not, so that no one drew suspicion by asserting their e-mail privacy with encryption. Think of it as a form of solidarity.

Today, if the Government wants to violate the privacy of ordinary citizens, it has to expend a certain amount of expense and labor to intercept and steam open and read paper mail, and listen to and possibly transcribe spoken telephone conversation. This kind of labor-intensive monitoring is not practical on a large scale. This is only done in important cases when it seems worthwhile.

More and more of our private communications are being routed through electronic channels. Electronic mail is gradually replacing conventional paper mail. E-mail messages are just too easy to intercept and scan for interesting keywords. This can be done easily, routinely, automatically, and undetectably on a grand scale. International cablegrams are already scanned this way on a large scale by the NSA.

We are moving toward a future when the nation will be crisscrossed with high capacity fiber optic data networks linking together all our increasingly ubiquitous personal computers. E-mail will be the norm for everyone, not the novelty it is today. The Government will protect our e-mail with Government-designed encryption protocols. Probably most people will trust that. But perhaps some people will prefer their own protective measures.

Senate Bill 266, a 1991 omnibus anticrime bill, had an unsettling measure buried in it. If this non-binding resolution had become real law, it would have forced manufacturers of secure communications equipment to insert special "trap doors" in their products, so that the Government can read anyone's encrypted messages. It reads: "It is the sense of Congress that providers of electronic communications services and manufacturers of electronic communications service equipment shall insure that communications systems permit the Government to obtain the plain text contents of voice, data, and other communications when appropriately authorized by law." This measure was defeated after rigorous protest from civil libertarians and industry groups.

In 1992, the FBI Digital Telephony wiretap proposal was introduced to Congress. It would require all manufacturers of communications equipment to build in special remote wiretap ports that would enable the FBI to remotely wiretap all forms of electronic communication from FBI offices. Although it never attracted any sponsors in Congress because of citizen opposition, it will be reintroduced in 1993.

Most alarming of all is the White House's bold new encryption policy initiative, under development at NSA for four years, and unveiled April 16th, 1993. The centerpiece of this initiative is a Government-built encryption device, called the "Clipper" chip, containing a new classified NSA encryption algorithm. The Government is encouraging private industry to design it into all their secure communication products, like secure phones, secure FAX, etc. AT&T is now putting the Clipper into all their secure voice products. The catch: At the time of manufacture, each Clipper chip will be loaded with its own unique key, and the

Government gets to keep a copy, placed in escrow. Not to worry, though—the Government promises that they will use these keys to read your traffic only when duly authorized by law. Of course, to make Clipper completely effective, the next logical step would be to outlaw other forms of cryptography.

If privacy is outlawed, only outlaws will have privacy. Intelligence agencies have access to good cryptographic technology. So do the big arms and drug traffickers. So do defense contractors, oil companies, and other corporate giants. But ordinary people and grassroots political organizations mostly have not had access to affordable "military grade" public-key cryptographic technology. Until now.

PGP empowers people to take their privacy into their own hands. There's a growing social need for it. That's why I wrote it.

12

Crypto Rebels

Steven Levy

The office atmosphere of Cygnus Support, a fast-growing Silicon Valley company that earns its dollars by providing support to users of free software, seems like a time warp to the days when hackers ran free. Though Cygnus is located in a mall-like business park within earshot of U.S. 101, it features a spacious cathedral ceiling overhanging a cluttered warren of workstation cubicles arranged in an irregular spherical configuration. A mattress is nestled in the rafters. In a hallway behind the reception desk is a kitchen laden with snack food and soft drinks.

Today, a Saturday, only a few show up for work. The action instead is in a small conference room overlooking the back of the complex—a "physical meeting" of a group whose members most often gather in the corridors of cyberspace. Their mutual interest is the arcane field of cryptography—the study of secret codes and cyphers. The very fact that this group exists, however, is indication that the field is about to shift into overdrive. This is crypto with an attitude, best embodied by the group's moniker: Cypherpunks.

The one o'clock meeting doesn't really get underway until almost three. By that time around fifteen techie-cum-civil libertarians are sitting around a table, wandering around the room, or just lying on the floor staring at the ceiling while listening to the conversations. Most have beards and long hair—Smith Brothers gone digital.

The talk today ranges from reports on a recent cryptography conference to an explanation of how entropy degrades information systems. There is an ad hoc demonstration of a new product, an AT&T "secure" phone, supposedly the first conversation-scrambler that's as simple to use as a standard-issue phone. The group watches in amusement as two of their number, including one of the country's best cryptographic minds, have trouble making the thing work. (This is sort of like watching Eric Clapton struggle with a new, easy-to-play guitar.) There is discussion of random number generators. Technical stuff, but everything has an underlying, if not explicitly articulated, political theme: the vital importance of getting this stuff out to the world for the public weal.

The people in this room hope for a world where an individual's informational footprints—everything from an opinion on abortion to the medical record of an actual abortion—can be traced only if the individual involved chooses to reveal them; a world where coherent messages shoot around the globe by network and microwave, but intruders and feds trying to pluck them out of the vapor find only gibberish; a world where the tools of prying are transformed into the instruments of privacy.

There is only one way this vision will materialize, and that is by widespread use of cryptography. Is this technologically possible? Definitely. The obstacles are political—some of the most powerful forces in government are devoted to the control of these tools. In short, there is a war going on between those who would liberate crypto and those who would suppress it. The seemingly innocuous bunch strewn around this conference room represents the vanguard of the pro-crypto forces. Though the battleground seems remote, the stakes are not: The outcome of this struggle may determine the amount of freedom our society will grant us in the 21st century. To the Cypherpunks, freedom is an issue worth some risk.

"Arise," urges one of their numbers, "You have nothing to lose but your barbed-wire fences."

Crashing the Crypto Monopoly

As the Cold War drifts into deep memory, one might think that the American body charged with keeping our secret codes and breaking the codes of our enemies—the National Security Agency (NSA)—might finally breathe easy for the first time in its 30-year existence. Instead, it is sweating out its worst nightmare.

The NSA's cryptographic monopoly has evaporated. Two decades ago, no one outside the government, or at least outside the government's control, performed any serious work in cryptography. That ended abruptly in 1975 when a 31-year-old computer wizard named Whitfield Diffie came up with a new system, called "public-key" cryptography, that hit the world of cyphers with the force of an unshielded nuke. The shock wave was undoubtedly felt most vividly in the fortress-like NSA headquarters at Fort Meade, Maryland.

As a child, Diffie devoured all the books he could find on the subject of cryptography. Certainly there is something about codes—secret rings, intrigue, Hardy Boys mysteries—that appeals to youngsters. Diffie, son of an historian, took them very seriously. Though his interest went dormant after he exhausted all the offerings of the local city college library, it resurfaced in the mid-1960s, when he became part of the computer hacker community at the Massachusetts Institute of Technology.

Even as a young man, Diffie's passion for technical, math-oriented problems was matched by a keen interest in the privacy of individuals. So it was natural that as one of the tenders of a complicated multi-user computer system at MIT, he became troubled with the problem of how to make the system, which held a person's work and sometimes his or her intimate secrets, truly secure. The traditional, top-down approach to the problem—protecting the files by user passwords, which in turn were stored in the electronic equivalent of vaults tended by trusted system administrators—was not satisfying. The weakness of the system was clear: The user's privacy depended on the degree to which the administrators were willing to protect it. "You may have protected files, but if a subpoena was served to the system manager, it wouldn't do you any good," Diffie notes with withering accuracy. "The administrators would sell you out, because they'd have no interest in going to jail."

Diffie recognized that the solution rested in a decentralized system in which each person held the literal key to his or her own privacy. He tried to get people interested in taking on the mathematical challenge of discovering such a system, but there were no takers. It was not until the 1970s, when the people running the ARPAnet (destined to become the Internet) were exploring security options for their members, that Diffie decided to take it on himself. By then he was at Stanford, under the thrall of David Kahn's 1967 work, *The Codebreakers*. It was a revelatory, well-written, and meticulously documented history of cryptography, focusing on 20th century American military activities, including those at the NSA.

"It brought people out of the woodwork and I certainly was one of them," recalls Diffie. "I probably read it more carefully than anyone had ever read it. By the end of 1973, I was thinking about nothing else." He embarked on what was planned to be a worldwide journey in search of information on the subject. Gaining access to it was a difficult task, since almost everything about modern cryptography was classified, available only to NSA-types and academics. Diffie's sojourn took him as far as the East Coast, where he met the woman he would eventually marry. With his future bride, he moved back to Stanford. It was then that he created a revolution in cryptography.

Specifically, the problem with the existing system of cryptography was that secure information traveled over insecure channels. In other words, a message could be intercepted before reaching its recipient. The traditional methods for securing information involved encoding an original message—known as a "plaintext," by use of a "key." The key would change all the letters of the message so anyone who tried to read it would see only an impenetrable "cyphertext." When the cyphertext message arrived at its destination, the recipient would use the same key to decipher the code, rendering it once again to plaintext. The difficulty with this scheme was getting the key from one party to another—if you sent it over an insecure channel, what's to stop someone from intercepting it and using it to decode all subsequent messages?

The problem got even thornier when one tried to imagine encryption employed on a massive scale. The only way to do it, really, was to have registries, or digital repositories, where keys would be stored. As far as Diffie was concerned, that system was screwed—you wound up having to trust the people in charge of the registry. It negated the very essence of cryptography: to maintain total privacy over your own communications.

Diffie also foresaw the day when people would be not only communicating electronically, but conducting business that way as well. They would need the digital equivalent of contracts and notarized statements. But how could this "digital signature," etched not in paper but in easily duplicated blocks of ones and zeros, possibly work?

In May 1975, collaborating with Stanford computer scientist Martin Hellman, Diffie cracked both problems. His scheme was called public-key cryptography. It was a brilliant breakthrough: Every user in the system has two keys—a public key and a private key. The public key can be widely distributed without compromising security; the private key, however, is held more closely than an ATM password—you don't let nobody get at it. For relatively arcane mathematical reasons, a message encoded with either key can be decoded with the other. For instance, if I want to send you a secure letter, I encrypt it with your public key (which I have with your blessing), and send you the cyphertext. You decipher it using your private key. Likewise, if you send a message to me, you can encrypt it with my public key, and I'll switch it back to plaintext with my private key.

This principle can also be used for authentication. Only one person can encrypt text with my private key—me. If you can decode a message with my public key, you know beyond a doubt that it's straight from my machine to yours. The message, in essence, bears my digital signature.

Public-key cryptography, in the words of David Kahn, was not only "the most revolutionary new concept in the field since . . . the Renaissance," but it was generated totally outside of the government's domain—by a privacy fanatic, no less! By the time Diffie and Hellman started distributing pre-prints of their scheme in late 1975, an independent movement in cryptography, centered in academia, was growing. These new cryptographers had read Kahn's book, but more important, they realized that the accelerating use of computers was going to mean a growth surge in the field. This expanding community soon had regular conferences and eventually published its own scientific journal.

By 1977, three members of this new community created a set of algorithms that implemented the Diffie-Hellman scheme. Called RSA for its founders—MIT scientists Rivest, Shamir, and Adleman—it offered encryption that was likely to be stronger than the Data Encryption Standard (DES), a government-approved alternative that does not use public keys. The actual strength of key-based cryptographic systems rests largely in the size of the key—in other words, how many bits of information make up the key. The larger the key, the harder it is to break the code. While DES, which was devised at IBM's research lab, limits key size to 56 bits, RSA keys could be any size. (The trade-off was that bigger keys are unwieldy, and RSA runs much more slowly than DES.) But DES had an added burden: Rumors abounded that the NSA had forced IBM to intentionally weaken the system so that the government could break DES-encoded messages. RSA did not have that stigma. (The NSA has denied these rumors.)

All that aside, the essential fact about RSA is that it was a working public-key system, and thus did not suffer from the dire flaw of all previous systems: the need to safely exchange private keys. It was flexible enough to be used to address the massive requirements of the crypto future. The algorithms were eventually patented and licensed to RSA Data Security, whose corporate mission was to create privacy and authentication tools.

As holder of the public-key patents, RSA Data Security is ideally placed to sell its privacy and authentication wares to businesses. Customers who plan to integrate RSA software in their systems include Apple, Microsoft, WordPerfect, Novell, and AT&T. RSA's president, Jim Bidzos, a non-cryptographer, is a compelling spokesperson for the need for privacy. He has cast himself as an adversary of the NSA, fighting legal restrictions on the export of his product. He even has been known to broadly hint that the NSA has used back-channels to retard the flow of his products.

Yet a number of privacy activists regard Bidzos and his company with caution. Some, like Jim Warren, the PC pioneer who chaired the first Computers, Freedom, and Privacy conference in 1991, are unhappy that a single company holds the domestic rights to such a broad concept as public-key cryptography. Others are even more concerned that RSA, a respectable business, will be unable to successfully resist any government pressure to limit the strength of the cryptography it sells.

In the Cypherpunk mind, cryptography is too important to leave to governments or even well-meaning companies. In order to insure that the tools of privacy are available to all, individual acts of heroism are required. Which brings us to Phil Zimmermann.

The Pretty Good Revolution

Phil Zimmermann is no stranger to political action. His participation in antinuke sit-ins has twice led to jailings. He has been a military policy analyst to political candidates. But his vocation is computers, and he has always been fascinated with cryptography. When he first heard about public-key crypto he was handling two jobs, one as a programmer and another unpaid post "saving the world." He was about to find a way to combine the two. Why not implement a public-key system on personal computers, using RSA algorithms?

Zimmermann posed this question around 1977, but didn't begin serious work to answer it until 1984. The more he thought about the issues, though, the more important the project became. As he later wrote in the product documentation:

> You may be planning a political campaign, discussing your taxes, or having an illicit affair. Or you may be doing something that you feel shouldn't be illegal, but is. Whatever it is, you don't want your private electronic mail or confidential documents read by anyone else. There's nothing wrong with asserting your privacy. Privacy is as apple-pie as the Constitution.
>
> What if everyone believed that law-abiding citizens should use postcards for their mail? If some brave soul tried to assert his privacy by using an envelope for his mail, it would draw suspicion. Perhaps the authorities would open his mail to see what he's hiding. Fortunately, we don't live in that kind of world, because everyone protects most of their mail with envelopes. So no one draws suspicion by asserting their privacy with an envelope. There's safety in numbers. Analogously, it would be nice if everyone routinely used encryption for all their e-mail, innocent or not, so that no one drew suspicion by asserting their e-mail privacy with encryption. Think of it as a form of solidarity. . . .
>
> If privacy is outlawed, only outlaws will have privacy. Intelligence agencies have access to good cryptographic technology. So do the big arms and drug traffickers. . . . But ordinary people and grass-roots political organizations mostly have not had access to affordable military grade public-key cryptographic technology. Until now.

Not being a professional cryptographer, Zimmermann moved slowly. By 1986, he had implemented RSA, and a year later wrote a scrambling function he called Bass-O-Matic, in homage to a *Saturday Night Live* commercial for a blender that liquifies fish. Piece by piece he built his program. In June, 1991, it was ready for release. He named his software PGP, for Pretty Good Privacy. Though at one time he mused about asking users for a fee, he subsequently became concerned that the government would one day outlaw the use of cryptography. Since Zimmermann wanted the tools for privacy disseminated widely before that day came, he decided to give PGP away. No strings.

This required some personal sacrifice. Zimmermann missed five mortgage payments producing PGP. "I came within an inch of losing my house," he says.

But the effort was worth it. PGP was unprecedented. It was, Zimmermann claims, faster than anything else available. And despite troublesome details like patent law and export code, it was very available.

Zimmermann put his first version, which ran only on PCs, on computer bulletin-board systems and gave it to a friend who posted it on the Internet. "Like thousands of dandelion seeds blowing in the wind," he wrote, PGP spread throughout cyberspace. Within hours, people were downloading it all over the country and beyond. "It was overseas the day after the release," he said. "I've gotten mail from just about every country on Earth."

PGP won no popularity contests at RSA Data Security. Jim Bidzos was incensed that Zimmermann, whom he considers not an altruistic activist but an opportunist who still hopes to make a buck off stealing intellectual property, had blithely included RSA's patented algorithms in PGP. Zimmermann's defense was that he wasn't selling PGP, but distributing it as a sort of research project. (Some people think that PGP, by spreading the gospel of public key cryptography, is the best thing that ever happened to RSA.)

In any case, the legal situation is still hazy, with Zimmermann now refraining from distributing the software (though he updates the user's guide and provides guidance and encouragement to those who have chosen to revise the software).

What does the NSA think about Phil Zimmermann's Johnny Appleseed-like attempt to bring the world crypto tools? Zimmermann has heard no formal complaint, even though many believe that PGP's strength in protecting data is such that it would never be approved for export to foreign shores. Zimmermann, of course, did not submit PGP to such scrutiny because he required no export license for international sales—after all, he was not selling it. In any case, Zimmermann himself never shipped the software overseas, warning users that it was their business if they chose to.

To be extra careful, Zimmermann arranged for the more powerful version 2.0, released last September, to be distributed from New Zealand "into" the United States, so there would be no question about exporting forbidden tools. (Due to some regulatory oddities, RSA is patented "only" in the United States, and thus PGP is a potential patent infringer only within U.S. borders.)

An uncounted number of U.S. users, probably thousands, have PGP in its various incarnations—on DOS, Macintosh, Amiga, Atari ST, or VAX/VMS computers.

At first the silence from the NSA actually worried Zimmermann. He wondered if it meant that PGP had some sort of weakness, a "trap door" that the government had identified. But after a session with a world-class cryptographer, Zimmermann was assured that while PGP had many inefficiencies, it offered protection at least as strong as the government-standard DES. It truly was "pretty good" protection. So people could evaluate it on their own, Zimmermann allowed free distribution of the source code—something one does not enjoy with alternative encryption products. And most of the inefficiencies are addressed in version 2.0.

(It was only as this article was being prepared, in February 1993, that Zimmermann was questioned about PGP by two U.S. Customs officials who flew from California to ask about how the program might have found its way out of the country. As of press time, it seems that this investigation might be still active. Jim Bidzos of RSA, obviously not a disinterested source, claims that not only Zimmermann, but anyone using PGP, is at risk. He scoffs at Zimmermann's efforts to stay within the letter of the law, charging that the use of PGP is "an illegal activity that violates patent and export law." Bidzos has written to institutions like Stanford and MIT, informing them that any copies of PGP on their computers would put them on the wrong side of the law, and he says that the universities have subsequently banned PGP.)

Still, PGP has changed the world of crypto. It is not a solution to the problem by any means—using it adds a degree of difficulty to e-mail and file transfers—but it has developed a cult among those motivated to use it. It's sort of a badge of honor to include one's PGP public key with e-mail messages.

And until the long-awaited alternative for electronic crypto on the Internet, Privacy Enhanced Mail (PEM), is released—after five years of planning, the release seems near—PGP is one of the only games in town. (Other alternatives include an RSA-approved product called RIPEM.) Even then, many users may stick to PGP. "PEM is technically cleaner but is bogged down in bureaucracy—for instance, before you use PEM you must first register a key with something called a policy certification authority," says crypto-activist and Cypherpunk John Gilmore. "PGP is portable, requires no bureaucracy, and has more than a year's head-start."

Ultimately, the value of PGP is in its power to unleash the possibilities of cryptography. Tom Jennings, founder of the FIDO-net matrix of computer bulletin boards, finds the software useful, but becomes positively rapturous as he contemplates its psychic influence. To Jennings, a gay activist, cryptography has the potential to be a powerful force in protecting the privacy of targeted individuals.

"People who never have had cops stomping through their house don't care about this," Jennings said. He believes that public awareness of these issues will be raised only by making the tools available. "If you can't demonstrate stuff, it's hard to explain." On the other hand, said Jennings, "If we flood the world with these tools, that's going to make a big difference."

The Empire Strikes Back

The flood to which Jennings refers is now only a trickle. But you don't have to be a cryptographer to know which way the code will flow. The flood indeed is coming, and the agency charged with safeguarding and mastering encryption technologies is about to be thrust into a cypher age in which messages that once were clear will require tedious cracking—and may not be crackable at all. While it is impossible to read the government's mind concerning the prospects of this scenario (see "The NSA Remains Cryptic"), its actions are telling. The strategy is one of resistance. The feds are stepping up the war between crypto activists and crypto suppressors.

The conflict actually began in the late 1970s. As wars go, this one was more cloak than dagger, with no disappearances in the night—unlikely to inspire a movie starring Steven Seagal, or even Robert Redford. As Diffie explains, "the whole thing has been conducted in a gentlemanly fashion." Yet the stakes are high: in one view, our privacy; in the other view, our national security. The government was not above implicitly threatening independent cryptographers with jail.

According to *The Puzzle Palace,* James Bamford's classic NSA expose, the first salvo in the conflict was a letter written in July 1977 by an NSA employee named Joseph A. Meyer. It warned those planning to attend an upcoming symposium on cryptography that participation might be unlawful under an Arms Regulation law, which controls weapons found on the U.S. Munitions List (cryptographic tools, it turns out, are classified right alongside tanks and bomber planes). Though the ensuing controversy in this case blew over, it became clear that the NSA regarded what came from the minds of folks like Whit Diffie to be contraband. In an unprecedented interview, the then-new NSA Director Bobby Inman floated the idea that his agency might have the same control over crypto as the Department of Energy has over nukes. In 1979, Inman gave an address that came to be known as "the sky is falling" speech, warning that "non-governmental cryptologic activity and publication . . . poses clear risks to the national security."

Through the 1980s, both sides became entrenched in their views—but it was by far the alternative crypto movement that gathered strength. Not only was the community growing to the point where government crypto specialists came to terms with the phenomenon, but computers—the devices destined to be crypto engines—became commonplace. Just as it was obvious that all communication and data storage was going digital, it was a total no-brainer that effective cryptography was essential to the maintenance of even a semblance of the privacy and security people and corporations enjoyed in the pre-digital era.

In fact, our personal information—medical information, credit ratings, income—lies unencrypted on databases. Our most intimate secrets rest on our hard disks, sitting ducks. Our phone conversations bounce off satellites, easily pluckable by those sophisticated enough to sort these things out. Our cellular phone conversations are routinely overheard by any goofus with a broadband radio—just ask Prince Charles.

And if things are tough for individuals, corporations are in worse shape—even their (weakly) encrypted secret plans are being swiped by competitors. Recently, the head of the French intelligence service quite cheerfully admitted intercepting confidential IBM documents and handing them over to French-government-backed competitors. (In cases like these, weak encryption—which gives a false sense of security—is worse than no encryption at all.)

In the face of this apparent inevitability—crypto for the masses!—what's a secret government agency to do? Throw in the towel, let the market determine the strength of the people's algorithms, and grumpily adjust to the new realities? No way. The government has chosen this moment to dig in and take its last stand. The future of crypto, and our ability to protect our information to the fullest extent, hangs in the balance.

The specter of what one Cypherpunk calls "Crypto Anarchy"—where strong, easy-to-use encryption is accessible to all—terrifies those accustomed to the old reality. Perhaps the best expression of these fears comes from Donn Parker, a think-tank computer security specialist who is in synch with the government mindset. "We have the capability of 100-percent privacy," he says. "But if we use this I don't think society can survive."

A somewhat less apocalyptic yet equally stern conclusion comes from Georgetown University Professor Dorothy Denning, a respected figure in academic crypto circles: "If we fail to enact legislation that will ensure a continued capability for court-ordered electronic surveillance," Denning writes, "systems fielded without an adequate provision for court-ordered intercepts would become sanctuaries for criminality wherein Organized Crime leaders, drug dealers, terrorists, and other criminals could conspire and act with impunity. Eventually, we could find ourselves with an increase in major crimes against society, a greatly diminished capacity to fight them, and no timely solution."

Denning has spoken favorably of a plan that sends chills up Cypherpunk spines: It allows people access to public-key cryptography only if they agree to "escrow" their private keys in a repository controlled by a third party who would, under a judge's order or other dire circumstance, give it to some government or police body.

Key registries, of course, would require crypto users to trust self-interested third parties, the very paradox that led Diffie to develop public-key cryptography. Diffie did not intend private keys to be shared—not with colleagues, not with spouses, and certainly not with some swiftie in a suit who would flip it over to the cops at the first flash of a warrant. As

Electronic Frontier Foundation co-founder John Perry Barlow put it, "You can have my encryption algorithm. . . when you pry my cold dead fingers from my private key."

But Dorothy Denning has a point. Unfettered cryptography does have its trade-offs. The same codes that protect journalists and accountants will abet the security of mobsters, child molesters, and terrorists. And if everyone encrypts, there certainly would be a weakening of our intelligence agencies, and possibly our national security.

As far as the NSA is concerned, its very mission is to establish and maintain superiority in making and breaking codes. If strong cryptography enters common usage, this task will be greatly complicated, if not rendered nearly impossible.

The government itself has taken action on three fronts:

• The first is a continuation of the secrecy with which it guards all information concerning cryptography. Traditionally, the NSA argument for this has been unimpeachable: Anything, even a seemingly innocuous fact about what we are doing, or even what we know, gives a potential adversary an advantage that it would not otherwise enjoy. Thus for years, even the very existence of the NSA (nicknamed No Such Agency by some) was denied. However, as cryptography becomes more essential for the protection of both individuals and corporations, the "anything-we-disclose-helps-our-enemies" argument is under attack. One of the most diligent prodders of the National Security Agency in this regard is John Gilmore (see "His Crime: Checking Out a Book").

• The second front is the ingenious use of export controls to limit the strength of cryptography within this country. Despite the desires of the NSA, U.S. law currently protects the way people communicate within the boundaries of the country. Practically speaking however, only the most motivated communicators take the trouble to employ the cumbersome measures necessary to encrypt their own data. Routine encryption can be made easy—so painless that it happens automatically. But for that to happen, the mass producers of software would have to include it as a default standard in their products.

• Here's where the export catch kicks in—companies like Microsoft, Apple, and WordPerfect find it unprofitable to produce two versions of their wares, one for domestic use and one for sales abroad. The path of least resistance is to adhere to the weak-encryption export standards ostensibly designed to deny strong encryption to our enemies. As a result, domestic users have less security than they would have otherwise.

• The third front is a legislative initiative known as Digital Telephony, in which the FBI has taken center stage as the lead actor in limiting not only crypto, but any system that would pose a problem for government agents implementing legal wiretaps. The deal proposed to the public is tempting—if we don't limit our high-tech communications so that government agents can easily plug in (and by association this means limiting crypto), drug smugglers, terrorists, and white-collar criminals will run rampant. ACLU lawyer Janlori Goldman contends, however, that by effectively "dumbing down" our entire communications structure, the law will put a halt to our economy's most competitive industries.

While defending Digital Telephony on ABC's *Nightline,* FBI chief William Sessions claimed that the law would merely allow law enforcement to keep pace with technology. But as Whit Diffie notes, "The most important impact of technology on communications security is that it draws better and better traffic into vulnerable channels."

In other words, Digital Telephony, if passed, would grant law-enforcement access not only to phone conversations, but a whole range of personal information previously stored in hard copy but ripe for plucking in the digital age. And if law enforcement can get at it, so can others—either government agents over-stepping their legal authority, or crooks.

In one sense this debate is moot, because the crypto genie is out of the bottle. The government may limit exports, but strong encryption software packages literally are being sold on the streets of Moscow. The NSA may keep its papers classified, but a whole generation of independent cryptographers is breaking ground and publishing freely. And then there are the crypto-guerrillas, who have already penetrated deep into the territory of their adversaries.

The Promise of Crypto Anonymity

The first physical Cypherpunk meeting occurred early last autumn at the instigation of two software engineers who had developed an interest in crypto. One was Tim May, a former Intel physicist who "retired" several years ago, at age 34, with stock options sufficient to assure that he would never flip a burger for Wendy's. May, who reluctantly permits journalists to pigeon-hole him as a libertarian, is the in-house theoretician, and author of the widely circulated "Crypto Anarchist

Manifesto." The other founder, Eric Hughes, has become the moderator of the physical meetings, maintaining an agenda that mixes technical issues of Cypherpunk works-in-progress with reports from the political front.

It would be wrong to think of Cypherpunks as a formal group. It's more a gathering of those who share a predilection for codes, a passion for privacy, and the gumption to do something about it. Anyone who decides to spread personal crypto or its gospel is a traveler in the territory of Cypherpunk.

The real action in that realm occurs via The List, an electronic posting ground which commonly generates more than 50 messages a day. People on The List receive the messages on their Internet mailboxes and can respond. The List is sort of a perpetual conversation pit from which gossip is exchanged, schemes are hatched, fantasies are outlined, and code is swapped. The modus operandi of Cypherpunks is a familiar one to hackers—*If you build it, they will come.*

As Eric Hughes posted on The List:

> Cypherpunks write code. They know that someone has to write code to defend privacy, and since it's their privacy they're going to write it. . . . Cypherpunks don't care if you don't like the software they write. Cypherpunks know that software can't be destroyed. Cypherpunks know that a widely dispersed system can't be shut down. Cypherpunks will make the networks safe for privacy.

As the Cypherpunks see it, the magic of public-key crypto can be extended far beyond the exchange of messages with secrecy. Ultimately, its value will be to provide anonymity, the right most threatened by a fully digitized society. Our transactions and conversations are now more easily traced by the digital trails we leave behind. By following the electronic links we make, one can piece together a depressingly detailed profile of who we are: Our health records, phone bills, credit histories, arrest records, and electronic mail all connect our actions and expressions to our physical selves. Crypto presents the possibility of severing these links. It is possible to use cryptography to actually limit the degree to which one can track the trail of a transaction.

This is why certain Cypherpunks are hard at work creating remailers that allow messages to be sent without any possible means of tracing who sent the message. Ideally, if someone chooses a pseudonym in one of these systems, no one else can send mail under that name. This allows for the possibility of a true digital persona—an "identity" permanently disembodied from one's physical being.

Cryptographic techniques can also potentially assure anonymity in more prosaic exchanges. For instance, in a system designed to protect privacy, a prospective employer requesting proof of a college degree will have access to records with that information—but will only be able to verify that sole datum. Cypherpunks even discuss certain cases in which a person's name would be one of the pieces protected—for instance, a police officer checking one's license need not know a driver's name, but only whether he or she is licensed to drive. The ultimate Crypto Anarchy tool would be anonymous digital money, an idea proposed and being implemented by cryptographer David Chaum. (Chaum also first proposed the idea of remailers—a good example of how the Cypherpunks are using academic research from the crypto community to build new privacy tools.)

In essence, the Cypherpunks propose an alternative to the continuation of the status quo, where cryptography is closely held and privacy is an increasingly rare commodity. Ultimately, the lessons taught by the Cypherpunks, as well as the tools they produce, are designed to help shape a world where cryptography runs free—a Pac-Man-like societal maneuver in which the digital technology that previously snatched our privacy is used, via cryptography, to snatch it back.

Tim May admits that if the whole cryptography matter were put to a vote among his fellow Americans, his side would lose. "Americans have two dichotomous views held exactly at the same time," he claims. "One view is, 'None of your damn business, a man's home is his castle. What I do is my business.' And the other is, 'What have you got to hide? If you didn't have anything to hide, you wouldn't be using cryptography.' There's a deep suspicion of people who want to keep things secret."

There's also a legitimate fear that with the anonymous systems proposed by crypto activists, illegal activities could be conducted more easily, and crucial messages our government now easily intercepts might never be noticed. But, as May says, these fears are ultimately irrelevant. Crypto Anarchy, he believes, is inevitable, despite the forces marshaled against it. "I don't see any chance that it will be done politically," says the Cypherpunk. "[But] it will be done technologically. It's already happening."

The NSA Remains Cryptic: The Official Reply

At one time, the National Security Agency would not even admit that it existed. Now, it has a Public Affairs Staff whose usual modus operandi is to reply to faxed questions from journalists. Attempting to get the NSA view of the alternative crypto movement, we asked the NSA the following six questions:

1 In the past two decades, a considerable community of serious cryptographers, in both academia and commerce, has emerged. What is the NSA's role in this evolutionary broadening of the field?

2 In light of the increasing need for privacy of communications, does the NSA anticipate less stringent secrecy concerning cryptography materials it controls?

3 What is the NSA's position on the desirability of strong cryptographic methods in individual domestic communications (e-mail, voice-mail, etc.)? Would it impede your work?

4 Does the NSA believe that the use of encryption by U.S. citizens and others communicating across borders impedes its mission?

5 Does the NSA endorse the idea of a mandatory private-key registry, accessible to the government in cases when a judge orders it suitable, for those using public-key cryptography?

6 Many people I speak to assume that all international communications are in some way monitored by the NSA. Some people have even speculated that the NSA routinely captures and in some way scans the entire traffic volume of the Internet (mail and/or news groups). Are these claims apocryphal?

Here, in its entirety, is the NSA reply:

The emergence of cryptography in the public sector has stemmed from the rapid growth in communications and information systems for private and commercial applications, and efforts to ensure that these systems are safe from hackers, viruses, and unauthorized access. One of NSA's primary responsibilities in this arena is to provide the means of protecting vital U.S. government and military communications and information systems of a classified nature. NSA maintains a high degree of expertise in cryptographic technology and keeps abreast of advancements, domestically and abroad, in order to better protect vital government communications.

Regarding questions two and three, as we have just stated, NSA is responsible for protecting U.S. government classified information systems. We do not anticipate relaxing security and integrity of these government systems since such disclosure could reduce the effectiveness of these measures. As for domestic use of cryptography, we have always supported the use of cryptographic products by U.S. businesses operating domestically and overseas to protect their sensitive and proprietary information.

Finally, as a policy matter, NSA does not discuss details of its signals intelligence operations, including the types of communications it monitors. Please note, however, that our signals intelligence operations are exclusively limited to producing foreign intelligence information considered vital to the security interest of the U.S. We, therefore, offer no comment to questions four and six.

In regard to question five and the idea of mandatory key registration, we defer to the Department of Justice/FBI.

His Crime: Checking Out a Book

One day last November, the Justice Department called John Gilmore's lawyer. The message they left: Gilmore was on the verge of violating the Espionage Act. A conviction could send him to jail for ten years. His crime? Basically, showing people a library book.

It was a fight that Gilmore instigated. As Sun Microsystems employee number five, Gilmore retired with a bankroll in the millions. Later, he had the opportunity not only to co-found a new company—called Cygnus Support—but to commit acts of public service. "As I get older," says the 37-year-old computer programmer, "I realize how limited our time on Earth is." His cause of choice was the liberation of cryptography, a field that had fascinated him since he was a boy.

"We aren't going to be secure in our persons, houses, papers, and effects unless we get a better understanding of cryptography," he says. "Our government is building some of those tools for its own use—there have been breakthroughs—but they're unavailable to us. We paid for them."

To remedy this situation, Gilmore and his lawyer, Lee Tien, have tried to rescue documents from the shroud of secrecy. Gilmore's first major coup was the distribution of a paper written by a Xerox cryptographer that the NSA had convinced Xerox not to publish. Gilmore posted the document on the Net, and within hours, thousands of people had a copy.

Gilmore's next action was to challenge the NSA's refusal to follow Freedom of Information Act (FOIA) protocols in releasing requested documents. The documents he sought were 30-year-old manuals written by William F. Friedman, the father of American cryptography. These seminal textbooks had been declassified, but later, for undisclosed reasons, reclassified. The NSA did not respond to Gilmore's request for their release within the required time-frame, so he took them to court. Meanwhile, a friend of Gilmore discovered copies of two of the documents: one in the Virginia Military Institute Library, the other on microfilm at Boston University. The friend gave copies to Gilmore, who then notified the judge hearing the FOIA appeal that the secret documents were actually on library shelves.

It was then that the government notified Gilmore that distribution of the Friedman texts would violate the Espionage Act, which dictated a possible ten-year prison sentence for violators. Gilmore sent a sealed copy to the judge, asking whether his First Amendment rights were being violated by the notice; he also alerted the press. Meanwhile, worried about whether the government might stage a surprise search of his house or business, he hid copies of the documents—one in an abandoned building. On November 25, 1992, an article about the case appeared in the *San Francisco Examiner*. Two days later, an NSA spokesperson announced that the agency had once again declassified the texts. (A Laguna Hills, California publisher, the Aegean Park Press, quickly printed and released the books, *Military Crypt-analysis,* Part III, and Part IV.)

Gilmore is still pressing his case, requesting a classified book called *Military Cryptanalytics,* Volume III. More important, he hopes to get a general court ruling that will force the NSA to adhere to FOIA rules, and possibly even a ruling that part of the Espionage Act, by using prior restraint to suppress free speech, is unconstitutional.

What if Gilmore wins, and the NSA is forced to reveal all but the most secret information about cryptography? Would national security be compromised, as the NSA claims? "I don't think so," says Gilmore. "We are not asking to threaten the national security. We're asking to discard a Cold War bureaucratic idea of national security which is obsolete. My response to the NSA is: Show us. Show the public how your ability to violate the privacy of any citizen has prevented a major disaster. They're abridging the freedom and privacy of all citizens—to defend us against a bogeyman that they will not explain. The decision to literally trade away our privacy is one that must be made by the whole society, not made unilaterally by a military spy agency."

Gilmore Speaks to Congress

John Gilmore presented the following "sound bites" to Congress for consideration as it debates technology policy:

- Government investment invariably brings government control, which is harmful to the development of a communications medium in a free and open society.
- The Government seized control of telegraphy, radio, and television early in their development, and they have never had full First Amendment protection.
- Private, interactive, electronic media involve Fourth and Fifth Amendment issues as well.
- The Executive Branch is already advocating broad wiretapping, and banning of privacy technologies, and they don't even own the network. If the government owned the network, there'd be no stopping them.
- The risk of moving society into media where individual rights are regularly abridged is too great. Economics is pushing us into individual electronic communication, regardless.
- If Congress truly believes in the Bill of Rights, it should get the hell out of the networking business and stay out of it.
- Privacy and authenticity technologies are key to reliable and trustworthy social and business interactions over networks.
- Current government policies actively prohibit and inhibit the research, design, manufacturing, sale, and use of these technologies.
- Taxpayers have been investing many billions of dollars per year in these technologies—in the NSA "black budget"—but have seen no return on this investment.

The Bedside Crypto Reader: Further Readings on Cypherpunk Topics

General

Kahn, David. *The Codebreakers*. Macmillan, 1967. The seminal cryptographic history.

Bamford, James. *Puzzle Palace*. Penguin, 1983. A classic exposé of the National Security Agency.

Books on Cryptographic Systems

Simmons, Gustavus J., ed. *Contemporary Cryptology.* IEEE Press, 1991. A fairly technical volume offering solid background on the subject, including a chapter on the history of public-key cryptography by Whitfield Diffie.

Denning, Dorothy. *Cryptography and Data Security.* Addison-Wesley, 1982. A good primer to the workings of crypto systems.

Sci-Fi Novels Beloved by Cypherpunks

Card, Orson Scott. *Ender's Game.* Tor, 1985. Some vivid scenarios in which crypto anonymity is crucial.

Brunner, John. *Shock-Wave Rider.* Ballantine, 1976. Chilling representation of an oppressive lack of privacy in a networked society.

Vinge, Werner. *True Names.* Blue Jay Books, 1984. A novel of cyberspace-style sojourns that outline links between electronic identity and physical identity.

13

Jackboots on the Infobahn

John Perry Barlow

On January 11, I managed to schmooze myself aboard Air Force 2. It was flying out of LA, where its principal passenger had just outlined his vision of the information superhighway to a suited mob of television, show-biz, and cable types who fervently hoped to own it one day—if they could ever figure out what the hell it was.

From the standpoint of the Electronic Frontier Foundation the speech had been wildly encouraging. The administration's program, as announced by Vice President Al Gore, incorporated many of the concepts of open competition, universal access, and deregulated common carriage that we'd been pushing for the previous year.

But he had said nothing about the future of privacy, except to cite among the bounties of the NII its ability to "help law enforcement agencies thwart criminals and terrorists who might use advanced telecommunications to commit crimes."

On the plane I asked Gore what this implied about administration policy on cryptography. He became as noncommittal as a cigar-store Indian. "We'll be making some announcements. . . . I can't tell you anything more." He hurried to the front of the plane, leaving me to troubled speculation.

Despite its fundamental role in assuring privacy, transaction security, and reliable identity within the NII, the Clinton administration has not demonstrated an enlightenment about cryptography up to par with the rest of its digital vision.

The Clipper Chip—which threatens to be either the goofiest waste of federal dollars since President Gerald Ford's great Swine Flu program or, if actually deployed, a surveillance technology of profound malignancy—seemed at first an ugly legacy of the Reagan-Bush modus operandi. "This is going to be our Bay of Pigs," one Clinton White House official told me at the time Clipper was introduced, referring to the disastrous plan to invade Cuba that Kennedy inherited from Eisenhower.

(Clipper, in case you're just tuning in, is an encryption chip that the National Security Agency and FBI hope will someday be in every phone and computer in America. It scrambles your communications, making them unintelligible to all but their intended recipients. All, that is, but the government, which would hold the "key" to your chip. The key would be separated into two pieces, held in escrow, and joined with the appropriate "legal authority.")

Of course, trusting the government with your privacy is like having a Peeping Tom install your window blinds. And, since the folks I've met in this White House seem like extremely smart, conscious freedom-lovers—hell, a lot of them are Deadheads—I was sure that after they were fully moved in, they'd face down the National Security Agency and the FBI, let Clipper die a natural death, and lower the export embargo on reliable encryption products.

Furthermore, the National Institutes of Standards and Technology and the National Security Council have been studying both Clipper and export embargoes since April. Given that the volumes of expert testimony they had collected overwhelmingly opposed both, I expected the final report would give the administration all the support it needed to do the right thing.

I was wrong. Instead, there would be no report. Apparently, they couldn't draft one that supported, on the evidence, what they had decided to do instead.

The Other Shoe Drops

On Friday, February 4, the other jackboot dropped. A series of announcements from the administration made it clear that cryptography would become their very own "Bosnia of telecommunications" (as one staffer put it). It wasn't just that the old Serbs in the National Security Agency and the FBI were still making the calls. The alarming new reality was that the invertebrates in the White House were only too happy to abide by them. Anything to avoid appearing soft on drugs or terrorism.

So, rather than ditching Clipper, they declared it a Federal Data Processing Standard, backing that up with an immediate government order for 50,000 Clipper devices. They appointed the National Institutes of Standards and Technology and the Department of Treasury as the "trusted" third parties that would hold the Clipper key pairs. (Treasury, by the way, is also home to such trustworthy agencies as the Secret Service and the Bureau of Alcohol, Tobacco, and Firearms.)

They reaffirmed the export embargo on robust encryption products, admitting for the first time that its purpose was to stifle competition to Clipper. And they outlined a very porous set of requirements under which the cops might get the keys to your chip. (They would not go into the procedure by which the National Security Agency could get them, though they assured us it was sufficient.)

They even signaled the impending return of the dread Digital Telephony, an FBI legislative initiative requiring fundamental reengineering of the information infrastructure; providing wiretapping ability to the FBI would then become the paramount design priority.

Invasion of the Body Snatchers

Actually, by the time the announcements thudded down, I wasn't surprised by them. I had spent several days the previous week in and around the White House.

I felt like I was in another remake of the *Invasion of the Body Snatchers*. My friends in the administration had been transformed. They'd been subsumed by the vast mindfield on the other side of the security clearance membrane, where dwell the monstrous bureaucratic organisms that feed on fear. They'd been infected by the institutionally paranoid National Security Agency's *Weltanschauung*.

They used all the telltale phrases. Mike Nelson, the White House point man on the NII, told me, "If only I could tell you what I know, you'd feel the same way I do." I told him I'd been inoculated against that argument during Vietnam. (And it does seem to me that if you're going to initiate a process that might end freedom in America, you probably need an argument that isn't classified.)

Besides, how does he know what he knows? Where does he get his information? Why, the National Security Agency, of course. Which, given its strong interest in the outcome, seems hardly an unimpeachable source.

However they reached it, Clinton and Gore have an astonishingly simple bottom line, to which even the future of American liberty and prosperity is secondary: They believe that it is their responsibility to eliminate, by whatever means, the possibility that some terrorist might get a nuke and use it on, say, the World Trade Center. They have been convinced that such plots are more likely to ripen to hideous fruition behind a shield of encryption.

The staffers I talked to were unmoved by the argument that anyone smart enough to steal a nuclear device is probably smart enough to use PGP or some other uncompromised crypto standard. And never mind that the last people who popped a hooter in the World Trade Center were able to get it there without using any cryptography and while under FBI surveillance.

We are dealing with religion here. Though only ten American lives have been lost to terrorism in the last two years, the primacy of this threat has become as much an article of faith with these guys as the Catholic conviction that human life begins at conception or the Mormon belief that the Lost Tribe of Israel crossed the Atlantic in submarines.

In the spirit of openness and compromise, they invited the Electronic Frontier Foundation to submit other solutions to the "problem" of the nuclear-enabled terrorist than key escrow devices, but they would not admit into discussion the argument that such a threat might, in fact, be some kind of phantasm created by the spooks to ensure their lavish budgets into the post-Cold War era.

As to the possibility that good old-fashioned investigative techniques might be more valuable in preventing their show-case catastrophe (as it was after the fact in finding the alleged perpetrators of the last attack on the World Trade Center), they just hunkered down and said that when wiretaps were necessary, they were damned well necessary.

When I asked about the business that American companies lose because of their inability to export good encryption products, one staffer essentially dismissed the market, saying that total world trade in crypto goods was still less than a billion dollars. (Well, right. Thanks more to the diligent efforts of the National Security Agency than to dim sales potential.)

I suggested that a more immediate and costly real-world effect of their policies would be to reduce national security by isolating American commerce, owing to a lack of international confidence in the security of our data lines. I said that Bruce Sterling's fictional data-enclaves in places like the Turks and Caicos Islands were starting to look real-world inevitable.

They had a couple of answers to this, one unsatisfying and the other scary. The unsatisfying answer was that the international banking community could just go on using DES, which still seemed robust enough to them. (DES is the old federal Data Encryption Standard, thought by most cryptologists to be nearing the end of its credibility.)

More frightening was their willingness to counter the data-enclave future with one in which no data channels anywhere would be secure from examination by one government or another. Pointing to unnamed other countries that were developing their own mandatory standards and restrictions regarding cryptography, they said words to the effect of, "Hey, it's not like you can't outlaw the stuff. Look at France."

Of course, they have also said repeatedly—and for now I believe them—that they have absolutely no plans to outlaw non-Clipper crypto in the U.S. But that doesn't mean that such plans wouldn't develop in the presence of some pending "emergency." Then there is that White House briefing document, issued at the time Clipper was first announced, which asserts that no U.S. citizen "as a matter of right, is entitled to an unbreakable commercial encryption product."

Now why, if it's an ability they have no intention of contesting, do they feel compelled to declare that it's not a right? Could it be that they are preparing us for the laws they'll pass after some bearded fanatic has gotten himself a surplus nuke and used something besides Clipper to conceal his plans for it?

If they are thinking about such an eventuality, we should be doing so as well. How will we respond? I believe there is a strong, though currently untested, argument that outlawing unregulated crypto would violate the First Amendment, which surely protects the manner of our speech as clearly as it protects the content.

But of course the First Amendment is, like the rest of the Constitution, only as good as the government's willingness to uphold it. And they are, as I say, in the mood to protect our safety over our liberty.

This is not a mind-frame against which any argument is going to be very effective. And it appeared that they had already heard and rejected every argument I could possibly offer.

In fact, when I drew what I thought was an original comparison between their stand against naturally proliferating crypto and the folly of King Canute (who placed his throne on the beach and commanded the tide to leave him dry), my government opposition looked pained and said he had heard that one almost as often as jokes about roadkill on the information superhighway.

I hate to go to war with them. War is always nastier among friends. Furthermore, unless they've decided to let the National Security Agency design the rest of the National Information Infrastructure as well, we need to go on working closely with them on the whole range of issues like access, competition, workplace privacy, common carriage, intellectual property, and such. Besides, the proliferation of strong crypto will probably happen eventually no matter what they do.

But then again, it might not. In which case we could shortly find ourselves under a government that would have the automated ability to log the time, origin and recipient of every call we made, could track our physical whereabouts continuously, could keep better account of our financial transactions than we do, and all without a warrant. Talk about crime prevention!

Worse, under some vaguely defined and surely mutable "legal authority," they also would be able to listen to our calls and read our e-mail without having to do any backyard rewiring. They wouldn't need any permission at all to monitor overseas calls.

If there's going to be a fight, I'd rather it be with this government than the one we'd likely face on that hard day.

Hey, I've never been a paranoid before. It's always seemed to me that most governments are too incompetent to keep a good plot strung together all the way from coffee break to quitting time. But I am now very nervous about the government of the United States of America.

Because Bill 'n' Al, whatever their other new-paradigm virtues, have allowed the very old-paradigm trogs of the Guardian Class to define as their highest duty the defense of America against an enemy that exists primarily in the imagination—and is therefore capable of anything.

To assure absolute safety against such an enemy, there is no limit to the liberties we will eventually be asked to sacrifice. And, with a Clipper Chip in every phone, there will certainly be no technical limit on their ability to enforce those sacrifices.

14

The Clipper Chip Will Block Crime

Dorothy E. Denning

Hidden among the discussions of the information highway is a fierce debate, with huge implications for everyone. It centers on a tiny computer chip called the Clipper, which uses sophisticated coding to scramble electronic communications transmitted through the phone system.

The Clinton administration has adopted the chip, which would allow law enforcement agencies with court warrants to read the Clipper codes and eavesdrop on terrorists and criminals. But opponents say that, if this happens, the privacy of law-abiding individuals will be at risk. They want people to be able to use their own scramblers, which the government would not be able to decode.

If the opponents get their way, however, all communications on the information highway would be immune from lawful interception. In a world threatened by international organized crime, terrorism, and rogue governments, this would be folly. In testimony before Congress, Donald Delaney, senior investigator with the New York State Police, warned that if we adopted an encoding standard that did not permit lawful intercepts, we would have havoc in the United States.

Moreover, the Clipper coding offers safeguards against casual government intrusion. It requires that one of the two components of a key embedded in the chip be kept with the Treasury Department and the other component with the Commerce Department's National Institute of Standards and Technology. Any law enforcement official wanting to wiretap would need to obtain not only a warrant but the separate components from the two agencies. This, plus the superstrong code and key system would make it virtually impossible for anyone, even corrupt government officials, to spy illegally.

But would terrorists use Clipper? The Justice Department has ordered $8 million worth of Clipper scramblers in the hope that they will become so widespread and convenient that everyone will use them. Opponents say that terrorists will not be so foolish as to use encryption to which the government holds the key but will scramble their calls with their own code systems. But then who would have thought that the World Trade Center bombers would have been stupid enough to return a truck that they had rented?

Court-authorized interception of communications has been essential for preventing and solving many serious and often violent crimes, including terrorism, organized crime, drugs, kidnaping, and political corruption. The FBI alone has had many spectacular successes that depended on wiretaps. In a Chicago case code-named RUKBOM, they prevented the El Rukn street gang, which was acting on behalf of the Libyan government, from shooting down a commercial airliner using a stolen military weapons system.

To protect against abuse of electronic surveillance, federal statutes impose stringent requirements on the approval and execution of wiretaps. Wiretaps are used judiciously (only 846 installed wiretaps in 1992) and are targeted at major criminals.

Now, the thought of the FBI wiretapping my communications appeals to me about as much as its searching my home and seizing my papers. But the Constitution does not give us absolute privacy from court-ordered searches and seizures, and for good reason. Lawlessness would prevail.

Encoding technologies, which offer privacy, are on a collision course with a major crime-fighting tool: wiretapping. Now the Clipper chip shows that strong encoding can be made available in a way that protects private communications but does not harm society if it gets into the wrong hands. Clipper is a good idea, and it needs support from people who recognize the need for both privacy and effective law enforcement on the information highway.

15

The Denning–Barlow Clipper Chip Debate

Dorothy E. Denning and John Perry Barlow

OnlineHost Good evening and welcome to the Time Online Odeon! Tonight we look from both sides at the Clipper Chip, a semiconductor device that the National Security Agency developed and wants installed in every telephone, computer modem and fax machine.

OnlineHost In his article in the current issue of *Time,* Philip Elmer-DeWitt writes: "The chip combines a powerful encryption algorithm with a "back door"—the cryptographic equivalent of the master key that opens schoolchildren's padlocks when they forget their combinations. A "secure" phone equipped with the chip could, with proper authorization, be cracked by the government.

OnlineHost "Law-enforcement agencies say they need this capability to keep tabs on drug runners, terrorists and spies. Critics denounce the Clipper—and a bill before Congress that would require phone companies to make it easy to tap the new digital phones—as Big Brotherly tools that will strip citizens of whatever privacy they still have in the computer age.

OnlineHost "Lined up on one side are the three-letter cloak-and-dagger agencies—the NSA, the CIA and the FBI—and key policymakers in the Clinton Administration (who are taking a surprisingly hard line on the encryption issue). Opposing them is an equally unlikely coalition of computer firms, civil libertarians, conservative columnists and a strange breed of cryptoanarchists who call themselves the cypherpunks."

RPTime Lined up on our stage tonight are John Perry Barlow, Dr. Dorothy Denning and Philip Elmer-DeWitt. Barlow is co-founder of the Electronic Frontier Foundation, which promotes freedom in digital media. A recognized commentator on computer security, he is arguing against the Clipper Chip. Dr. Denning is the chairperson of the Computer Science Department at Georgetown University. A leading expert on cryptography and data security, she favors the adoption of the Clipper Chip. Philip Elmer-DeWitt, *Time*'s technology editor will lead the questioning of our guests. Audience questions may be sent up using the Interact with Host function . . . Phil?

PhilipED Dr. Denning, could you *briefly* make the case for why we need the key escrow encryption system.

DDenning The government needs a new encryption standard to replace DES. They came up with a very strong algorithm called SKIPJACK. In making that available, they didn't want to do it in a way that could ultimately prove harmful to society. So they came up with the idea of key escrow so that if SKIPJACK were used to conceal criminal activity, they would be able to get access to the communications.

PhilipED Thanks. Mr. Barlow, could you briefly make the case *against* Clipper.

Barlow1 We'll see if I can be brief. We oppose Clipper in large part because of the traffic analysis which it makes possible. We believe that it is in the functional nature of the chip as designed to greatly enhance the ability of government to observe who we are calling, when, and from where, all fairly automatically and centrally. We also oppose Clipper because of the many ways in which we believe the escrow system could be compromised, by people and institutions both inside and outside of government.

PhilipED Dr. Denning, what about John's contention that Clipper makes it easier to detect calling patterns.

DDenning I don't buy this. First off, for law enforcement to access any communications, they need a court order. Even if the communications are encrypted. Second, with a court order, they can get access to call setup information and find out what other lines the subject of the investigation is talking to. This is of much more use than anything in the encrypted stream.

PhilipED John, is Dorothy right that you need a court order for call setup info?

Barlow1 Dorothy, the government asked for and received over 100,000 calling records last year without a court order. I see nothing in the Clipper documents which indicates that they would require a court order to get this kind of information, which each chip would make readily available to the entire network.

DDenning You need a court order to do implement pen registers and dialed number recorders in order to find out who is talking to whom.

Barlow1 Furthermore, my faith in court orders has been eroded by 30 years of government wiretap abuse.

PhilipED Aren't we talking about three different hurdles here, one for a wiretap . . .

Barlow1 But that's only with the present system where putting a pen register on a line requires physical entrance to a phone company site.

PhilipED One for a pen register (to track calling patterns in real time) and one for phone records.

RPTime Let's take a question from the audience . . . How would you guarantee that this facility will never be misused? If you can't make that guarantee, why should a democratic society, with a prohibition against prior restraint, consent to this? John Barlow?

Barlow1 There are three different sources of information, as you say. But there are not three "hurdles." That sounds like a question for Dorothy. I don't think we should, obviously.

RPTime Dr. Denning?

DDenning First of all, there has been no evidence of widespread abuse of wiretaps since passage of the 1968 and 1978 wiretap statutes. Second, there are a lot of security mechanisms going into it to protect against abuse. Third, it will provide much greater protection against illegal wiretaps than we have now, since almost all phone conversations are in the clear. It will make virtually all illegal wiretaps impossible. Fourth, if for some reason it doesn't provide adequate protection, we can destroy the key databases and everyone will have absolute privacy against government wiretaps. I don't think our society will tolerate that kind of abuse.

PhilipED John, isn't Dorothy right that you're better off with compromised encryption than none?

Barlow1 Gee, where to begin . . . First of all, there was plenty of abuse after 1968. Remember Watergate, Dorothy? Second, I believe that Clipper in the Net will dramatically *enhance* certain powers of . . .

DDenning I was talking specifically about wiretap abuses. And there hasn't been any evidence since the 1978 law.

Barlow1 . . . surveillance over current technical abilities. One of the reasons that wiretap hasn't been more abused is the bureaucratic overhead of current practices. Make it so that it doesn't require 50 agents to conduct a wire tap and you'll see a lot more of it. And Watergate included quite a number of wiretap violations. Indeed, the burglers were caught trying to install one. As to the assertion that we can always back up and destroy the databases if we don't like it, I can't imagine that someone as bright as yourself would believe that this is possible. Technology and power ratchet into positions which almost never retract without a complete change in the system of authority

RPTime Care to respond Dr. Denning?

DDenning Clipper would prevent the Watergate burglars from getting anywhere since they wouldn't have a court order. Clipper will not make wiretaps cheaper or easier. Wiretaps are becoming more difficult. And there will always be more agents involved because they have to follow exacting procedures, including minimization (throw out all conversations that are not specific to the crime at hand).

Barlow1 Dorothy, they were from the *Government,* remember? I can't imagine that Nixon wouldn't have been able to find a sympathetic ear from somebody at NIST and somebody else at Treasury. Further, you're not talking about the truly insidious element of this, which is dramatically improved traffic analysis. Content is less important than context, and most agents will support this.

RPTime Another question from the audience. JCMaille asks . . . Does the government have a constitutional right of access to my personal communications? Dr. Denning, why don't you go first?

DDenning The Supreme Court ruled that wiretaps with a court order are Constitutional. At one time, communications were not even protected under the 4th Amendment. The government could wiretap without a court order! Now a court order is required.

PhilipED To put the question another way, do citizens have a right to use powerful encryption?

DDenning Right now there are no laws preventing the use of any encryption. Clipper is voluntary. You can still use something else.

RPTime We have to apologize. John Barlow has temporarily lost his connection . . .

PhilipED Dr. Denning, in your opinion . . . would a law outlawing powerful encryption be unconstitutional?

DDenning I don't think so. But that doesn't mean it will happen.

RPTime John Barlow is back with us. Sorry for the interruption! Barlow, Denning just said she didn't think a law banning powerful encryption would be unconstitutional. What do you say?

Barlow1 Actually, I believe that our current export embargoes are a violation of the 1st Amendment which specifies speech without regard to the manner of speech. If we could restrict manner of speech, it would be constitutional to require that everyone speak English. Which of course it isn't.

PhilipED John, can you make the case why ordinary law-abiding citizens need powerful encryption?

Barlow1 Because it is in the nature of digitally networked communications to be quite visible. Every time we make any sort of transaction in a digital environment, we smear our fingerprints all over Cyberspace. If we are to have any privacy in the future, we will need virtual "walls" made of cryptography.

RPTime Another audience question . . . Isn't this like the gun argument? If guns are outlawed only criminals will have guns? Well, if Clipper is standardized, won't criminals be the ones *not* using it?

RPTime Dr. Denning?

DDenning If Clipper becomes the de facto standard, then it will be the chief method of encryption. That would be what you'd get at Radio Shack. What criminals use will depend on what is readily available and what their cohorts are using. Both parties of a conversation have to use the same thing. Criminals also talk to a lot of people outside their immediate circle—e.g., to buy goods and services. Also, they can be quite stupid at times. But the main thing is that criminals will not be able to take advantage of the SKIPJACK algorithm as a way of concealing their conversations. This is the whole point. It is not to catch criminals. It is to allow people access to a really high quality algorithm in a way that someone cannot use it to conceal criminal activity.

Barlow1 The gun analogy is excellent up to a point. I can't for the life of me imagine why we would think that even a stupid criminal would use Clipper if something else were available. And when I talk to people in the administration their big hobgoblin is the "nuclear-armed" terrorist. Any fanatic smart enough to assemble and detonate a nuclear device is going to be smart enough to download PGP from a bulletin board somewhere. Also, I'd like to point out that the gun analogy doesn't go the whole distance. Crypto is by its nature a purely *defensive* technology. You can't shoot people with it.

PhilipED Speaking of PGP, Dr. Denning, is that encryption system secure, in your opinion?

DDenning I don't know of anyone who's been able to break the IDEA algorithm that it uses.

RPTime Back to the audience for a question from SteveHW . . . This is for Dr. Denning. What is the evidence of harm if the Clipper proposal is not adopted?

DDenning The harm would be to the government. They would not be able to use it and would have to resort to something less secure. Also, Clipper is part of a larger project to make hardware available for encryption and digital signatures. This will be used, for example, in the Defense Message System. The goverment needs a new standard. I personally believe that making really powerful encryption like SKIPJACK available without key escrow could be harmful to society. Wiretaps have been essential for preventing and solving many serious crimes and terrorist activities.

Barlow1 Why on earth would the government have to use something else if they failed to get the rest of rest of us to buy into this folly? Hey, they are already using SKIPJACK. It's a government algorithm and has been in use for a . . .

DDenning CPSR and others are asking the government to drop Clipper.

Barlow1 . . . long time. There are plenty other algorithms which we can use which are truly protected . . . unless of course, this is only the first step in a process which will outlaw other forms of crypto. And I believe that it must be. Makes absolutely no sense otherwise. EFF is not asking the Government to drop Clipper, though we would vastly prefer they did. We're merely asking that no steps be taken to require it either by law or practice . . . as, for example, would be the case if you had to use a Clipper chip to file your tax return.

PhilipED Dr. Denning, do you think this is the "first step in a process to outlaw crypto"?

DDenning No I do not. The government has not been using SKIPJACK to my knowledge. The Clipper initiative represents the first time that the government has put one of their really good algorithms out there in the unclassified arena. They are trying to do this in a way that won't backfire against the public. Other NSA developed algorithms are not available for purchase by the public.

Barlow1 I appreciate their willingness to make some of that crypto research available to a public which has paid so much for it, but I'm afraid that I would never trust an algorithm which was given to me by any government. And I certainly don't trust a classified algorithm like SKIPJACK, even without a back door which everyone can see. I think I'll stick to systems which have been properly vetted to be clear of such compromises, like RSA. I hope others will do likewise and that RSA will become the standard which Clipper shouldn't be.

RPTime Time for one more question from our audience . . . To John Barlow. Isn't society becoming increasingly vulnerable to concerted criminal/terrorist disruption, requiring *stronger* law enforcement tools?

Barlow1 Gee. I don't know. It's a scary world. However, I'm willing to take my chances with the few terrorists and drug lords there are out there rather than trusting government with the kind of almost unlimited surveillance power which Clipper and Digital Telephony would give them. It's a tough choice. But when you look at the evil perpetrated by government over this century in the name of stopping crime, it far exceeds that done by other organized criminals.

RPTime Dr. Denning, hasn't remote listening technology enhanced police abilities to eavesdrop to the point . . . where the loss of a few wire taps won't mean much?

DDenning No. They need to get the cooperation of the service providers to implement a wiretap. The loss of some wiretaps could be costly indeed. As an example, wiretaps were used to help solve a case that involved plans by a Chicago gang from shooting down a commercial airliner.

There have been 2 cases where they helped save the lives of kids who were going to be kidnaped for the making of a snuff murder film. They helped solve a case where a man's house was going to be bombed. I could go on. If we take John's arguments about law enforcement to their logical conclusion, we'd just get rid of law enforcement. I think it's better to have it. The people in law enforcement hate it as much as the rest of us when some member of the community does something wrong. And they correct it, design new procedures and laws where necessary, and go on.

Barlow1 Oh, please. I'm not proposing eliminating police. I'm opposing giving them unlimited powers. Also, these are the same cases cited over and over by everyone from you to Judge Freeh. Surely, we aren't going to fundamentally change the balance of power in this country because of these two (undocumented, to my knowledge) stories.

DDenning Clipper is not going to change the balance of power. It does not give law enforcement any additional authority to do wiretaps.

Barlow1 Well, this is where we basically disagree, Dorothy. If we could continue the same level of LE capacity we presently have, I'd have no objection. But I believe, for reasons I'm not sure we have the bandwidth to discuss here, that we are talking about dramatically enhancing their abilities. For one thing, we would greatly reduce the bureaucratic overhead involved in wiretap, which is what keeps it under 900 cases nationwide at the present.

RPTime And that will have to be the last word on the matter for tonight . . .

DDenning The overhead of a wiretap is more likely to increase, not decrease.

PhilipED Not quite! Maybe not! ;-)

RPTime *That* will be the final word!

Barlow1 Well, let's get together and talk, Dorothy.

RPTime *Time* thanks Dr. Dorothy Denning and John Perry Barlow for being with us tonight . . . along with Philip Elmer-DeWitt. Thank you all, and goodnight! Thank you both. This was very interesting.

DDenning Thank you for the opportunity to be here!

16

Achieving Electronic Privacy

David Chaum

Every time you make a telephone call, purchase goods using a credit card, subscribe to a magazine or pay your taxes, that information goes into a data base somewhere. Furthermore, all these records can be linked so that they constitute in effect a single dossier on your life, not only your medical and financial history but also what you buy, where you travel and whom you communicate with. It is almost impossible to learn the full extent of the files that various organizations keep on you, much less to assure their accuracy or to control who may gain access to them.

Organizations link records from different sources for their own protection. Certainly it is in the interest of a bank looking at a loan application to know that John Doe has defaulted on four similar loans in the past two years. The bank's possession of that information also helps its other customers, to whom the bank passes on the cost of bad loans. In addition, these records permit Jane Roe, whose payment history is impeccable, to establish a charge account at a shop that has never seen her before.

That same information in the wrong hands, however, provides neither protection for businesses nor better service for consumers. Thieves routinely use a stolen credit card number to trade on their victims' good payment records; murderers have tracked down their targets by consulting government-maintained address records. On another level, the U.S. Internal Revenue Service has attempted to single out taxpayers for audits based on estimates of household income compiled by mailing-list companies.

The growing amounts of information that different organizations collect about a person can be linked because all of them use the same key in the U.S.—the social security number—to identify the individual in question. This identifier-based approach perforce trades off security against individual liberties. The more information that organizations have (whether the intent is to protect them from fraud or simply to target marketing efforts), the less privacy and control people retain.

Over the past eight years, my colleagues and I at CWI (the Dutch nationally funded Center for Mathematics and Computer Science in Amsterdam) have developed a new approach, based on fundamental theoretical and practical advances in cryptography, that makes this trade-off unnecessary. Transactions employing these techniques avoid the possibility of fraud while maintaining the privacy of those who use them.

In our system, people would in effect give a different (but definitively verifiable) pseudonym to every organization they do business with and so make dossiers impossible. They could pay for goods in untraceable electronic cash or present digital credentials that serve the function of a banking passbook, driver's license or voter registration card without revealing their identity. At the same time, organizations would benefit from increased security and lower record-keeping costs.

Recent innovations in microelectronics make this vision practical by providing personal "representatives" that store and manage their owners' pseudonyms, credentials and cash. Microprocessors capable of carrying out the necessary algorithms have already been embedded in pocket computers the size and thickness of a credit card. Such systems have been tested on a small scale and could be in widespread use by the middle of this decade.

The starting point for this approach is the digital signature, first proposed in 1976 by Whitfield Diffie, then at Stanford University. A digital signature transforms the message that is signed so that anyone who reads it can be sure of who sent it (see "The Mathematics of Public-Key Cryptography," by Martin E. Hellman, *Scientific American,* August 1979). These signatures employ a secret key used to sign messages and a public one used to verify them. Only a message signed with the private key can be verified by means of the public one. Thus, if Alice wants to send a signed message to Bob (these two are the cryptographic community's favorite hypothetical characters), she transforms it using her private key, and he applies her public key to make sure that it was she who sent it. The best methods known for producing forged signatures would require many years, even using computers billions of times faster than those now available.

To see how digital signatures can provide all manner of unforgeable credentials and other services, consider how they might be used to provide an electronic replacement for cash. The First Digital Bank would offer electronic bank notes: messages signed using a particular private key. All messages bearing one key might be worth a dollar, all those bearing a different key five dollars, and so on for whatever denominations were needed. These electronic bank notes could be authenticated using the corresponding public key, which the bank has made a matter of record. First Digital would also make public a key to authenticate electronic documents sent from the bank to its customers.

To withdraw a dollar from the bank, Alice generates a note number (each note bears a different number, akin to the serial number on a bill); she chooses a 100-digit number at random so that the chance anyone else would generate the same one is negligible. She signs the number with the private key corresponding to her "digital pseudonym" (the public key that she has previously established for use with her account). The bank verifies Alice's signature and removes it from the note number, signs the note number with its worth-one-dollar signature and debits her account. It then returns the signed note along with a digitally signed withdrawal receipt for Alice's records. In practice, the creation, signing and transfer of note numbers would be carried out by Alice's card computer. The power of the cryptographic protocols, however, lies in the fact that they are secure regardless of physical medium: the same transactions could be carried out using only pencil and paper.

When Alice wants to pay for a purchase at Bob's shop, she connects her "smart" card with his card reader and transfers one of the signed note numbers the bank has given her. After verifying the bank's digital signature, Bob transmits the note to the bank, much as a merchant verifies a credit card transaction today. The bank reverifies its signature, checks the note against a list of those already spent and credits Bob's account. It then transmits a "deposit slip," once again unforgeably signed with the appropriate key. Bob hands the merchandise to Alice along with his own digitally signed receipt, completing the transaction.

This system provides security for all three parties. The signatures at each stage prevent any one from cheating either of the others: the shop cannot deny that it received payment, the bank cannot deny that it issued the notes or that it accepted them from the shop for deposit, and the customer can neither deny withdrawing the notes from her account nor spend them twice.

This system is secure, but it has no privacy. If the bank keeps track of note numbers, it can link each shop's deposit to the corresponding withdrawal and so determine precisely where and when Alice (or any other account holder) spends her money. The resulting dossier is far more intrusive than those now being compiled. Furthermore, records based on digital signatures are more vulnerable to abuse than conventional files. Not only are they self-authenticating (even if they are copied, the information they contain can be verified by anyone), but they also permit a person who has a particular kind of information to prove its existence without either giving the information away or revealing its source. For example, someone might be able to prove incontrovertibly that Bob had telephoned Alice on 12 separate occasions without having to reveal the time and place of any of the calls.

I have developed an extension of digital signatures, called blind signatures, that can restore privacy. Before sending a note number to the bank for signing, Alice in essence multiplies it by a random factor. Consequently, the bank knows nothing about what it is signing except that it carries Alice's digital signature. After receiving the blinded note signed by the bank, Alice divides out the blinding factor and uses the note as before.

The blinded note numbers are "unconditionally untraceable" that is, even if the shop and the bank collude, they cannot determine who spent which notes. Because the bank has no idea of the blinding factor, it has no way of linking the note numbers that Bob deposits with Alice's withdrawals. Whereas the security of digital signatures is dependent on the difficulty of particular computations, the anonymity of blinded notes is limited only by the unpredictability of Alice's random numbers. If she wishes, however, Alice can reveal these numbers and permit the notes to be stopped or traced.

Blinded electronic bank notes protect an individual's privacy, but because each note is simply a number, it can be copied easily. To prevent double spending, each note must be checked on-line against a central list when it is spent. Such a verification procedure might be acceptable when large amounts of money are at stake, but it is far too expensive to use when someone is just buying a newspaper. To solve this problem, my colleagues Amos Fiat and Moni Naor and I have proposed a method for generating blinded notes that requires the payer to answer a random numeric query about each note when making a payment. Spending such a note once does not compromise unconditional untraceability, but spending it twice reveals enough information to make the payer's account easily traceable. In fact, it can yield a digitally signed confession that cannot be forged even by the bank.

Cards capable of such anonymous payments already exist. Indeed, DigiCash, a company with which I am associated, has installed equipment in two office buildings in Amsterdam that permits copiers, fax machines, cafeteria cash registers and even coffee vending machines to accept digital "bank notes." We have also demonstrated a system for automatic toll collection in which automobiles carry a card that responds to radioed requests for payment even as they are travelling at highway speeds.

My colleagues and I call a computer that handles such cryptographic transactions a "representative." A person might use different computers as representatives depending on which was convenient: Bob might purchase software (transmitted to him over a network) by using his home computer to produce the requisite digital signatures, go shopping with a "palm-top" personal computer and carry a smart credit card to the beach to pay for a drink or crab cakes. Any of these machines could represent Bob in a transaction as long as the digital signatures each generates are under his control.

Indeed, such computers can act as representatives for their owners in virtually any kind of transaction. Bob can trust his representative and Alice hers because they have each chosen their own machine and can reprogram it at will (or, in principle, build it from scratch). Organizations are protected by the cryptographic protocol and so do not have to trust the representatives.

The prototypical representative is a smart credit-card-size computer containing memory and a microprocessor. It also incorporates its own keypad and display so that its owner can control the data that are stored and exchanged. If a shop provided the keypad and display, it could intercept passwords on their way to the card or show one price to the customer and another to the card. Ideally, the card would communicate with terminals in banks and shops by a short-range communications link such as an infrared transceiver and so need never leave its owner's hands.

When asked to make a payment, the representative would present a summary of the particulars and await approval before releasing funds. It would also insist on electronic receipts from organizations at each stage of all transactions to substantiate its owner's position in case of dispute. By requiring a password akin to the PIN (personal identifying number) now used for bank cards, the representative could safeguard itself from abuse by thieves. Indeed, most people would probably keep backup copies of their keys, electronic bank notes and other data; they could recover their funds if a representative were lost or stolen.

Personal representatives offer excellent protection for individual privacy, but organizations might prefer a mechanism to protect their interests as strongly as possible. For example, a bank might want to prevent double spending of bank notes altogether rather than simply detecting it after the fact. Some organizations might also want to ensure that certain digital signatures are not copied and widely disseminated (even though the copying could be detected afterwards).

Organizations have already begun issuing tamperproof cards (in effect, their own representatives) programmed to prevent undesirable behavior. But these cards can act as "Little Brothers" in everyone's pocket.

We have developed a system that satisfies both sides. An "observer," a tamper-resistant computer chip, issued by some entity that organizations can trust, acts like a notary and certifies the behavior of a representative in which it is embedded. Philips Industries has recently introduced a tamper-resistant chip that has enough computing power to generate and verify digital signatures. Since then, Siemens, Thomson CSF and Motorola have announced plans for similar circuits, any of which could easily serve as an observer.

The central idea behind the protocol for observers is that the observer does not trust the representative in which it resides, nor does the representative trust the observer. Indeed, the representative must be able to control all data passing to or from the observer; otherwise the tamper-proof chip might be able to leak information to the world at large.

When Alice first acquires an observer, she places it in her smart-card representative and takes it to a validating authority. The observer generates a batch of public and private key pairs from a combination of its own random numbers and numbers supplied by the card. The observer does not reveal its numbers but reveals enough information about them so that the card can later check whether its numbers were in fact used to produce the resulting keys. The card also produces random data that the observer will use to blind each key.

Then the observer blinds the public keys, signs them with a special built-in key and gives them to the card. The card verifies the blinding and the signature and checks the keys to make sure they were correctly generated. It passes the blinded, signed keys to the validating authority, which recognizes the observer's built-in signature, removes it and signs the blinded keys with its own key. The authority passes the keys back to the card, which unblinds them. These keys, bearing the signature of the validating authority, serve as digital pseudonyms for future transactions; Alice can draw on them as needed.

An observer could easily prevent (rather than merely detect) double spending of electronic bank notes. When Alice withdraws money from her bank, the observer witnesses the process and so knows what notes she received. At Bob's shop, when Alice hands over a note from the bank, she also hands over a digital pseudonym (which she need use only once) signed by the validating authority. Then the observer, using the secret key corresponding to the validated pseudonym, signs a statement certifying that the note will be spent only once, at Bob's shop and at this particular time and date. Alice's card verifies the signed statement to make sure that the observer does not leak any information and passes it to Bob. The observer is programmed to sign only one such statement for any given note.

Many transactions do not simply require a transfer of money. Instead they involve "credentials," information about an individual's relationship to some organization. In today's identifier-based world, all of a person's credentials are easily linked. If Alice is deciding whether to sell Bob insurance, for example, she can use his name and date of birth to gain access to his credit status, medical records, motor vehicle file and criminal record, if any.

Using a representative, however, Bob would establish relationships with different organizations under different digital pseudonyms. Each of them can recognize him unambiguously, but none of their records can be linked.

In order to be of use, a digital credential must serve the same function as a paper-based credential such as a driver's license or a credit report. It must convince someone that the person attached to it stands in a particular relation to some issuing authority. The name, photograph, address, physical description and code number on a driver's license, for example, serve merely to link it to a particular person and to the corresponding record in a data base. Just as a bank can issue unforgeable, untraceable electronic cash, so too could a university issue signed digital diplomas or a credit-reporting bureau issue signatures indicating a person's ability to repay a loan.

When the young Bob graduates with honors in medieval literature, for example, the university registrar gives his representative a digitally signed message asserting his academic credentials. When Bob applies to graduate school, however, he does not show the admissions committee that message. Instead his representative asks its observer to sign a statement that he has a B.A. cum laude and that he qualifies for financial aid based on at least one of the university's criteria (but without revealing which ones). The observer, which has verified and stored each of Bob's credentials as they come in, simply checks its memory and signs the statement if it is true.

In addition to answering just the right question and being more reliable than paper ones, digital credentials would be both easier for individuals to obtain and to show and cheaper for organizations to issue and to authenticate. People would no longer need to fill out long and revealing forms. Instead their representatives would convince organizations that they meet particular requirements without disclosing any more than the simple fact of qualification. Because such credentials reveal no unnecessary information, people would be willing to use them even in contexts where they would not willingly show identification, thus enhancing security and giving the organization more useful data than it would otherwise acquire.

Positive credentials, however, are not the only kind that people acquire. They may also acquire negative credentials, which they would prefer to conceal: felony convictions, license suspensions or statements of pending bankruptcy. In many cases, individuals will give organizations the right to inflict negative credentials on them in return for some service. For instance, when Alice borrows books from a library, her observer would be instructed to register an overdue notice unless it had received a receipt for the books' return within some fixed time.

Once the observer has registered a negative credential, an organization can find out about it simply by asking the observer (through the representative) to sign a message attesting to its presence or absence. Although a representative could muzzle the observer, it could not forge an assertion about the state of its credentials. In other cases, organizations might simply take the lack of a positive credential as a negative one. If Bob signs up for skydiving lessons, his instructors may assume that he is medically unfit unless they see a credential to the contrary.

For most credentials, the digital signature of an observer is sufficient to convince anyone of its authenticity. Under some circumstances, however, an organization might insist that an observer demonstrate its physical presence. Otherwise, for example, any number of people might be able to gain access to nontransferable credentials (perhaps a health club membership) by using representatives connected by concealed communications links to another representative containing the desired credential.

Moreover, the observer must carry out this persuasion while its input and output are under the control of the representative that contains it. When Alice arrives at her gym, the card reader at the door sends her observer a series of single-bit challenges. The observer immediately responds to each challenge with a random bit that is encoded by the card on its way back to the organization. The speed of the observer's response establishes that it is inside the card (since processing a single bit introduces almost no delay compared with the time that signals take to traverse a wire). After a few dozen iterations the card reveals to the observer how it encoded the responses; the observer signs a statement including the challenges and encoded responses only if it has been a party to that challenge-response sequence. This process convinces the organization of the observer's presence without allowing the observer to leak information.

Organizations can also issue credentials using methods that depend on cryptography alone rather than on observers. Although currently practical approaches can handle only relatively simple queries, Gilles Brassard of the University of Montreal, Claude Cripeau of the École Normale Supérieure and I have shown how to answer arbitrary combinations of questions about even the most complex credentials while maintaining unconditional unlinkability. The concealment of purely cryptographic negative credentials could be detected by the same kinds of techniques that detect double spending of electronic bank notes. And a combination of these cryptographic methods with observers would offer accountability after the fact even if the observer chip were somehow compromised.

The improved security and privacy of digital pseudonyms exact a price: responsibility. At present, for example, people can disavow credit card purchases made over the telephone or cash withdrawals from an automatic teller machine (ATM). The burden of proof is on the bank to show that no one else could have made the purchase or withdrawal. If computerized representatives become widespread, owners will establish all their own passwords and so control access to their representatives. They will be unable to disavow a representative's actions.

Current tamper-resistant systems such as ATMs and their associated cards typically rely on weak, inflexible security procedures because they must be used by people who are neither highly competent nor overly concerned about security. If people supply their own representatives, they can program them for varying levels of security as they see fit. (Those who wish to trust their assets to a single four-digit code are free to do so, of course.) Bob might use a short PIN (or none at all) to authorize minor transactions and a longer password for major ones. To protect himself from a robber who might force him to give up his passwords at gunpoint, he could use a "duress code" that would cause the card to appear to operate normally while hiding its more important assets or credentials or perhaps alerting the authorities that it had been stolen.

A personal representative could also recognize its owner by methods that most people would consider unreasonably intrusive in an identifier-based system; a notebook computer, for example, might verify its owner's voice or even fingerprints. A supermarket checkout scanner capable of recognizing a person's thumbprint and debiting the cost of groceries from their savings account is Orwellian at best. In contrast, a smart credit card that knows its owner's touch and doles out electronic bank notes is both anonymous and safer than cash. In addition, incorporating some essential part of such identification technology into the tamperproof observer would make such a card suitable even for very high security applications.

Computerized transactions of all kinds are becoming ever more pervasive. More than half a dozen countries have developed or are testing chip cards that would replace cash. In Denmark, a consortium of banking, utility and transport companies has announced a card that would replace coins and small bills; in France, the telecommunications authorities have proposed general use of the smart cards now used at pay telephones. The government of Singapore has requested bids for a system that would communicate with cars and charge their smart cards as they pass various points on a road (as opposed to the simple vehicle identification systems already in use in the U.S. and elsewhere). And cable and satellite broadcasters are experimenting with smart cards for delivering pay-per-view television. All these systems, however, are based on cards that identify themselves during every transaction.

If the trend toward identifier-based smart cards continues, personal privacy will be increasingly eroded. But in this conflict between organizational security and individual liberty, neither side emerges as a clear winner. Each round of improved identification techniques, sophisticated data analysis or extended linking can be frustrated by widespread noncompliance or even legislated limits, which in turn may engender attempts at further control.

Meanwhile, in a system based on representatives and observers, organizations stand to gain competitive and political advantages from increased public confidence (in addition to the lower costs of pseudonymous record-keeping). And individuals, by maintaining their own cryptographically guaranteed records and making only necessary disclosures, will be able to protect their privacy without infringing on the legitimate needs of those with whom they do business.

The choice between keeping information in the hands of individuals or of organizations is being made each time any government or business decides to automate another set of transactions. In one direction lies unprecedented scrutiny and control of people's lives, in the other, secure parity between individuals and organizations. The shape of society in the next century may depend on which approach predominates.

Further Reading

Brassard, Gilles. Modern Cryptology: A Tutorial. *Lecture Notes in Computer Science* 325. Springer-Verlag, 1988.

Chaum, David. The Dining Cryptographers Problem: Unconditional Sender and Recipient Untraceability. *Journal of Cryptology* 1, no. 1, pp. 65–75; 1988.

Chaum, David. Privacy Protected Payments: Unconditional Payer and/or Payee Untraceability. *Smart Card 2000: The Future of IC Cards.* Edited by David Chaum and Ingrid Schaumueller-Bichl. North-Holland, 1989.

Chaum, David. Security Without Identification: Transaction Systems to Make Big Brother Obsolete. *Communications of the ACM* 28, no. 10, pp. 1030–1044; October 1985.

17

A Crypto Anarchist Manifesto

Cypherpunks of the World,

Several of you at the "physical Cypherpunks" gathering yesterday in Silicon Valley requested that more of the material passed out in meetings be available electronically to the entire readership of the Cypherpunks list, spooks, eavesdroppers, and all. (Gulp.)

Here's the "Crypto Anarchist Manifesto" I read at the September 1992 founding meeting. It dates back to mid-1988 and was distributed to some like-minded techno-anarchists at the "Crypto '88" conference and then again at the "Hackers Conference" that year. I later gave talks at Hackers on this in 1989 and 1990.

There are a few things I'd change, but for historical reasons I'll just leave it as is. Some of the terms may be unfamiliar to you . . . I hope the Crypto Glossary I just distributed will help. (This should explain all those cryptic terms in my .signature!)
—Tim May

The Crypto Anarchist Manifesto

A specter is haunting the modern world, the specter of crypto anarchy.

Computer technology is on the verge of providing the ability for individuals and groups to communicate and interact with each other in a totally anonymous manner. Two persons may exchange messages, conduct business, and negotiate electronic contracts without ever knowing the true name, or legal identity, of the other. Interactions over networks will be untraceable, via extensive re-routing of encrypted packets and tamper-proof boxes which implement cryptographic protocols with nearly perfect assurance against any tampering. Reputations will be of central importance, far more important in dealings than even the credit ratings of today. These developments will alter completely the nature of government regulation, the ability to tax and control economic interactions, the ability to keep information secret, and will even alter the nature of trust and reputation.

The technology for this revolution—and it surely will be both a social and economic revolution—has existed in theory for the past decade. The methods are based upon public-key encryption, zero-knowledge interactive proof systems, and various software protocols for interaction, authentication, and verification. The focus has until now been on academic conferences in Europe and the U.S., conferences monitored closely by the National Security Agency. But only recently have computer networks and personal computers attained sufficient speed to make the ideas practically realizable. And the next ten years will bring enough additional speed to make the ideas economically feasible and essentially unstoppable. High-speed networks, ISDN, tamper-proof boxes, smart cards, satellites, Ku-band transmitters, multi-MIPS personal computers, and encryption chips now under development will be some of the enabling technologies.

The State will of course try to slow or halt the spread of this technology, citing national security concerns, use of the technology by drug dealers and tax evaders, and fears of societal disintegration. Many of these concerns will be valid; crypto anarchy will allow national secrets to be traded freely and will allow illicit and stolen materials to be traded. An anonymous computerized market will even make possible abhorrent markets for assassinations and extortion. Various criminal and foreign elements will be active users of CryptoNet. But this will not halt the spread of crypto anarchy.

Just as the technology of printing altered and reduced the power of medieval guilds and the social power structure, so too will cryptologic methods fundamentally alter the nature of corporations and of government interference in economic transactions. Combined with emerging information markets, crypto anarchy will create a liquid market for any and all material which can be put into words and pictures. And just as a seemingly minor invention like barbed wire made possible the fencing-off of vast ranches and farms, thus altering forever the concepts of land and property rights in the frontier West, so too will the seemingly minor discovery out of an arcane branch of mathematics come to be the wire clippers which dismantle the barbed wire around intellectual property.

Arise, you have nothing to lose but your barbed wire fences!

Timothy C. May
tcmay@netcom.com
408-688-5409
W.A.S.T.E.: Aptos, CA
2^756839

Crypto Anarchy: encryption, digital money, anonymous networks, digital pseudonyms, zero knowledge, reputations, information markets, black markets, collapse of governments. Higher Power: PGP Public Key: by arrangement.

18

Introduction to BlackNet

Timothy C. May

Your name has come to our attention. We have reason to believe you may be interested in the products and services our new organization, Black-Net, has to offer.

BlackNet is in the business of buying, selling, trading, and otherwise dealing with *information* in all its many forms.

We buy and sell information using public key cryptosystems with essentially perfect security for our customers. Unless you tell us who you are (please don't!) or inadvertently reveal information which provides clues, we have no way of identifying you, nor you us.

Our location in physical space is unimportant. Our location in cyber-space is all that matters. Our primary address is the PGP key location: "BlackNet<nowhere@cyberspace.nil>" and we can be contacted (preferably through a chain of anonymous remailers) by encrypting a message to our public key (contained below) and depositing this message in one of the several locations in cyberspace we monitor. Currently, we monitor the following locations: alt.extropians, alt.fan.david-sternlight, and the "Cypherpunks" mailing list.

BlackNet is nominally nonideological, but considers nation-states, export laws, patent laws, national security considerations and the like to be relics of the pre-cyberspace era. Export and patent laws are often used to explicitly project national power and imperialist, colonialist state fascism. BlackNet believes it is solely the responsibility of a secret holder to keep that secret—not the responsibilty of the State, or of us, or of anyone else who may come into possession of that secret. If a secret's worth having, it's worth protecting.

BlackNet is currently building its information inventory. We are interested in information in the following areas, though any other juicy stuff is always welcome. "If you think it's valuable, offer it to us first."

• trade secrets, processes, production methods (esp. in semiconductors)

• nanotechnology and related techniques (esp. the Merkle sleeve bearing)

• chemical manufacturing and rational drug design (esp. fullerines and protein folding)

• new product plans, from children's toys to cruise missiles (anything on "3DO"?)

• business intelligence, mergers, buyouts, rumors

BlackNet can make anonymous deposits to the bank account of your choice, where local banking laws permit, can mail cash directly (you assume the risk of theft or seizure), or can credit you in "CryptoCredits," the internal currency of BlackNet (which you then might use to buy *other* information and have it encrypted to your special public key and posted in public places).

If you are interested, do *not* attempt to contact us directly (you'll be wasting your time), and do *not* post anything that contains your name, your e-mail address, etc. Rather, compose your message, encrypt it with the public key of BlackNet (included below), and use an anonymous remailer chain of one or more links to post this encrypted, anonymized message in one of the locations listed (more will be added later). Be sure to describe what you are selling, what value you think it has, your payment terms, and, of course, a special public key (*not* the one you use in your ordinary business, of course!) that we can use to get back in touch with you. Then watch the same public spaces for a reply.

(With these remailers, local PGP encryption within the remailers, the use of special public keys, and the public postings of the encrypted messages, a secure, two-way, untraceable, and fully anonymous channel has been opened between the customer and BlackNet. This is the key to BlackNet.)

A more complete tutorial on using BlackNet will soon appear, in plaintext form, in certain locations in cyberspace.

Join us in this revolutionary—and profitable—venture.

BlackNet<nowhere@cyberspace.nil>

- - -BEGIN PGP PUBLIC KEY BLOCK- - -Version: 2.3

mQCPAixusCEAAAEEAJ4/hpAPevOuFDXWJ0joh/y6zAwklEPige7N
9WQMYSaWrmbiXJ0/MQXCABNXOj9sR3GOlSF8JLOPInKWbo4i
HunNnUczU7pQUKnmu VpkY014M5ClPnzkKPk2mlSDOqRanJZCky
Be2jjHXQMhasUngReGxNDMjW1IBzuUFqioZRpABEBAAG0IEJsY
WNrTmV0PG5vd2hlcmVAY3liZXJzcGFjZS5uaWw+ =Vmmy

- - -END PGP PUBLIC KEY BLOCK- - -

19

BlackNet Worries[1]

Timothy C. May

X makes some comments about the dangers (I call them benefits) of systems like "BlackNet," the hypothetical-but-inevitable entity I described last fall. These dangers/benefits have been apparent to me since around 1988 or so and are the main motivator of my interest in "crypto-anarchy," the set of ideas that I espouse.

(I don't often dwell on them on this list, partly because I already have in the past, and in the "Crypto Anarchist Manifesto" and other rants at the soda.berkeley.edu archive site, and partly because the Cypherpunks list is somewhat apolitical—apolitical in the sense that we have libertarians, anarcho-syndicalists, anarcho-capitalists, neo-Pagans, Christian fundamentalists, and maybe even a few unreconstructed Communists on the list, and espousing some particular set of beliefs is discouraged by common agreement.)

However, since X has raised some issues, and the general issues of data havens, anonymous information markets, espionage, and other "illegal" markets have been raised, I'll comment . . .

First, a legal caveat. I openly acknowledge having written the BlackNet piece—proof is obvious. But I did *not* post it to Cypherpunks, nor to any other mailing lists and certainly not to Usenet. Rather, I dashed it off one night prior to a nanotechnology discussion in Palo Alto, as a concrete example of the coming future and how difficult it will be to "bottle up" new technologies (a point X alludes to). I sent this note off to several of my associates, via anonymous remailers, so as to make the point in a more tangible way. I also printed out copies and passed them out at the nanotech meeting, which was around last September or so.

Someone decided to post this (through a remailer) to the Cypherpunks list. Kevin Kelly and John Markoff told me they've seen it on numerous other lists and boards, and of course Y has recently posted it to dozens of newsgroups (though it got canceled and only the "echoes" remain in most places—a few folks forwarded copies to other sites, with comments, so they were not affected by the cancellation message).

My legal protection, my point here, is that I did not post the BlackNet piece, it does not exist as an actual espionage or data haven entity, and my point was rhetorical and is clearly protected by the First Amendment (to the Constitution of the country in which I nominally reside).

[quotes from X elided]

Yes, military intelligence will become much more "fungible" in the future I envision. It already is, of course, a la the Walkers, but computer-mediated markets and secure encryption will make it so much more efficient and liquid. Buyers will be able to advertise their wants and their prices. Ditto for sellers. Of course, decoys, disinformation, and the like come to the fore.

To pick a trivial example, someone sits above a busy port and watches ship movements from the privacy of his apartment. He summarizes these, then sells them for a paltry-but-comfortable $3000 a month to some other nation. (The ease of doing this means others will get into the market. Prices will likely drop. Hard to predict the final prices—the beauty of free markets.)

The motivation for thinking about BlackNet, which is what I dubbed this capability in late 1987, was a discussion with the late Phil Salin that year about his as-yet-unfunded company, "AMIX," the American Information Exchange. I played the Devil's Advocate and explained why I thought corporate America—his main target for customers—would shun such a system. My thinking?

Corporations would not allow employees to have corporate accounts, as it would make leakage of corporate information too easy.

(Example: "We will pay $100,000 for anyone who knows how to solve the charge buildup problem during ion implant of n-type wafers." Many corporations spend millions to solve this, others do not. A "market" for such simple-to-answer items would revolutionize the semiconductor industry—but would also destroy the competitive advantage obtained by those who first solved the problems. . . . An information market system like AMIX means "digital moonlighting," a system corporations will not lightly put up with.)

If information markets spread, even "legit" ones like AMIX (not featuring anonymity), I expect many corporations to make non-participation in such markets a basis for continuing employment. (The details of this, the legal issues, I'll leave for later discussions.)

[X comments on the difficulty of keeping military secrets in a BlackNet environment.]

Yes, which is why I always used to use "B-2 Stealth Bomber blueprints for sale" as my canonical example of a BlackNet ad. Hundreds of folks at Northrup had access to various levels of B-2 secrets. The "problem" for them was that military intelligence (Defense Intelligence Agency, Office of Naval Intelligence, CIA, NDA, etc.) was watching them (and they knew this) and monitoring the local bars and after-work hangouts. Read "The Falcon and the Snowman," or rent the movie, for some details on this.

Anonymous markets completely change the equation!

(By the way, many other "tradecraft" aspects of espionage are similarly changed forever—and probably already have been changed. Gone will be the messages left in Coke cans by the side of the road, the so-called "dead drops" so favored by spies for communicating microfilm, microdots, and coded messages. What I call "digital dead drops" already allow nearly untraceable, unrestricted communication. After all, if I can use a remailer to reach St. Petersburg. . . . Or if I can place message bits in the LSB of an image and then place this on Usenet for world-wide distribution. (I described this in my first message on using LSBs of audio and picture files in 1988, in sci.crypt). The world has already changed for the spy. And Mafia guys on the run are using CompuServe to communicate with their wives—the Feds can't tap these ever-changing systems—a likely motivation for current Clipper/Capstone/Tessera/Digital Telephony schemes.)

"Classified classifieds," so to speak. "No More Secrets." At least, no more secrets that you don't keep yourself! (A subtle point: crypto anarchy doesn't mean a "no secrets" society; it means a society in which individuals must protect their own secrets and not count on governments or corporations to do it for them. It also means "public secrets," like troop movements and Stealth production plans, or the tricks of implanting wafers, will not remain secret for long.)

Are there negative implications of this, even more negative than the selling of corporate and military secrets?

We discussed this several times on the Extropians list, especially with regard to what most folks consider an even more disturbing use of BlackNet-type services: liquid markets for killings and extortion. Pun intended. Buyers and sellers of "hits" can get in contact anonymously, place money (digicash) in escrow with "reputable escrow services" ("Ace's Anonymous Escrow—You slay, we pay"), and the usual methods of stopping such hits fail.

(The Mob rarely is stopped, as they use their own hitters, usually brought in from distant cities for just the one job. And reputations are paramount. Amateurs usually are caught because they get in contact with potential hitters by "asking around" in bars and the like—and somebody calls the cops and the FBI then stings 'em. Anonymous markets, digital cash, escrow services, and reputation services all change the equation dramatically. If the hit is made, the money get transferred. If the hit is not made, no money is transferred. In any case, the purchaser of the hit is fairly safe. Implication of the purchaser can still happen, but by means other than the usual approach of setting up a sting.)

Is the NSA aware of such dangers? I think so. If I could think all this stuff up in 1987–88, so can a lot of others. It was clear to me, at the Crypto Conference in 1988, that David Chaum had thought of these uses and was deliberately navigating around them in his scenarios for digicash. He just raised his eyebrows and nodded when I discussed a few of the less fearsome applications.

To the governments of the world, facing these and other threats to their continued ways of doing business, the existence of strong encryption in the hands of the population is indeed a mortal threat.

They'll cite the "unpopular" uses: kiddie porn nets, espionage, selling of trade secrets (especially to "foreigners"), the bootlegging of copyrighted material, "digital fences" for stolen information, liquid markets in liquidations, and on and on. They won't mention a basic principle of western civilization: that just because *some* people misuse a technology that is no reason to bar others.

Just because some people misuse camcorders to film naked children is no reason to ban cameras, camcorders, and VCRs. Just because some folks misuse free speech is no reason to ban free speech. And just because some will misuse encryption—in the eyes of government—is not a good reason to ban encryption.

In any case, it's too late. The genie's nearly completely out of the bottle. National borders are just speed bumps on the information highway.

The things I've had in my .sig for the past couple of years are coming.

Timothy C. May tcmay@netcom.com 408-688-5409 W.A.S.T.E.: Aptos, CA Power: 2^859433	Crypto Anarchy: encryption, digital money, anonymous networks, digital pseudonyms, zero knowledge, reputations, information markets, black markets, collapse of governments. Higher Public Key: PGP and MailSafe available.

"National borders are just speed bumps on the information superhighway."

Note

1. The following was originally posted to the cypherpunks list in Feb. 1994. This version has been edited somewhat by T. May. References to interlocutors and some of their comments have been elided.—PL

IV

Censorship and Sysop Liability

This section takes up the difficult issue of censorship on the Internet. As the reading from *Computer and Academic Freedom News* shows, even in academia any number of items have been subject to censorship by various universities. Sometimes sexually explicit materials are censored, sometimes hate speech is censored, sometimes students are barred from having certain kinds of computer code in their accounts.

In the main, however, censorship tends to be directed at sexually explicit materials. One recent case of such censorship is the banning of certain Usenet user groups by Carnegie Mellon University (see the *Time* article by Philip Elmer-Dewitt). Fearing a lawsuit, the university originally banned some 80 newsgroups in the alt.sex hierarchy. Some of these usergroups contained digitized photographs, but they also included newsgroups that were dedicated to discussions of safe sex, sexual problems, and such matters. The university soon restored the groups devoted to discussion, but many observers found it remarkable that the administration of a university such as CMU did not initially see that such discussions were constitutionally protected free speech (see the ACLU press release).

In a sense, the initial action by CMU belies an unspoken assumption that seems to have widespread currency—an assumption that electronic forms of speech should not enjoy the same protections that the printed and spoken word do. There is a reluctance to see that the sexually explicit material being banned in electronic form is often available in the campus library or the campus bookstore, or is possibly being assigned in freshman literature courses. Why should the electronic word be exempt from constitutional protections?

Strictly speaking, of course, there is no serious answer to the above question. Protected speech should be protected speech, no matter what its form (see the reading by Shallit for a discussion of this point). Speech in electronic form presents more of a threat, however, and this is perhaps what lies at the bottom of a number of censorship actions. The threat is that electronic words and images are so readily located, copied, and transmitted.

Consider the college student set on extracting graphic S&M literature from the campus library. Where would the student begin? That is not so clear. On the Internet, however, the student might simply drop in on the alt.sex.bondage usergroup. There is a sense in which the Internet makes information too available, too "in your face."

This, of course, suggests that free access to information was never taken seriously. It was perhaps acceptable to allow underground presses to grind out a few hundred pamphlets, but it is quite another for such radical information to be available to everyone in the world, and at virtually no expense. Likewise, it is one thing to allow certain books to be housed in libraries so long as they are lost in the stacks with millions of other volumes, but to have sexually explicit or radical material so readily available on the Internet appears to evoke considerable concern, not only from university administrators, but from government legislators as well. It may be that many institutions tolerate free expression only so long as there are structural barriers limiting its distribution and influence. In other words, perhaps they were never advocates of free expression in the first place.

A good example of this is the recent media hand-wringing over the presence of bomb recipes on the Internet. Sometimes the concern is that minors might get access to such recipes, but one also hears the concern voiced that this sort of information need not be protected and that it ought to be banned. Of course bomb recipes have been circulated among children for years, and I remember injuries to children from pipe bombs and so forth being common when I was in grade school (long before the Internet came into existence). For all we know, the distribution of technical information about bomb making has slowed since children got onto the Internet and began pursuing other technical interests. So what is the real concern? It appears to be that the Internet makes this information just too *available* (quite apart from the issue of whether the information is actually used). That is, the real danger is perceived to lie in the information itself (not in the bombs that may be constructed) and in particular in the ready availability of that information.

Ease of access seems to be the subtext in a number of discussions about troublesome materials on the Internet. Parents will claim that pornographic materials, bomb recipes, and so on, are, in a sense, being broadcast directly into their homes. It is not like the old days when Junior had to cross the tracks and go to the other side of town to find such materials. Now the materials are available to children with computers with Internet access, and that means upper-middle-class children (hence the keen interest by the media).

In a sense the parents are right when they think that the materials are coming right into their homes. True, in some cases the child must FTP or Gopher to some remote site, but it is increasingly possible to use a graphical interface such as Netscape, in which one merely points and clicks on an icon. Phenomenologically, the selected materials may as well be in a desktop computer. Indeed, users may have no idea what the remote location is, nor, in many cases, will they even care.

The transparent feel of the new interfaces is bound to exacerbate other problems—in particular the problem of maintaining community standards. For example, it is possible that a web site in New York could contain images that would violate community standards in Eagle Grove, Iowa. What happens when the citizens of Eagle Grove learn that these materials (which local standards take to be obscene) are available at the click of a button?

Even without transparent interfaces, problems of this nature have arisen. In "Virtual Community Standards" Godwin discusses one such recent case, in which a U.S. attorney in Memphis charged the operators of a Milpitas, California, BBS with violating Memphis community standards. The BBS did indeed carry hard-core pornography, some of which allegedly violated Memphis standards of decency and which was downloaded by a Tennessee postal inspector. In this case, however, the California site was not on the Internet, and hence there was no transparent interface. Indeed, the postal inspector had to telephone California in order to log on and download the materials. In Godwin's judgment, the decision to prosecute in this case turned the whole community standards principle on its head.

> The case sends a frightening message to virtual communities: "It doesn't matter if you're abiding by your own community's standards—you have to abide by Memphis's as well."

But, on the assumption that there is a genuine problem here, what is to be done about it? Should we ban everything that isn't safe for children and the residents of Memphis? That hardly seems like an appropriate response, but it is not without advocates (although the advocates would probably describe their positions in other ways). Alternatively, should children and the residents of Memphis be banned from the electronic frontier? Again, this hardly seems appropriate.

One approach has been to hold that BBS system operators should be responsible for who logs onto the system. In the article on the Memphis case, Godwin touches on the problems with trying to screen users in this way. Consider the difficulty of keeping minors off of the system. In a world where minors routinely enter bars with fake IDs, there are bound to be loopholes in any such screening process.

That isn't the only problem that system operators have, however. System operators are also routinely held responsible for ensuring that illegal material such as child pornography is not uploaded onto their systems. But it is far from clear that a sysop is able to screen everything that is uploaded onto a system. Some electronic bulletin boards are vast, with hundreds if not thousands of files being posted daily. It is possible that a user might upload pilfered credit information, even child pornography, without the knowledge of the sysop (see Godwin's "Sex and the Single Sysadmin"). Yet it appears that, for all practical purposes, the government holds the system operator responsible for the material posted on the system. Just how fair is this? After all, we wouldn't hold the telephone company responsible if pilfered credit information were transmitted via telephone, nor would we hold the post office responsible if child pornography were sent via mail. So why is the sysop responsible for everything that appears on his or her system (a point that applies also to pirated software, by the way)?

There are intermediate positions here. One might argue that sysops be responsible for seeing that their systems are not routinely used for distributing certain materials, while excusing them for the odd file that gets posted to the system. Drawing the line is difficult here, however, as it is not always clear where the odd upload ends and a policy of tolerating such uploads begins.

This discussion has granted a certain assumption—that censorship is possible on the electronic frontier. There are those who would argue otherwise, suggesting that there are just too many ways to bypass attempted censorship. For example, if CMU had banned the alt.sex hierarchy, it would have been a simple matter to telnet to a remote system that continued to carry it. Even if we were to ban the alt.sex hierarchy from every system in the United States it would still be possible to telnet to a remote location in, say Denmark, which continued to carry the "offending" material.

This, then, is the problem that concerned parents and university administrators must face. They can hardly police every Usenet and FTP site in the world. Nor is it reasonable to suppose that every country in the world is going to be interested in preventing 17-year-old CMU students from seeing pictures of naked bodies. It seems that the only solution is to block Internet access altogether, or to constantly monitor the activities of each student. Whether such draconian measures are feasible remains to be seen. If they are, one has to ask the question whether such measures do not do greater harm than potential encounters with images and ideas that some perceive to be dangerous.

20

Censoring Cyberspace

Philip Elmer-Dewitt

The steam began rising for Carnegie Mellon University four weeks ago, when one of its research associates, Martin Rimm, informed the administration that a draft of his study of pornography on the computer networks was about to be released. Rimm had made an elaborate analysis of the sexually oriented material available online. Not only had he put together a picture collection that rivaled Bob Guccione's (917,410 in all), but by tracking how many times each image had been retrieved by computer users (a total of 6.4 million downloads), he had obtained a measure of the consumer demand for different categories of sexual content, some of them, as a faculty adviser put it, "extremely rough." [The Rimm study has since been discredited by its numerous flaws in research methodology. Visit http://www2000.ogsm.vanderbilt.edu/cyberporn.debate.cgi for details.—PL]

The problem, from the Pittsburgh, Pennsylvania, university's point of view, was not that Rimm had found sexually explicit content on the computer networks; there is sex in every medium, from comic books to videotapes. Nor was it even that he had found some of it on CMU's own computers; every university connected to the Internet is a conduit, however unwitting, for gigabytes of salacious words and pictures. The immediate issue was that Rimm had brought it to the administration's attention, pointing out that some of the images on CMU's machines—digitized pictures of men and women having sex with animals, for example—had been declared obscene by a Tennessee court a few months before.

William Arms, vice president of CMU's computing services department, spent an hour reviewing the questionable material "with the law of Pennsylvania in one hand and a mouse in the other" and decided that the university was in deep trouble. It is illegal in the state to knowingly distribute sexually explicit material to anyone under the age of 18—as many freshmen are—or to distribute obscene material at all, no matter what the consumer's age. Fearing that the university would be open to prosecution—and the worst kind of publicity—CMU's academic council hurriedly voted to shut down those areas of the computer system that carried discussions or depictions of sex. The plug was scheduled to be pulled last Tuesday.

Thus the lines were drawn for a battle over the preservation of free speech in the new interactive media—a battle that not only raised tricky questions about how to balance openness with good taste, but also managed, on a campus not noted for activism, to rouse something resembling a student protest movement. CMU casts a long shadow in cyberspace. It was one of the first universities to join the Arpanet (the precursor to the Internet) and the first to wire up its dorms. It even provides Internet access to some of its bathrooms. Using the computer networks to spread the word and muster support, the students quickly organized a "Protest for Freedom in Cyberspace" that drew 350 students and faculty members. (Pittsburgh in the 1990s, though, is hardly Berkeley in the '60s: the protesters last week politely applauded their opponents and then retired to a reception with cheese and fruit.)

At the core of the CMU dispute is a question that goes beyond the campus and could touch every media and entertainment company that wants to do business on the info highway: to what extent can the operators of interactive media be held responsible for the material that moves through their systems? Are they common carriers, like the phone companies, which must ignore the content of the messages? Are they like TV stations, whose broadcasts are monitored by the government for fairness and suitability? Or are they like bookstores, which the courts have ruled can't be expected to review the content of every title on their shelves? And what happens when that content hops over borders and lands in a different city—or country—whose laws and community standards may differ?

The last issue came to a head most dramatically last July, after a U.S. postal inspector, posing as a customer in Tennessee, downloaded X-rated pictures from an adult computer bulletin board in California. Though the images might have been acceptable by California standards, they were judged obscene in the Bible Belt, and the owners of the bulletin board were convicted of transporting obscene material across state lines. Their appeal may be headed for the Supreme Court.

There's more to free speech than sexy words and pictures, of course. Publishers who venture onto international networks like the Internet are particularly concerned about libel and slander. The rules of libel in England, for example, are considerably more restrictive than those in the U.S.; what might be considered a fair crack at a public figure in New York City could be actionable in London. Conversely, the muzzles that are slapped on reporters covering trials in Commonwealth countries can't be placed so easily on writers living abroad, as Canadian officials learned to their dismay last year when foreign press reports of a particularly sensitive homicide case in Ontario began drifting back into Canada through the Internet.

All sorts of subversive materials have found their way onto the computer networks, from secret spy codes to instructions for making long-range rocket bombs. As if to provoke the authorities, some college students have posted collections of electronic pamphlets that include Suicide Methods, an instruction manual for self-destruction, and The School Stopper's Textbook, which tells students how to blow up toilets, short-circuit electrical wiring and "break into your school at night and burn it down."

High schools pose a special problem for administrators, who want to give students the benefits of computer networking without exposing minors to everything that washes up online. Many lower schools have adopted the CMU approach, cutting off access to the electronic discussion groups where the most offensive material is carried.

At CMU, the administration determined that its problem was centered in a collection of discussion groups, called Usenet newsgroups, with awkward but functional titles like alt.sex, rec.arts.erotica and alt.binaries.pictures.erotica. The "binary" groups are the most controversial, for they contain codes that savvy computer users can translate into pictures and movie clips. The university's initial decision was to pull the plug on all the major "sex" newsgroups and their subsidiary sections—more than 80 categories altogether.

That decision drew fire from all sides. The student council pointed out that the administration was restricting the reading matter of adults to what was acceptable for children. The American Civil Liberties Union complained that the ban was overly broad and included discussions of sexual matters that were clearly protected speech. Mike Godwin, staff counsel for the Electronic Frontier Foundation, made a distinction between words and pictures, arguing that while images are still sometimes found obscene, words never are—a view confirmed by the Allegheny county assistant district attorney, who told *Time* there was "not a chance in a million" his office could win an obscenity case based on a written work.

But the central objection was more fundamental: that the university had ignored decades of constitutional law and abrogated its responsibility as a center for free inquiry. "I'm deeply ashamed that Carnegie Mellon capitulated so spinelessly," said one CMU student in a radio call-in debate. "Some lawyer told them they might someday be dragged into court, and they just decided, 'To hell with the First Amendment.'"

By midweek, the university had begun to back down. First it seized on Godwin's formula, banning the binaries and leaving the text in place—pending review by a student-faculty committee. Then, on Thursday night, the faculty senate voted to recommend restoration of all the newsgroups, including the binaries.

But the issue will not go away. There is material on the networks—child pornography, in particular—that has been targeted for prosecution by U.S. Attorney General Janet Reno. Unless computer users exercise some self-restraint, control could be imposed from the outside. If that happens, the next generation of interactive media may not have the freedom and openness that today's users value so highly.

Reported by John F. Dickerson/New York and Douglas Root/Pittsburgh

21

ACLU Letter to CMU on alt.sex Newsgroups

ACLU Urges Carnegie Mellon to Reverse Internet Censorship; Letter to University President Says Students Must Have Access to Information

For IMMEDIATE RELEASE

November 8, 1994

In a strongly worded letter to the President of Carnegie Mellon University, the American Civil Liberties Union today urged the university to reconsider and reverse its decision to prohibit student access to six network news groups that deal with sexual topics on the Internet.

"Carnegie Mellon has a well deserved reputation in higher education as a leader on technology issues," said Barry Steinhardt, Associate Director of the ACLU. "You have already recognized the extraordinary potential of networked communications to enhance and democratize speech.

"But if the full potential is to be reached, it is important that leaders like Carnegie Mellon stand strong for free and open access to information and that you resist the urge to censor," Steinhardt concluded.

In its letter, the ACLU said that Carnegie Mellon officials based their decision to remove the news groups on a broad misreading of Pennsylvania obscenity law. The vast majority of information on these news groups has never been challenged as obscene, the ACLU said, nor could the university be held liable for distributing this material through the Internet.

"Your policy sweeps far too broadly," the letter said. "Out of fear that your students may be exposed to a few unprotected works, you have cut off access to a large volume of protected ideas and information."

A copy of the letter to Carnegie Mellon is attached.

November 8, 1994

Dr. Robert Mehrabian
President
Carnegie Mellon University
5000 Forbes Ave. Warner Hall
Pittsburgh, PA 15213

Dear President Mehrabian:

We write on behalf of the American Civil Liberties Union (ACLU) to urge Carnegie Mellon University to reconsider and reverse the decision to prohibit student access to six network news groups which deal with sexual topics. We believe that the University's plan is inconsistent with the principles of academic freedom and free speech, which a great University must defend, and is based on a serious misreading of relevant laws.

Carnegie Mellon's decision to offer its students broad access to the Internet and its thousands of news groups was a farsighted recognition that networked communications will increasingly provide the means for academic research and the forum for the free exchange of ideas. Like your decision to establish and nurture a library, it was a decision to give your students access to the widest variety of information and to allow them to make their own judgements about their worth.

Your decision to revoke access to the six news groups deprives your students of the opportunity to judge for themselves the value of these groups.

As we understand the rationale for your decision, the University is concerned about its potential liability under Pennsylvania's obscenity law and particularly its provisions relating to minors. We believe that the conclusions you have drawn are mistaken and misperceive your role in providing student access to the Internet. This also seems surprising since there has apparently been no effort by any governmental entity to assert the existence of any such liability.

To begin with, these news groups are not "obscene" merely because they contain sexually explicit materials. Most sexually explicit speech is protected by the First Amendment and only a small portion of sexually explicit materials can constitutionally be deemed obscene. A jury applying the three-part test of Miller v. California must decide on a case by case basis whether a particular work is obscene. There are literally thousands of postings to these news groups every year and only a small fraction have ever been challenged as obscene.

Your policy sweeps far too broadly. Out of fear that your students may be exposed to a few works that a court might ultimately find unprotected, you have cut off access to a large volume of protected ideas and information.

In fact, you have cut off access to information that is clearly of significant value to your students and deals with serious societal issues. For example, in barring access to the alt.sex news group, you have deprived students of access to all of its branches, including alt.sex.safe, which discusses responsible sexual behavior.

The University's conclusion that you must cut off access to these news groups because "it is a criminal offense to knowingly disseminate sexually explicit material to minors . . ." is equally troubling.

First, it is not illegal to distribute any "sexually explicit" material to minors. The state can only ban the distribution to minors of materials that satisfies the classic three part Miller test, as modified for minors. A careful reading of Pennsylvania law makes this clear. 18 Pa. C.S.A. 5903 applies only to those types of sexually explicit materials which satisfy the modified test and are "harmful to minors."

Secondly, even assuming that some of the material posted to these news groups might properly be restricted to adults, it is a well established principle that obscenity policies cannot reduce adults to reading only that which is fit for children. But that is precisely the effect of the new policy.

The vast majority of your students are undoubtedly over the age of 18 and legally adults. The policy effectively treats them as children and limits their access to materials deemed suitable for children.

That is not what the law requires and we do not think that you would draw this conclusion in other contexts. Surely, you don't believe that Pennsylvania law requires that the University library and bookstore, or for that matter your literature classes, must be purged of all sexually explicit material because there may be minors on campus or minors may access the imagery.

Finally, by its terms, the Pennsylvania obscenity law cannot be applied to the University's provision of Internet access; nor should it be. The

Pennsylvania statute provides that a party can only be held liable for the content of material . . . which is reasonably susceptible of examination by the defendant." (Sec 5903 (b))

By its very nature, the Internet is vast and chaotic. There are millions of speakers and countless speeches. The Internet is so large and disorderly that the University could never reasonably be expected to examine the content of every message available to your students.

Nor could you reasonably be expected to be able to control all access to any particular group of messages. One of the unique features of the Internet is that there are many paths to the same destination.

CMU's students are smart and technologically savvy. They will quickly learn how to use the access provided by the University to subscribe to Internet "mailing lists," to download archival files or to link with other networks to obtain exactly the same material that is available in the banned news groups.

The new policy assumes that the University has an obligation to prevent its students from obtaining access to any possibly illegal materials about which the University has knowledge. If that assumption is correct, then you have not gone far enough in simply blocking access to a few news groups. To meet such a heavy burden you would need to take the draconian steps of either monitoring all student communications or cutting off all access to the Internet.

Fortunately, the law does not impose that burden. The law properly holds speakers and publishers liable for the content of their messages. By offering your students access to thousands of news groups and hundreds of millions of postings, you are neither a speaker, nor a publisher. At most, you are acting as a distributor providing access to information, exactly in the same way that you provide access to library books, and could not and should not be held liable, for example, if a 17-year-old freshman happens to check out a book with "sexually explicit" content.

In fact, Subsection (j) of the Pennsylvania obscenity law explicitly exempts "any library of any school, college or university . . ." from its reach. The Legislature recognized that universities and libraries have special protections as access providers to knowledge and that you should not be chilled in your mission by the specter of criminal or civil prosecution of an obscenity law that you cannot be reasonably expected to enforce.

While your connection to the Internet may not be housed in your library building, it is no less deserving of the protection offered by Subsection (j). By providing wide access to the Internet, you are, in effect, functioning as electronic librarians and the exemption should apply. Furthermore, as a well established principle of constitutional due process, any doubts about applicability of Pennsylvania obscenity laws must be resolved in your favor.

Indeed, we would think and hope that the University would want to lay vigorous claim to this exemption in order to protect future concepts of academic freedom. A library free from government control is an essential component of a vibrant university. As technology changes the ways in which we store and access information, it seems beyond dispute that the digital library of the next century will bear far greater resemblance to the Internet than to today's brick and mortar constructs. As the technology changes, it is essential that we not lose sight of core principles of academic freedom.

Carnegie Mellon has a well-deserved reputation in higher education as a leader on technology issues. You have already recognized the extraordinary potential of networked communications to enhance and democratize speech. But if the full potential is to be reached, it is important that leaders like CMU stand strong for free and open access to information and that you resist the urge to censor.

We strongly urge you to reconsider the new policy. It is our understanding that the University's decision was made without consultation with your counsel. We hope that you will now take that step. We would be happy to provide your attorneys with additional citations and materials to facilitate a reconsideration.

Thank you for your consideration of our views.

Sincerely,

Barry Steinhardt
Associate Director, ACLU

Marjorie Heins
Director, ACLU Arts Censorship Project
Witold Walczak
Executive Director, ACLU Greater Pittsburgh Chapter

22

Virtual Community Standards: BBS Obscenity Case Raises New Legal Issues

Mike Godwin

At first glance, the obscenity prosecution of Robert and Carleen Thomas of Milpitas seemed little different from the average obscenity prosecution. Sure, this case involves a computer bulletin board system (BBS), but there's nothing new about prosecuting pornography distributors in conservative states like Tennessee, is there?

Except that this BBS wasn't in Tennessee. It was in California. But that didn't stop Tennessee prosecutors from going after it. Because of the way BBSs normally operate, a conservative jurisdiction like Memphis may be in a position to dictate what's allowable on BBSs all over the country, from New York City to San Francisco. For this reason, the prosecution of the Thomases and their "Amateur Action BBS" calls into question the continuing validity of the Supreme Court's obscenity decision in Miller v. California, now more than 20 years old. That case, which was designed to allow communities to set their own standards of what is acceptable and what is obscene, has now been used for just the opposite purpose—it has allowed a Memphis prosecutor to dictate the content of a computer system in California.

Memphis Reaches Out to Touch Someone

The facts of the case are straightforward. The Thomases are the system operators (sysops) of an adults-only sexually oriented BBS in Milpitas, California. The operator of a BBS typically dedicates a computer and one or more phone lines at his home or business for the use of a "virtual community" of users. Each user calls up the BBS (using a modem connected to his or her telephone) and leaves public messages that can be read by all other users and/or private mail that can be read by a particular user. BBSs become forums—digital nightclubs, salons, and Hyde Park corners—for their users, and users with similar interests can associate with one another without being hindered by the accidents of geography. A BBS also can be used to trade in computer files, programs, and digital images, including sexually graphic images.

A Tennessee postal inspector, working closely with an assistant U.S. attorney in Memphis, became a member of the Thomases' BBS. Once he had become a member, he did three things: he downloaded sexually oriented images, ordered a videotape (which was delivered via UPS), and sent an unsolicited child-porn video to the Thomases. This led to a federal indictment with a dozen obscenity counts, most based on the downloading of the computer images.

The indictment also included one child-pornography count, based on the unsolicited video. At trial, the Memphis jury convicted the Thomases on all the obscenity counts, but acquitted them on the child-porn count. (A reporter at the scene who interviewed jurors said they believed the child-porn count smacked of entrapment.) The Thomases now face sentencing on the 11 obscenity convictions, each carrying a maximum sentence of five years in prison and $250,000 in fines.

The Thomases' lawyer says they will appeal, based at least in part on a claim that the jury instructions as to "community standards" were incorrect. "This case would never have gone to trial in California," he has said.

Community Standards and BBSs

It has long been held that obscenity is not protected by the First Amendment, but what qualifies as "obscenity" has not always been clear. After Miller v. California, a 1973 Supreme Court case, there has been no national standard as to what is obscene. In that case, the Court stated that material is "obscene" (and therefore not protected by the First Amendment) if 1) the average person, applying contemporary community standards, would find the materials, taken as a whole, arouse immoral lustful desire (or, in the Court's language, appeals to the "prurient interest"), 2) the materials depict or describe, in a patently offensive way, sexual conduct specifically prohibited by applicable state law, and 3) the work, taken as a whole, lacks serious literary, artistic, political or scientific value.

To put it in layman's terms, the trial court would ask something like these four questions:

1. Is it designed to be sexually arousing?
2. Is it arousing in a way that one's local community would consider unhealthy or immoral?
3. Does it depict acts whose depictions are specifically prohibited by state law?
4. Does the work, when taken as a whole, lack significant literary, artistic, scientific, or social value?

If the answer to all four questions is "yes," the material will be judged obscene, and it will be constitutional to prosecute someone for distributing it. (It should be noted in passing that pictures of the "hardness" of *Playboy* and *Penthouse* photography are never found to be obscene—their appearance in digital form on Usenet sites may create copyright problems, but they won't create obscenity problems. Remember also that "pornography" and "obscenity" are not identical categories—much pornography is not legally obscene.)

Normally, an appeal on the issue of obscenity will focus on one or more of the answers to the four questions. If, for example, a Robert Mapplethorpe photo is found obscene at a trial, defense on appeal might argue that, even if the photo is sexually arousing in a way that violates community standards and state law, the work's social value renders it protected by the First Amendment. In hardcore porn cases, the defense might argue that, in fact, the community is highly tolerant of such images (in adult bookstores, films, and the like).

It has long been held to be constitutional to prosecute any porn vendors located in more liberal jurisdictions who have knowingly or intentionally distributed obscenity into conservative jurisdictions. Many large-scale commercial porn vendors have made deliberate decisions not to distribute their materials into jurisdictions likely to prosecute—postal inspectors frequently engage in "sting" operations in order to test whether a vendor will send obscene material into their states.

This case is different, however. Consider: a seller of adult magazines normally makes a conscious decision to send his product into the jurisdiction in which he's prosecuted, thus establishing criminal intent for the purpose of an obscenity-distribution prosecution. In contrast, a BBS operator may be wholly unaware of the distribution—it may occur overnight, for example—due to the automatic operation of his software.

What's more, even if the Thomases were to attempt to screen their users on a state-by-state basis, there's no guarantee that this attempt would protect them—a user could simply lie about which state he is calling from, or he could obtain a membership while living in California yet maintain it after he moved to Tennessee. Since a BBS operator cannot block out calls from conservative jurisdictions, there is inherent vulnerability for a BBS operator that exceeds that for traditional pornography distributors.

While the Thomases' conviction with regard to the UPS-delivered video is likely to stand on traditional grounds, their convictions with regard to the downloaded images raise a number of critical issues. For example, does it make sense for a court to infer a defendant's criminal intent to distribute obscenity into Tennessee merely because neither he nor his BBS can ensure that someone cannot download that material into the state?

More importantly, the case turns the whole community-standards doctrine on its head. The Supreme Court was attempting, in Miller v. California, to prevent the standards of acceptability in New York City or San Francisco from dictating the standards of Kansas City or Norman, Oklahoma. Yet if it's wrong for New York City to set the standards for Norman, it's surely just as wrong for Memphis to set the standards for Milpitas.

Finally, the case raises the question of whether it makes sense to define "community standards" solely in terms of geographic communities. Now that an increasing number of Americans find themselves participating in "virtual communities" on services such as America Online, CompuServe, Prodigy, and the WELL, does it make sense to have what those citizens are allowed to bring into their own homes be dictated by the arbitrary fact of where their physical homes happen to be?

It's time for the courts to revisit the Miller obscenity standard. In the face of changes in communications media and the evolving nature of "community," the courts should modify the application of the Miller standard to prevent this kind of prosecutorial overreaching. Failing that, the courts should abandon the "community standards" approach altogether.

Until these issues are addressed, this case will create a "chilling effect" all over the country, as BBSs either censor themselves or cease operations in order to avoid prosecution. The case sends a frightening message to virtual communities: "It doesn't matter if you're abiding by your own community's standards—you have to abide by Memphis's as well."

23

Public Networks and Censorship

Jeffrey Shallit

Good afternoon. Thank you very much for the opportunity to speak to the Ontario Library Association on the subject of public networks and censorship.

1 Librarians and Computers

I had planned to start off with something sententious such as, "We stand today at an information delivery crossroads," but the truth is, that we have already passed this crossroads and are heading into the information age at very high speed. The crossroads, I think, was traversed back in 1989—when, for the first time, the number of videotapes rented exceeded the number of books checked out of public libraries.

The old concept of the library, as we have known and loved it, is dying. Now I'm not saying that books will cease to be published, or that traditional library concerns such as shelf space and book theft will disappear tomorrow. But I *am* saying that there is an enormous flood of information and communication that is about to be unleashed, that is already being unleashed, and that librarians and the principles they have developed and fought hard for, are desperately needed in the new world as "information intermediaries."

The librarians of yesterday were valued by the general public for, among other things, their abilities to determine just *where* in that intimidating building full of books, magazines, newspapers, and scholarly journals the particular piece of desired information resided. The librarians of tomorrow will be equally valued, but now much of the information lies in cyberspace. Yesterday, the *Reader's Guide to Periodical Literature* and *Ulrich's;* today, the Lexis/Nexis search service; tomorrow . . . ?

The librarians of yesterday were also known as guardians of intellectual freedom and the freedom to read. The principles of their profession can be found in statements produced by such groups as the American Library Association (for example, Library Bill of Rights, the Freedom to Read Statement, and the Intellectual Freedom Statement); the Canadian Library Association (Statement on Intellectual Freedom); and the Canadian Association of Research Libraries.

Let's take a look at just one of those statements, the Intellectual Freedom Statement of the Canadian Library Association [15]:

> All persons in Canada have the fundamental right, as embodied in the nation's Bill of Rights and the Canadian Charter of Rights and Freedoms, to have access to all expressions of knowledge, creativity and intellectual activity, and to express their thoughts publicly. . . .
>
> Libraries have a basic responsibility for the development and maintenance of intellectual freedom.
>
> It is the responsibility of libraries to guarantee and facilitate access to all expressions of knowledge and intellectual activity, including those which some elements of society may consider to be unconventional, unpopular or unacceptable. To this end, libraries shall acquire and make available the widest variety of materials. . . .
>
> Libraries should resist all efforts to limit the exercise of these responsibilities while recognizing the right of criticism by individuals and groups. . . .

I find those words very inspiring, and I hope you do, too. The question I would like to pose to you today is: as the libraries of yesterday are transformed into the libraries of tomorrow, will these principles govern electronic communication technologies such as the Internet?

2 Shallit's Three Laws

Before we begin discussion of fundamental freedoms on computer networks and the challenges to those freedoms, I'd like to tell you about what I modestly call Shallit's Three Laws of New Media. Shallit's first Law is the following:

Every new medium of expression will be used for sex.

Now you might say that I'm overstating my case, but think about it for a moment: some of the very earliest sculptures we know about are fertility symbols, such as the Venus of Laussel (c. 20,000 BC). One of the earliest books printed after Gutenberg invented the printing press was Bocaccio's erotic classic, *The Decameron.* Shortly after the introduction of photography, there was a thriving trade in pornographic pictures. And some anthropologists have even claimed that speech evolved so quickly in humans because it facilitated seduction! And this brings me to Shallit's Second Law:

Every new medium of expression will come under attack, usually because of Shallit's First Law.

Before I get to Shallit's Third Law of New Media, I'd like to tell you a story from a really terrific book, Carolyn Marvin's *When Old Technologies Were New: Thinking About Electric Communication in the Late Nineteenth Century.* Marvin's book is largely concerned with the societal impact of the telegraph and telephone, and, as we will see, neither was exempt from Shallit's Three Laws.

As Marvin observes

> New forms of communication created unprecedented opportunities not only for courting and infidelity, but for romancing unacceptable persons outside one's own class, and even one's own race, in circumstances that went unobserved by the regular community. The potential for illicit sexual behaviour had obvious and disquieting power to undermine accustomed centers of moral authority and social order. [7, p. 70]

Now here's that story I promised: in the summer of 1886, in New Jersey,

> a "nice young man" from the city met "one of the rustic beauties of the place" and they fell in love. They corresponded, and she invited him to visit. One day a telegram appeared with news of his impending arrival.
>
> Somehow—nobody ever will know just how—fifteen minutes after the message clicked into the [telegraph] office every person in town knew that young Blake was coming to see Miss Trevette. Every young lady of the town made up her mind to catch a glimpse of this rash young man who sent telegrams, and every man determined to be there to see that everything went smoothly.
>
> When young Blake alighted from his carriage . . . an audience of 499 villagers had gathered to watch. They observed while he paid the driver, studied him as he asked directions to the young lady's house, and followed his progress up the hill.

Panicked by the approaching procession, Miss Trevette sent word of her absence, halting the romance at a blow. [7, pp. 70–71]

An amusing story—but with a cautionary moral. Today's new communications technology—electronic mail—does not yet enjoy any of the legal or societal protections we associate with communication by more traditional means. While employers would think twice before opening an employee's mail delivered by Canada Post, e-mail is another matter. For example, Nissan Corporation dismissed a man for "inappropriate jokes and language" found in his e-mail. Epson, a computer company, dismissed a woman after she reported on a co-worker who was reading another employee's e-mail—apparently with the blessing of management. [8]

And this brings up Shallit's Third Law of New Media:

Protection afforded for democratic rights and freedoms in traditional media will rarely be understood to apply to new media.

Shallit's Third Law can be rephrased as the fallacy of focusing on the medium and not the message. A good illustration is the regulation of radio and television broadcasting. We tolerate content restrictions on television, for example, that would be intolerable if they were applied to print media [9]. When asked why, most people cite the supposed scarcity of the airwaves as a justification for government regulation of content. The truth is that this scarcity itself is a product of government intervention. The technology now exists to make possible hundreds or even thousands of broadcast stations in any metropolitan area. You don't hear much about this, because broadcasters are understandably less than enthusiastic about new competition, and the CRTC doesn't wish to relinquish its control on content. As Jonathan Emord shows, in his excellent book *Freedom, Technology, and The First Amendment*, regulations on broadcasting were historically enacted with little understanding of the technology and its capabilities [3].

3 Threats and Challenges to Freedom

We see that traditional democratic freedoms, such as freedom of expression and privacy, are under threat when these freedoms are asserted electronically.

And make no mistake, there is indeed a threat. One danger is that the new medium will be regulated to death before it is firmly established. For example, in November 1994, Reform MP Myron Thompson issued a press release alleging "highly pornographic, illegal stories available on Internet . . . that are reaching our children" and saying, "this smut must be stopped." (Shallit's Second Law again!)

Also, in a report recently presented to the Canadian Parliament, the Justice Committee recommended changes to the legal definition of "obscenity" to include "undue exploitation or glorification of horror, cruelty, or violence." In addition to cards and games, the report names "music, videos, comics, posters, and computer bulletin boards" as forms of communication that need to be controlled by the government. Communication that falls within this expanded definition and has "no redeeming cultural or social value" would be prohibited. The Internet is at risk, but books are safe . . . at least for the time being.

One reason for this difference in legal protection is that the print medium has existed for more than five hundred years, and libraries have existed for thousands of years. During that time, librarians have earned a good reputation for their craft, and have developed intellectual freedom principles that are well-respected. In contrast, electronic computers have existed for barely fifty years, and computer networks for barely twenty years. Computer system administrators have their own conferences and their own journals, but to my knowledge, they have no statement of duties, responsibilities, or ethics even remotely like the ALA's *Intellectual Freedom Manual* [2].

Within the next ten years, I predict that the power of many computer system administrators to regulate content on the machines they administer will wane. They will still be needed to help plan day-to-day use, install new software, and fix bugs, but the responsibility for such public forums such as Usenet news, etc., will move to people trained in principles of acquisition and intellectual freedom.

It may be that in the near future, the sheer volume of information flow will make selection much more necessary than it is today. When this happens, shouldn't the decisions on what electronic materials to subscribe to be based on the acquisition principles that librarians have worked so hard to enunciate? I hope so.

4 Censorship Incidents

As I pointed out, freedom of expression is at risk on the Internet. I think it's worthwhile to make this concrete by examining some censorship incidents in detail. Since I am most familiar with one Canadian institution, the University of Waterloo, I will focus on that university.

First, a little background. Due primarily to historical accident, universities are currently one of the principal locations where people have free and unlimited access to the Internet, one part of the so-called Information Highway. The Internet is also one of the principal places where Usenet news may be accessed.

Usenet consists of thousands of bulletin boards called "newsgroups," on a variety of topics—a kind of shared electronic mailbox. Users may read messages that have been posted on a particular topic, reply to those messages (by sending electronic mail directly to the poster), or "follow-up" (post a reply to the newsgroup itself). Usenet has existed for about fifteen years, and readership estimates for some newsgroups are in the millions or hundreds of thousands.

Usenet censorship can take place in a variety of ways, some more subtle than others. For example, it is possible for a local system administrator to expurgate a news feed, so that only certain newsgroups get through, and others are blocked. When this is done, the user is typically not informed. It is also possible to block certain postings locally from certain newsgroups, as has recently been done at the University of Kentucky [6]. Finally, messages do not stay forever on the bulletin boards they are posted to: something called an "expire time" governs how long they are available to the public. By differentially setting the expire times, it is possible to control locally which newsgroups actually get read.

The first censorship incident at Waterloo took place in 1988. Brad Templeton, a UW alumnus and operator of a Waterloo-area computer company, moderated a newsgroup called rec.humor.funny, a bulletin board devoted to jokes. People from all over the world sent him jokes; he chose the best ones, and posted them to the Internet. When an ethnic joke offended a student at MIT, he complained to the local newspaper, the Kitchener-Waterloo Record, and the Waterloo administration responded by banning the newsgroup. Ironically, after the ban, compilations of the jokes from the newsgroup could still be found for sale in Waterloo's own bookstore. (Shallit's Third Law!)

More recently, the University administration discovered that some of those thousands of newsgroups dealt with sex. In today's climate—as Trent University professor John Fekete calls it, an atmosphere of "moral panic" [4]—such a thing has become unacceptable.

To give you some idea of what we're dealing with, here are some of the newsgroups you can find on the Internet:

alt.sex.bestiality
alt.sex.bondage
alt.sex.stories
alt.sex.stories.d [d = discussion]
alt.tasteless
rec.arts.erotica
alt.sex.anal
alt.sex.breast
alt.sex.exhibitionism
alt.sex.fetish.feet
alt.sex.fetish.tickling
alt.sex.intergen
alt.sex.masturbation
alt.sex.pedophilia
alt.sex.safe
alt.sex.services
alt.sex.pictures
alt.sex.spanking
alt.binaries.pictures.erotica
alt.binaries.pictures.erotica.fetish
alt.binaries.pictures.tasteless
alt.binaries.multimedia.erotica
ont.personals.whips.and.rubber.chickens

For reasons known only to that arcane bureaucracy known as a University administration, all these newsgroups are currently available at the University of Waterloo, except for the first five. I should point out that all five groups are groups in which text, not pictures, is primarily distributed. The newsgroups in which pictures are distributed are not yet banned at Waterloo.

How did this censorship happen at Waterloo and other Ontario universities, and why is it being tolerated? I believe (although I cannot prove it) that it started with this September 1992 memo from Bernard Shapiro, Deputy Minister for Colleges and Universities from the Ontario Ministry of Education [19]:

> It has recently come to my attention that computer systems at Ontario's colleges and universities, normally used for the exchange of information between academics and scientific researchers, may be providing access to pornographic and/or racist material through international computer networks.
>
> It is the ministry's position that publicly-funded postsecondary institutions in Ontario should have appropriate policies and procedures in place to discourage the use of their computing systems for purposes of accessing or sending racist or pornographic materials. Furthermore, offensive material should be removed when it is identified, and appropriate sanctions should be in place to deal with offences. . . .
>
> . . . I do not believe that publicly-funded institutions should be seen to support either access to, or distribution of offensive material. . . .

I find this memo bizarre for a number of reasons. First of all, it exhibits no comprehension of the current purpose or use of the Internet. The Internet is not simply used for the "exchange of information between academics and scientific researchers."

Second, the memo exhibits the fallacy of "the medium, not the message." Pornography—a word that is often used pejoratively, but should not be—just means material that is intended to cause an erotic response in the viewer. Pornography is not, per se, illegal in Canada. Many pornographic materials in the print medium are freely available in many Ontario libraries. For example, the University of Waterloo library carries a subscription to *Playboy*, and the University of Waterloo bookstore carries a book called *Women's Erotic Dreams* [16]. Where is the concern and outrage over these materials?

Third, the memo asks for the suppression of *offensive materials* at Ontario universities. I was under the impression (in Clark Kerr's words) that the purpose of a University was to make students safe for ideas, not to make ideas safe for students. If you haven't been offended by *some* idea put forward at a university, then you haven't been paying attention.

Again, my university contains books in its library that are patently offensive to many, including *The Protocols of the Learned Elders of Zion*, Bret Easton Ellis' *American Psycho*, and Arthur Butz's *The Hoax of the Twentieth Century*, a book that claims that the Holocaust is a massive Jewish hoax. Butz's book is banned from importation into Canada, but it is nevertheless freely available in the Waterloo library.

It was not long after the Shapiro memo that action began to happen at Ontario universities. At Waterloo, the University Ethics Committee was empowered to investigate the Internet and decide what material might possibly break Canadian obscenity laws. In February, 1994, based on an opinion from the Ethics Committee, the University administration banned the five newsgroups previously listed. Here is part of the memo from the President of the University, James Downey [17]:

> Last fall I became aware that certain newsgroups on the Internet carried material which was almost certainly obscene and therefore contrary to the Criminal Code. Advice from the University solicitor was unequivocal: under the Criminal Code it is an offence for anyone to publish or distribute obscene material, and the University is running a risk of prosecution if it knowingly receives and distributes obscene material. In these circumstances I felt the University had to act to protect itself. . . .
>
> I am aware, of course, that this is a sensitive area: there is no precise and agreed-on measurement of where on the scale of human taste pornography begins. . . .
>
> I am now authorizing implementation of the following process:
>
> Complaints concerning newsgroups which contain material considered to be obscene are to be referred to the Ethics Committee. The Ethics Committee, with advice from legal counsel as appropriate, will make a recommendation to the Vice-President, Academic & Provost for the removal of any newsgroups it judges to be carrying obscene material. . . .

This memo also troubles me. First, the muddled conflation of "pornography" with "obscenity." Again, pornography is not illegal in Canada—only certain kinds of pornography are illegal. Second, a quick glance at the Criminal Code informs you that one cannot be convicted under obscenity law if "the public good was served by the acts" [18]. Surely guaranteeing free expression at a university is a case of the public good. Third, notice that the stated goal is simply to avoid legal liability. This would be a reasonable objective for a business or corporation, but not for a university, whose hallmark is the guarantee of freedom of expression.

Finally, obscenity law is traditionally among the most vexing and difficult to interpret of all the criminal laws, even with the recent *Butler* decision to give guidance. As Ontario Judge Stephen Borins once remarked, "Judge or jurors lacking experience in the field of pornography and the attitudes of others toward it face a substantial challenge in making the findings demanded by the law." [14]

Because of this difficulty, the American Library Association offered the following interpretation of its Challenged Materials policy [2]:

> Particularly when sexually explicit materials are the object of censorship efforts, librarians and boards of trustees are often unaware of the legal procedures required to effect the removal of such items. Many attorneys, even when employed by state and local governing bodies, are not aware of the procedures to determine whether or not a work is obscene under the law. According to U.S. Supreme Court decisions, a work is not obscene until found to be so by a court of law, and only after an adversary hearing to determine the question of obscenity. Until a work is specifically found to be unprotected by the First Amendment, the title remains a legal library acquisition and need not be removed.

Although this policy is written for the United States, its principles are equally valid in Canada. Material in Canada is not obscene until declared so by a court; until then it enjoys the protection of the Charter of Rights and Freedoms.

This point was driven home by Canadian Supreme Court Justice John Sopinka, in a November 26, 1994 speech at the University of Waterloo. Mr. Justice Sopinka, author of the *Butler* decision, said:

> Difficult issues also arise in the context of universities which take action to ban certain communications found to be offensive and undesirable. First, one must ask whether it is not preferable to permit the expression and allow the criminal or civil law to deal with the individual who publishes obscene, defamatory or hateful messages rather than prevent speech before it can be expressed. Otherwise, individuals may be putting themselves in the positions of courts to determine what is obscene and what is acceptable. [10]

Isn't this precisely what happened at Waterloo? No Internet newsgroup or message has ever been declared obscene by a court of law. Nevertheless, five newsgroups were banned from the campus.

There is an interesting historical parallel. Back in 1961, four copies of Henry Miller's *Tropic of Cancer* were acquired from Grove Press by the

Toronto Public Library. The Department of National Revenue, having declared the book obscene and unfit for importation into Canada, demanded that the Toronto Public Library hand over all copies of the book.

But chief librarian Henry C. Campbell refused. [11] As he pointed out, no Canadian court had declared the book obscene. The *Toronto Star* editorialized, "If the authorities deem *Tropic of Cancer* pornographic, they should test that belief in court. . . . Censorship guided by open court hearings, even on the basis of imperfect law, is preferable to any attempt at censorship by official decree." [12]

Unfortunately, Campbell's principled refusal to turn the book over to the censors at National Revenue was later overruled by Toronto Public Library Board Chair W. Harold Male. But the inner workings of the censorious mind may be judged by the following: Male huffed that "any self-respecting public library shouldn't have it on its shelves," and then was forced to admit that he had never even read the Miller novel. [13]

The sad conclusion: librarians understand the principles of intellectual freedom better than some university administrators.

5 A Simple Principle

We have seen that, true to Shallit's Third Law, the current public perception is that communication on the Internet does not merit protection under the Charter of Rights and Freedoms.

In the meantime, what are we to do? One possibility is to establish and debate fundamental principles on which policy can be based. To that end, I would like to bring your attention to a principle of intellectual freedom for electronic bulletin boards, as enunciated by Carl Kadie. The principles of intellectual freedom developed by libraries should be applied to the administration of information material on computers. [5]

Let us try to apply this principle to two specific cases, and see what results.

First, the case of access to the Internet by minors. As we have seen, people like Reform MP Myron Thomson are worried that children might gain access to pornographic material. Now, as I have pointed out, many public and university libraries in Canada already contain pornographic materials. For example, the Cambridge Public Library purchased two copies of Madonna's recent book, *Sex*. Following Kadie's principle, we must ask, what special actions have been taken by librarians to restrict access by minors to this kind of pornography?

The answer is, nothing. For example, the American Library Association has a policy on access to library material by minors that reads, in part,

> Library policies and procedures which effectively deny minors equal access to all library resources available to other users violate the LIBRARY BILL OF RIGHTS. The American Library Association opposes all attempts to restrict access to library services, materials, and facilities based on the age of library users. . . .
>
> Every restriction on access to, and use of, library resources, based solely on the chronological age, educational level, or legal emancipation of users violates Article V. . . .
>
> The selection and development of library resources should not be diluted because of minors having the same access to library resources as adult users. Institutional self-censorship diminishes the credibility of the library in the community, and restricts access for all library users. [1]

Although this is an American policy, it is generally adhered to by Ontario libraries. Most Ontario public libraries, including the Cambridge Public Library, have ended their two-tier library card system and now only offer a single library card. Madonna's *Sex* is now freely available to any child with a library card in Cambridge (but they'll have to wait in line to see it, since there is currently a waiting list of 100 people). If parents are worried about the kinds of materials their child might borrow, they are free to refuse permission for their child to obtain a library card. Ontario librarians recognize the right of parents to control their children's reading, but they refuse to act in loco parentis.

In the same way, schools and libraries that provide Internet access should refuse to provide a two-tier service in which some newsgroups are censored or suppressed for children. Should parents worry about the kinds of material their children might encounter on the Internet, they are free to deny access entirely for their children; for example, by not telling them the password.

Let us now examine another problem, that of requesting new newsgroups. In some systems, users are forced to make their request for new newsgroups in public—at the University of Waterloo, for example, some newsgroups are automatically subscribed to, but as of this writing others must be requested by posting to a newsgroup called uw.newsgroups. The result is that some newsgroups—particularly those dealing with sexual topics—may end up not being subscribed to because users are too embarrassed to make their request in front of everyone.

If we apply the intellectual freedom principles enunciated by libraries, however, we see that some other method for requesting newsgroups should be provided. For example, Article III of the ALA's "Librarian's Code of Ethics" states [2]: Librarians must protect each user's right to privacy with respect to information sought or received and materials consulted, borrowed, or acquired.

I believe that the principles librarians have developed for traditional media are a good basis for the protection of the new electronic media.

6 Why EFC?

The Internet and related communications technologies are going to change the way we communicate and research in the 21st century. Rules will be needed to make sure that everyone has a chance to participate, and to prevent abuse of the technology. But those rules should be made with careful thought, by people informed about the possibilities, limitations, and dangers of the technology. It is with this goal in mind that the Electronic Frontier Foundation was founded in the United States in July 1990. But until recently, there was no similar organization in Canada. Professor David Jones (then of McGill University and now of McMaster University) and I founded Electronic Frontier Canada in January 1994. Here is our raison d'etre (based on a similar statement from the Electronic Frontier Foundation): Electronic Frontier Canada (EFC) was founded to ensure that the principles embodied in the Canadian Charter of Rights and Freedoms are protected as new computing, communications, and information technologies emerge.

EFC is working to shape Canada's computing and communications infrastructure and the policies that govern it, in order to maintain privacy, freedom of speech, and other democratic values. Our work focuses on the establishment of:

- clear institutional policies and new laws that guarantee citizens' basic rights and freedoms on the electronic frontier;

• a policy of common carriage requirements for all network providers so that all forms of speech and expression, no matter how controversial, will be carried without discrimination;

• a diverse electronic community that enables all citizens to have a voice in the information age.

I hope that EFC will become a voice for reason and education as the electronic frontier becomes more civilized. And I also hope that librarians and their understanding of intellectual freedom principles will be at the forefront of the civilizing process. We need you.

References

1. American Library Association, "Free Access to Libraries for Minors: An Interpretation of the Library Bill of Rights," July 3, 1991. (Available by gopher or anonymous FTP to gopher.eff.org.)

2. American Library Association, *Intellectual Freedom Manual*, 3rd edition, 1989. (Sections also available by gopher or anonymous FTP to gopher.eff.org.)

3. Jonathan Emord, *Freedom, Technology, and the First Amendment*, Pacific Research Institute for Public Policy, 1991.

4. John Fekete, *Moral Panic: Biopolitics Rising*, Robert Davies Publishing, 1994.

5. Carl Kadie, "Content: The Academic Freedom Model," paper delivered at the *Third Conference on Computers, Freedom, and Privacy*, Burlingame, California, March 1993. Full text available at ftp://ftp.eff.org/pub/CAF/statements/cfp93.kadie.

6. Carl Kadie, "Applying Library Intellectual Freedom Principles to Public and Academic Computers," paper delivered at the *Fourth Conference on Computers, Freedom, and Privacy*, March 1994. Full text available at http://www.eff.org/CAF/cfp94.kadie.html.

7. Carolyn Marvin, *When Old Technologies Were New: Thinking About Electric Communication in the Late Nineteenth Century*, Oxford University Press, 1988.

8. Corey L. Nelson and Bonnie Brown, "Is E-mail Private or Public?" *Computerworld*, June 27, 1994, pp. 135–137.

9. Ithiel de Sola Pool, *Technologies of Freedom*, Belknap Press of Harvard University Press, 1983.

10. John Sopinka, "Freedom of Speech and Privacy in the Information Age," text of speech delivered at the University of Waterloo, November 26, 1994. Text available at gopher://insight.mcmaster.ca/00/org/efc/doc/sfsp/sopinka.

11. "Librarian Refuses to Give Banned Novel to Customs," *Toronto Globe & Mail*, October 30, 1961, p. 5.

12. "Censorship by Decree," *Toronto Star*, October 31, 1961, p. 6.

13. "Banned Book," *Toronto Globe & Mail*, November 27, 1961, p. 6.

14. Quoted in Lynn King, "Censorship and Law Reform" in *Women Against Censorship*, Varda Burstyn, ed., Douglas & McIntyre, 1985, p. 86.

15. Canadian Library Association, Intellectual Freedom Statement. Full text available at gopher://insight.mcmaster.ca/00/org/efc/library/library-cla-policy.

16. Celeste T. Paul, *Women's Erotic Dreams (and What They Mean)*, Grafton Books, London, 1988.

17. Memo from University of Waterloo President James Downey, January 31, 1994. Full text available at gopher://insight.mcmaster.ca/00/org/efc/univ/waterloo/uw.memo.netnews.31jan94.

18. Criminal Code of Canada, Section 163 (3). Full text available from http://insight.mcmaster.ca/org/efc/pages/law/cc/cc.163.html.

19. Memo from Bernard Shapiro, September 1992. Full text available from gopher://insight.mcmaster.ca:70/00/org/efc/univ/ontario.univ-ministry.memo.

24

Sex and the Single Sysadmin: The Risks of Carrying Graphic Sexual Materials

Mike Godwin

It's the kind of nightmare that will cause any sysadmin to bolt upright in bed, shaking, gripping the sheets with white-knuckled fingers.

In this nightmare scenario, the facts are simple: you hear a knock at the door, you answer to discover grim-faced law-enforcement agents holding a search warrant, and you are forced to stand by helplessly while they seize your system to search it for obscene or child-pornographic images.

In some versions of the nightmare, you may not even have known your hard disk contained such images; in others, your lack of knowledge may prove to be no defense in a criminal prosecution for possession of child pornography.

A Wave of Concern about Porn

In recent months, the Legal Services Department here at EFF (the Electronic Frontier Foundation) has faced a wave of concern in the United States about the legal issues raised by online obscenity and child pornography. Most recently, a nationwide federal investigation into the importing of child-pornographic computer files led first to several well-publicized searches and seizures of computers and bulletin-board systems (BBSs) and later to a number of indictments of computer users on charges relating to possession or distribution of this material. One result has been that a large number of BBS operators and network site administrators have contacted EFF with questions and concerns about their potential liability under obscenity and child-pornography laws.

Why so much concern? Partly, it's that, thanks to the availability of cheap image scanners, fast modems, and capacious hard disks, a large number of this country's BBSs and network sites carry GIF (Graphic Interchange Format) files or other kinds of graphic images with sexual content. These images can range from centerfold-type nudes to "hard-core" pornography. (For the sake of simplicity, I will refer to all graphic-image files as GIFs, although there are a number of other formats commonly available.)

Just as the growth of the consumer VCR market was linked to a growth in the market for adult videos, the increasing availability of certain kinds of consumer computer technology has led to a rapid increase in GIF-file traffic. System operators who might never consider opening an adult book or video store have either allowed or encouraged sexually oriented images to be exchanged on their systems. To understand this difference in attitudes one has to understand how online conferencing systems are generally run—as forums for their users to talk to each other, and to trade computer programs and files with each other.

How Porn Gets Online

Although these problems pervade the world of the Internet, the easiest case to understand is the microcomputer-based BBS. The operator of a BBS typically dedicates a computer and one or more phone lines at her home or business for the use of a "virtual community" of users. Each user calls up the BBS and leaves public messages (or, in many cases, GIFs) that can be read by all other users or private mail (which may include GIFs) that can be read by a particular user or both. BBSs become forums—digital public houses, salons, and Hyde Park corners—for their users, and users with similar interests can associate with one another without being hindered by the accidents of geography. By some estimates, there are currently in excess of 40,000 BBSs throughout North America, ranging from low-end free-access BBSs with only one or two phone lines to BBSs run by companies, government agencies, user groups, and other organizations.

A step up from the BBS in complexity is the conferencing system or information service. These systems differ in capacity from BBSs: they have the capability of serving dozens, or hundreds, of users at the same time. But they're like BBSs in that uploaded files can be found at a fixed geographic location. A further step up are entities like Fidonet and Usenet, which, because they're highly distributed, decentralized conferencing systems, add complications to the legal issues raised by the computerization of sexual images.

Internet nodes and the systems that connect to them, for example, may carry such images unwittingly, either through uuencoded mail or through uninspected Usenet newsgroups. The store-and-forward nature of message distribution on these systems means that such traffic may exist on a system at some point in time even though it did not originate there, and even though it won't ultimately end up there. What's more, even if a sysadmin refuses to carry the distributed forums most likely to carry graphic images, she may discover that sexually graphic images have been distributed through a newsgroup that's not obviously sexually oriented.

Depending on the type of system he or she runs, a system operator may not know (and may not be able to know) much about the system's GIF-file traffic, especially if his or her system allows GIFs to be traded in private mail. Other operators may devote all or part of their systems to adult-oriented content, including image files.

Regardless of how their systems are run, though, operators often create risks for themselves under the mistaken assumption that a) since this kind of material is commonplace, it must be legal, and b) even if it's illegal, they can't be prosecuted for something they don't know about. EFF's Legal Services Department has been working actively to educate system operators about the risks of making these assumptions.

What Counts as "Obscene"?

First of all, we've explained that the fact that graphic sexual material is common on BBSs doesn't mean that it's not legally obscene and illegal in their jurisdiction.

As Judge Richard Posner comments in the October 18, 1993, issue of *The New Republic,* "Most "hard-core" pornography—approximately, the photographic depiction of actual sex acts or of an erect penis—is illegal," even though it is also widely available. (Let me emphasize the word "approximately"—Posner knows that there are countless exceptions to this general rule.) That is, distribution of most of this material is prohibited under state or federal anti-obscenity law because it probably would meet the Supreme Court's test for defining obscenity.

But what precisely is the Court's definition of obscenity? In Miller v. California (1973), the Court stated that material is "obscene" (and therefore not protected by the First Amendment) if 1) the average person, applying contemporary community standards, would find the materials, taken as a whole, arouse immoral lustful desire (or, in the Court's language, appeals to the "prurient interest"), 2) the materials depict or describe, in a patently offensive way, sexual conduct specifically prohibited by applicable state law, and 3) the work, taken as a whole, lacks serious literary, artistic, political or scientific value.

This is a fairly complex test, but most laymen remember only the "community standards" part of it, which is why some system operators are under the mistaken impression that if the material is common and available, "community standards" and the law must allow it.

The Perils of Online Obscenity

In theory, most "hardcore" pornography qualifies as "obscenity" under the Supreme Court's test. Yet theoretically obscene material is commonly available in many urban areas—this signifies, perhaps, that the relevant laws, when they do exist, are underenforced. At EFF, however, we have been telling system operators that there is no *legal* basis for their assuming that the laws will remain underenforced when it comes to online forums.

For one thing, most of this country's law-enforcement organizations have only recently become aware of the extent that such material is traded and distributed online—now that they're aware of it, they're aware of the potential for prosecution. In a recent case, an Oklahoma system operator was charged under state law for distribution of obscene materials, based on a CD-ROM of sexual images that he'd purchased through a mainstream BBS trade magazine. He was startled to find out that something he'd purchased through normal commercial channels had the potential of leading to serious criminal liability.

Still another issue, closely related to obscenity law, is whether an online system creates a risk that children will have access to adult materials. States in general have a special interest in the welfare of children, and they may choose to prohibit the exposure of children to adult materials, even when such materials are not legally obscene. (Such materials are often termed "indecent"—that is, they violate some standard of "decency," but nevertheless are constitutionally protected. If this category seems vague, that's because it is.) In Ginsberg v. State of New York (1968), the Supreme Court held a state statute of this sort to be constitutional.

Although there is no general standard of care for system operators who want to prevent children from having such access, it seems clear that, for a system in a state with such a statute, an operator must make a serious effort to bar minors from access to online adult materials. (A common measure—soliciting a photocopy of a driver's license—is inadequate in my opinion. There's no reason to think a child would be unable to send in a photocopy of a parent's driver's license.)

It's worth noting that, in addition to the risk, there are also some protections for system operators who are concerned about obscene materials. For example, the system operator who merely possesses, but does not distribute, obscene materials cannot constitutionally be prosecuted—in the 1969 case Stanley v. Georgia, the Supreme Court held the right to possess such materials in one's own home is constitutionally protected. Thus, even if you had obscene materials on the Internet node you run out of your house, you're on safe ground so long as they're not accessible by outsiders who log into your system.

And, in the 1959 case Smith v. California, the Court held that criminal obscenity statutes, like the great majority of all criminal laws, must require the government to prove "scienter" (essentially, "guilty knowledge" on the defendant's part) before that defendant can be found guilty. So, if the government can't prove beyond a reasonable doubt that a system operator knew or should have known about the obscene material on the system, the operator cannot be held liable for an obscenity crime.

In short, you can't constitutionally be convicted merely for possessing obscene material, or for distributing obscene material you didn't know about.

Child Pornography—Visual Images That Use Children

When the issue is child pornography, however, the rules change. Here's one of the federal child-porn statutes:

18 USC 2252: Certain activities relating to material involving the sexual exploitation of minors.

(a) Any person who—

(1) knowingly transports or ships in interstate or foreign commerce by any means including by computer or mails, any visual depiction, if—

(A) the producing of such visual depiction involves the use of a minor engaging in sexually explicit conduct; and

(B) such visual depiction is of such conduct; or

(2) knowingly receives, or distributes, any visual depiction that has been transported or shipped in interstate or foreign commerce by any means including by computer or mailed or knowingly reproduces any visual depiction for distribution in interstate or foreign commerce by any means including by computer or through the mails if—

(A) the producing of such visual depiction involves the use of a minor engaging in sexually explicit conduct; and

(B) such visual depiction is of such conduct;

shall be punished as provided in subsection (b) of this section.

(b) Any individual who violates this section shall be fined not more than $100,000, or imprisoned not more than 10 years, or both, but, if such individual has a prior conviction under this section, such individual shall be fined not more than $200,000, or imprisoned not less than five years nor more than 15 years, or both. Any organization which violates this section shall be fined not more than $250,000.

(N.B. For the purposes of federal law, "minor" means "under age 18"—it does not refer to the age of consent in a particular state.)

This statute illustrates some of the differences between the world of obscenity law and that of child-pornography law. For one thing, the statute does not address the issue of whether the material in question is "obscene." There's no issue of community standards or of "serious" artistic value. For all practical purposes, the law of child pornography is wholly separate from the law of obscenity.

Here's the reason for the separation: "obscenity" laws are aimed at forbidden expression—they assume that some things are socially harmful by virtue of being expressed or depicted. Child-porn laws, in contrast, are not aimed at *expression* at all—instead, they're designed to promote the protection of children by trying to destroy a market for materials the production of which requires the sexual use of children.

This rationale for the child-pornography laws has a number of legal consequences. First of all, under the federal statute, material that depicts child sex, but in which a child has not been used, does not qualify as child pornography. Such material would include all textual depictions of such activity, from Nabokov's novel *Lolita* to the rankest, most offensive newsgroups on Usenet, all of which are protected by the First Amendment (assuming that, in addition to not being child pornography, they're also not obscene).

Secondly, the federal child-porn statute is limited to visual depictions (this is not true for all state statutes), but does not apply to *all* visual depictions: computer-generated or -altered material that *appears* to be child pornography, but which did not in fact involve the sexual use of a real child, would not be punishable under the federal statute cited above. This makes sense in light of the policy—if real children aren't being sexually abused, the conduct these statutes are trying to prevent has not occurred. Although prosecutors have had little trouble up to now in proving at trial that actual children have been used to create the child-porn GIF images at issue, we can anticipate that, as computer-graphics tools grow increasingly powerful, a defendant will someday argue that a particular image was created by computer rather than scanned from a child-porn photograph.

Third, since the laws are aimed at destroying the market for child pornography, and since the state has a very powerful interest in the safety of children, even the mere possession of child porn can be punished. (Compare: mere possession of obscene materials is constitutionally protected.)

The fourth consequence of the child-protection policy that underlies child-porn statutes is that the federal law, as interpreted by most federal courts, does not require that the defendant be proved to have known that a "model" is a minor. In most jurisdictions, a defendant can be convicted for possession of child porn even if he can prove that he believed the model was an adult. If you can prove that you did not even know you possessed the image at all, you should be safe. If your knowledge falls somewhere in between—you knew you had the image, but did not know what it depicted, or that it was sexual in its content—the law is less clear. (In other words, it's not yet clear whether it is a defense for a system administrator to claim he didn't even know he possessed the image, either because it had been uploaded by a user without his knowledge, or because it had appeared in "pass-through" mail or through a Usenet newsfeed.)

In sum, then, the child-porn statutes create additional problems for the system administrator who wants to avoid criminal liability and minimize the risk of a disruptive search and seizure.

What You Can Do

The first thing to do is not to overreact at this discussion of the risks. It would amount to a serious "chilling effect" on freedom of expression if a sysadmin—in order to eliminate the risk of prosecution for distribution of obscenity, or for possession or distribution of child pornography—decided to eliminate all newsgroups with sexual content. The textual content of such newsgroups is constitutionally protected, as is much of the GIF content.

What's worse is that the tactic wouldn't eliminate the risks—it's always possible for someone to post illegal material to an innocuous newsgroup, like sci.astro or rec.arts.books, so that it would get to your system anyway. Similarly, an illegal image might be uuencoded and included in e-mail, which, if you're a system covered by the Electronic Communications Privacy Act, you're not allowed to read.

You should begin with the knowledge that nothing you can do as a sysadmin will eliminate altogether the risks of prosecution or of a disruptive search and seizure. But a few sensible measures can reduce the risks of a search or an arrest, and at the same time preserve the freedom of expression of your users and of those users who transmit material through your system.

• If you plan to carry graphic sexual material, look up your state's obscenity laws. A lawyer or librarian can help you find the relevant state statutes. Find out what, specifically, your state tries to prohibit. (If the state statute seems inconsistent with what I've written here, consider seeking legal advice—it may be that the statute predates the Supreme Court's decisions on obscenity and child pornography but has not yet been challenged.) You may also want to consult local adult bookstores—they often have clear, practical information about avoiding obscenity prosecutions.

• If you're running an online forum local to your system, and that forum has an upload/download area, prescreen graphic images before making them publicly available for downloads. While "calendar" and "foldout" images are constitutionally protected, you may want to consider deleting "hardcore" images that might be found "obscene" in your community. You also want to delete anything that looks like child pornography.

• If you're running a Usenet node, and you are informed by users that an obscene or child-porn image has been posted to a newsgroup you carry, examine it and consider deleting it. If there's any ambiguity, err on the conservative side—remember, if you guess wrong about the age of the model, you can be convicted anyway.

• Take pains on your system to limit childrens' access to adult material, even if that material is not legally obscene (it may still be "indecent"). This includes textual material dealing with adult topics. Hint: asking for a photocopied driver's license in the mail is probably not an adequate safeguard—too easy for industrious minors to circumvent. A good set of rules to follow is spelled out in an FCC regulation applicable to phone-sex providers—47 CFR 64.201. The easiest FCC suggestions for a for-pay BBS, online service, or Internet access provider is to require payment by credit card; the easiest for a nonpay system is have an application process that reasonably ascertains whether an applicant for access is an adult, and to have a procedure whereby one can instantly cut off that access when informed that a user is in fact a minor.

• Don't delete discussions of sexual topics—they're constitutionally protected. And even though the Supreme Court has not limited the definition of "obscenity" to visual depictions, as a practical matter, there is little legal risk in carrying textual narratives ("stories") on sexual themes.

• Don't inspect individuals' e-mail without their consent—unless they're employees of your company, their mail is probably protected by the Electronic Communications Privacy Act.

• If you're a university site, or if you're simply interested in the law of freedom of speech, consult the Computers and Academic Freedom (CAF) archive, which is part of the EFF archive at ftp.eff.org. If you have gopher, the archive is at gopher.eff.org; if you are limited to e-mail access, send e-mail to archive-server@eff.org, and include the line

send acad-freedom/law

The CAF archive has a number of instructional materials that deal with obscenity and child-pornography law.

These measures won't guarantee that you'll never have legal troubles—nothing can guarantee that. (And if you have particular legal worries, you should consult a lawyer in your jurisdiction.) But they can reduce the risks you face as a system administrator and as a carrier and distributor of information. At the same time, they'll minimize the extent to which you interfere with your users' freedom to communicate—which is, after all, one of the chief reasons they're online in the first place.

25

Computer and Academic Freedom News's List of Banned Computer Material on College Campuses

Inspired by Banned Book Week '92, this is a list of computer material that was banned or challenged in academia in 1992. Iowa State University has the dubious distinction of being listed most often (three times).

The list proper starts after a list of the academic institutions where bans or challenges have occurred. The list proper is followed by instructions on how to get more information about specific incidents and then by instructions on how to get general information about computers and academic freedom.

Please send reports, corrections, and updates to either caf-talk@eff.org (a public mailing list) or kadie@eff.org (private).

Carl Kadie, kadie@eff.org,
co-editor, *Computer and Academic Freedom News*
Disclaimer: I do not represent EFF; this is just me.
version: 1.09

Academic Institutions

USA

Ball State University
Boston University (i)
Carnegie Mellon University
Iowa State University (i)
North Dakota State University
Princeton

University of California at Berkeley (site of an unsuccessful challenge)
University of Nebraska-Lincoln
University of Wyoming
Virginia Public Education Network
Virginia Tech
Williams College (the college not directly involved)

Canada

Canadian Universities
Simon Fraser University
University of British Columbia
University of Manitoba
University of Toronto (site of an unsuccessful challenge)
University of Ottawa
Wilfrid Laurier University (i)
Wilfrid Laurier University (ii)

Europe

Irish universities
German universities
Middle East Technical University in Turkey
United Kingdom Net

Updates

Iowa State University (ii)
University of Illinois at Urbana-Champaign (ban ended)

Continuing

Boston University (ii)
Iowa State University (iii)
James Madison University
Pennsylvania State University
University of Newcastle
University of Texas
University of Toledo
Western Washington University (& University of Washington)

List of Banned Computer Materials

USA

Computer code at *Ball State University* to crack passwords . . . even if it is never run. During a system-wide search, an administrator found the computer code. The user says "[i]t really bothers me that I'm going to get in a lot of trouble (probably anyway) just for the mere possession of a program."

Reference:
news/cafv02n11:<9202161945.AA24863@bsu-cs.bsu.edu>

Lyrics to Ice-T's "Cop Killer" in a .plan file at *Boston University*.

"Two people have complained to my department's chair. . . . He asked me informally to remove it. I told him I would not do so voluntarily."

news/cafv02n35:<JBW.92Jul16195814@bigbird.bu.edu>

Articles in an open bulletin board at *Carnegie Mellon University* if they offend.

The University threatened to investigate the author on charges of sexual harassment unless he stopped writing.

news/cafv02n11:<46750.298C2BB3@psycho.fidonet.org>
news/cafv02n08:<1992Jan28.223429.20426@eff.org>

Material from the rec.arts.erotica newsgroup at *Iowa State University*.

To protest the University's ban of this newsgroup, a student reposted some of the articles to newsgroup isu.newsgroups. He was summarily expelled from the University computers. Later his account was restored. The incident made the front page of the student newspaper.

news/cafv02n30:<1992May6.033143.16713@eff.org>
news/cafv02n30:<1992May8.064304.8364@news.iastate.edu>

All "offensive" material at *North Dakota State University* banned by the Policy on Misuse of Computer Facilities.

news/cafv02n20:<1992Apr27.214917.13402@eff.org>

Any electronic posting at *Princeton* that demeans a person because of his or her beliefs banned by Princeton's Guidelines for the use of Campus and Network Computing Resources and the more general Rights, Rules, Responsibilities Policy.

news/cafv02n20:<199204292110.AA23705@eff.org>

news/cafv02n20:<1992Apr29.213206.24214@eff.org>

Anti-Semitic material available at the *University of California at Berkeley* via the Internet . . . challenged by a student, but the University and the Anti-Defamation League of B'nai B'rith said that censorship would be inappropriate.

news/cafv02n07:<kpgo3cINNvq@news.bbn.com>

All the alternative newsgroups (even alt.censorship) at the *University of Nebraska-Lincoln* . . . because someone might find some of the articles in some of the newsgroups "objectionable." On April 6th the UNL Academic Senate Executive Committee voted to request restoration of the majority of the alt.* groups, but none have been restored.

news/cafv02n22:<1992Mar26.214421.26447@sparky.imd.sterling .com>

news/cafv02n22:<9203212232.AA24018@cse.unl.edu>

news/cafv02n23:<1992Apr1.192701.28737@eff.org>

news/cafv02n23:<9205040334.AA04565@cse.unl.edu>

news/cafv02n23:<fwd.9204201540.AA12109@herodotus.cs.uiuc .edu>

news/cafv02n30:<1992May5.005813.281@eff.org>

Computer code at the *University of Wyoming* for Internet Relay Chat. A student was told that if university searches turned up IRC code in his possession, he "would be disusered without hope for reinstatement."

news/cafv02n08: <3803321809011992_A11466_POSSE_11614C9 F3200 @mrgate.uwyo.edu>

Any network use on *Virginia Public Education Network* that violates "generally accepted social standards." Such use is defined as "obscene" and is banned by PEN's Acceptable Use Policy.

policies/virginia.pen.edu

policies/virginia.pen.edu.critique

Any "unwarranted annoyance" or "unsolicited e-mail" at *Virginia Tech* . . . banned by the Information System's Appropriate Use Policy. The policy is currently being revised.

news/cafv02n20:<1992Apr27.214917.13402@eff.org>

The phrase "George Bush and his people need a bullet in the head" posted to the Net from *Williams College*. The posting led to a U.S. Secret Service and grand jury investigation.

news/cafv02n29:<1992Jun11. 001601.29258@morrow.stanford.edu>

Canada

alt.sex.bondage and other "pornographic writing" anywhere in *Canada*. . . . challenged in a CBC Radio show reporting that some police consider these legally obscene, and would like to suppress them if possible. (The police haven't acted, but their statements may have caused some sites to ban material.)

news/cafv02n30:<telecom12.427.9@eecs.nwu.edu>

All Netnews discussions of sex at *Simon Fraser University*

The *Globe and Mail* quotes the director of academic computing services: "It's the same as if somebody wants *Playboy* or *Penthouse*. We don't have them in the university library." In fact, SFU has *Playboy* in its library.

news/cafv02n38:<1992Jul21.164722.252@jarvis.csri.toronto.edu>
news/cafv02n37:<philip.12@SMU.StMarys.CA>

All "vulgar," "reprehensible," "pornographic," or "poison[ous]" material that might be accessed from, created on, or stored on *University of British Columbia* computing equipment starting with newsgroups alt.sex and rec.arts.erotica . . . banned by order of the president of the University.

news/cafv02n39:<DALTON.92Jul31231305@oligo.Geop.UBC.CA>

All Netnews discussions of sex at the *University of Manitoba* . . . banned the day after a critical article in the *Winnipeg Free Press*.
news/cafv02n21:<1992May10.093635.27536@ccu.umanitoba.ca>
news/cafv02n38:<1992Jul21.164722.252@jarvis.csri.toronto.edu>
news/cafv02n37:<philip.12@SMU.StMarys.CA>
news/cafv02n26:<1992May28.010057.18609@cs.sfu.ca>
news/cafv02n30:<1992May31.080939.25516@clarinet.com>

All on-line material related to sex at *University of Toronto* . . . challenged in a broadcast by CITY-TV (an independent Toronto television station) that suggested the U. of Toronto should deal with the "problem" like U. of Manitoba did, that is, by banning the material. The U. of Toronto resisted the challenge and refused to censor the material.
news/cafv02n34:<1992Jul7.150830.27316@ccu.umanitoba.ca>
policies/utoronto.ca
news/cafv02n37:<philip.12@SMU.StMarys.CA>
news/cafv02n33:<1992Jun16.045026.15800@gpu.utcs.utoronto. ca>

The alt.sex* newsgroups at the *University of Ottawa*.
cases/wlu.ca

All "profane" computer file names at *Wilfrid Laurier University*.
news/cafv02n40:<1992Aug13.182157.5688@m.cs.uiuc.edu>

The alt.sex* newsgroups at *Wilfrid Laurier University* . . . because the administration thinks they are "offensive" and "puerile."
cases/wlu.ca

Europe

Newsgroups at *many German universities* that discuss sex, including discussion of recovery from sexual abuse . . . banned in response to an article in the German paper *Emma*.
news/cafv02n23:<199204201927.AA07124@eff.org>

Netnews discussion in *Ireland* of abortion.
news/cafv02n11:<1992Feb24.222848.12187@maths.tcd.ie>

Netnews discussion via Switzerland's *Switch* of gay rights, of drugs and drug policy, and of sex and recovery from sexual abuse. Also, United Press International articles related to terrorism or sex. *Switch* is an academic network consortium. The official rational is that this information *might* be illegal under Swiss law.
news/cafv02n22:<1992Mar2.135005.14877@neptune.inf.ethz.ch>
news/cafv02n11:<1992Feb20.180752@sic.epfl.ch>
news/cafv02n13:<16825.9203091724@pyr.swan.ac.uk>

All on-line political or religions "activism" at *Middle East Technical University in Turkey.*
news/cafv02n21:<1992May4.223243.28741@eff.org>

Newsgroups alt.sex*, alt.drugs, alt.evil, alt.tasteless and rec.arts.erotica on *United Kingdom Net.*
UKNet is a commercial network that connects most academic institutions in the United Kingdom. They say that they fear UK law.
news/cafv02n33:<1992Jun08.165434.4998@bas-a.bcc.ac.uk>
news/cafv02n30:<1992May19.093311.105@rdg.dec.com>

Updates

Most on-line discussion of sex at *Iowa State University* restricts access to these newsgroups. The rational for the restriction is Iowa's obscenity law. That law, however, explicitly exempts universities. Since the original restrictions were started, rec.arts.erotica has been added to the restricted list, while discussions of drugs and drug policy were removed.
news/cafv02n11:<1992Feb23.201324.12799@m.cs.uiuc.edu>
news/cafv02n11:<3198@ecicrl.ocunix.on.ca>
news/cafv02n08:<1992Jan24.160039.20161@news.iastate.edu>
news/cafv02n30:<1992May11.132630.23905@news.iastate.edu>

E-mail sent to or from the National Center for Supercomputer Applications (NCSA) that verbally attacks the Center or the *University of Illinois at Urbana-Champaign.* No longer grounds for a computer file search.
cases/ncsa.email
news/cafv02n33:<1992Jun2.011050.15719@m.cs.uiuc.edu>

No Changes Reported
Any computer files at *Boston University* that anyone else finds offensive or annoying. The rules at Boston University prohibit a computer user from "making accessible offensive [or] annoying . . . material."
news/cafv01n10

All rude articles at *Iowa State University.* On-line rudeness is prohibited by Iowa State computer policy. A student was reprimanded for posting a rude article to the net.
news/cafv01n38
news/cafv02n23:<1992Apr2.174625.23219@eff.org>

All e-mail containing "offensive" material at *James Madison University.*
news/cafv01n39

The alt.sex* hierarchy on PSUVM, the main general purpose computer at *Pennsylvania State University.*
news/cafv01n34

All offensive messages at *University of Newcastle.*
news/cafv01n39

All email or Netnews articles that "bring discredit" to the *University of Texas* or its Computer Science Department.
news/cafv01n37

The alt.sex newsgroup at the *University of Toledo.*
batch/oct_06_1991

More than a dozen newsgroups, including alt.sex, at *Western Washington University*. They were removed from Western Washington University on the order of one person, the Vice Provost for "information and communication." Alt.sex remains at the *University of Washington*, but other newsgroups were removed right before a negative article was printed in the Seattle *Post Intelligencer*.

news/cafv01n33
news/cafv01n36
news/cafv01n35
news/cafv01n41

How to Get More Information about an Incident

Following each item in the list above is one or more references.

For example:
news/cafv02n11:<9202161945.AA24863@bsu-cs.bsu.edu>
news/cafv01n10
policies/virginia.pen.edu
cases/wlu.ca
batch/oct_06_1991

In the first example, "news/cafv02n11" is the name of a file and "<9202161945.AA24863@bsu-cs.bsu.edu> is a message-id within the file. The other example references consist of just file names. If a reference includes a message-id, retrieve the named file first, then edit it and do a text search for that message-id.

The files are available by anonymous FTP (the preferred method) and by e-mail. To get the files via FTP, do an anonymous FTP to ftp.eff.org (192.77.172.4), and "get" the files.

For example:
get pub/academic/news/cafv02n11
get pub/academic/news/cafv01n10
get pub/academic/policies/virginia.pen.edu
get pub/academic/cases/wlu.ca

get pub/academic/batch/oct_06_1991

To get the files by email, send email to archive-server@eff.org. For the files in the example, the email should contain the lines:

send acad-freedom/news cafv02n11
send acad-freedom/news cafv01n10
send acad-freedom/policies virginia.pen.edu
send acad-freedom/cases wlu.ca
send acad-freedom/batch oct_06_1991

V

Self and Community Online

In this section we take up issues surrounding the nature of self and community on the electronic frontier. Consider first, our online selves. It might seem odd to suppose that there is a distinct notion of self that one has when online. Isn't the self identical to the physical body? And therefore isn't it somewhat silly to talk about there being selves in cyberspace? Isn't it rather the case that our selves (since they are identical to our physical bodies) remain in chairs typing on terminals? So even if we are MUDding, our selves remain in the real world (RW) and we are engaged in communications with others in which we create fictional characters, right? Surely it would be a blunder to say that these fictional characters are in any way to be identified with our true selves—surely that is just a conflation of fiction with reality. Well, matters are not so simple.

We might be tempted to identify ourselves with our RW bodies, but even if that is a reasonable identification to make, it assumes some sort of clear conception of what bodies are. But is there such a clear conception? That is doubtful. For example, a great deal of contemporary philosophical writing on the nature of the body casts doubt on any conception of body as the biological organism bordered by the skin. The reasoning is that when we act in the world we do so with the aid of tools, and these tools can be construed as extensions of our physical bodies. To give a widely discussed example, the experienced carpenter may not even reflect on the fact that a hammer is being used as an instrument in some task (any more than he or she would reflect on the fact that his or her arm or index finger was involved in the same task). The instrument becomes, in effect, an extension of the body.

Now consider that tools need not be discrete objects we can hold in the palm of our hand. Communications devices, like telephones, computers, and modems, must certainly count as tools. It is also reasonable to suppose that tools include data structures (bits of computer code) that allow us to present our thoughts in the guise of a virtual reality (VR) character. So, for example, if I have constructed and registered a permanent character on a particular MUD or MOO, that character becomes a kind of tool that I manipulate, often without reflection. Like the carpenter who uses the hammer without reflection, I might use my VR character without reflection. But if the hammer is an extension of the body, is it not just as reasonable to suppose that the VR character (or at least the data structure that encodes it) is also an extension of my body? Maybe, when MUDding, my body is not confined to my chair but through the mediation of my computer and the Internet extends all the way to Xerox PARC, or to some nonlocalizable location in cyberspace.

In a sense, the VR character has an even better claim to being an extension of my body than a hammer does. The hammer, after all, only participates in my interactions with nails and wood, but my VR character is a tool through which I communicate with other persons—a highly complex tool at that. With my VR character I can project a certain physical description, emotions, and so forth. But there is more. Depending upon how my VR character is modified, I may receive different kinds of feedback from my VR friends. It thus serves as an important feedback mechanism in my interpersonal relations.

This last point takes on particular importance if we take seriously a number of contemporary theories that regard the self as socially constructed in some sense. So, for example, such theories would reject the broadly Cartesian view that there is a core portion of me that is situated in my body and uses my body to interact with a distinct external world. Instead, according to such theories, the self does not come first but is rather the product of social mediation. This is not a simple point about nature vs. nurture. It is rather a deeper point about how the self is defined by the social relations in which it participates.

This point might seem abstract, so let's consider a particular property that we suppose RW individuals to have: gender. It might seem that our gender is whatever it is, and that's the end of it (barring some form of radical surgery). That view, however, rests upon the assumption that gender is essentially a biological category—an assumption that some have called into question. The alternative assumption would be that gender is a *social* concept—a way of dividing the population into two groups that is grounded in certain social practices and institutions. Functional explanations for this division might be offered—for example, that gender plays the role of forcing certain individuals into kinds of work or social roles that they might otherwise find unrewarding or demeaning. Crucially, however, according to this view people are not born gendered, but rather become gendered via their social contacts; gender is the product of a feedback loop between individuals and the social settings in which they are situated.

It should be clear that the above analysis of gender has very strong consequences for the notion of online gender. If the bulk of my social contacts are in VR rather than the RW, then why wouldn't VR have greater claim to the construction of my gender? That is, if social institutions determine gender and if the bulk of the social institutions in which I participate are VR institutions, then why isn't my VR gender my "real" gender?

Provisos are necessary here. The claim is not that if an RW male temporarily assumes female gender in his VR character he will become, ipso facto, a female. On the contrary, it would be necessary for the individual to be accepted as a female in his VR community, and this would no doubt require a very extended period of enculturation. But once that is accomplished we might seriously raise questions about the actual gender of the individual. (See the Bruckman reading for further discussion of these issues.)

As noted in Reid's piece "Identity and the Cyborg Body," VR gender possibilities are substantially more complex than the simple binary opposition male/female. More generally, the kinds of forms we may take on to represent ourselves are virtually unlimited. Thus we have the existence of cyberspace locales like FurryMuck, where participants create characters that are, in effect, furry animals. Of course, no one is claiming that by building a character that looks like a woodchuck one becomes a woodchuck. Rather, the claim is that by describing your character you are projecting certain properties to the other MUD denizens. Your true properties depend not on the definition you provide, but rather on how you are viewed by the members of the MUD.

A number of writers have been quick to criticize cases where individuals have allegedly conflated reality and fiction or identified too closely with their VR characters, but it seems to me that these criticisms are easily turned around. Perhaps the critics are showing undue deference to RW. Or even more strongly, perhaps the critics have failed to see that RW is itself a social construction, having no more, and in some cases less, claim to authenticity that a number of robust VR communities.

One such robust community is the famous LambdaMoo run at Xerox PARC (see the description in the reading by Pavel), and one of the most famous examples of how seriously VR events can be taken is chronicled in Dibbell's "Rape in Cyberspace." The incident involved a character, Mr. Bungle, who took advantage of the possibility of "spoofing" on other LambdaMoo characters (i.e., temporarily taking control of their words and actions). By doing so, Mr. Bungle was able to perpetrate acts of fictive sexual assault against the VR denizens of LambdaMoo. No one involved was under the illusion that actual rape had taken place, but it did seem to a number of participants that this attack had been more than theater—they held that in some sense it had been a kind of attack against their cyborg bodies.

The Mr. Bungle case is interesting in that it not only illustrates the sense of embodiment that certain persons can have in cyberspace, but also shows how the self is intertwined with community in c-space. For the members of LambdaMoo, the Bungle incident represented a kind of crisis in their virtual community—one that helped to galvanize it.

MUDs and MOOs are not the only sorts of locations that might give rise to VR communities. In the second reading by Reid ("Communication and Community on IRC") we find a description of the kinds of communities that emerge on Internet Relay Chat, and in the reading by Rheingold there is a description of the WELL BBS, Rheingold's home in cyberspace. While authors such as Rheingold at times can border on the utopian in their descriptions of their virtual homes, there are plenty of individuals who are less positive in their assessments of virtual communities. The reading (i.e., rant) from humdog is one such antiutopian statement. In it, humdog, once a highly visible member of the WELL, explains why she left that community. Finally, the essay by DiGiovanna suggests that other utopian myths about cyberspace communities must also fall—in particular the myth that c-space is a place, like the old American west, where we can all be individuals and where our voices can be heard. Contrary to these myths, DiGiovanna argues, in cyberspace you quickly fade into the background. Even the words that you leave there, if not ignored completely, will quickly mutate into some new form, expressing new thoughts quite different from what you originally intended to say. Indeed, rather than carving out some identity for yourself, you are much more likely to be erased.

26

Gender Swapping on the Internet

Amy S. Bruckman[1]

I Gender Swapping on the Internet

On the television show *Saturday Night Live,* a series of skits concerned a character named Pat, who has no apparent gender. The audience is tempted with the promise of clues. In one episode, Pat gets his or her hair cut. A sign in the salon says that men's haircuts are $7, and women's haircuts are $9. The audience waits in suspense: when Pat goes to pay, his or her true gender will be revealed. The humor of the series lies in the fact that those hopes are constantly foiled; in this instance, Pat leaves $10 and says to keep the change.

Gender is so fundamental to human interactions, that the idea of a person without gender is absurd. The audience thinks that surely some clue must reveal Pat's gender, but none ever does. Many who have never seen *Saturday Night Live* know about Pat.[2] The character has become a kind of cultural icon. Pat's popularity is revealing.

On many MUDs, it is possible to create gender neutral characters. It is possible not only to meet Pat, but also to be Pat. When I[3] first met an ungendered character, I felt a profound sense of unease. How should I relate to this person? Most unsettling was my unease about my unease: why should this matter? I am having a casual conversation with a random stranger; why should I feel a need to know his or her gender?

The experience highlights two things: the ways in which gender structures human interactions, and, more importantly, the ways in which MUDs help people to understand these phenomena by experiencing them. This paper briefly introduces the technology called MUDs, and then analyzes a community discussion about the role of gender in human social interaction which was inspired by the participants' experiences in MUDs. Gender swapping is one example of how the Internet has the potential to change not just work practice but also culture and values.

II What Are MUDs?

A MUD is a text-based multi-user virtual-reality environment. As of April 16th, 1993, there were 276 publicly announced MUDs based on twenty different kinds of software on the Internet. I will use the term "MUD," which stands for "Multi-User Dungeon," to refer to all the various kinds.[4] The original MUDs were adventure games; however, the technology has been adapted to a variety of purposes.

When a person first logs onto a MUD, he or she creates a character. The person selects the character's name and gender, and writes a description of what the character looks like. It is possible for a character to be male or female, regardless of the gender of the player. In many MUDs, a character can also be neuter or even plural. A plural character could, for example, be called swarm_of_bees or Laurel&Hardy.

MUDs are organized around the metaphor of physical space. You can "talk" to anyone in the same virtual room. When you connect to a MUD at the Media Lab called MediaMOO,[5] you see the description:

>connect guest

Okay, . . . guest is in use. Logging you in as "Green_Guest"

*** Connected ***

The LEGO Closet

It's dark in here, and there are little crunchy plastic things under your feet! Groping around, you discover what feels like a doorknob on one wall.
Obvious exits: out to The E&L Garden

MediaMOO is a virtual representation of the MIT Media Lab. Typing "out" gets you to the "E&L Garden," a central work area for the lab's Epistemology and Learning research group:

>out

The E&L Garden

The E&L Garden is a happy jumble of little and big computers, papers, coffee cups, and stray pieces of LEGO.

Obvious exits: hallway to E&L Hallway, closet to The LEGO Closet, and sts to STS Centre Lounge

You see a newspaper, a Warhol print, a Sun SPARCstation IPC, Projects Chalkboard, and Research Directory here. Amy is here.

>say hi

You say, "hi"
Amy says, "Hi Green_Guest! Welcome!"

The earliest MUDs such as "MUD1" and "Scepter of Goth" were based on the role-playing game Dungeons and Dragons, and were written in late 1978 to 1979.[6] They were also based on early single-user text adventure games, such as the original ADVENT by Crowther and Woods [7]. In adventure-based MUDs, the object is to kill monsters and obtain treasure in order to gain "experience points." As a character gains experience, he/she/it becomes more powerful.

In 1989, a graduate student at Carnegie Mellon University named James Aspnes decided to see what would happen if the monsters and magic swords were removed. He created a new type of MUD, called "TinyMUD," which was not an adventure game. Instead of spending time killing virtual monsters, participants work together to help extend the virtual world using a simple programming language. Langdon Winner remarks that "social activity is an ongoing process of world-making" [9]. In MUDs, this is true in a literal sense.

In most MUDs, characters are anonymous. People who become friends can exchange real names and email addresses, but many choose not to. Conventions about when it is acceptable to talk about "real life" vary between communities. In most MUDs, people begin to talk more about real life when they get to know someone better. However, in some communities such as those based on the Dragonriders of Pern series of books by Anne McCaffrey, talking about real life is taboo.

MUDs are increasingly being used for more "serious" purposes. Pavel Curtis of Xerox PARC has developed a MUD to enhance professional community amongst astrophysicists called AstroVR [4]. The MediaMOO project, which I began in fall of 1992, is designed to enhance professional community amongst media researchers [2]. MediaMOO currently has over 500 participants from fourteen countries and is growing rapidly.

MUDs also have an intriguing potential as an educational environment. Since 1990, Barry Kort has been running a MUD for children called MicroMUSE.[7] I am currently in the process of designing a MUD language and interface to make the technology more usable by children as part of my dissertation research. I hope to use this technology to encourage ten to twelve year-old girls to be more interested in computers.

III A Public Debate about Gender

Gender pervades human interactions in such basic ways that its impact is often difficult to observe. Phenomena that are subtle in real life become obvious in MUDs, and are a frequent topic of discussion on USENET newsgroups about MUDs. For example, men are often surprised at how they are treated when they log on as a female character. Andrew writes on the newsgroup rec.games.mud:[8]

"Back when I had time for MUD, I, too, played female characters. I found it extraordinarily interesting. It gave me a slightly more concrete understanding of why some women say, 'Men suck.' It was both amusing and disturbing."

Female characters are often besieged with attention. By using the who command, it is possible to get a list of all characters logged on. The page command allows one to talk to people not in the same room. Many male players will get a list of all present, and then page characters with female names. Unwanted attention and sexual advances create an uncomfortable atmosphere for women in MUDs, just as they do in real life.

Many people, both male and female, enjoy the attention paid to female characters. Male players will often log on as female characters and behave suggestively, further encouraging sexual advances. Pavel Curtis has noted that the most promiscuous and sexually aggressive women are usually played by men. If you meet a character named "FabulousHot-Babe," she is almost certainly a he in real life [3].

Perhaps more damaging than unwanted sexual advances are unrequested offers of assistance. Carol, an experienced programmer who runs a MUD in Britain, writes on rec.games.mud:

> What I *do* think is funny is this misconception that women can't play muds, can't work out puzzles, can't even type "kill monster" without help. (Okay, I admit we have it on this side of the Atlantic too . . .) Thanks, guys. . . . I log on, they work out I am female, and then the fun begins. Oh joy! After all, I don't log on to see whether people have found bugs with my little area, or to dispense arbitrary justice ("Please, Miss, he stole my sword!") or to find a friend. I call Aber-o-rama[9] (for this is the place) expressly to meet little spods who think (I assume) that because I am female I need help. People offering me help to solve puzzles *I* wrote are not going to get very far.
>
> Do you think all women in real life too are the same? We don't squeak and look helpless *all* the time (in my case, only when I am tired and can't be bothered to wire the plug, change a fuse or remove the centipede from the bath [I really should move house . . .]).

The constant assumption that women need help can be damaging to a woman's sense of self esteem and competence. If people treat you like an incompetent, you may begin to believe it. Carol here is honest and astute enough to admit that women as well as men help create this problem—sometimes she acts helpless when she's simply "tired and can't be bothered" to complete an uninteresting or unpleasant task.

In the same netnews discussion, Dennis concurs with Carol:

> I played a couple of MUDS as a female, one making up to wizard level. And the first thing I noticed was that the above was true. Other players start showering you with money to help you get started, and I had never once gotten a handout when playing a male player. And then they feel they should be allowed to tag along forever, and feel hurt when you leave them to go off and explore by yourself. Then when you give them the knee after they grope you, they wonder what your problem is, reciting that famous saying "What's your problem? It's only a game." Lest you get the wrong idea, there was nothing suggesting about my character, merely a female name and the appropriate pronouns in the bland description. Did I mention the friendly wizard who turned cold when he discovered I was male in real life? I guess some people are jerks in real life too.

Male characters often expect sexual favors in return for technical assistance. A male character once requested a kiss from me after answering a question. A gift always incurs an obligation. Offering technical help, like picking up the check at dinner, can be used to try to purchase rather than win a woman's favor. While this can be subtle and sometimes overlooked in real life, in MUDs it is blatant, directly experienced by most, and openly discussed in public forums such as this USENET discussion.

Ellen provides an interesting counter point:

> This is very odd. I played LPmud[10] once, just to find out what it was like. Since most LP's do something hideous with my preferred capitalization of my preferred name, I chose a different name, and thought, what the heck, I'd try genderbending and find out if it was true that people would be nasty and kill me on sight and other stuff I'd heard about on r.g.m.[11] But, no, everyone was helpful (I was truly clueless and needed the assistance); someone gave me enough money to buy a weapon and armor and someone else showed me where the easy-to-kill newbie[12] monsters were. They definitely went out of their way to be nice to a male-presenting newbie. . . . (These were all male-presenting players, btw.[13])
>
> One theory is that my male character (Argyle, description "A short squat fellow who is looking for his socks") was pretty innocuous. Maybe people are only nasty if you are "A broad-shouldered perfect specimen of a man" or something of that nature, which can be taken as vaguely attacking. People are nice if they don't view you as a threat.

Ellen's point is intriguing, and takes the discussion to a new level of sophistication. In *Group Psychology and Analysis of the Ego,* Sigmund Freud suggests that "love relationships . . . constitute the essence of the group mind" [5]. Issues of sexual power structure interpersonal interactions, and are more complex than "boy chases girl." Argyle's description invites a phallic interpretation—he is short and squat, and the reference to socks carries a connotation of limpness. Since Argyle is clearly not a sexual threat, he receives kinder treatment.

One cannot fail to be impressed by the quality of the netnews discussion. For the participants, MUDding throws issues of the impact of gender on human relations into high relief. Fundamental to its impact is the fact that it allows people to experience rather than merely observe what it feels like to be the opposite gender or have no gender at all.

Without makeup, special clothing, or risk of social stigma, gender becomes malleable in MUDs. When gender becomes a property that can be reset with a line of code, one bit in a data structure, it becomes an "object to think with," to use Seymour Papert's terminology [6]. In public forums like rec.games.mud, people reflect the values that our society attaches to gender. In private experiences, people can explore the impact of gender on their lives and their constructions of themselves.

V Conclusion

Gender is just one example of an aspect of personal identity that people explore on MUDs. Examples abound. Jack is a British student studying in America. He logs onto MUDs in the morning when it is afternoon in Britain and many British players are on. He enjoys confusing them—he tells them he is in America, but displays a detailed knowledge of Britain. On further questioning, Jack tells me he is trying to decide whether to return to Britain or continue his studies in America. What does it mean to be British or American? Jack is exploring his sense of national identity in virtual reality. MUDs are an identity workshop.

Gender swapping is an extreme example of a fundamental fact: the network is in the process of changing not just how we work, but how we think of ourselves—and ultimately, who we are.

Notes

1. Amy Bruckman is with the MIT Media Laboratory. She may be reached at asb@media-lab.media.mit.edu.

2. In fact, I retell this story second hand; the details may not exactly reflect the television show.

3. I have chosen to write in the first person, because many of the ideas in this paper are based on my experiences as a participant-observer, and because notions of identity are part of my topic.

4. On March 6th, 1992 there were 143 MUDs based on 13 kinds of software. This is an increase of 93% in number of MUDs and 54% in number of types of software over slightly more than a year. MUDs are constantly being created and destroyed. A current list is regularly posted to the USENET news group rec.games.mud.announce.

5. To connect to MediaMOO, type "telnet purple-crayon.media.mit.edu 8888" from a UNIX system on the Internet. Send electronic mail to mediamoo-registration@media.mit.edu for more information.

6. The earliest multi-player games existed on stand-alone time-sharing systems. In 1977, Jim Guyton adapted a game called "mazewar" to run on the ARPAnet. Participants in mazewar could duck around corners of a maze and shoot at one another, but could not communicate in any other fashion [email conversation

with Jim Guyton, March 1992]. Numerous multi-user games based on the Dungeons and Dragons role playing game appeared in 1978-1979 including Scepter of Goth by Alan Klietz and MUD1 by Roy Trubshaw and Richard Bartle [email conversation with Alan Klietz, March 1992].

7. MicroMUSE is at chezmoto.ai.mit.edu 4201.

8. This is an excerpt from a USENET discussion about MUDs. Communications technologies have complex interactions. Since most MUDders have read USENET groups about MUDding for at least some period of time, the culture of USENET and of MUDs are in some ways linked. Social conventions evolve in the context of the complete set of technologies in use, including email, netnews, surface mail, telephones, answering machines, voice mail, television, radio, newspapers, magazines, books, and the like. Email, netnews, and MUDs have especially complex interactions.

9. The name of the MUD has been changed.

10. LPMUDs are a type of adventure-game-style MUD.

11. The abbreviation "r.g.m" stands for "rec.games.mud," the USENET newsgroup on which this discussion is taking place.

12. A newbie is a new player with little experience. According to Raymond [7], the term comes from British slang for "new boy," and first became popular on the Net in the group talk.bizarre. A newbie monster is a monster that a low-level player could defeat.

13. This is an abbreviation for "by the way."

References

[1]. A. Bruckman. "Identity Workshop: Emergent Social and Psychological Phenomena in Text-based Virtual Reality." Unpublished manuscript, 1992. Available via anonymous ftp from media.mit.edu in pub/asb/papers/identity-workshop.ps.Z, rtf.Z}.

[2]. A. Bruckman and M. Resnick. "Virtual Professional Community: Results from the MediaMOO Project." Presented at the Third International Conference on Cyberspace in Austin, Texas on May 15th, 1993. Available via anonymous ftp from media.mit.edu in pub/asb/papers/MediaMOO-3cyberconf. ps.Z, rtf.Z, txt}.

[3]. P. Curtis. "MUDding: Social Phenomena in Text-based Virtual Realities." Proceedings of DIAC '92. Available via anonymous ftp from parcftp.xerox.com, pub/MOO/papers/DIAC92.ps, txt}. [Chapter 28 in this book.]

[4]. P. Curtis and D. Nichols. "MUDs Grow Up: Social Virtual Reality in the Real World." Presented at the Third International Conference on Cyberspace in Austin, Texas on May 15th, 1993. Available via anonymous ftp from parcftp.xerox.com in pub/MOO/papers/MUDsGrowUp.ps, txt}.

[5]. S. Freud. *Group Psychology and Analysis of the Ego*. New York: W. W. Norton & Company, 1989.

[6]. S. Papert. *Mindstorms: Children, Computers, and Powerful Ideas*. New York: Basic Books, 1980.

[7]. E. Raymond. *The New Hackers Dictionary*. Cambridge, MA: MIT Press, 1991.

[8]. S. Turkle. *The Second Self: Computers and the Human Spirit*. New York: Simon & Schuster, 1984.

[9]. L. Winner. *The Whale and the Reactor*. Chicago: University of Chicago Press, 1986.

Acknowledgments

I'd like to thank MIT Professors Sherry Turkle, Mitchel Resnick, and Glorianna Davenport for their support of this research. Warren Sack and Lenny Foner read drafts of this paper. Most importantly, I'd like to thank the MUDders who have shared their experiences with me.

27

Text-based Virtual Realities: Identity and the Cyborg Body

Elizabeth M. Reid

MUD systems, with all the factors of anonymity, distance and flexibility brought into play, allow people to say what they want. That freedom is not always exercised to the approval of other players, and social systems which maintain cohesion amongst members of a MUD community have arisen. But the nature of what people do on MUDs does not provide a complete explanation of such systems—the nature of the people is just as important. A player of a MUD system is not a transparent medium, providing nothing but a link between external and internal cultural patterns, between actual and virtual realities. The player is the most problematic of all virtual entities, for his or her virtual manifestation has no constant identity. MUD characters need not be of any fixed gender or appearance, but may evolve, mutate, morph, over time and at the whim of their creator. All of these phenomena place gender, sexuality, identity and corporeality beyond the plane of certainty. They become not merely problematic but unresolvable. If anonymity on MUDs allows people to do and say whatever they wish, it also allows them to be whatever they wish. It is not only the MUD environment that is a virtual variable—the virtual manifestation of each player is similarly alterable, open to change and re-interpretation. The player does not constitute a fixed reference point in the MUD universe. Players do not enter into the system and remain unchanged by it. Players do not, in essence, "enter" the virtual landscape—they are manifested within it by their own imaginative effort.

In everyday life, our efforts at self-presentation usually assume that we cannot change the basics of our appearance. Physical characteristics, although open to cosmetic or fashionable manipulation, are basically unalterable. What we look like, we have to live with, and this fixity underpins our social institutions. Social structures based on bias toward or prejudice against differing portions of humanity depend on the ease with which we can assess each other's bodies, and ascribe identities to physical form. Male, female, white, black, young, old, poor and affluent are all terms that resonate through our culture, and each depends in part on the fixity of physical form, and our ability to affix meaning to that form. These kinds of assumptions go beyond the level of non-verbal communication—they make up not the outward form of our culture but the substructure of it. Just as we notice—if such an almost subconscious perception can be called "noticing"—the gender of our interlocutors before we notice their facial expressions, the symbolism of the body underpins and shapes our culture. On MUDs, however, the body is not an immutable property. How one MUD player "looks" to another player is entirely dependent upon information that they choose to give. The boundaries delineated by cultural constructions of the body are both subverted and given free rein in virtual environments. With the body freed from the physical, it completely enters the realm of symbol. It becomes an entity of pure meaning, but is simultaneously meaningless, stripped of any fixed referent.

The MUD system does not dictate to players the form of their virtual persona. The process of character creation is at all times in the hands, or imaginations, of the player, although different systems may make the process less or more complex.[1] Players may manifest themselves in any way they please, unbounded by the physical measures that limit our self-presentation in actual life. MUD characters are much more than a few bytes of computer data—they are cyborgs, a manifestation of the self beyond the realms of the physical, existing in a space where identity is self-defined rather than pre-ordained. The consequences of this for the sub-cultures that form on MUDs are enormous. They begin with a challenge to the ties between body and self, and lead to subversions of the categories of gender and sexuality which are so dominant in the actual world.

Self-Made People

MUD players create their own virtual personas, their own characters. They create, initially, a name. Their first contact with the MUD program is to direct it to create a database entry which will serve as their window into the virtual universe, the informational node to which they will connect in order to experience the virtual reality contained in a MUD system. Players rarely choose to give their real name to their virtual persona. Most choose to manifest themselves under a name that forms the central focus of what becomes a virtual disguise. These names can be almost anything that the player chooses to make them. They can be conventional names such as Chris, Jane or Smith. In many cases, the names have clearly been borrowed from characters from books, films or television shows—Gandalf, AgentCooper and PrincessLeia. Other names, such as Love, funky, Moonlight and blip, reflect ideas, symbols and emotions, while many more, such as FurryMUCK's felinoid Veronicat and LambdaMOO's yudJ, involve plays upon language and conventional naming systems.[2] The name a player chooses is the beginning point of his or her virtual self. On top of that name, the player builds a virtual body, endowing the new-born and newly-christened database entry with characteristics that mimic actuality. Players attach textual descriptions to those entries, clothing and defining the would-be physical form of their character, giving them possessions, and attaching to them symbols of those aspects of identity to which we give great importance in actual life—characters are gendered, sexed, identified.

The subversion of the body begins in small ways on MUDs. At the least end of the virtual surgery that players may perform upon themselves lies the cosmetic. It is possible to by-pass the boundaries delineated by cultural constructs of beauty, ugliness and fashion. Players can appear to be as they would wish. Such changes that a player might make to his or her perceived identity can be small, a matter of realising in others' minds a desire to be attractive, impressive and popular:

Lirra is a short young woman with long blonde hair, an impish grin and a curvaceous figure. Her clear blue eyes sparkle as she looks back at you. She is wearing a short red skirt, a white t-shirt, black fishnet stockings, and black leather boots and jacket.

Lirra whispers, "my desc is pretty real, but I'm a bit plumper than that" to you.

Lirra whispers, "and maybe i don't always wear such sexy clothes ;)" to you.[3]

Such manifestations remain within the realm of the bodily constructs with which we are familiar in actual life. They may enable the player to side-step the normal requirements of entry into glamour, but they do not subvert the concept. Rather, such descriptions call upon our pre-conceived notions about the human appearance to sustain their power. They do not free players from the shackles of the beauty myth, but they allow them to redefine themselves in accordance with that myth.

Beyond the bounds of beauty, other players shape their virtual selves to emulate the signs of influence and affluence which we pay heed to in our actual lives. Such characters are usually beautiful, but their beauty is at most a setting, the background for social status rather than the reason for it:

Darklighter
A lean Man standing a metre 73, weighing about 70 kilos. His hair is golden brown with hints of red that frames his angelic face. Deep set are two emerald eyes that peer back at you. His vestiage is all in black with a cloak concealing him. You see on his right hand an emerald colored ring of peculiar origin. You realize that it is that of a Green Lantern. You can tell he is the sort of man who can see the strings that bind the universe together and mend them when they break.[4]

At the core of such characters is their possession of influential and even superhuman attributes. Curtis describes this phenomenon in player description as simply being a case of wish-fulfilment—"I cannot count," he says, "the number of "mysterious but unmistakably powerful" figures I have seen wandering LambdaMOO."[5] In many cases this may be true—certainly the majority of people in everyday life are neither as extraordinary nor as powerful as many MUD characters present themselves to be. However, it must be remembered that their personal description is the only method open to players to substitute for what, in everyday life, would be a complex mixture of non-verbal social context cues such as accent, dress and race. If many descriptions show exaggerated, even fantastical, attempts to indicate social acceptability, it is at least in part a reflection of the degree to which players feel it necessary to compensate for the lack of non-textual communication channels. Without reference to the senses on which we normally rely to provide information, such socio-emotional cues must be made explicit in textual descriptions. The social information usually spread out over several different sensual channels is concentrated into one channel and therefore exaggerated.

Whatever the reasons for such cases of virtual cosmetic surgery, be they dramaturgical or egoistical, their effect upon the MUD universe is to free it from conventions of power that rely on physical manifestation. When everyone can be beautiful, there can be no hierarchy of beauty. This freedom, however, is not necessarily one that undermines the power of such conventions. Indeed, such freedom to be beautiful tends to support these conventions by making beauty not unimportant but a prerequisite. The convention becomes conventional—MUD worlds are free from the stigma of ugliness not because appearance ceases to matter but because no one need be seen to be ugly. The cosmetic nature of virtual worlds is, however, the least of their ability to operate upon our physically-centred prejudices. In the realms of gender and sexuality, MUD systems go beyond the escapist and become creative.

Ungrounding Gender

Of the cultural factors that are most important in encounters in Western society—typified by the big three of gender, race and class—all may be "hard-coded" into MUD programs. Race and class are generally the least problematised of these three, and their representations offer a link between the cosmetic and the radical ends of cultural surgery. Race and class on MUDs are generally the concern of systems that are adventure-oriented, and the choices available are likely to be within the realms of fantasy. Choices of race are more likely to be between Dwarvish, Elvish and Klingon than between Asian, Black and Caucasian; choices of class are more likely to be between Warrior, Magician and Thief than between white or blue-collar. This essential racial and class blindness is very likely the effect of the pre-selection criteria which the actual world places on those who would have access to the Internet. MUD players are necessarily people who have access to the Internet computer network. They are most likely to live in the industrialised and largely English-speaking countries that form the greater part of the Internet. They are also most likely to be either employed by an organisation with an interest in computing, or be attending an educational institution. People who fit these requirements are overwhelmingly likely to be affluent and white.[6] Uniformity decreases visibility, and thus for a large percentage of players, race and class are taken as a given and so seem to be invisible.

Gender, however, is brought very much to the fore on MUDs. All MUDs allow—and some insist—that players set their "gender flag," a technical property of MUD characters that controls which set of pronouns are used by the MUD program in referring to the character. Most MUDs allow only three choices—male, female and neuter—which decide between the families of pronouns containing him, her or it. A few MUDs demand that a player select either male or female as their gender, and do not allow a player with an unset gender flag to enter the MUD. Other MUDs allow many genders—male, female, plural, neuter, hermaphrodite, and several unearthly genders lifted from the pages of science fiction novels. It is obviously easy for players to choose to play a character with a gender different from their own. At least, it is technically easy, but not necessarily socially easy since there is a lively controversy surrounding the issue of cross-gendered playing. The subject is one that regularly recurs on the Usenet newsgroups relating to MUDs. Indeed, the times when the topic is not being debated are far outnumbered by the times when it is—it is a subject that evokes strong feelings from a very large number of MUD players.

Almost without exception such debates begin with the instance, either actual or hypothetical, of a male player controlling a female character. It is very rare for the reverse situation, that of a woman playing a man, to be brought up, at least in the first instance. This one-sidedness runs in parallel to a common claim that male-to-female cross-gendering is far more common than the reverse, a claim that rests in part on the notion, common lore amongst MUD players, that most of their number are in fact male. This may well be so. The cultural pre-selection process which ensures that most MUD players are white and affluent is also in operation in defining the sex of the average player. Although the gap is slowly closing, most people employed as computer programmers and computer engineers are male, and most of the students likely to have access to the Internet (those studying Computer Science, or Software Engineering) are also male. It is therefore quite likely that the folklore on the subject is correct, and that the majority of MUD players are male.[7] Since female and male presenting characters are about equally common, it follows that some of those female characters are controlled by male players.

Whether or not most players are male, the one-sidedness in the cross-gender debate is strongly related to players' perception of women as being the minority of their number, and to notions of gender-specific behaviour found in the external culture. Female-presenting players are treated very differently to male-presenting players. They are often subjected to virtual forms of those two hoary sides of a male-dominated society—harassment and chivalry. The latter can give female characters an advantage in the game world. Players newly connecting to a MUD system will inevitably require help in navigating the virtual terrain, and in learning the commands particular to that system. Players who present themselves as female are more likely than their male counterparts to find help easily, or to be offered it spontaneously. On adventure-oriented systems, in which the goodwill of other players can mean the life or death of a character, female-presenting characters are likely to be offered help in the form of money and other objects helpful for survival. This special treatment is not always, however, meted out in a spirit of pure altruism. Players offering help, expensive swords and amulets of protection generally want something in return. At the least, they might expect to be offered friendship; sometimes they may expect less platonic favours to be showered upon them.

Sex is, of course, at the root of this special treatment. As well as being white and male, the average MUD player might be likely to be young, since the Internet primarily serves educational institutions and thus students who are generally in their late teens or early twenties.[8] Such young people might well be expected to engage in romantic and sexual exploration, and the anonymous virtual environment allows this kind of exploration a safety that could only make it all the more attractive a site for it. It is hardly unusual for young people to utilise social situations to form relationships with members of the appropriate sex; since MUD systems provide a social environment it is not surprising that they are sometimes used in such ways, and successful liaisons can be intensely felt and emotionally fulfilling. Romantic attentions are not, however, always welcome or appropriate. In cases where they are not, the attention paid to female-presenting characters can fall into the realms of sexual harassment. As I have described, aggression can as easily be played out on MUDs as can affection. The sexual harassment of female characters is not uncommon, and is often closely tied to what may begin as a chivalrous offer of help, as this adventure MUD player describes:

> I played a couple of muds as a female, one making up to wizard level. Other players start showering you with money to help you get started, and I had never once gotten a handout when playing a male player. And then they feel they should be allowed to tag along forever, and feel hurt when you leave them to go off and explore by yourself. Then when you give them the knee after they grope you, they wonder what your problem is, reciting that famous saying "What's your problem? It's only a game."[9]

For others the cry of "it's only a game" is itself justification for permitting cross-gendered playing: "I just paged through about 15 articles on this cross-gender topic. GEEZ guys get a life. Who cares if someone plays a female or male character and who cares what sex they are in real life! This is a game, and if someone enjoys playing the opposite sex, so what."[10]

However, and despite claims such as this one, for most players gender is of great moment, far more so than the imagined race or profession of the player. The simple fact is that no player presenting him or herself as a Dwarvish warrior-image is likely to be one in actual life, but a female or male-presenting character could be controlled by a player of that sex. There is no cause for branding role-playing a Dwarf as deception when a reasonable person could not truly be deceived; it is only where virtual existence holds close parallels to actual life that the possibility and accusations of deception enter the equation. The ethics of this kind of "deception" are subject to debate amongst MUD players. Opinion is sharply divided. Some players feel that cross-gendering, particularly in the case of male players controlling female characters, is a despicable and even perverted practice:

> Well, I think it *is* sick for guys to play female characters. Most only do it to fool some poor guy into thinking he's found the lady of his dreams, and then turn around and say "Ha! Ha! I'm really male!" Real mature. I think if you get off on pretending to be female you should go and dress up and go to some club in San Fran where they like perverts—just don't go around deceiving people on muds.[11]

There are three issues which those who oppose cross-gendering are concerned about. Firstly, they feel that it is "cheating" for a male player to take advantage of the favouritism and chivalry that is commonly showered upon female-presenting players in order to get special privileges in the game. Secondly, many feel that such impersonations are, by virtue of being "lies," unethical. Lastly, many players obviously feel very uncomfortable and at a disadvantage in interacting with others whose gender is unclear, and feel even more discomforted on discovering that they have been interacting under false assumptions.

For some, this is where cyberspace ceases to be a comfortable place. We are so used to being provided with information about each other's sex that the lack of it can leave many players feeling set adrift. Gender roles are so ingrained in our culture that for many people they are a necessity, and acting without reference to them seems impossible. Many people are simply unable to negotiate social encounters without needing to fix, at least in assumption, the genders of their interlocutors. It is indeed a truly disorienting experience the first time one finds oneself being treated as a member of the opposite sex. My own forays into the realm of virtual masculinity were at first frightening experiences. Much as some of us may deplore what we see as the negative sides of our culture's sexual politics, we are brought up to align ourselves with gender-specific social navigation mechanisms. Once deprived of the social tools which I, as female, was used to deploying and relying on, I felt rudderless, unable to negotiate the most simple of social interactions. I did not know how to speak, whether to women or to "other" men, and I was thrown off balance by the ways in which other people spoke to me. It took much practice to learn to navigate these unfamiliar channels, an experience that gave me a greater understanding of the mechanics of sexual politics than any other I have ever had.

For some players it is precisely this chance to swim unfamiliar seas that attracts them to cross-gendered playing. If it had not been for my intellectual interest I would probably not have persevered with my attempts as male self-presentation since it was often stressful and bewildering. Others, perhaps more adventurous and less self-conscious than I, claim this as the most rewarding aspect of virtual existence. The chance to see how the other half lives is enjoyed by many as liberating and enlightening, as is the opportunity to take a holiday from the confines of one's actual gender. The demands of masculinity, or femininity, can be daunting to those not brought up to them, and even those who are can appreciate the chance to side-step them:

Melina says, "What I really liked about having a female character was that I didn't have to do all the masculine bullshit—all the penis-waving." Melina giggles. "Penis-waving . . . I love that phrase . . ."

Melina says, "I could just chat with people! It was great! No having to compete, no *pressures,* no feeling like I'd be made fun of for talking about my feelings."[12]

The ability to adopt and adapt to the erosion of gender requires a great deal of cultural and psychological flexibility. At its best it might help those who can play this game to understand the problems experienced by actual members of the opposite sex. Men who have experienced first hand the kinds of sexual harassment that for women have often been, as Gloria Steinem described it on a televised interview, "just part of life," may be less likely to perpetuate the social structures that enable such harassment. At the same time, such virtual fluidity acts to erode the places from which many of us speak. What, for instance, will it mean for feminist politics that in cyberspace men can not only claim to speak for women, but can speak *as* women, with no one able to tell the difference? The subversion of gender is not always a happy or enlightening experience. The problematising of identity, and of the speaking positions which are so crucial to our politics aside, many cross-gendered players experience the opposite of liberation—they are caught in a backlash against it:

There are also those who think it is an abomination to be playing a character of a different gender . . . and if it becomes known that a female character is actually being played by a guy, some of these guys will hunt down and kill the female character repeatedly for the "crime" of being a genderbender.[13]

The tools utilised by MUD players to enforce and maintain social structures and social coherence can be used to support any number of different ethical and moral systems. If methods of enforcing such systems can be called into effect in an effort to shore up the virtual holes in players' perceptions of traditional gender roles, they can also be used to enforce a different kind of "political correctness":

I am female. I choose to play female chars on muds. And people do harass you. Its not just casual convo or compliment. I stopped playing muds where playerkilling is not legal. People tend to value their characters. If they really start harassing you, you, or some other high level, killing them a few times tends to stop it short. On the muds i play im happy to kill people for harassment [. . .] But i went on a few no pk muds recently and it was constant harassment. I was getting tells like "How big are your tits" or "You want to mudfuck" which is really annoying. So to the females who have problems, head to the player killing muds where you can avenge yourself.[14]

The structure of MUD programs destroys the usually all but insurmountable confines of sex. Gender is self-selected. This freedom opens up a wealth of possibilities, for gender is one of the more "sacred" institutions in our society, a quality whose fixity is so assumed that enacted or surgical reassignment has and does involve complex rituals, taboos, procedures and stigmas. This fixity, and the common equation of gender with sex, becomes problematic when gender reassignment can be effected by a few touches at a keyboard. MUDs become the arena for experimentation with gender specific social roles, and debate over the ethics of such experimentation. The flexibility of self-presentation provided by MUDs makes it possible for players to experiment with aspects of behaviour and identity that it would not normally be possible to play with. Players are able to create a virtual self outside the normally assumed boundaries of gender, race, class and age. The possibility of such experimentation governs the expectations of all players of MUDs. Some find the lack of fixity intimidating; others show a willingness to accept this phenomenon, and to join in the games that can be played within it. Whether an individual player enjoys the situations that come of this potential, or is resentful and wary of them, exploitation of it is an accepted part of the MUD environment. Most players seem to be aware, and some have learnt through bitter experience, that not all characters reflect the identity of the player. MUDs challenge and obscure the boundaries between some of our most deeply felt cultural significances, and force the creation of new cultural expectations to accommodate this.

MUDs both erode gender and bring it to the fore. In the instant that a player assigns a sex to his or her character, that split has been recognised. The need for conscious assignment makes gender meaningless as a reference point in some claimed reality, but it also marks it as a vital cultural referent. On MUDs sex and gender are subverted by the whims of imagination. The attributes and social options society allocates each gender offer both negative and positive experiences. The chance to experience life on the other side of what is usually an all but insurmountable divide can make the MUD world into a stage for inventive and subversive cultural games. At their most liberal, systems where this playful subversion is an accepted by-product of virtual existence can be dynamic and challenging places.

Nevertheless, as Stone has also noted, the gender-specific roles that our culture prescribes have not been changed by this virtual freedom from the shackles of gender, but the rules delineating who may use which social mode have been clouded. The appropriation of the other is an accepted, though not always liked, feature of the virtual terrain. The virtual colonisation of the body of the other in the often culturally uncharted waters of the cyberspatial frontier, to offer a mix of landscapes and similes only possible in virtual reality, is commonplace. Gender is divorced from the body, and given a purely social significance. The man who can behave as a woman, and the woman who can behave as a man, are virtually accepted as legitimately owning such presented identities. The cyborg entity, to paraphrase Sylvia Plath, walks wary through the virtual landscape, sceptical of the "real world" significance of what is culturally signposted, yet politic, amenable to the games played within that space. The gendered subject is separated from the sexed body, if not finally divorced from it. MUDs do not grant a *decree nisi* to the gender roles that permeate our social existence, but they do offer equal opportunity casting.

Cyborg Sexuality

Stone tells us that, in describing the act of computer-mediated communication, people she had interviewed would "move their hands expressively as though typing, emphasising the gestural quality and essential tactility of the virtual mode."[15] Communication through the fingertips rather than through sound, a necessarily tactile connection, a social touch, albeit one distanced by computer cable, is the breed of sociality expressed on MUDs. The pose command and the feelings commands are the most richly used of all those communicative tools available on MUD systems. This obsession with the physical in a non-physical environment is hardly contradictory—a consensual hallucination is, after all, in part a sensual hallucination. Spanning the senses as well as the imaginations of the participants, MUDs are as grimily sensual as their name suggests, and can be a stage for sexual expression.

FurryMUCK is one of the most popular social MUDs on the Internet, and one that has a reputation for being rampant with sexual activity. I cannot say whether this is deserved or not—MUDsex seems to happen on all systems, and it is impossible for me to say whether it is more or less common on FurryMUCK. However, questions of social and sexual identity, and of the unfixed and unfixable nature of the cyborg body, are prominent on FurryMUCK. The very theme of the MUD draws these questions to the fore, for every character on Furry is inhuman, and most are anthropomorphised animals clad only in virtual fur. Cats and bears are legion, most of them sleek-furred and svelte or broad and brawny. The nature and culture of the body is the primary theme of FurryMUCK, and the ideal is animalistic allure. Sexuality is a vital aspect of this kind of cyborg body, and most character descriptions reflect this. There are few "mysterious but powerful" image-warriors on FurryMUCK, but many flashes of velvet-pelted thighs, glints of slitted pupils and touches of sharp-taloned paws.

"Touches" is indeed the operative word. FurryMUCK is by far the most "physical" of the MUDs I have encountered. There is much back-scratching, fur-patting, hugging and kissing between Furries, that being the name by which they are both called and self-identified. This virtual touching is rarely overtly sexual when performed in the more public areas of the FurryMUCK world. It is always affectionate, and indeed FurryMUCK is one of the most friendly MUDs I have used. Nevertheless, beneath the affectionate snugging and purring is a strong undercurrent of revelry in the decidedly beautiful and sensual nature of Furry bodies. If one looks for them, areas where semi-public sexual play is common are not hard to find. The FurryMUCK hot-tubs are both popular and well sign-posted with warnings about the nature of the behaviour both allowed and to be expected inside them. The Truth or Dare games played in their own specially designed and, again, sign-posted, areas are a deliberate invitation for sexual expression. Just as the games of Truth or Dare played by actual humans, as many adolescent memories will attest, nearly always concern themselves with questions about desires and dares to act on them, so do the games played by Furries.

The mechanics of sexual activity on MUDs are very simple. It is a form of co-authored interactive erotica. The players involved in a particular virtual sexual act type out their actions and utterances:

Arista continues to nip little kisses back down your neck.

Pete mmmms, his hands stroking a little at your sides.

Arista presses her body to yours, rubbing herself like a cat over you.

Pete groans softly, laying back on the long seat, writhing softly under you.

Arista moves her mouth down over your chest slowly.

Arista plants open mouth kisses over your left nipple as she flicks her tongue over it gently.

Pete's body arches up towards your mouth, softly.[16]

From all accounts MUDsex can be a lot of fun for the participants, and many a crude reference has been made in the MUD-related newsgroups as to the manner in which it improves a player's ability to type one-handed. Beyond its mechanics MUDsex—or tinysex as it is often called, in erroneous implication that most of it occurs on social-style MUDs—is not at all simple. MUDsex falls into a realm between the actual and the virtual. Players can become emotionally involved in the virtual actions of their characters, and the line between virtual actions and actual desires can become blurred.

Virtual sex is the least and the most expressive of virtual interactions. In its descriptions of purely would-be physical interaction, it is the least overtly cultural of interactions. It draws most heavily on external cultural factors in its dramaturgical nature, and it is without doubt among the most dramatically affective of virtual happenings. Real desire and arousal are evoked between participants, a reaction hugely dependant upon each person's external cultural experience. As Stone describes the relationship between phone sex workers and clients, the speaker—or typist—textually codes for gesture, appearance, or proclivity, and expresses these as tokens, sometimes in no more than a smiley, and the listener, or reader, uncompresses the tokens and constructs a dense, complex interactive image.[17] In these interactions, Stone continues, "desire appears as a product of the interaction between embodied reality and the emptiness of the token."[18] That emptiness is filled with the cultural and personal expectations of the virtual lovers—good cybersex consists of the empathetic understanding of and response to the cultural symbols represented by a partner's symbolic tokens. Such descriptors are loaded with assumptions and meanings; that they can be transmitted along with the text is a tribute not only to the linguistic skill of the interlocutors but to the facility of the virtual medium for such dramatic and intimate play. The human body is represented through narrow bandwidth communication in all its culturally laden fleshiness through the coding of cultural expectations as linguistic tokens of meaning. Desire is no longer grounded in physicality in cyberspace, in triumphant confirmation of the thesis that the most important human erogenous zone is the mind. MUD sex may never replace actual sex, but it does provide some erotic satisfaction to those who participate in it.

"Textuality as striptease" is no longer just a jibe directed by the script writers of the BBC production "Small World" at a particular breed of American postmodern cultural critics.[19] The textual nature of MUDs strips the confines of a particular body from players, and allows them the freedom to play with, in and through any body they desire. Cyborg bodies are not, as Stone claims, "preorgasmic."[20] The "erotic ontology of cyberspace" lies most clearly in its concentration of the erogenous into the imaginative.[21] Cyborg bodies are, in many ways, superior to their actual counterparts. They cannot tire, stumble, or subject their inhabitants to any of the embarrassments or failures that flesh is prone to. Thus cyborg sex is a concentration of the erotic, a purifying of prurient imagination, a romantic idealisation of sexual encounters worthy of the most airbrushed Hollywood art.

The Cyborg Self

Cyborgs are born out of virtual sex. At the moment of virtual orgasm the line between player and character is the most clouded and the most transparent. Who it is that is communicating becomes unclear, and whether passion is being simulated on or transmitted through the MUD becomes truly problematic. Born from primeval MUD, these cyborgs redefine gender, identity and the body. In this part of cyberspace, a place as far divorced from the natural world and the animal, as far from the flesh as human inventiveness can get, the lines between the animal and the conscious are erased.

FurryMUCK seems almost too good for cultural analysis to be true—an imaginary world populated by conscious animals consciously sensualised, all represented by pure linguistic symbolism and represented within the confines of electricity, silicon and magnetism. At the margins of physicality, these Furry cyborgs play with the margins of sexuality. They have none of the boundaries of the actual to confine them. They may take on any physiology that passion and imagined convenience invites. Any configuration of human and animal components may be mixed to create as many sexual possibilities as can be imagined. Bisexual, multisexual, polysexual—they can be all, but always consensual. For the players there is always the off-button; for the cyborg characters, implements of sensual overload are as controlled or as uncontrolled, as gentle or as cruel, as the simulation demands. Perversion is as common on MUDs as in the "real world," but in cyberspace perversion can be perverted into any form. In the dim recesses of Internet cyberspace, there are MUDs, known only by word of mouth—or touch of keyboard—with themes as controversial as that of any specialist brothel. Kinks of any kind can be found if looked for, all bent to the demands of the cyborg entities who portray them for the amusement of the humans shadowed behind their technologies. FurryMUCK is the lightest side of this twisting of cyborg gender and sex—the fluffiest and the snuggliest. Darker cyberspaces can be found, painted not in cartoon colours and textured with fur, but depicted in the dark techno-organicism of H. R. Giger and texted with all the danger and poetry of Pauline Reage.

The cyborgs on MUDs do not, as Donna Haraway suggests in her "Cyborg Manifesto," have "no truck with bisexuality, pre-oedipal symbiosis . . . or other seductions to organic wholeness."[22] Although, in partial confirmation of Haraway's comments, they are literally the illegitimate offspring of militarism and patriarchal capitalism—of the US Department of Defense and the bastions of higher education—MUD cyborgs do not reject the labels of the father culture. There is no escape from labelling for these cyborgs—they are constructed entirely from the most evident of labels. Their commitment to "particularity, irony, intimacy and perversity" is expressed through the flaunting of cultural symbols and the literal inscription upon their virtual bodies of the signs of who they want to be.[23] Transsexual, transvestite, bisexual, superhuman and anthropomorphic—MUD bodies can embrace and be embraced by each of these richly coded definitions.

At the heart of this play with identity is always the question of how dichotomous cyborg and actual identities are. Where are the lines drawn between representation, simulation and actualisation? How far do genuine feelings draw virtual actions into the realm of the actual? These are questions for the legislators and philosophers of our new computerised world, and not questions that will be answered easily, for the one constant of cyberspatial existence is that it is different for everyone. Current political and legal trends, with talk of "hostile environments" and "hate speech," may lead to the notion that biotechnological politics move beyond the regulation of actions upon the body and into actions upon the spirit. The ultimate reduction of the physical—the microelectronic—may become the realm of the disembodied spirit. If criminality, or even immorality, can be discovered in cyberspace it will entail a greater recognition of amorphic harm. The most intimate of MUD interactions already involve that recognition. Negotiation, and behind-the-scenes direction, almost always ride in tandem with expression. In the mechanics of the act, cyborg lovers whisper messages between their players, directing what is acceptable and what is not, defining and creating the virtual experience with determination and consent. The most highly practised inhabitants of MUD spaces make their intentions and desires clear. Flirtation is more highly specified than it is in the pubs and parties of the "real world." Raised eyebrows and tilted cigarettes are replaced by direct requests. This is cyberspatial intimacy at its best.

These cyborgs do not exist in a "post-gender world."[24] They are only quasi-disembodied. They do not attempt to posit their identities as amorphous, but instead revel in the possibilities of body-hopping. Play is not with escape from the claims of the flesh, but with the cultural meanings attached to different bodies. The adoption of masculinity, femininity, androgyny, animality or the more fantastical meanings attributed to fictional races or genders, is as easily accomplished as might be the donning of a new set of clothes. Thus clothed in the borrowed trappings of other's cultural expectations and imaginings, cyborg selves interact in fashions that are based both on superficial appearances and on an acceptance of whatever the individual wants to be. They do not reject gender, or any other signs of identity, but play a game with them, freeing symbols from their organic referents and grafting the meanings of those symbols onto their virtual descriptors.

Notes

1. See appendix 7 in "Cultural Formations in Text-based Virtual Realities," MA thesis, Cultural Studies Program, University of Melbourne, January 1994, for examples of simple and complex character creation systems.

2. These names have been selected from the character lists of the four MUDs which I have concentrated on in this thesis.

3. From a log taken of a session on LambdaMOO on July 10th, 1992. The name of the player concerned has been changed at her request.

4. From a log taken of a session on LambdaMOO on January 17th, 1992.

5. Pavel Curtis, "MUDding: Social Phenomena in Text-Based Virtual Realities," chapter 28 in this volume.

6. Many Asian countries (including Japan, Malaysia, Taiwan, and Thailand) are represented on the Internet. However the different computer platforms needed to transmit and receive Asian and Roman character sets often mean that users from Asian and Western countries are, unless they are able to arrange special access to the appropriate platforms, unlikely to meet on any common virtual ground.

7. In the survey carried out on LambdaMOO, 76.6% of respondents claimed to be male in real life and 23.4% claimed to be female.

8. The results of the LambdaMOO survey indicated that the mean age of players was 23.6, the median age was 21, and the greatest number of players (90) claimed to be 19. 50% of players claimed to be aged between 19 and 23. The youngest age given was 12 and the oldest 54.

9. From: djohnson@elvis.ucsd.edu (Darin Johnson); Newsgroups: rec.games. mud; Subject: Re: MUD practical jokes?; Date: 27 Jan 92 20:27:50 GMT.

10. From: anonymous; Newsgroups: rec.games.mud; Subject: Cross-gender thing!; Date: 4 Mar 92 00:16:30 GMT.

11. From: anonymous; Subject: Re: Gender Issues: "Real World" Warning; Newsgroups: rec.games.mud; Date: 4 Jun 92 08:27:53 GMT.

12. From a log taken of a session on FurryMUCK on June 21st, 1993. The name of the player has been changed at "her" request.

13. From: dst@hardy.u.washington.edu (Trif); Newsgroups: rec.games. mud.admin; Subject: Re: sex roles; Date: 21 Nov 1993 22:59:27 GMT.

14. From: valkyrie@shell.portal.com (Kristen–Taylor); Newsgroups: rec.games. mud.misc; Subject: Re: Muding Girlfriends?; Date: Fri, 10 Dec 1993 03:09:47 GMT.

15. Allucquere Rosanne Stone, "Will the Real Body Please Stand Up? Boundary Stories about Virtual Cultures," in *Cyberspace: First Steps*, ed. Michael Benedikt (Cambridge, Mass.: The MIT Press, 1991), p. 90.

16. From: jadawin@world.std.com; To: emr@ee.mu.oz.au; Subject: 141 lines . . . pick a few; Date: Mon, 3 Jan 94 8:05:03 EST.

17. Stone, 103.

18. Stone, 103.

19. For those who have not seen this hilarious series, it followed the adventures of a naive young Irish poet as he accompanied three seasoned academics on the literary conference circuit. These three academics each gave exactly the same paper at each conference: the American Postmodernist speaking on "Textuality as Striptease," the English Traditionalist speaking on "The Love of Books," and the European Marxist giving a "Criticisme of Capitalisme."

20. Stone, 104.

21. This phrase has been taken from Michael Heim, "The Erotic Ontology of Cyberspace," in *Cyberspace: First Steps,* ed. Michael Benedikt (Cambridge, Mass.: The MIT Press, 1991).

22. "A Cyborg Manifesto: Science, Technology, and Socialist-Feminism in the Late Twentieth Century" is contained in Chapter Eight of Donna Haraway, *Simians, Cyborgs, and Women: The Reinvention of Nature* (London: Free Association Books, 1991). This quotation is taken from page 150.

23. Haraway, 151.

24. Haraway, 150.

28

MUDding: Social Phenomena in Text-based Virtual Realities

Pavel Curtis

1 A Brief Introduction to MUDding

The Machine did not transmit nuances of expression. It only gave a general idea of people—an idea that was good enough for all practical purposes.
—E.M. Forster [1]

A MUD is a software program that accepts "connections" from multiple users across some kind of network (e.g., telephone lines or the Internet) and provides to each user access to a shared database of "rooms," "exits," and other objects. Each user browses and manipulates this database from "inside" one of those rooms, seeing only those objects that are in the same room and moving from room to room mostly via the exits that connect them. A MUD, therefore, is a kind of virtual reality, an electronically-represented "place" that users can visit.

MUDs are not, however, like the kinds of virtual realities that one usually hears about, with fancy graphics and special hardware to sense the position and orientation of the user's real-world body. A MUD user's interface to the database is entirely text-based; all commands are typed in by the users and all feedback is printed as unformatted text on their terminal. The typical MUD user interface is most reminiscent of old computer games like Adventure and Zork [5]; a typical interaction is shown in Figure 28.1.

Three major factors distinguish a MUD from an Adventure-style computer game, though:

• A MUD is not goal-oriented; it has no beginning or end, no "score," and no notion of "winning" or "success." In short, even though users

>look

Corridor

The corridor from the west continues to the east here, but the way is blocked by a purple-velvet rope stretched across the hall. There are doorways leading to the north and south.
You see a sign hanging from the middle of the rope here.

>read sign

This point marks the end of the currently-occupied portion of the house.
Guests proceed beyond this point at their own risk.

— The residents >go east

You step disdainfully over the velvet rope and enter the dusty darkness of the unused portion of the house.

Figure 28.1.
A typical MUD database interaction

of MUDs are commonly called players, a MUD isn't really a game at all.

• A MUD is extensible from within; a user can add new objects to the database such as rooms, exits, "things," and notes. Certain MUDs, including the one I run, even support an embedded programming language in which a user can describe whole new kinds of behavior for the objects they create.

• A MUD generally has more than one user connected at a time. All of the connected users are browsing and manipulating the same database and can encounter the new objects created by others. The multiple users on a MUD can communicate with each other in real time.

This last factor has a profound effect on the ways in which users interact with the system; it transforms the activity from a solitary one into a social one.

Most inter-player communication on MUDs follows rules that fit within the framework of the virtual reality. If a player "says" something (using the say command), then every other player in the same room will "hear" them. For example, suppose that a player named Munchkin typed the command

say Can anyone hear me?

Then Munchkin would see the feedback

You say, "Can anyone hear me?"

and every other player in the same room would see

Munchkin says, "Can anyone hear me?"

Similarly, the emote command allows players to express various forms of "non-verbal" communication. If Munchkin types

emote smiles.

then every player in the same room sees
Munchkin smiles.

Most interplayer communication relies entirely on these two commands.[1]

There are two circumstances in which the realistic limitations of say and emote have proved sufficiently annoying that new mechanisms were developed. It sometimes happens that one player wishes to speak to another player in the same room, but without anyone else in the room being aware of the communication. If Munchkin uses the whisper command

whisper "I wish he'd just go away . . ." to Frebble

then only Frebble will see

Munchkin whispers, "I wish he'd just go away . . ."

The other players in the room see nothing of this at all.

Finally, if one player wishes to say something to another who is connected to the MUD but currently in a different and perhaps "remote" room, the page command is appropriate. It is invoked with a syntax very like that of the whisper command and the recipient sees output like this:

You sense that Munchkin is looking for you in The Hall.

He pages, "Come see this clock, it's tres cool!"

Aside from conversation, MUD players can most directly express themselves in three ways: by their choice of player name, by their choice of gender, and by their self-description.

When a player first connects to a MUD, they choose a name by which the other players will know them. This choice, like almost all others in MUDs, is not cast in stone; any player can rename themself at any time, though not to a name currently in use by some other player. Typically, MUD names are single words, in contrast to the longer "full" names used in real life.

Initially, MUD players appear to be neuter; automatically-generated messages that refer to such a player use the family of pronouns including "it," "its," etc. Players can choose to appear as a different gender, though, and not only male or female. On many MUDs, players can also choose to be plural (appearing to be a kind of "colony" creature: "Chup-Chups leave the room, closing the door behind them"), or to use one of several sets of gender-neutral pronouns (e.g., "s/he," "him/her" and "his/her," or "e," "em" and "eir").

Every object in a MUD optionally has a textual description which players can view with the look command. For example, the description of a room is automatically shown to a player when they enter that room and can be seen again just by typing "look." To see another player's description, one might type "look Bert." Players can set or change their descriptions at any time. The lengths of player descriptions typically vary from short one-liners to dozen-line paragraphs.

Aside from direct communication and responses to player commands, messages are printed to players when other players enter or leave the same room, when others connect or disconnect and are already in the same room, and when objects in the virtual reality have asynchronous behavior (e.g., a cuckoo clock chiming the hours).

MUD players typically spend their connected time socializing with each other, exploring the various rooms and other objects in the database, and adding new such objects of their own design. They vary widely in the amount of time they spend connected on each visit, ranging from only a minute to several hours; some players stay connected (and almost always idle) for days at a time, only occasionally actively participating.

This very brief description of the technical aspects of MUDding suffices for the purposes of this paper. It has been my experience, however, that it is quite difficult to properly convey the "sense" of the experience in words. Readers desiring more detailed information are advised to try MUDding themselves, as described in the final section of this paper.

2 Social Phenomena Observed on One MUD

Man is the measure.
—Ibid.

In October of 1990, I began running an Internet-accessible MUD server on my personal workstation here at PARC. Since then, it has been running continuously, with interruptions of only a few hours at most. In January of 1991, the existence of the MUD (called LambdaMOO[2]) was announced publicly, via the Usenet newsgroup rec.games.mud. As of this writing, well over 3,500 different players have connected to the server from over a dozen countries around the world and, at any given time, over 750 players have connected at least once in the last week. Recent statistics concerning the number of players connected at a given time of day (Pacific Standard Time) appear in Figure 28.2.

LambdaMOO is clearly a reasonably active place, with new and old players coming and going frequently throughout the day. This popularity has provided me with a position from which to observe the social patterns of a fairly large and diverse MUD clientele. I want to point out to the reader, however, that I have no formal training in sociology, anthropology, or psychology, so I cannot make any claims about methodology or even my own objectivity. What I relate below is merely my personal observations made over a year of mudding. In most cases, my discussions of the motivations and feelings of individual players is based upon in-MUD conversations with them; I have no means of checking the veracity of their statements concerning their real-life genders, identities, or (obviously) feelings. On the other hand, in most cases, I also have no reason to doubt them.

I have grouped my observations into three categories: phenomena related to the behavior and motivations of individual players, phenomena related to interactions between small groups of players (especially observations concerning MUD conversation), and phenomena related to the behavior of a MUD's community as a whole.

Cutting across all of these categories is a recurring theme to which I would like to draw the reader's attention in advance. Social behavior on MUDs is in some ways a direct mirror of behavior in real life, with mechanisms being drawn nearly unchanged from real-life, and in some

4 AM *** 10-1/2
5 AM ****** 12-1/4
6 AM ******** 14
7 AM *************** 18-3/4
8 AM ******************* 21-1/4
9 AM ************************ 25-1/4
10 AM **************************** 28
11 AM ********************************** 32-1/4
noon *** 37
1 PM *** 41-1/4
2 PM *** 39-3/4
3 PM ************************************** 35
4 PM *** 39-1/2
5 PM *** 40-3/4
6 PM *** 39-3/4
7 PM ** 40-1/2
8 PM *** 42-1/2
9 PM ** 44-1/4
10 PM ** 37-3/4
11 PM ********************************* 31
midnight *************************** 26-3/4
1 AM ****************** 20-3/4
2 AM ******** 13-3/4
3 AM **** 10-3/4
4 AM *** 10-1/2

Figure 28.2.
Average number of connected players on LambdaMOO, by time of day

ways very new and different, taking root in the new opportunities that MUDs provide over real life.

2.1 Observations about Individuals

The MUDding Population

The people who have an opportunity to connect to LambdaMOO are not a representative sample of the world population; they all read and write

English with at least passable proficiency and they have access to the Internet. Based on the names of their network hosts, I believe that well over 90% of them are affiliated with colleges and universities, mostly as students and, to a lesser extent, mostly undergraduates. Because they have Internet access, it might be supposed that the vast majority of players are involved in the computing field, but I do not believe that this is the case. It appears to me that no more than half (and probably less) of them are so employed; the increasing general availability of computing resources on college campuses and in industry appears to be having an effect, allowing a broader community to participate.

In any case, it appears that the educational background of the MUDding community is generally above average and it is likely that the economic background is similarly above the norm. Based on my conversations with people and on the names of those who have asked to join a mailing list about programming in LambdaMOO, I would guess that over 70% of the players are male; it is very difficult to give any firm justification for this number, however.

Player Presentation

As described in the introduction to MUDding, players have a number of choices about how to present themselves in the MUD; the first such decision is the name they will use. Figure 28.3 shows some of the names used by players on LambdaMOO.

One can pick out a few common styles for names (e.g., names from or inspired by myth, fantasy, or other literature, common names from real life, names of concepts, animals, and everyday objects that have representative connotations, etc.), but it is clear that no such category includes a majority of the names. Note that a significant minority of the names are in lower case; this appears to be a stylistic choice (players with such names describe the practice as "cool") and not, as might be supposed, an indication of a depressed ego.

Players can be quite possessive about their names, resenting others who choose names that are similarly spelt or pronounced or even that are taken from the same mythology or work of literature. In one case, for example, a player named "ZigZag" complained to me about other players taking the names "ZigZag!" and "Zig."

Toon	Gemba	Gary_Severn	Ford	Frand
li'ir	Maya	Rincewind	yduJ	funky
Grump	Foodslave	Arthur	EbbTide	Anathae
yrx	Satan	byte	Booga	tek
chupchups	waffle	Miranda	Gus	Merlin
Moonlight	MrNatural	Winger	Drazz'zt	Kendal
RedJack	Snooze	Shin	lostboy	foobar
Ted_Logan	Xephyr	King_Claudius	Bruce	Puff
Dirque	Coyote	Vastin	Player	Cool
Amy	Thorgeir	Cyberhuman	Gandalf	blip
Jayhirazan	Firefoot	JoeFeedback	ZZZzzz . . .	Lyssa
Avatar	zipo	Blackwinter	viz	Kilik
Maelstorm	Love	Terryann	Chrystal	arkanoiv

Figure 28.3.
A selection of player names from LambdaMOO

The choice of a player's gender is, for some, one of great consequence and forethought; for others (mostly males), it is simple and without any questions. For all that this choice involves the fewest options for the player (unlike their name or description, which are limited only by their imagination), it is also the choice that can generate the greatest concern and interest on the part of other players.

As I've said before, it appears that the great majority of players are male and the vast majority of them choose to present themselves as such. Some males, however, taking advantages of the relative rarity of females in MUDs, present themselves as female and thus stand out to some degree. Some use this distinction just for the fun of deceiving others, some of these going so far as to try to entice male-presenting players into sexually-explicit discussions and interactions. This is such a widely-noticed phenomenon, in fact, that one is advised by the common wisdom to assume that any flirtatious female-presenting players are, in real life, males. Such players are often subject to ostracism based on this assumption.

Some MUD players have suggested to me that such transvestite flirts are perhaps acting out their own (latent or otherwise) homosexual urges or fantasies, taking advantage of the perfect safety of the MUD situation to see how it feels to approach other men. While I have had no personal experience talking to such players, let alone the opportunity to delve into their motivations, the idea strikes me as plausible given the other ways in which MUD anonymity seems to free people from their inhibitions. (I say more about anonymity later on.)

Other males present themselves as female more out of curiosity than as an attempt at deception; to some degree, they are interested in seeing "how the other half lives," what it feels like to be perceived as female in a community. From what I can tell, they can be quite successful at this.

Female-presenting players report a number of problems. Many of them have told me that they are frequently subject both to harassment and to special treatment. One reported seeing two newcomers arrive at the same time, one male-presenting and one female-presenting. The other players in the room struck up conversations with the putative female and offered to show her around but completely ignored the putative male, who was left to his own devices.

In addition, probably due mostly to the number of female-presenting males one hears about, many female players report that they are frequently (and sometimes quite aggressively) challenged to "prove" that they are, in fact, female. To the best of my knowledge, male-presenting players are rarely if ever so challenged.

Because of these problems, many players who are female in real life choose to present themselves otherwise, choosing either male, neuter, or gender-neutral pronouns. As one might expect, the neuter and gender-neutral presenters are still subject to demands that they divulge their real gender.

Some players apparently find it quite difficult to interact with those whose true gender has been called into question; since this phenomenon is rarely manifest in real life, they have grown dependent on "knowing where they stand," on knowing what gender roles are "appropriate." Some players (and not only males) also feel that it is dishonest to present oneself as being a different gender than in real life; they report feeling "mad" and "used" when they discover the deception.

While I can spare no more space for this topic, I enthusiastically encourage the interested reader to look up Van Gelder's fascinating article [3] for many more examples and insights, as well as the story of a remarkably successful deception via "electronic transvestism."

The final part of a player's self-presentation, and the only part involving prose, is the player's description. This is where players can, and often do, establish the details of a persona or role they wish to play in the virtual reality. It is also a significant factor in other players' first impressions, since new players are commonly looked at soon after entering a common room.

Some players use extremely short descriptions, either intending to be cryptic (e.g., "the possessor of the infinity gems") or straightforward (e.g., "an average-sized dark elf with lavender eyes") or, often, just insufficiently motivated to create a more complex description for themselves. Other players go to great efforts in writing their descriptions; one moderately long example appears in Figure 28.4.

A large proportion of player descriptions contain a degree of wish fulfillment; I cannot count the number of "mysterious but unmistakably powerful" figures I have seen wandering around in LambdaMOO. Many players, it seems, are taking advantage of the MUD to emulate various attractive characters from fiction.

Given the detail and content of so many player descriptions, one might expect to find a significant amount of role-playing, players who adopt a coherent character with features distinct from their real-life personalities. Such is rarely the case, however. Most players appear to tire of such an effort quickly and simply interact with the others more-or-less straightforwardly, at least to the degree one does in normal discourse. One factor might be that the roles chosen by players are usually taken from a

You see a quiet, unassuming figure, wreathed in an oversized, dull-green Army jacket which is pulled up to nearly conceal his face. His long, unkempt blond hair blows back from his face as he tosses his head to meet your gaze. Small round gold-rimmed glasses, tinted slightly grey, rest on his nose. On a shoulder strap he carries an acoustic guitar and he lugs a backpack stuffed to overflowing with sheet music, sketches, and computer printouts. Under the coat are faded jeans and a T-Shirt reading "Paranoid CyberPunks International." He meets your gaze and smiles faintly, but does not speak with you. As you surmise him, you notice a glint of red at the rims of his blue eyes, and realize that his canine teeth seem to protrude slightly. He recoils from your look of horror and recedes back into himself.

Figure 28.4.
A moderately long player description.

particular creative work and are not particularly viable as characters outside of the context of that work; in short, the roles don't make sense in the context of the MUD.

A notable exception to this rule is one particular MUD I've heard of, called "PernMUSH." This appears to be a rigidly-maintained simulacrum of the world described in Ann McCaffrey's celebrated "Dragon" books. All players there have names that fit the style of the books and all places built there are consistent with what is shown in the series and in various fan materials devoted to it. PernMUSH apparently holds frequent "hatchings" and other social events, also derived in great detail from McCaffrey's works. This exception probably succeeds only because of its single-mindedness; with every player providing the correct context for every other, it is easier for everyone to stay more-or-less "in character."

Player Anonymity

It seems to me that the most significant social factor in MUDs is the perfect anonymity provided to the players. There are no commands available to the players to discover the real-life identity of each other and, indeed, technical considerations make such commands either very difficult or impossible to implement.

It is this guarantee of privacy that makes players' self-presentation so important and, in a sense, successful. Players can only be known by what they explicitly project and are not "locked into" any factors beyond their easy control, such as personal appearance, race, etc. In the words of an old military recruiting commercial, MUD players can "be all that you can be."[3]

This also contributes to what might be called a "shipboard syndrome," the feeling that since one will likely never meet anyone from the MUD in real life, there is less social risk involved and inhibitions can safely be lowered.

For example, many players report that they are much more willing to strike up conversations with strangers they encounter in the MUD than in real life. One obvious factor is that MUD visitors are implicitly assumed to be interested in conversing, unlike in most real world contexts. Another deeper reason, though, is that players do not feel that very much is at risk. At worst, if they feel that they've made an utter fool of themself, they can always abandon the character and create a new one, losing only the name and the effort invested in socially establishing the old one. In effect, a "new lease on life" is always a ready option.

Players on most MUDs are also emboldened somewhat by the fact that they are immune from violence, both physical and virtual. The permissions systems of all MUDs (excepting those whose whole purpose revolves around adventuring and the slaying of monsters and other players) generally prevent any player from having any kind of permanent effect on any other player. Players can certainly annoy each other, but not in any lasting or even moderately long-lived manner.

This protective anonymity also encourages some players to behave irresponsibly, rudely, or even obnoxiously. We have had instances of severe and repeated sexual harassment, crudity, and deliberate offensiveness. In general, such cruelty seems to be supported by two causes: the offenders believe (usually correctly) that they cannot be held accountable for their actions in the real world, and the very same anonymity makes it easier for them to treat other players impersonally, as other than real people.

Wizards

Usually, as I understand it, societies cope with offensive behavior by various group mechanisms, such as ostracism, and I discuss this kind of effect in detail in Section 2.3. In certain severe cases, however, it is left to the "authorities" or "police" of a society to take direct action, and MUDs are no different in this respect.

On MUDs, it is a special class of players, usually called wizards or (less frequently) gods, who fulfill both the "authority" and "police" roles. A wizard is a player who has special permissions and commands available, usually for the purpose of maintaining the MUD, much like a "system administrator" or "superuser" in real-life computing systems. Players can only be transformed into wizards by other wizards, with the maintainer of the actual MUD server computer program acting as the first such.

On most MUDs, the wizards' first approach to solving serious behavior problems is, as in the best real-life situations, to attempt a calm dialog with the offender. When this fails, as it usually does in the worst cases of irresponsibility, the customary response is to punish the offender with "toading." This involves (a) either severely restricting the kinds of actions the player can take or else preventing them from connecting at all, (b) changing the name and description of the player to present an unpleasant appearance (often literally that of a warty toad), and (c) moving the player to some very public place within the virtual reality. This public humiliation is often sufficient to discourage repeat visits by the player, even in a different guise.

On LambdaMOO, the wizards as a group decided on a more low-key approach to the problem; we have, in the handful of cases where such a severe course was dictated, simply "recycled" the offending player, removing them from the database of the MUD entirely. This is a more permanent solution than toading, but also lacks the public spectacle of toading, a practice none of us were comfortable with.

Wizards, in general, have a very different experience of mudding than other players. Because of their palpable and extensive extra powers over other players, and because of their special role in MUD society, they are frequently treated differently by other players.

Most players on LambdaMOO, for example, upon first encountering my wizard player, treat me with almost exaggerated deference and respect. I am frequently called "sir" and players often apologize for "wasting" my time. A significant minority, however, appear to go to great lengths to prove that they are not impressed by my office or power, speaking to me quite bluntly and making demands that I assist them with their problems using the system, sometimes to the point of rudeness.

Because of other demands on my time, I am almost always connected to the MUD but idle, located in a special room I built (my "den") that players require my permission to enter. This room is useful, for example, as a place in which to hold sensitive conversations without fear of interruption. This constant presence and unapproachability, however, has had significant and unanticipated side-effects. I am told by players who get more circulation than I do that I am widely perceived as a kind of mythic figure, a mysterious wizard in his magical tower. Rumor and hearsay have spread word of my supposed opinions on matters of MUD policy. One effect is that players are often afraid to contact me for fear of capricious retaliation at their presumption.

While I find this situation disturbing and wish that I had more time to spend out walking among the "mortal" members of the LambdaMOO community, I am told that player fears of wizardly caprice are justified on certain other MUDs. It is certainly easy to believe the stories I hear of

MUD wizards who demand deference and severely punish those who transgress; there is a certain ego boost to those who wield even simple administrative power in virtual worlds and it would be remarkable indeed if no one had ever started a MUD for that reason alone.

In fact, one player sent me a copy of an article, written by a former MUD wizard, based on Machiavelli's *The Prince;* it details a wide variety of more-or-less creative ways for wizards to make ordinary MUD players miserable. If this wizard actually used these techniques, as he claims, then some players' desires to avoid wizards are quite understandable.

2.2 Observations about Small Groups

MUD Conversation

The majority of players spend the majority of their active time on MUDs in conversation with other players. The mechanisms by which those conversations get started generally mirror those that operate in real life, though sometimes in interesting ways.

Chance encounters between players exploring the same parts of the database are common and almost always cause for conversation. As mentioned above, the anonymity of MUDs tends to lower social barriers and to encourage players to be more outgoing than in real life. Strangers on MUDs greet each other with the same kinds of questions as in real life: "Are you new here? I don't think we've met." The very first greetings, however, are usually gestural rather than verbal: "Munchkin waves. Lorelei waves back."

The @who (or WHO) command on MUDs allows players to see who else is currently connected and, on some MUDs, where those people are. An example of the output of this command appears in Figure 28.5.

This is, in a sense, the MUD analog of scanning the room in a real-life gathering to see who's present.

Players consult the @who list to see if their friends are connected and to see which areas, if any, seem to have a concentration of players in them. If more than a couple of players are in the same room, the presumption is that an interesting conversation may be in progress there; players are thus more attracted to more populated areas. I call this phenomenon "social gravity"; it has a real-world analog in the tendency

Player name	Connected	Idle time	Location
Haakon (#2)	3 days	a second	Lambda's Den
Lynx (#8910)	a minute	2 seconds	Lynx' Abode
Garin (#23393)	an hour	2 seconds	Carnival Grounds
Gilmore (#19194)	an hour	10 seconds	Heart of Darkness
TamLin (#21864)	an hour	21 seconds	Heart of Darkness
Quimby (#23279)	3 minutes	2 minutes	Quimby's room
koosh (#24639)	50 minutes	5 minutes	Corridor
Nosredna (#2487)	7 hours	36 minutes	Nosredna's Hideaway
yduJ (#68)	7 hours	47 minutes	Hackers' Heaven
Zachary (#4670)	an hour	an hour	Zachary's Workshop
Woodlock (#2520)	2 hours	2 hours	Woodlock's Room

Total: 11 players, 6 of whom have been active recently.

Figure 28.5.
Sample output from LambdaMOO's @who command.

of people to be attracted to conspicuous crowds, such as two or more people at the door of a colleague's office.

It is sometimes the case on a MUD, as in real life, that one wishes to avoid getting into a conversation, either because of the particular other player involved or because of some other activity one does not wish to interrupt. In the real world, one can refrain from answering the phone, screen calls using an answering machine, or even, in copresent situations, pretend not to have heard the other party. In the latter case, with luck, the person will give up rather than repeat themself more loudly.

The mechanisms are both similar and interestingly different on MUDs. It is often the case that MUD players are connected but idle, perhaps because they have stepped away from their terminal for a while. Thus, it often happens that one receives no response to an utterance in a MUD simply because the other party wasn't really present to see it. This commonly-understood fact of MUD life provides for the MUD equivalent of pretending not to hear. I know of players who take care after such a pretense not to type anything more to the MUD until the would-be conversant has left, thus preserving the apparent validity of their excuse.

Another mechanism for avoiding conversation is available to MUD players but, as far as I can see, not to people in real life situations. Most MUDs provide a mechanism by which each player can designate a set of other players as "gagged"; the effect is that nothing will be printed to the gagging player if someone they've gagged speaks, moves, emotes, etc. There is generally no mechanism by which the gagged player can tell a priori that someone is gagging them; indeed, unless the gagged player attempts to address the gagging player directly, the responses from the other players in the room (who may not be gagging the speaker) may cause the speaker never even to suspect that some are not hearing them.

We provide a gagging facility on LambdaMOO, but it is fairly rarely used; a recent check revealed only 45 players out of almost 3,000 who are gagging other players. The general feeling appears to be that gagging is quite rude and is only appropriate (if ever) when someone persists in annoying you in spite of polite requests to the contrary. It is not clear, though, quite how universal this feeling is. For example, I know of some players who, on being told that some other players were offended by their speech, suggested that gagging was the solution: "If they don't want to hear me, let them gag me; I won't be offended." Also, I am given to understand that gagging is much more commonly employed on some other MUDs.

The course of a MUD conversation is remarkably like and unlike one in the real world. Participants in MUD conversations commonly use the emote command to make gestures, such as nodding to urge someone to continue, waving at player arrivals and departures, raising eyebrows, hugging to apologize or soothe, etc. As in electronic mail (though much more frequently), players employ standard "smiley-face" glyphs (e.g., ":-)," ":-(," and ":-|") to clarify the "tone" with which they say things. Utterances are also frequently addressed to specific participants, as opposed to the room as a whole (e.g., "Munchkin nods to Frebble. 'You tell 'em!'").

The most obvious difference between MUD conversations and those in real life is that the utterances must be typed rather than simply spoken. This introduces significant delays into the interaction and, like nature, MUD society abhors a vacuum.

Even when there are only two participants in a MUD conversation, it is very rare for there to be only one thread of discussion; during the pause while one player is typing a response, the other player commonly thinks of something else to say and does so, introducing at least another level to the conversation, if not a completely new topic. These multi-topic conversations are a bit disorienting and bewildering to the uninitiated, but it appears that most players quickly become accustomed to them and handle the multiple levels smoothly. Of course, when more than two players are involved, the opportunities for multiple levels are only increased. It has been pointed out that a suitable punishment for truly heinous social offenders might be to strand them in a room with more than a dozen players actively conversing.

This kind of cognitive time-sharing also arises due to the existence of the page command. Recall from the introduction that this command allows a player to send a message to another who is not in the same room. It is not uncommon (especially for wizards, whose advice is frequently sought by "distant" players) to be involved in one conversation "face-to-face" and one or two more conducted via page. Again, while this can be overwhelming at first, one can actually come to appreciate the relief from the tedious long pauses waiting for a fellow conversant to type.

Another effect of the typing delay (and of the low bandwidth of the MUD medium) is a tendency for players to abbreviate their communications, sometimes past the point of ambiguity. For example, some players often greet others with "hugs" but the "meanings" of those hugs vary widely from recipient to recipient. In one case the hug might be a simple friendly greeting, in another it might be intended to convey a very special affection. In both cases, the text typed by the hugger is the same (e.g., "Munchkin hugs Frebble."); it is considered too much trouble for the hugger to type a description of the act sufficient to distinguish the "kind" of hug intended. This leads to some MUD interactions having much more ambiguity than usually encountered in real life, a fact that some mudders consider useful.

The somewhat disjointed nature of MUD conversations, brought on by the typing pauses, tends to rob them of much of the coherence that makes real-life conversants resent interruptions. The addition of a new conversant to a MUD conversation is much less disruptive; the "flow" being disrupted was never very strong to begin with. Some players go so far as to say the interruptions are simply impossible on MUDs; I think that this is a minority impression, however. Interruptions do exist on MUDs; they are simply less significant than in real life.

Other Small-Group Interactions

I would not like to give the impression that conversation is the only social activity on MUDs. Indeed, MUD society appears to have most of the same social activities as real life, albeit often in a modified form.

As mentioned before, PernMUSH holds large-scale, organized social gatherings such as "hatchings" and they are not alone. Most MUDs have at one time or another organized more or less elaborate parties, often to celebrate notable events in the MUD itself, such as an anniversary of its founding. We have so far had only one or two such parties on LambdaMOO, to celebrate the "opening" of some new area built by a player; if there were any other major parties, I certainly wasn't invited!

One of the more impressive examples of MUD social activity is the virtual wedding. There have been many of these on many different MUDs; we are in the process of planning our first on LambdaMOO, with me officiating in my role as archwizard.

I have never been present at such a ceremony, but I have read logs of the conversations at them. As I do not know any of the participants in the ceremonies I've read about, I cannot say much for certain about their emotional content. As in real life, they are usually very happy and celebratory occasions with an intriguing undercurrent of serious feelings. I do not know and cannot even speculate about whether or not the main participants in such ceremonies are usually serious or not, whether or not the MUD ceremony usually (or even ever) mirrors another ceremony in the real world, or even whether or not the bride and groom have ever met outside of virtual reality.

In the specific case of the upcoming LambdaMOO wedding, the participants first met on LambdaMOO, became quite friendly, and eventually decided to meet in real life. They have subsequently become romantically involved in the real world and are using the MUD wedding as a celebration of that fact. This phenomenon of couples meeting in virtual reality and then pursuing a real-life relationship, is not uncommon; in one notable case, they did this even though one of them lived in Australia and the other in Pittsburgh!

It is interesting to note that the virtual reality wedding is not specific to the kinds of MUDs I've been discussing; Van Gelder [7] mentions an on-line reception on CompuServe and weddings are quite common on Habitat [4], a half-graphical, half-textual virtual reality popular in Japan.

The very idea, however, brings up interesting and potentially important questions about the legal standing of commitments made only in virtual reality. Suppose, for example, that two people make a contract in virtual reality. Is the contract binding? Under which state's (or country's) laws? Is it a written or verbal contract? What constitutes proof of signature in such a context? I suspect that our real-world society will have to face and resolve these issues in the not-too-distant future.

Those who frequent MUDs tend also to be interested in games and puzzles, so it is no surprise that many real-world examples have been implemented inside MUDs. What may be surprising, however, is the extent to which this is so.

On LambdaMOO alone, we have machine-mediated Scrabble, Monopoly, Mastermind, Backgammon, Ghost, Chess, Go, and Reversi boards. These attract small groups of players on occasion, with the Go players being the most committed; in fact, there are a number of Go players who come to LambdaMOO only for that purpose. I say more about these more specialized uses of social virtual realities later on. In many ways, though, such games so far have little, if anything, to offer over their real-world counterparts except perhaps a better chance of finding an opponent.

Perhaps more interesting are the other kinds of games imported into MUDs from real life, the ones that might be far less feasible in a non-virtual reality. A player on LambdaMOO, for example, implemented a facility for holding food fights. Players throw food items at each other, attempt to duck oncoming items, and, if unsuccessful, are "splattered" with messes that cannot easily be removed. After a short interval, a semi-animate "Mr. Clean" arrives and one-by-one removes the messes from the participants, turning them back into the food items from which they came, ready for the next fight. Although the game was rather simple to implement, it has remained enormously popular nearly a year later.

Another player on LambdaMOO created a trainable Frisbee, which any player could teach to do tricks when they threw or caught it.

Players who used the Frisbee seemed to take great pleasure in trying to out-do each other's trick descriptions. My catching description, for example, reads "Haakon stops the frisbee dead in the air in front of himself and then daintily plucks it, like a flower." I have also heard of MUD versions of paint-ball combat and fantastical games of Capture the Flag.

2.3 Observations about the MUD Community as a Whole

MUD communities tend to be very large in comparison to the number of players actually active at any given time. On LambdaMOO, for example, we have between 700 and 800 players connecting in any week but rarely more than 40 simultaneously. A good real-world analog might be a bar with a large number of "regulars," all of whom are transients without fixed schedules.

The continuity of MUD society is thus somewhat tenuous; many pairs of active players exist who have never met each other. In spite of this, MUDs do become true communities after a time. The participants slowly come to consensus about a common (private) language, about appropriate standards of behavior, and about the social roles of various public areas (e.g., where big discussions usually happen, where certain "crowds" can be found, etc.).

Some people appear to thrive on the constant turnover of MUD players throughout a day, enjoying the novelty of always having someone new to talk to. In some cases, this enjoyment goes so far as to become a serious kind of addiction, with some players spending as much as 35 hours out of 48 constantly connected and conversing on MUDs. I know of many players who have taken more-or-less drastic steps to curtail their participation on MUDs, feeling that their habits had gotten significantly out of control.

One college-student player related to me his own particularly dramatic case of MUD addiction. It seems that he was supposed to go home for the Christmas holidays but missed the train by no less than five hours because he had been unable to tear himself away from his MUD conversations. After calling his parents to relieve their worrying by lying about the cause of his delay, he eventually boarded a train for home. However, on arrival there at 12:30 AM the next morning, he did not go directly to his parents' house but instead went to an open terminal room in the local university, where he spent another two and a half hours connected before finally going home. His parents, meanwhile, had called the police in fear for their son's safety in traveling.

It should not be supposed that this kind of problem is the now commonly-understood phenomenon of "computer addiction"; the fact that there is a computer involved here is more-or-less irrelevant. These people are not addicted to computers, but to communication; the global scope of Internet MUDs implies not only a great variety in potential conversants, but also 24-hour access. As Figure 28.2 shows, the sun never really sets on LambdaMOO's community.

While it is at the more macroscopic scale of whole MUD communities that I feel least qualified to make reliable observations, I do have one striking example of societal consensus having concrete results on LambdaMOO.

From time to time, we wizards are asked to arbitrate in disputes among players concerning what is or is not appropriate behavior. My approach generally has been to ask a number of other players for their opinions and to present the defendant in the complaint with a precis of the plaintiff's grievance, always looking for the common threads in their responses. After many such episodes, I was approached by a number of players asking that a written statement on LambdaMOO "manners" be prepared and made available to the community. I wrote up a list of those rules that seemed implied by the set of arbitrations we had performed and published them for public comment. Very little comment has ever been received, but the groups of players I've asked generally agree that the rules reflect their own understandings of the common will. For the curious, I have included our list of rules in Figure 28.6; the actual "help manners" document goes into a bit more detail about each of these points.

It should be noted that different MUDs are truly different communities and have different societal agreements concerning appropriate behavior. There even exist a few MUDs where the only rule in the social contract is that there is no social contract. Such "anarchy" MUDs have appeared a few times in my experience and seem to be quite popular for a time before eventually fading away.

• Be polite. Avoid being rude. The MOO is worth participating in because it is a pleasant place for people to be. When people are rude or nasty to one another, it stops being so pleasant.

• "Revenge is ours," sayeth the wizards. If someone is nasty to you, please either ignore it or tell a wizard about it. Please don't try to take revenge on the person; this just escalates the level of rudeness and makes the MOO a less pleasant place for everyone involved.

• Respect other players' sensibilities. The participants on the MOO come from a wide range of cultures and backgrounds. Your ideas about what constitutes offensive speech or descriptions are likely to differ from those of other players. Please keep the text that players can casually run across as free of potentially-offensive material as you can.

• Don't spoof. Spoofing is loosely defined as "causing misleading output to be printed to other players." For example, it would be spoofing for anyone but Munchkin to print out a message like "Munchkin sticks out his tongue at Potrzebie." This makes it look like Munchkin is unhappy with Potrzebie even though that may not be the case at all.

• Don't shout. It is easy to write a MOO command that prints a message to every connected player. Please don't.

• Only teleport your own things. By default, most objects (including other players) allow themselves to be moved freely from place to place. This fact makes it easier to build certain useful objects. Unfortunately, it also makes it easy to annoy people by moving them or their objects around without their permission. Please don't.

• Don't teleport silently or obscurely. It is easy to write MOO commands that move you instantly from place to place. Please remember in such programs to print a clear, understandable message to all players in both the place you're leaving and the place you're going to.

• Don't hog the server. The server is carefully shared among all of the connected players so that everyone gets a chance to execute their commands. This sharing is, by necessity, somewhat approximate. Please don't abuse it with tasks that run for a long time without pausing.

• Don't waste object numbers. Some people, in a quest to own objects with "interesting" numbers (e.g., #17000, #18181, etc.) have written MOO programs that loop forever creating and recycling objects until the "good" numbers come up. Please don't do this.

Figure 28.6.
The main points of LambdaMOO manners.

3 The Prospects for Mudding in the Future

The clumsy system of public gatherings had been long since abandoned; neither Vashti nor her audience stirred from their rooms. Seated in her arm-chair, she spoke, while they in their arm-chairs heard her, fairly well, and saw her, fairly well.

—Ibid.

A recent listing of Internet-accessible MUDs showed almost 200 active around the world, mostly in the United States and Scandinavia. A conservative guess that these MUDs average 100 active players each gives a total of 20,000 active mudders in the world today; this is almost certainly a significant undercount already and the numbers appear to be growing as more and more people gain Internet access.

In addition, at least one MUD-like area exists on the commercial CompuServe network in the United States and there are several more commercial MUDs active in the United Kingdom. Finally, there is Habitat [4], a half-graphical, half-textual virtual reality in Japan, with well over 10,000 users.

I believe that text-based virtual realities and wide-area interactive "chat" facilities [6] are becoming more and more common and will continue to do so for the foreseeable future. Like CB radios and telephone party lines before them, MUDs seem to provide a necessary social outlet.

The MUD model is also being extended in new ways for new audiences. For example, I am currently involved in adapting the LambdaMOO server for use as an international teleconferencing and image database system for astronomers. Our plans include allowing scientists to give on-line presentations to their colleagues around the world, complete with "slides" and illustrations automatically displayed on the participants' workstations. The same approach could be used to create on-line meeting places for workers in other disciplines, as well as for other non-scientific communities. I do not believe that we are the only researchers planning such facilities. In the near future (a few years at most), I expect such specialized virtual realities to be commonplace, an accepted part of at least the academic community.

On another front, I am engaged with some colleagues in the design of a MUD for general use here at Xerox PARC. The idea here is to use virtual reality to help break down the geographical barriers of a large building, of people increasingly working from their homes, and of having a sister research laboratory in Cambridge, England. In this context, we intend to investigate the addition of digital voice to MUDs, with the conventions of the virtual reality providing a simple and intuitive style of connection management: if two people are in the same virtual room, then their audio channels are connected. Some virtual rooms may even overlap real-world rooms, such as those in which talks or other meetings are held.

Of course, one can expect a number of important differences in the social phenomena on MUDs in a professional setting. In particular, I would guess that anonymity might well be frowned upon in such places, though it may have some interesting special uses, for example in the area of refereeing papers.

Some of my colleagues have suggested that the term "text-based virtual reality" is an oxymoron, that "virtual reality" refers only to the fancy graphical and motion-sensing environments being worked on in many places. They go on to predict that these more physically-involving systems will supplant the text-based variety as soon as the special equipment becomes a bit more widely and cheaply available. I do not believe that this is the case.

While I agree that the fancier systems are likely to become very popular for certain applications and among those who can afford them, I believe that MUDs have certain enduring advantages that will save them from obsolescence.

The equipment necessary to participate fully in a MUD is significantly cheaper, more widely available, and more generally useful than that for the fancy systems; this is likely to remain the case for a long time to come. For example, it is already possible to purchase palm-sized portable computers with network connectivity and text displays, making it possible to use MUDs even while riding the bus, etc. Is similarly-flexible hardware for fancy virtual realities even on the horizon?

It is substantially easier for players to give themselves vivid, detailed, and interesting descriptions (and to do the same for the descriptions and behavior of the new objects they create) in a text-based system than in a graphics-based one. In McLuhan's terminology [3], this is because MUDs are a "cold" medium, while more graphically-based media are "hot";

that is, the sensorial parsimony of plain text tends to entice users into engaging their imaginations to fill in missing details while, comparatively speaking, the richness of stimuli in fancy virtual realities has an opposite tendency, pushing users' imaginations into a more passive role. I also find it difficult to believe that a graphics-based system will be able to compete with text for average users on the metric of believable detail per unit of effort expended; this is certainly the case now and I see little reason to believe it will change in the near future.

Finally, one of the great strengths of MUDs lies in the users' ability to customize them, to extend them, and to specialize them to the users' particular needs. The ease with which this can be done in MUDs is directly related to the fact that they are purely text-based; in a graphics-based system, the overhead of creating new moderate-quality graphics would put the task beyond the inclinations of the average user. Whereas, with MUDs, it is easy to imagine an almost arbitrarily small community investing in the creation of a virtual reality that was truly customized for that community, it seems very unlikely that any but the largest communities would invest the greatly-increased effort required for a fancier system.

4 Conclusions

Vashti was seized with the terrors of direct experience. She shrank back into her room, and the wall closed up again.

—Ibid.

The emergence of MUDs has created a new kind of social sphere, both like and radically unlike the environments that have existed before. As they become more and more popular and more widely accessible, it appears likely that an increasingly significant proportion of the population will at least become familiar with mudding and perhaps become frequent participants in text-based virtual realities.

It thus behooves us to begin to try to understand these new societies, to make sense of these electronic places where we'll be spending increasing amounts of our time, both doing business and seeking pleasure. I would hope that social scientists will be at least intrigued by my amateur observations and perhaps inspired to more properly study MUDs and their players. In particular, as MUDs become more widespread, ever more people are likely to be susceptible to the kind of addiction I discuss in an earlier section; we must, as a society, begin to wrestle with the social and ethical issues brought out by such cases.

Those readers interested in trying out MUDs for themselves are encouraged to do so. The Usenet news group rec.games.mud periodically carries comprehensive lists of publicly-available, Internet-accessible MUDs, including their detailed network addresses. My own MUD, LambdaMOO, can be reached via the standard Internet telnet protocol at the host lambda.parc.xerox.com (the numeric address is 13.2.116.36), port 8888. On a UNIX machine, for example, the command

telnet lambda.parc.xerox.com 8888

will suffice to make a connection. Once connected, feel free to page me; I connect under the names "Haakon" and "Lambda."

Acknowledgments

I was originally prodded into writing down my MUDding experiences by Eric Roberts. In trying to get a better handle on an organization for the material, I was aided immeasurably by my conversations with Francoise Brun-Cottan; she consistently brought to my attention phenomena that I had become too familiar with to notice. Susan Irwin and David Nichols have been instrumental in helping me to understand some of the issues that might arise as MUDs become more sophisticated and widespread. The reviewers of this paper provided several pointers to important related work that I might otherwise never have encountered. Finally, I must also give credit to the LambdaMOO players who participated in my on-line brainstorming session; their ideas, experiences, and perceptions provided a necessary perspective to my own understanding.

Notes

1. In fact, these two commands are so frequently used that single-character abbreviations are provided for them. The two example commands would usually be typed as follows:

"Can anyone hear me?

:smiles.

2. The "MOO" in "LambdaMOO" stands for "MUD, Object-Oriented." The origin of the "Lambda" part is more obscure, based on my years of experience with the Lisp programming language.

3. Kiesler and her colleagues [2] have investigated the effects of electronic anonymity on the decision-making and problem-solving processes in organizations; some of their observations parallel mine given here.

References

[1]. Forster, E. M. "The Machine Stops." In Ben Bova, editor, *The Science Fiction Hall of Fame,* Vol. IIB, Avon, 1973. Originally in E. M. Forster, *The Eternal Moment and Other Stories.* Harcourt Brace Jovanovich, 1928.

[2]. Kiesler, Sara, et al. "Social Psychological Aspects of Computer-Mediated Communication," in *Computerization and Controversy,* ed. Charles Dunlop and Robert Kling. Academic Press, 1991.

[3]. McLuhan, Marshall. *Understanding Media.* McGraw-Hill, 1964.

[4]. Morningstar, Chip, and F. Randall Farmer. "The Lessons of Lucasfilm's Habitat," in *Cyberspace,* ed. Michael Benedikt. MIT Press, 1991.

[5]. Raymond, Eric S., ed. *The New Hacker's Dictionary.* MIT Press, 1991.

[6]. Reid, Elizabeth M. "Electropolis: Communication and Community on Internet Relay Chat." *Intertek* 3, no. 3, Winter 1992. [Chapter 30 in this book.]

[7]. Van Gelder, Lindsy. "The Strange Case of the Electronic Lover," in Charles Dunlop and Robert Kling, editors, *Computerization and Controversy.* Academic Press, 1991.

29

A Rape in Cyberspace; or How an Evil Clown, a Haitian Trickster Spirit, Two Wizards, and a Cast of Dozens Turned a Database into a Society

Julian Dibbell

They say he raped them that night. They say he did it with a cunning little doll, fashioned in their image and imbued with the power to make them do whatever he desired. They say that by manipulating the doll he forced them to have sex with him, and with each other, and to do horrible, brutal things to their own bodies. And though I wasn't there that night, I think I can assure you that what they say is true, because it all happened right in the living room—right there amid the well-stocked bookcases and the sofas and the fireplace—of a house I've come to think of as my second home.

Call me Dr. Bombay. Some months ago—let's say about halfway between the first time you heard the words *information superhighway* and the first time you wished you never had—I found myself tripping with compulsive regularity down the well-traveled information lane that leads to LambdaMOO, a very large and very busy rustic chateau built entirely of words. Nightly, I typed the commands that called those words onto my computer screen, dropping me with what seemed a warm electric thud inside the mansion's darkened coat closet, where I checked my quotidian identity, stepped into the persona and appearance of a minor character from a long-gone television sitcom, and stepped out into the glaring chatter of the crowded living room. Sometimes, when the mood struck me, I emerged as a dolphin instead.

I won't say why I chose to masquerade as Samantha Stevens's outlandish cousin, or as the dolphin, or what exactly led to my mild but so-far incurable addiction to the semifictional digital otherworlds known around the Internet as multi-user dimensions, or MUDs. This isn't my story, after all. It's the story of a man named Mr. Bungle, and of the ghostly sexual violence he committed in the halls of LambdaMOO, and most importantly of the ways his violence and his victims challenged the 1000 and more residents of that surreal, magic-infested mansion to become, finally, the community so many of them already believed they were.

That I was myself one of those residents has little direct bearing on the story's events. I mention it only as a warning that my own perspective is perhaps too steeped in the surreality and magic of the place to serve as an entirely appropriate guide. For the Bungle Affair raises questions that—here on the brink of a future in which human life may find itself as tightly enveloped in digital environments as it is today in the architectural kind—demand a clear-eyed, sober, and unmystified consideration. It asks us to shut our ears momentarily to the techno-utopian ecstasies of West Coast cyberhippies and look without illusion upon the present possibilities for building, in the on-line spaces of this world, societies more decent and free than those mapped onto dirt and concrete and capital. It asks us to behold the new bodies awaiting us in virtual space undazzled by their phantom powers, and to get to the crucial work of sorting out the socially meaningful differences between those bodies and our physical ones. And most forthrightly it asks us to wrap our late-modern ontologies, epistemologies, sexual ethics, and common sense around the curious notion of rape by voodoo doll—and to try not to warp them beyond recognition in the process.

In short, the Bungle Affair dares me to explain it to you without resort to dime-store mysticisms, and I fear I may have shape-shifted by the digital moonlight one too many times to be quite up to the task. But I will do what I can, and can do no better I suppose than to lead with the facts. For if nothing else about Mr. Bungle's case is unambiguous, the facts at least are crystal clear.

The facts begin (as they often do) with a time and a place. The time was a Monday night in March, and the place, as I've said, was the living room—which, due to the inviting warmth of its decor, is so invariably packed with chitchatters as to be roughly synonymous among

LambdaMOOers with a party. So strong, indeed, is the sense of convivial common ground invested in the living room that a cruel mind could hardly imagine a better place in which to stage a violation of LambdaMOO's communal spirit. And there was cruelty enough lurking in the appearance Mr. Bungle presented to the virtual world—he was at the time a fat, oleaginous, Bisquick-faced clown dressed in cum-stained harlequin garb and girdled with a mistletoe-and-hemlock belt whose buckle bore the quaint inscription "KISS ME UNDER THIS, BITCH!" But whether cruelty motivated his choice of crime scene is not among the established facts of the case. It is a fact only that he did choose the living room.

The remaining facts tell us a bit more about the inner world of Mr. Bungle, though only perhaps that it couldn't have been a very comfortable place. They tell us that he commenced his assault entirely unprovoked, at or about 10 PM Pacific Standard Time. That he began by using his voodoo doll to force one of the room's occupants to sexually service him in a variety of more or less conventional ways. That this victim was legba, a Haitian trickster spirit of indeterminate gender, brown-skinned and wearing an expensive pearl gray suit, top hat, and dark glasses. That legba heaped vicious imprecations on him all the while and that he was soon ejected bodily from the room. That he hid himself away then in his private chambers somewhere on the mansion grounds and continued the attacks without interruption, since the voodoo doll worked just as well at a distance as in proximity. That he turned his attentions now to Starsinger, a rather pointedly nondescript female character, tall, stout, and brown-haired, forcing her into unwanted liaisons with other individuals present in the room, among them legba, Bakunin (the well-known radical), and Juniper (the squirrel). That his actions grew progressively violent. That he made legba eat his/her own pubic hair. That he caused Starsinger to violate herself with a piece of kitchen cutlery. That his distant laughter echoed evilly in the living room with every successive outrage. That he could not be stopped until at last someone summoned Zippy, a wise and trusted old-timer who brought with him a gun of near wizardly powers, a gun that didn't kill but enveloped its targets in a cage impermeable even to a voodoo doll's powers. That Zippy fired this gun at Mr. Bungle, thwarting the doll at last and silencing the evil, distant laughter.

These particulars, as I said, are unambiguous. But they are far from simple, for the simple reason that every set of facts in virtual reality (or VR, as the locals abbreviate it) is shadowed by a second, complicating set: the "real-life" facts. And while a certain tension invariably buzzes in the gap between the hard, prosaic RL facts and their more fluid, dreamy VR counterparts, the dissonance in the Bungle case is striking. No hideous clowns or trickster spirits appear in the RL version of the incident, no voodoo dolls or wizard guns, indeed no rape at all as any RL court of law has yet defined it. The actors in the drama were university students for the most part, and they sat rather undramatically before computer screens the entire time, their only actions a spidery flitting of fingers across standard QWERTY keyboards. No bodies touched. Whatever physical interaction occurred consisted of a mingling of electronic signals sent from sites spread out between New York City and Sydney, Australia. Those signals met in LambdaMOO, certainly, just as the hideous clown and the living room party did, but what was LambdaMOO after all? Not an enchanted mansion or anything of the sort—just a middlingly complex database, maintained for experimental purposes inside a Xerox Corporation research computer in Palo Alto and open to public access via the Internet.

To be more precise about it, LambdaMOO was a MUD. Or to be yet more precise, it was a subspecies of MUD known as a MOO, which is short for "MUD, Object-Oriented." All of which means that it was a kind of database especially designed to give users the vivid impression of moving through a physical space that in reality exists only as descriptive data filed away on a hard drive. When users dial into LambdaMOO, for instance, the program immediately presents them with a brief textual description of one of the rooms of the database's fictional mansion (the coat closet, say). If the user wants to leave this room, she can enter a command to move in a particular direction and the database will replace the original description with a new one corresponding to the room located in the direction she chose. When the new description scrolls across the user's screen it lists not only the fixed features of the room but all its contents at that moment—including things (tools, toys, weapons) and other users (each represented as a "character" over which he or she has sole control).

As far as the database program is concerned, all of these entities—rooms, things, characters—are just different subprograms that the program allows to interact according to rules very roughly mimicking the laws of the physical world. Characters may not leave a room in a given direction, for instance, unless the room subprogram contains an "exit" at that compass point. And if a character "says" or "does" something (as directed by its user-owner), then only the users whose characters are also located in that room will see the output describing the statement or action. Aside from such basic constraints, however, LambdaMOOers are allowed a broad freedom to create—they can describe their characters any way they like, they can make rooms of their own and decorate them to taste, and they can build new objects almost at will. The combination of all this busy user activity with the hard physics of the database can certainly induce a lucid illusion of presence—but when all is said and done the only thing you *really* see when you visit LambdaMOO is a kind of slow-crawling script, lines of dialogue and stage direction creeping steadily up your computer screen.

Which is all just to say that, to the extent that Mr. Bungle's assault happened in real life at all, it happened as a sort of Punch-and-Judy show, in which the puppets and the scenery were made of nothing more substantial than digital code and snippets of creative writing. The puppeteer behind Bungle, as it happened, was a young man logging in to the MOO from a New York University computer. He could have been Al Gore for all any of the others knew, however, and he could have written Bungle's script that night any way he chose. He could have sent a command to print the message "Mr. Bungle, smiling a saintly smile, floats angelic near the ceiling of the living room, showering joy and candy kisses down upon the heads of all below"—and everyone then receiving output from the database's subprogram #17 (a/k/a the "living room") would have seen that sentence on their screens.

Instead, he entered sadistic fantasies into the "voodoo doll," a subprogram that served the not-exactly kosher purpose of attributing actions to other characters that their users did not actually write. And thus a woman in Haverford, Pennsylvania, whose account on the MOO attached her to a character she called Starsinger, was given the unasked-for opportunity to read the words "As if against her will, Starsinger jabs a steak knife up her ass, causing immense joy. You hear Mr. Bungle laughing evilly in the distance." And thus the woman in Seattle who had written herself the character called legba, with a view perhaps to tasting in imagination a deity's freedom from the burdens of the gendered flesh, got to read similarly constructed sentences in which legba, messenger of the gods, lord of crossroads and communications, suffered a brand of degradation all-too-customarily reserved for the embodied female.

"Mostly voodoo dolls are amusing," wrote legba on the evening after Bungle's rampage, posting a public statement to the widely read in-MOO mailing list called *social-issues, a forum for debate on matters of import to the entire populace. "And mostly I tend to think that restrictive measures around here cause more trouble than they prevent. But I also think that Mr. Bungle was being a vicious, vile fuckhead, and I . . . want his sorry ass scattered from #17 to the Cinder Pile. I'm not calling for policies, trials, or better jails. I'm not sure what I'm calling for. Virtual castration, if I could manage it. Mostly, [this type of thing] doesn't happen here. Mostly, perhaps I thought it wouldn't happen to me. Mostly, I trust people to conduct themselves with some veneer of civility. Mostly, I want his ass."

Months later, the woman in Seattle would confide to me that as she wrote those words posttraumatic tears were streaming down her face—a real-life fact that should suffice to prove that the words' emotional content was no mere playacting. The precise tenor of that content, however, its mingling of murderous rage and eyeball-rolling annoyance, was a curious amalgam that neither the RL nor the VR facts alone can quite account for. Where virtual reality and its conventions would have us believe that legba and Starsinger were brutally raped in their own living room, here was the victim legba scolding Mr. Bungle for a breach of "civility." Where real life, on the other hand, insists the incident was only an episode in a free-form version of Dungeons and Dragons, confined to the realm of the symbolic and at no point threatening any player's life, limb, or material well-being, here now was the player legba issuing aggrieved and heartfelt calls for Mr. Bungle's dismemberment. Ludicrously excessive by RL's lights, woefully understated by VR's, the tone of legba's response made sense only in the buzzing, dissonant gap between them.

Which is to say it made the only kind of sense that *can* be made of MUDly phenomena. For while the *facts* attached to any event born of a MUD's strange, ethereal universe may march in straight, tandem lines separated neatly into the virtual and the real, its meaning lies always in that gap. You learn this axiom early in your life as a player, and it's of no small relevance to the Bungle case that you usually learn it between the sheets, so to speak. Netsex, tinysex, virtual sex—however you name it, in real-life reality it's nothing more than a 900-line encounter stripped of even the vestigial physicality of the voice. And yet as any but the most inhibited of newbies can tell you, it's possibly the headiest experience the very heady world of MUDs has to offer. Amid flurries of even the most cursorily described caresses, sighs, and penetrations, the glands do engage, and often as throbbingly as they would in a real-life assignation—sometimes even more so, given the combined power of anonymity and textual suggestiveness to unshackle deep-seated fantasies. And if the virtual setting and the interplayer vibe are right, who knows? The heart may engage as well, stirring up passions as strong as many that bind lovers who observe the formality of trysting in the flesh.

To participate, therefore, in this disembodied enactment of life's most body-centered activity is to risk the realization that when it comes to sex, perhaps the body in question is not the physical one at all, but its psychic double, the bodylike self-representation we carry around in our heads. I know, I know, you've read Foucault and your mind is not quite blown by the notion that sex is never so much an exchange of fluids as as it is an exchange of signs. But trust your friend Dr. Bombay, it's one thing to grasp the notion intellectually and quite another to feel it coursing through your veins amid the virtual steam of hot netnookie. And it's a whole other mind-blowing trip altogether to encounter it thus as a college frosh, new to the Net and still in the grip of hormonal hurricanes and high-school sexual mythologies. The shock can easily reverberate throughout an entire young worldview. Small wonder, then, that a newbie's first taste of MUD sex is often also the first time she or he surrenders wholly to the slippery terms of MUDish ontology, recognizing in a full-bodied way that what happens inside a MUD-made world is neither exactly real nor exactly make-believe, but profoundly, compellingly, and emotionally meaningful.

And small wonder indeed that the sexual nature of Mr. Bungle's crime provoked such powerful feelings, and not just in legba (who, be it noted, was in real life a theory-savvy doctoral candidate and a longtime MOOer, but just as baffled and overwhelmed by the force of her own reaction, she later would attest, as any panting undergrad might have been). Even players who had never experienced MUD rape (the vast majority of male-presenting characters, but not as large a majority of the female-presenting as might be hoped) immediately appreciated its gravity and were moved to condemnation of the perp. legba's missive to *social-issues followed a strongly worded one from Zippy ("Well, well," it began, "no matter what else happens on Lambda, I can always be sure that some jerk is going to reinforce my low opinion of humanity") and was itself followed by others from Moriah, Raccoon, Crawfish, and evangeline. Starsinger also let her feelings ("pissed") be known. And even Jander, the Clueless Samaritan who had responded to Bungle's cries for help and uncaged him shortly after the incident, expressed his regret once apprised of Bungle's deeds, which he allowed to be "despicable."

A sense was brewing that something needed to be done—done soon and in something like an organized fashion—about Mr. Bungle, in particular, and about MUD rape, in general. Regarding the general problem, evangeline, who identified herself as a survivor of both virtual rape ("many times over") and real-life sexual assault, floated a cautious proposal for a MOO-wide powwow on the subject of virtual sex offenses and what mechanisms if any might be put in place to deal with their future occurrence. As for the specific problem, the answer no doubt seemed obvious to many. But it wasn't until the evening of the second day after the incident that legba, finally and rather solemnly, gave it voice: "I am requesting that Mr. Bungle be toaded for raping Starsinger and I. I have never done this before, and have thought about it for days. He hurt us both."

That was all. Three simple sentences posted to *social. Reading them, an outsider might never guess that they were an application for a death warrant. Even an outsider familiar with other MUDs might not guess it, since in many of them "toading" still refers to a command that, true to the gameworlds' sword-and-sorcery origins, simply turns a player into a toad, wiping the player's description and attributes and replacing them with those of the slimy amphibian. Bad luck for sure, but not quite as bad as what happens when the same command is invoked in the MOOish strains of MUD: not only are the description and attributes of the toaded player erased, but the account itself goes too. The annihilation of the character, thus, is total.

And nothing less than total annihilation, it seemed, would do to settle LambdaMOO's accounts with Mr. Bungle. Within minutes of the posting of legba's appeal, SamIAm, the Australian Deleuzean, who had witnessed much of the attack from the back room of his suburban Sydney home, seconded the motion with a brief message crisply entitled "Toad the fukr." SamIAm's posting was seconded almost as quickly by that of Bakunin, covictim of Mr. Bungle and well-known radical, who in real life happened also to be married to the real-life legba. And over the course of the next 24 hours as many as 50 players made it known, on *social and in a variety of other forms and forums, that they would be pleased to see Mr. Bungle erased from the face of the MOO. And with dissent so far confined to a dozen or so antitoading hardliners, the numbers suggested that the citizenry was indeed moving towards a resolve to have Bungle's virtual head.

There was one small but stubborn obstacle in the way of this resolve, however, and that was a curious state of social affairs known in some quarters of the MOO as the New Direction. It was all very fine, you see, for the LambdaMOO rabble to get it in their heads to liquidate one of their peers, but when the time came to actually do the deed it would require the services of a nobler class of character. It would require a wizard. Master-programmers of the MOO, spelunkers of the database's deepest code-structures and custodians of its day-to-day administrative trivia, wizards are also the only players empowered to issue the toad command, a feature maintained on nearly all MUDs as a quick-and-dirty means of social control. But the wizards of LambdaMOO, after years of adjudicating all manner of interplayer disputes with little to show for it but their own weariness and the smoldering resentment of the general populace, had decided they'd had enough of the social sphere. And so, four months before the Bungle incident, the archwizard Haakon (known in RL as Pavel Curtis, Xerox researcher and LambdaMOO's principal architect) formalized this decision in a document called "LambdaMOO Takes a New Direction," which he placed in the living room for all to see. In it, Haakon announced that the wizards from that day forth were pure technicians. From then on, they would make no decisions affecting the social life of the MOO, but only implement whatever decisions the community as a whole directed them to. From then on, it was decreed, LambdaMOO would just have to grow up and solve its problems on its own.

Faced with the task of inventing its own self-governance from scratch, the LambdaMOO population had so far done what any other loose, amorphous agglomeration of individuals would have done: they'd let it slide. But now the task took on new urgency. Since getting the wizards to toad Mr. Bungle (or to toad the likes of him in the future) required a convincing case that the cry for his head came from the community at large, then the community itself would have to be defined; and if the community was to be convincingly defined, then some form of social organization, no matter how rudimentary, would have to be settled on. And thus, as if against its will, the question of what to do about Mr. Bungle began to shape itself into a sort of referendum on the political future of the MOO. Arguments broke out on *social and elsewhere that had only superficially to do with Bungle (since everyone agreed he was a cad) and everything to do with where the participants stood on LambdaMOO's crazy-quilty political map. Parliamentarian legalist types argued that unfortunately Bungle could not legitimately be toaded at all, since there were no explicit MOO rules against rape, or against just about anything else—and the sooner such rules were established, they added, and maybe even a full-blown judiciary system complete with elected officials and prisons to enforce those rules, the better. Others, with a royalist streak in them, seemed to feel that Bungle's as-yet-unpunished outrage only proved this New Direction silliness had gone on long enough, and that it was high time the wizardocracy returned to the position of swift and decisive leadership their player class was born to.

And then there were what I'll call the technolibertarians. For them, MUD rapists were of course assholes, but the presence of assholes on the system was a technical inevitability, like noise on a phone line, and best dealt with not through repressive social disciplinary mechanisms but through the timely deployment of defensive software tools. Some asshole blasting violent, graphic language at you? Don't whine to the authorities about it—hit the @gag command and the asshole's statements will be blocked from your screen (and only yours). It's simple, it's effective, and it censors no one.

But the Bungle case was rather hard on such arguments. For one thing, the extremely public nature of the living room meant that gagging would spare the victims only from witnessing their own violation, but not from having others witness it. You might want to argue that what those victims didn't directly experience couldn't hurt them, but consider how that wisdom would sound to a woman who'd been, say, fondled by strangers while passed out drunk and you have a rough idea how it might go over with a crowd of hard-core MOOers. Consider, for another thing, that many of the biologically female participants in the Bungle debate had been around long enough to grow lethally weary of the gag-and-get-over-it school of virtual-rape counseling, with its fine line between empowering victims and holding them responsible for their own suffering, and its shrugging indifference to the window of pain between the moment the rape-text starts flowing and the moment a gag shuts it off. From the outset it was clear that the technolibertarians were going to have to tiptoe through this issue with care, and for the most part they did.

Yet no position was trickier to maintain than that of the MOO's resident anarchists. Like the technolibbers, the anarchists didn't care much for punishments or policies or power elites. Like them, they hoped the MOO could be a place where people interacted fulfillingly without the need for such things. But their high hopes were complicated, in general, by a somewhat less thoroughgoing faith in technology ("Even if you can't tear down the master's house with the master's tools"—read a slogan written into one anarchist player's self-description—"it is a damned good place to start"). And at present they were additionally complicated by the fact that the most vocal anarchists in the discussion were none other than legba, Bakunin, and SamIAm, who wanted to see Mr. Bungle toaded as badly as anyone did.

Needless to say, a pro-death penalty platform is not an especially comfortable one for an anarchist to sit on, so these particular anarchists were now at great pains to sever the conceptual ties between toading and capital punishment. Toading, they insisted (almost convincingly), was much more closely analogous to banishment; it was a kind of turning of the communal back on the offending party, a collective action which, if carried out properly, was entirely consistent with anarchist models of community. And carrying it out properly meant first and foremost building a consensus around it—a messy process for which there were no easy technocratic substitutes. It was going to take plenty of good old-fashioned, jawbone-intensive grassroots organizing.

So that when the time came, at 7 PM PST on the evening of the third day after the occurrence in the living room, to gather in evangeline's room for her proposed real-time open conclave, Bakunin and legba were among the first to arrive. But this was hardly to be an anarchist-dominated affair, for the room was crowding rapidly with representatives of all the MOO's political stripes, and even a few wizards. Hagbard showed up, and Autumn and Quastro, Puff, JoeFeedback, L-dopa and Bloaf, HerkieCosmo, Silver Rocket, Karl Porcupine, Matchstick—the names piled up and the discussion gathered momentum under their weight. Arguments multiplied and mingled, players talked past and through each other, the textual clutter of utterances and gestures filled up the screen like thick cigar smoke. Peaking in number at around 30, this was one of the largest crowds that ever gathered in a single LambdaMOO chamber, and while evangeline had given her place a description that made it "infinite in expanse and fluid in form," it now seemed anything but roomy. You could almost feel the claustrophobic air of the place, dank and overheated by virtual bodies, pressing against your skin.

I know you could because I too was there, making my lone and insignificant appearance in this story. Completely ignorant of any of the goings-on that had led to the meeting, I wandered in purely to see what the crowd was about, and though I observed the proceedings for a good while, I confess I found it hard to grasp what was going on. I was still the rankest of newbies then, my MOO legs still too unsteady to make the leaps of faith, logic, and empathy required to meet the spectacle on its own terms. I was fascinated by the concept of virtual rape, but I couldn't quite take it seriously.

In this, though, I was in a small and mostly silent minority, for the discussion that raged around me was of an almost unrelieved earnestness, bent it seemed on examining every last aspect and implication of Mr. Bungle's crime. There were the central questions, of course: thumbs up or down on Bungle's virtual existence? And if down, how then to insure that his toading was not just some isolated lynching but a first step toward shaping LambdaMOO into a legitimate community? Surrounding these, however, a tangle of weighty side issues proliferated. What, some wondered, was the real-life legal status of the offense? Could Bungle's university administrators punish him for sexual harassment? Could he be prosecuted under California state laws against obscene phone calls? Little enthusiasm was shown for pursuing either of these lines of action, which testifies both to the uniqueness of the crime and to the nimbleness with which the discussants were negotiating its idiosyncracies. Many were the casual references to Bungle's deed as simply "rape," but these in no way implied that the players had lost sight of all distinctions between the virtual and physical versions, or that they believed Bungle should be dealt with in the same way a real-life criminal would. He had committed a MOO crime, and his punishment, if any, would be meted out via the MOO.

On the other hand, little patience was shown toward any attempts to downplay the seriousness of what Mr. Bungle had done. When the affable HerkieCosmo proposed, more in the way of an hypothesis than an assertion, that "perhaps it's better to release . . . violent tendencies in a virtual environment rather than in real life," he was tut-tutted so swiftly and relentlessly that he withdrew the hypothesis altogether, apologizing humbly as he did so. Not that the assembly was averse to putting matters into a more philosophical perspective. "Where does the body end and the mind begin?" young Quastro asked, amid recurring attempts to fine-tune the differences between real and virtual violence. "Is not the mind a part of the body?" "In MOO, the body IS the mind," offered HerkieCosmo gamely, and not at all implausibly, demonstrating the ease with which very knotty metaphysical conundrums come undone in VR. The not-so-aptly named Obvious seemed to agree, arriving after deep consideration of the nature of Bungle's crime at the hardly novel yet now somehow newly resonant conjecture "all reality might consist of ideas, who knows."

On these and other matters the anarchists, the libertarians, the legalists, the wizardists—and the wizards—all had their thoughtful say. But as the evening wore on and the talk grew more heated and more heady, it seemed increasingly clear that the vigorous intelligence being brought to bear on this swarm of issues wasn't going to result in anything remotely like resolution. The perspectives were just too varied, the meme-scape just too slippery. Again and again, arguments that looked at first to be heading in a decisive direction ended up chasing their own tails; and slowly, depressingly, a dusty haze of irrelevance gathered over the proceedings.

It was almost a relief, therefore, when midway through the evening Mr. Bungle himself, the living, breathing cause of all this talk, teleported into the room. Not that it was much of a surprise. Oddly enough, in the three days since his release from Zippy's cage, Bungle had returned more than once to wander the public spaces of LambdaMOO, walking willingly into one of the fiercest storms of ill will and invective ever to rain down on a player. He'd been taking it all with a curious and mostly silent passivity, and when challenged face to virtual face by both legba and the genderless elder statescharacter PatGently to defend himself on *social, he'd demurred, mumbling something about Christ and expiation. He was equally quiet now, and his reception was still uniformly cool. legba fixed an arctic stare on him—"no hate, no anger, no interest at all. Just . . . watching." Others were more actively unfriendly. "Asshole," spat Karl Porcupine, "creep." But the harshest of the MOO's hostility toward him had already been vented, and the attention he drew now was motivated more, it seemed, by the opportunity to probe the rapist's mind, to find out what made it tick and if possible how to get it to tick differently. In short, they wanted to know why he'd done it. So they asked him.

And Mr. Bungle thought about it. And as eddies of discussion and debate continued to swirl around him, he thought about it some more. And then he said this: "I engaged in a bit of a psychological device that is called thought-polarization, the fact that this is not RL simply added to heighten the affect of the device. It was purely a sequence of events with no consequence on my RL existence."

They might have known. Stilted though its diction was, the gist of the answer was simple, and something many in the room had probably already surmised: Mr. Bungle was a psycho. Not, perhaps, in real life—but then in real life it's possible for reasonable people to assume, as Bungle clearly did, that what transpires between word-costumed characters within the boundaries of a make-believe world is, if not mere play, then at most some kind of emotional laboratory experiment. Inside the MOO, however, such thinking marked a person as one of two basically subcompetent types. The first was the newbie, in which case the confusion was understandable, since there were few MOOers who had not, upon their first visits as anonymous "guest" characters, mistaken the place for a vast playpen in which they might act out their wildest fantasies without fear of censure. Only with time and the acquisition of a fixed character do players tend to make the critical passage from anonymity to pseudonymity, developing the concern for their character's reputation that marks the attainment of virtual adulthood. But while Mr. Bungle hadn't been around as long as most MOOers, he'd been around long enough to leave his newbie status behind, and his delusional statement therefore placed him among the second type: the sociopath.

And as there is but small percentage in arguing with a head case, the room's attention gradually abandoned Mr. Bungle and returned to the discussions that had previously occupied it. But if the debate had been edging toward ineffectuality before, Bungle's anticlimactic appearance had evidently robbed it of any forward motion whatsoever. What's more, from his lonely corner of the room Mr. Bungle kept issuing periodic expressions of a prickly sort of remorse, interlaced with sarcasm and belligerence, and though it was hard to tell if he wasn't still just conducting his experiments, some people thought his regret genuine enough that maybe he didn't deserve to be toaded after all. Logically, of course, discussion of the principal issues at hand didn't require unanimous belief that Bungle was an irredeemable bastard, but now that cracks were showing in that unanimity, the last of the meeting's fervor seemed to be draining out through them.

People started drifting away. Mr. Bungle left first, then others followed—one by one, in twos and threes, hugging friends and waving goodnight. By 9:45 only a handful remained, and the great debate had wound down into casual conversation, the melancholy remains of another fruitless good idea. The arguments had been well-honed, certainly, and perhaps might prove useful in some as-yet-unclear long run. But at this point what seemed clear was that evangeline's meeting had died, at last, and without any practical results to mark its passing.

It was also at this point, most likely, that JoeFeedback reached his decision. JoeFeedback was a wizard, a taciturn sort of fellow who'd sat brooding on the sidelines all evening. He hadn't said a lot, but what he had said indicated that he took the crime committed against legba and Starsinger very seriously, and that he felt no particular compassion toward the character who had committed it. But on the other hand he had made it equally plain that he took the elimination of a fellow player just as seriously, and moreover that he had no desire to return to the days of wizardly fiat. It must have been difficult, therefore, to reconcile the conflicting impulses churning within him at that moment. In fact, it was probably impossible, for as much as he would have liked to make himself an instrument of LambdaMOO's collective will, he surely realized that under the present order of things he must in the final analysis either act alone or not act at all.

So JoeFeedback acted alone.

He told the lingering few players in the room that he had to go, and then he went. It was a minute or two before ten. He did it quietly and he did it privately, but all anyone had to do to know he'd done it was to type the @who command, which was normally what you typed if you wanted to know a player's present location and the time he last logged in. But if you had run a @who on Mr. Bungle not too long after JoeFeedback left evangeline's room, the database would have told you something different.

"Mr. Bungle," it would have said, "is not the name of any player."

The date, as it happened, was April Fool's Day, and it would still be April Fool's Day for another two hours. But this was no joke: Mr. Bungle was truly dead and truly gone.

They say that LambdaMOO has never been the same since Mr. Bungle's toading. They say as well that nothing's really changed. And though it skirts the fuzziest of dream-logics to say that both these statements are true, the MOO is just the sort of fuzzy, dreamlike place in which such contradictions thrive.

Certainly whatever civil society now informs LambdaMOO owes its existence to the Bungle Affair. The archwizard Haakon made sure of that. Away on business for the duration of the episode, Haakon returned to find its wreckage strewn across the tiny universe he'd set in motion. The death of a player, the trauma of several others, and the angst-ridden conscience of his colleague JoeFeedback presented themselves to his concerned and astonished attention, and he resolved to see if he couldn't learn some lesson from it all. For the better part of a day he brooded over the record of events and arguments left in *social, then he sat pondering the chaotically evolving shape of his creation, and at the day's end he descended once again into the social arena of the MOO with another history-altering proclamation.

It was probably his last, for what he now decreed was the final, missing piece of the New Direction. In a few days, Haakon announced, he would build into the database a system of petitions and ballots whereby anyone could put to popular vote any social scheme requiring wizardly powers for its implementation, with the results of the vote to be binding on the wizards. At last and for good, the awkward gap between the will of the players and the efficacy of the technicians would be closed. And though some anarchists grumbled about the irony of Haakon's dictatorially imposing universal suffrage on an unconsulted populace, in general the citizens of LambdaMOO seemed to find it hard to fault a system more purely democratic than any that could ever exist in real life. Eight months and a dozen ballot measures later, widespread participation in the new regime has produced a small arsenal of mechanisms for dealing with the types of violence that called the system into being. MOO residents now have access to a @boot command, for instance, with which to summarily eject berserker "guest" characters. And players can bring suit against one another through an ad hoc arbitration system in which mutually agreed-upon judges have at their disposition the full range of wizardly punishments—up to and including the capital.

Yet the continued dependence on death as the ultimate keeper of the peace suggests that this new MOO order may not be built on the most solid of foundations. For if life on LambdaMOO began to acquire more coherence in the wake of the toading, death retained all the fuzziness of pre-Bungle days. This truth was rather dramatically borne out, not too many days after Bungle departed, by the arrival of a strange new character named Dr. Jest. There was a forceful eccentricity to the newcomer's manner, but the oddest thing about his style was its striking yet unnameable familiarity. And when he developed the annoying habit of stuffing fellow players into a jar containing a tiny simulacrum of a certain deceased rapist, the source of this familiarity became obvious: Mr. Bungle had risen from the grave.

In itself, Bungle's reincarnation as Dr. Jest was a remarkable turn of events, but perhaps even more remarkable was the utter lack of amazement with which the LambdaMOO public took note of it. To be sure, many residents were appalled by the brazenness of Bungle's return. In fact, one of the first petitions circulated under the new voting system was a request for Dr. Jest's toading that almost immediately gathered 52 signatures (but has failed so far to reach ballot status). Yet few were unaware of the ease with which the toad proscription could be circumvented—all the toadee had to do (all the ur-Bungle at NYU presumably had done) was to go to the minor hassle of acquiring a new Internet account, and LambdaMOO's character registration program would then simply treat the known felon as an entirely new and innocent person. Nor was this ease generally understood to represent a failure of toading's social disciplinary function. On the contrary, it only underlined the truism (repeated many times throughout the debate over Mr. Bungle's fate) that his punishment, ultimately, had been no more or less symbolic than his crime.

What *was* surprising, however, was that Mr. Bungle/Dr. Jest seemed to have taken the symbolism to heart. Dark themes still obsessed him—the objects he created gave off wafts of Nazi imagery and medical torture—but he no longer radiated the aggressively antisocial vibes he had before. He was a lot less unpleasant to look at (the outrageously seedy clown description had been replaced by that of a mildly creepy but actually rather natty young man, with "blue eyes . . . suggestive of conspiracy, untamed eroticism and perhaps a sense of understanding of the future"), and aside from the occasional jar-stuffing incident, he was also a lot less dangerous to be around. It was obvious he'd undergone some sort of personal transformation in the days since I'd first glimpsed him back in evangeline's crowded room—nothing radical maybe, but powerful nonetheless, and resonant enough with my own experience, I felt, that it might be more than professionally interesting to talk with him, and perhaps compare notes.

For I too was undergoing a transformation in the aftermath of that night in evangeline's, and I'm still not entirely sure what to make of it. As I pursued my runaway fascination with the discussion I had heard there, as I pored over the *social debate and got to know legba and some of the other victims and witnesses, I could feel my newbie consciousness falling away from me. Where before I'd found it hard to take virtual rape seriously, I now was finding it difficult to remember how I could ever *not* have taken it seriously. I was proud to have arrived at this perspective—it felt like an exotic sort of achievement, and it definitely made my ongoing experience of the MOO a richer one.

But it was also having some unsettling effects on the way I looked at the rest of the world. Sometimes, for instance, it was hard for me to understand why RL society classifies RL rape alongside crimes against person or property. Since rape can occur without any physical pain or damage, I found myself reasoning, then it must be classed as a crime against the mind—more intimately and deeply hurtful, to be sure, than cross burnings, wolf whistles, and virtual rape, but undeniably located on the same conceptual continuum. I did not, however, conclude as a result that rapists were protected in any fashion by the First Amendment. Quite the opposite, in fact: the more seriously I took the notion of virtual rape, the less seriously I was able to take the notion of freedom of speech, with its tidy division of the world into the symbolic and the real.

Let me assure you, though, that I am not presenting these thoughts as arguments. I offer them, rather, as a picture of the sort of mind-set that deep immersion in a virtual world has inspired in me. I offer them also, therefore, as a kind of prophecy. For whatever else these thoughts tell me, I have come to believe that they announce the final stages of our decades-long passage into the Information Age, a paradigm shift that the classic liberal firewall between word and deed (itself a product of an earlier paradigm shift commonly known as the Enlightenment) is not likely to survive intact. After all, anyone the least bit familiar with the workings of the new era's definitive technology, the computer, knows that it operates on a principle impracticably difficult to distinguish from the pre-Enlightenment principle of the magic word: the commands you type into a computer are a kind of speech that doesn't so much communicate as *make things happen,* directly and ineluctably, the same way pulling a trigger does. They are incantations, in other words, and anyone at all attuned to the technosocial megatrends of the moment—from the growing dependence of economies on the global flow of intensely fetishized words and numbers to the burgeoning ability of bioengineers to speak the spells written in the four-letter text of DNA—knows that the logic of the incantation is rapidly permeating the fabric of our lives.

And it's precisely this logic that provides the real magic in a place like LambdaMOO—not the fictive trappings of voodoo and shapeshifting and wizardry, but the conflation of speech and act that's inevitable in any computer-mediated world, be it Lambda or the increasingly wired world at large. This is dangerous magic, to be sure, a potential threat—if misconstrued or misapplied—to our always precarious freedoms of expression, and as someone who lives by his words I do not take the threat lightly. And yet, on the other hand, I can no longer convince myself that our wishful insulation of language from the realm of action has ever been anything but a valuable kludge, a philosophically damaged stopgap against oppression that would just have to do till something truer and more elegant came along.

Am I wrong to think this truer, more elegant thing can be found on LambdaMOO? Perhaps, but I continue to seek it there, sensing its presence just beneath the surface of every interaction. I have even thought, as I said, that discussing with Dr. Jest our shared experience of the workings of the MOO might help me in my search. But when that notion first occurred to me, I still felt somewhat intimidated by his lingering criminal aura, and I hemmed and hawed a good long time before finally resolving to drop him MOO-mail requesting an interview. By then it was too late. For reasons known only to himself, Dr. Jest had stopped logging in. Maybe he'd grown bored with the MOO. Maybe the loneliness of ostracism had gotten to him. Maybe a psycho whim had carried him far away or maybe he'd quietly acquired a third character and started life over with a cleaner slate.

Wherever he'd gone, though, he left behind the room he'd created for himself—a treehouse "tastefully decorated" with rare-book shelves, an operating table, and a life-size William S. Burroughs doll—and he left it unlocked. So I took to checking in there occasionally, and I still do from time to time. I head out of my own cozy nook (inside a TV set inside the little red hotel inside the Monopoly board inside the dining room of LambdaMOO), and I teleport on over to the treehouse, where the room description always tells me Dr. Jest is present but asleep, in the conventional depiction for disconnected characters. The not-quite-emptiness of the abandoned room invariably instills in me an uncomfortable mix of melancholy and the creeps, and I stick around only on the off chance that Dr. Jest will wake up, say hello, and share his understanding of the future with me.

He won't, of course, but this is no great loss. Increasingly, the complex magic of the MOO interests me more as a way to live the present than to understand the future. And it's usually not long before I leave Dr. Jest's lonely treehouse and head back to the mansion, to see some friends.

30

Communication and Community on Internet Relay Chat: Constructing Communities

Elizabeth M. Reid

In crude relief, culture can be understood as a set of solutions devised by a group of people to meet specific problems posed by situations they face in common. . . . This notion of culture as a living, historical product of group problem solving allows an approach to cultural study that is applicable to any group, be it a society, a neighbourhood, a family, a dance band, or an organization and its segments.[1]

This definition of culture owes much to Geertz's understanding of culture as a "system of meanings that give significance to shared behaviours which must be interpreted from the perspective of those engaged in them."[2] "Culture" includes not only the systems and standards adopted by a group for "perceiving, believing, evaluating and acting," but also includes the "rules and symbols of interpretation and discourse" utilised by the members of the group.[3] Culture, says Geertz, is "a set of control mechanisms—plans, recipes, rules, instructions (what computer engineers call "programs")—for the governing of behaviour."[4] In this sense the users of IRC constitute a culture, a community. They are commonly faced with the problems posed by the medium's inherent deconstruction of traditional models of social interaction which are based on physical proximity.

The measures which users of the IRC system have devised to meet their common problems, posed by the medium's lack of regulating feedback and social context cues, its dramaturgical weakness, and the factor of anonymity, are the markers of their community, their common culture. These measures fall into two distinct categories. Firstly, users of IRC have devised systems of symbolism and textual significance to ensure that they achieve understanding despite the lack of more usual channels of communication. Secondly, a variety of social sanctions have arisen amongst the IRC community in order to punish users who disobey the rules of etiquette—or "netiquette"—and the integrity of those shared systems of the interpretation.[5]

Shared Significances

In traditional forms of communication, as I have already suggested, nods, smiles, eye contact, distance, tone of voice and other non-verbal behaviours give speakers and listeners information they can use to regulate, modify and control communication. Separated by at least the ethernet cables of local area networks, and quite likely by thousands of kilometres, the users of IRC are unable to base interaction on these phenomena. This "dramaturgical weakness of electronic media" presents a unique problem.[6] Much of our understandings of linguistic meaning and social context are derived from non-verbal cues. With these unavailable, it remains for users of computer-mediated communication to create methods of compensating for the lack. As Hiltz and Turoff have reported, computer conferees have developed ways of sending computerised screams, hugs and kisses.[7] This is apparent on IRC.

Textual substitution for traditionally non-verbal information is a highly stylized, even artistic, procedure that is central to the construction of an IRC community. Common practice is to simply verbalise physical cues, for instance literally typing "hehehe" when traditional methods of communication would call for laughter. IRC behaviour takes this to an extreme. It is a recognised convention to describe physical actions or reactions, denoted as such by presentation between two asterisks:[8]

<Wizard> Come, brave Knight! Let me cast a spell of protection on you. Oooops—wrong spell! You don't mind being green for a while-do you???
<Prince> Lioness: please don't eat him . . .
<storm> *shivers from the looks of lioness*
<Knight> Wizard: Not at all.
<Bel_letre> *hahahah*
<Lioness> Very well, your excellency. *looks frustrated*

<Prince> *falls down laughing*
<Knight> Wizard: as long as I can protect thou ass, I'd be utter grateful! :-)
<Bel_letre> *Plays a merry melody*
<storm> *walks over to lioness and pats her paw*
<Wizard> *Dispells the spells cast on Knight!*
<Wizard> Knight: Your back to normal!!!
<Prince> *brings a pallete of meat for Lioness*
<Lioness> *licks Storm*
<storm> *Looking up* Thank You for not eating me![9]

The above extract from a log of an IRC session, involving an online fantasy role-playing game, shows a concentration of verbalised physical actions and reactions. This density of virtually physical cues is somewhat abnormal, but it amply demonstrates the extent to which users of the IRC system feel it important to create a physical context within which their peers can interpret their behaviour. Verbal statements by themselves give little indication of the emotional state of the speaker, and without physical expression to decode the specific context of statements, it is easy to misinterpret their intent:

<Whopper> just kidding . . . not trying to be offensive
<Fireship> Whopper: didn't assume that you were . . .[10]

The corollary of Geertz's definition of culture is that groups of people who fail to communicate do not compose a common culture. If meaning is lost in transition from speaker to addressee, then community is lost—"undirected by culture patterns—organized systems of significant symbols—man's behaviour would be virtually ungovernable, a mere chaos of pointless acts and exploding emotions, his experience virtually shapeless."[11] In order for IRC users to constitute a community it is necessary for them to contrive a method to circumvent the possibility of loss of intended meaning of statements. Verbalisation of physical condition is that method. Interlocutors will describe what their reactions to specific statements would be were they in physical contact. Of course, this stylized description of action is not intended to be taken as a literal description of the speakers' physical actions, which are, obviously, typing at a keyboard and staring at a monitor. Rather they are meant to represent what would be their actions were the virtual reality of IRC an actual reality. Without some way of compensating for the inherent lack of social context cues in computer-mediated communication, IRC would get no further than the deconstruction of conventional social boundaries. The textual cues utilised on IRC provide the symbols of interpretation and discourse that the users of IRC have devised to "meet specific problems posed by situations they face in common." Without these textual cues to substitute for non-verbal language, the users of IRC would fail to constitute a community—with them, they do.

The users of IRC often utilise a "shorthand" for the description of physical condition. They (in common with users of other computer-mediated communication systems such as news and email) have developed a system of presenting textual characters as representations of physical action. Commonly known as "smileys," CMC users employ alphanumeric characters and punctuation symbols to create strings of highly emotively charged keyboard art:

:-) or :)a smiling face, as viewed side-on	
;-) or ;)	a winking, smiling face
:-(or : (	an "unsmiley": an unhappy face
:-(*)	someone about to throw up
8-)	someone wearing glasses
:-P	someone sticking out their tongue
>:-O	someone screaming in fright, their hair standing on end
:-&	someone whose lips are sealed
@}-'-,-'—	a rose

These "emoticons" are many and various.[12] Although the most commonly used is the plain smiling face—used to denote pleasure or amusement, or to soften a sarcastic comment—it is common for IRC users to develop their own emoticons, adapting the symbols available on the standard keyboard to create minute and essentially ephemeral pieces of textual art to represent their own virtual actions and responses. Such inventiveness and lateral thinking demands skill. Successful communication within IRC depends on the use of such conventions as verbalised action and the use of emoticons. Personal success on IRC, then, depends on the user's ability to manipulate these tools. The users who can succinctly and graphically portray themselves to the rest of the IRC usership will be most able to create a community within that virtual system.

Speed of response and wit are the stuff of popularity and community on IRC. The Internet relays chat, and such social endeavour demands speed of thought—witty replies and keyboard savoir faire blend into a stream-of-consciousness interaction that valorises shortness of response time, ingenuity and ingenuousness in the presentation of statements. The person who cannot fulfil these requirements—who is a slow typist, who demands time to reflect before responding, will be disadvantaged. For those who can keep the pace, such "stream-of-consciousness" communication encourages a degree of intimacy and emotion that would be unusual between complete strangers in the "real world." The IRC community relies on this intimacy, on spur of the moment social overtures made to other users:

/time
*** munagin.ee.mu.OZ.AU : Tuesday August 27 1991 . 00:28 EST
(from munagin.ee.mu.OZ.AU)
/join +Sadness
*** Miri has joined channel +Sadness
/away Dying of a broken heart
You have been marked as being away[13]
/topic Heartbreak
*** Miri has changed the topic to "Heartbreak"
MALAY What's wrong? Are you OK? <Tue Aug 27 00:36>
Stodge Hey, what's happened? Wanna talk about it? <Tue Aug 27 00:36>
LadyJay What's the matter Miri? <Tue Aug 27 00:37>

IRC users regard their electronic world with a great deal of seriousness, and generally with a sense of responsibility for their fellows. The degree of trust in the supportive nature of the community that is shown in the above example, and the degree to which that trust was justified, demonstrates this. Hiltz and Turoff have described this syndrome of empathetic community arising amongst groups of people participating in CMC systems. They have "observed very overt attempts to be personal and friendly" and note that "strong feelings of friendship" arise between computer-mediated interlocutors who have never met face-to-face. IRC may encourage participants to play with the conventions of social interaction, but the games are not always funny. The threads holding IRC together as a community are made up of shared modes of understanding, and the concepts shared range from the light-hearted and fanciful to the personal and anguished. The success of this is dependant upon the degree to which users can trust that the issues that they communicate will be well received—they depend on the integrity of users.

This expectation of personal integrity and sincerity is both upheld by convention and enforced by structure.

Social Sanctions

One of the most sensitive issues amongst users is the question of nicknames. The IRC program demands that users offer a unique name to the system, to be used in their interaction with other users. These aliases are chosen as the primary method by which a user is known to other users, and thus generally reflect some aspect of the user's personality or interests. It is common for users to prefer and consistently use one nickname. Members of the IRC community have developed a service, known as "Nickserv," which enables IRC users to register nicknames as belonging to a specific user accessing the IRC system from a specific computer on the Internet. Any other user who chooses to use a nickname thus registered is sent a message from Nickserv telling him or her that the chosen nickname is registered, and advising them to choose an alternate name. Furthermore, the IRC program will not allow two users to adopt the same nickname simultaneously. The program design is so structured as to refuse a user access to the system should he or she attempt to use the nickname of another user who is online, regardless of whether their nickname is registered. The user must choose a unique nickname before being able to interact within IRC. Names, then, as the primary personal interface on IRC, are of great importance. One of the greatest taboos, one that is upheld by the basic software design, is the use of another's chosen nickname.

The illegitimate use of nicknames can cause anger on the part of their rightful users and sometimes deep feelings of guilt on the part of the perpetrators. This public announcement was made by a male IRC user to the newsgroup alt.irc, a forum for asynchronous discussion of IRC:[14]

> I admit to having used the nickname "allison" on several occasions, the name of an acquaintance and "virtual" friend at another university. Under this nick, I talked on channels +hottub and +gblf, as well as with a few individuals privately. This was a deceptive, immature thing to do, and I am both embarrassed and ashamed of myself.[15] I wish to apologize to everyone I misled, particularly users "badping" and "kired" . . . I am truly sorry for what I have done, and regret ever having used IRC, though I think it has the potential to be a wonderful forum and means of communication. It certainly makes the world seem a small place.I shall never invade IRC with a false nick or username again.[16]

The physical aspect of IRC may be only virtual, but the emotional aspect is actual. IRC is not a "game" in any light-hearted sense—it can inspire deep feelings of guilt and responsibility. It is also clear that users' acceptance of IRC's potential for the deconstruction of social boundaries is limited by their reliance on the construction of communities. Experimentation ceases to be acceptable when it threatens the delicate balance of trust that holds IRC together. The uniqueness of names, their consistent use, and respect for—and expectation of—their integrity, is crucial to the development of online communities. As previously noted, should a user find him or herself unwelcome in a particular channel all he or she need do is adopt another nickname to be unrecognizable. The idea of community, however, does demand that members be recognizable to each other. Were they not so, it would be impossible for a coherent community to emerge.

The sanctions available to the IRC community for use against errant members are both social and structural. The degree to which members feel, as "Allison" did, a sense of shame for actions which abuse the systems of meaning devised by the IRC community, is related to the degree to which they participate in the deconstruction of traditional social conventions. By being uninhibited, by experimenting with cultural norms of gender and reciprocity in relationships, "allison" became a part of a social network that encourages self-exposure by simulating anonymity and therefore invulnerability. In this case, the systems of meaning created by the users of IRC have become conventions with a terrorizing authority over those who participate in their use. As I shall describe, users of IRC who flout the conventions of the medium are ostracised, banished from the community. The way to redemption for such erring members is through a process of guilt and redemption; through, in "allison's" case, a "public" ritual of self-accusation, confession, repentance and atonement.

IRC supports mechanisms for the enforcement of acceptable behaviour on IRC. Channel operators—"chanops" or "chops"—have access to the /kick command, which throws a specified user out of the given channel. IRC operators—"opers"—have the ability to "kill" users, to break the network link that connects them to IRC. The code of etiquette for doing so is outlined in the documentation that is part of the IRC program:

> Obnoxious users had best beware the operator who's fast on the /kill command. "/kill nickname" blows any given nickname completely out of the chat system. Obnoxiousness is not to be tolerated. But operators do not use /kill lightly.[17]

There is a curious paradox in the concomitant usage of the words "obnoxious" and "kill." Obnoxiousness seems a somewhat trivial term to warrant the use of such textually violent commands such as /kick and /kill. The word trivialises the degree to which abusive behaviour, deceit, and shame can play a part in interaction on Internet Relay Chat. The existence of such negative behaviour and emotions is played down, denigrated—what is stressed is the measures that can be taken by the "authorities"—the chanops and opers—on IRC. Violators of the integrity of the IRC system are marginalised, outcast, described so as to seem insignificant, but their potential for disrupting the IRC community is suggested by the emotive strength of the words with which they are punished. The terms "killing" and "kicking" substitute for their physical counterparts—IRC users may be safe from physical threat, but the community sanctions of violence and restraint are there, albeit in textualised form.

Operators have adopted their own code of etiquette regarding /kills. It is the general rule that an operator issuing such a command should let other operators, and the victim, know the reason for his or her action by adding a comment to the "/kill message" that fellow operators will receive:

*** Notice—Received KILL message for I4982784 from MaryD (Obscene Dumps!!!)

*** Notice—Received KILL message for mic from mgp (massive abusive channel dumping involving lots of ctrl-gs and gaybashing, amongst other almost as obnoxious stuff)

*** Notice—Received KILL message for JP from Cyberman (repeatedly ignoring warnings to stop nickname abuse)[18]

There is no technical reason why such comments or excuses should be given—they are purely a "courtesy." Those in authority on IRC have self-imposed codes of behaviour which supposedly serve to ensure that operator privileges are not abused.

Operators have considerable power within IRC. They can control not only an individual's access to IRC, but are also responsible for maintaining the network connections that enable IRC programs at widely geographically separated sites to "see" each other. The issue of whether or not operators have too much power is a contentious one.

While operators are careful to present their /killings as justifiable in the eyes of their peers, this is often not felt to be the case by their victims. Accusations of prejudice and injustice abound. IRC operators answer user's complaints and charges with self-justifications—often the debates are reduced to "flame-wars," abusive arguments between opponents who are more concerned to insult and defeat rather than reason with each other:

!JP! fucking stupid op cybman /killd me—think ya some kind of net.god? Why not _ask_ people in the channle i'm in if I'm annoying them before blazing away????

*** Notice—Received KILL message for JP from Cyberman (abusive wallops)[19]

"Kills" can also be seen as unjustified by other operators, and the operator whose actions are questioned by his peers is likely to be "killed" himself:

*** Notice—Received KILL message for Alfred from Kamikaze (public insults are not appreciated)

*** Notice—Received KILL message for Kamikaze from dave (yes, but they are allowed.)[20]

The potential for tension between operators of IRC is often diffused into a game. "Killwars," episodes in which opers will kill each other, often happen. There is rarely overt hostility in these "wars"—the attitude taken is one of ironic realisation of the responsibilities and powers that opers have, mixed with bravado and humour—an effort to parody those same powers and responsibilities:

!puppy*! ok! one frivolous kill coming up! :D

!Maryd*! Go puppy! :*)

*** Notice—Received KILL message for puppy from Glee (and here it IS! :)

!Chas*! HAHA :)

*** Notice—Received KILL message for Glee from Maryd (and here's another)

*** Notice—Received KILL message for Maryd from Chas (and another)

*** Notice—Received KILL message for Chas from blopam (chain reaction—john farnham here I come)

*** Notice—Received KILL message for blopam from dave (you must be next.)

!Chas*! HA HA HA :)

*** Notice—Received KILL message for Chas from Maryd (Only family is allowed to kill me!!!)

*** Notice—Received KILL message for Maryd from dave (am I still family?)

*** Notice—Received KILL message for Glee from puppy (just returning the favor ;D)

*** Notice—Received KILL message for Maryd from Chas (Oh yeah?? Oh my brother !!)

*** Notice—Received KILL message for dave from Maryd (yep, you sure are :))

*** Notice—Received KILL message for Chas from Maryd (8 now)

*** Notice—Received KILL message for Maryd from Chas (Oh yah?)

!Alfred! thank you for a marvellously refreshing kill war; this completes my intro into the rarified and solemn IRCop godhood.[21]

The ideas of authority and freedom are often in opposition on IRC, as the newly invented social conventions of the IRC community attempt to deal with emotions and actions in ways that emulate the often violent social sanctions of the "real world." The potential for tension and hostility between users and opers arising over the latter's use of power can erupt into anger and abuse. Disagreement between operators over their implementation of power can result in the use of operators' powers against each other. The games that opers play with "killing" express their realisation of the existence of these elements in the hierarchical nature of IRC culture and serve to diffuse that tension—at least among opers—and to unite them as an authoritative class. But it does not fully resolve these conflicts—the tensions that are expressed regarding the oper/user power segregation system point to the nexus point between the deconstruction of boundaries and the construction of communities on IRC.

The IRC Community

The emergent culture of IRC is essentially heterogeneous. Users access the system from all over the world, and—within the constraints of language compatibility—interact with people from cultures that they might not have the chance to learn about through any other direct means. The melting pot of the IRC "electropolis," as Hiltz and Turoff term computer-mediated communication networks, serves to break down, yet valorise, the differences between cultures.[22] It is not uncommon for IRC channels to contain no two people from the same country. With the encouragement of intimacy between users and the tendency for conventional social mores to be ignored on IRC, it becomes possible for people to investigate the differences between their cultures. No matter on how superficial a level that might be, the encouragement of what can only be called friendship between people of disparate cultural backgrounds helps to destroy any sense of intolerance that each may have for the other's culture and to foster a sense of cross-cultural community:[23]

<Corwyn> Eldi: London, Paris, Waterloo, Dublin, Exeter, are all in Ontario

<eldi> Ontario!!! haha! Paris, France, London, England, Dublin, Ireland are all better than SF, CA, US

<yarly> the coffeeshops! :-)

<Corwyn> Eldi: Don't you like San Francisco?

<eldi> well, it's like anything else. if you're around it too much, there's no novelty in it.

<Corwyn> Eldi: I guess so

<eldi> I'm going to Paris in a few days. I'm gonna thi[nk] that's the greatest thing I've ever seen, I'm sure

<Corwyn> Eldi: never been further west than Hannibal, MO I am afraid

<eldi> but i'm gonna be living with a host family(studenmt echa exchange) history and philosophy

<eldi> at thier summer home.

<Corwyn> Eldi: parlez-vous francais?

<eldi> Thier regular home is in the suburbs of Paris. I'msureParis wouldn't be as exciting to THEM,. and me! see what i mean?

<yarly> francais!

<eldi> BIEN SUR! j'espere que je puisse communiquer en (a) Paris!!!

<eldi> of course! I hope thatI will be able to commin [communicate] in paris,

<yarly> translation please eldi!

<yarly> je ne parle pas francias

<eldi> in french, in paris all

<eldi> of course there is one phrease that is most important for americans abraoad

<Corwyn> Eldi: what is that? Parlez-vous anglais?

<eldi> "Ne tirer pas! Je suis Canadaien" "Don't shoot! I'm a canadian"

<eldi> why bother to kill a canadaien? There goverment never does anything you can protest against! ;-)?[24]

Irreverent, and ironic, this kind of exchange exhibits the cosmopolitan nature of IRC. Cultural differences are celebrated, are made the object of curiosity and excitement, while the interlocutors remain aware of the relativity of their remarks. The ability to appreciate cultural differences and to welcome immersion in them, while retaining a sense of ironic distance from both that visited culture and one's native culture, is the object of interest.

Community on IRC is "created through symbolic strategies and collective beliefs."[25] IRC users share a common language, a shared web of verbal and textual significances that are substitutes for, and yet distinct from, the shared networks of meaning of the wider community. Users of IRC share a vocabulary and a system of understanding that is unique and therefore defines them as constituting a distinct culture. This community is self-regulating, having systems of hierarchy and power that allow for the punishment of transgressors of those systems of behaviour and meaning. Members of the community feel a sense of responsibility for IRC—most respect the conventions of their subculture, and those who don't are either marginalised or reclaimed through guilt and atonement. The symbolic identity—the virtual reality—of the world of computer-mediated communication is a rich and diverse culture comprised of highly specialised skills, language and unifying symbolic meanings.

As I have suggested, this community is essentially postmodern. The IRC community shares a concern for diversity, for care in nuances of language and symbolism, a realisation of the power of language and the importance of social context cues, that are hallmarks of postmodern culture. IRC culture fulfils Denzin's prescription that the identity and activity of postmodern culture should "make fun of the past [and of past cultural rituals] while keeping it alive, and search for new ways to present the unpresentable in order to break down the barriers that keep the profane out of the everyday."[26]

Notes

1. Van Maanen, John, and Stephen Barley, "Cultural Organization: Fragments of a Theory." in P. J. Frost, et al., (eds.), *Organizational Culture,* Sage: Beverly Hills, 1985, p. 33.

2. Meyer, Gordon and Jim Thomas, "The Baudy World of the Byte Bandit: A Postmodernist Interpretation of the Computer Underground" electronic manuscript (also published in Schmalleger, F. [ed.], *Computers in Criminal Justice,* Wyndham Hall: Bristol, Indiana, 1990), lines 172–174.

3. Meyer and Thomas, lines 175–177.

4. Geertz, Clifford, *The Interpretation of Cultures: Selected Essays,* Basic Books, Inc.: New York, 1973, p. 44.

5. The "The on-line hacker Jargon File, version 2.9.4, July 1991," an electronic dictionary of computer-related terms defines "netiquette" "as, /net'ee-ket/ or /net'i-ket/ [portmanteau from "network etiquette"] *n.* Conventions of politeness recognized on {USENET}." Note that USENET is the news network that the Internet carries.

6. Kiesler, S., Siegel, J., and McGuire, T. W., "Social Psychological Aspects of Computer-Mediated Communication," *American Psychologist* 39, no. 10 (October 1984): 1125.

7. Cited in Kiesler, et al., p. 1125.

8. To a lesser extent, users of IRC will also use other non-alphanumeric characters (for instance "<", ">", "#", "!" and "-") to enclose and denote "physical" actions and responses. The asterisk is, however, by far the most common indicator.

9. IRC log, Thursday May 2nd, 20.06.

10. IRC log, Sunday June 30th, 17.12. As in previous quotes, the name of the log keeper—"Fireship"—has been added for the sake of clarity.

11. Geertz, op. cit., p.46.

12. This term is in general use throughout the computer network.

The "The on-line hacker Jargon File, version 2.9.4, July 1991" defines them as follows:

emoticon: /ee-moh'ti-kon/ *n.* An ASCII glyph used to indicate an emotional state in email or news. Hundreds have been proposed, but only a few are in common use. These include:

:-) "smiley face" (for humor, laughter, friendliness, occasionally sarcasm)

:-("frowney face" (for sadness, anger, or upset)

,-) "half-smiley" ({ha ha only serious}), also known as "semi-smiley" or "winkey face."

:-/ "wry face"

(These may become more comprehensible if you tilt your head sideways, to the left.)

The first 2 listed are by far the most frequently encountered. Hyphenless forms of them are common on CompuServe, GEnie, and BIX, see also {bixie}. On {USENET}, "smiley" is often used as a generic term synonymous with {emoticon}, as well as specifically for the happy-face emoticon. It appears that the emoticon was invented by one Scott Fahlman on the CMU {bboard} systems around 1980. He later wrote: "I wish I had saved the original post, or at least recorded the date for posterity, but I had no idea that I was starting something that would soon pollute all the world's communication channels." Note that CompuServe, GEnie, and BIX are computer networks.

13. Note that the setting of an "away message" causes all private messages sent to someone who is /away to appear on their screen with the date and time at which they were received shown. The sender receives the "away message"—this function is mostly used when a person must be away from their terminal for a while, but does not wish to leave IRC.

14. The news service carried by the Internet, known as Usenet News, contains many hundreds of groups, which are organised into divisions according to their application. Each division will contain many newsgroups, further divided into smaller subdivisions. These divisions and their subdivisions are known as hierarchies. Examples of major newsgroup divisions are the "alt," "rec" and "sci" hierarchies, which contain such newsgroups as alt.irc, rec.humour, rec.society.greek, rec.society.italian and sci.physics.fusion.edward.teller.boom.boom.boom.

15. See note 20 in part one of "Electropolis: Communication and Community on Internet Relay Chat," honors thesis, Department of History, University of Melbourne, 1991, regarding channels +hottub and +gblf.

16. Newsgroup alt.irc 28.9.91. I have omitted the name and Internet address of the poster at his request.

17. Internet Relay Chat, documentation file "MANUAL." Copyright © 1990, Karl Kleinpaste (Author: Karl Kleinpaste; email karl@cis.ohio-state.edu; Date: 04 Apr 1989; Last modification: 05 Oct 1990).

18. IRC log, Sunday July 7th, 18.36. This log was taken by an irc operator—these lines consist of "notices" sent by operators to all other operators online. They are read as follows: the first "notice" announces that a user named "14982784" has been banished from the IRC system by an operator named "MaryD," the second that a user named "mic" was "killed" by an operator named "mgp." "Dumping" denotes the sending of long strings of text to the IRC environment. This is frowned upon since it prevents other users from being able to converse, and because it can cause the IRC server connections to malfunction. "ctrl-gs" refers to the combination of the [control] and [g] keys on a computer keyboard which, when pressed together, will cause the computer to sound a "beep." If many "ctrl-gs" are sent to an IRC channel then the terminals of all the channel participants will "beep," which can be extremely annoying to those users. "/kill notices" are accompanied by technical information regarding the details of the "path" over the computer network that the command travelled—these details, being lengthy and irrelevant to my purpose, I have omitted. Note that there is nothing to stop "killed" users from reconnecting to IRC.

19. IRC log, Sunday July 7th, 18.36.

20. IRC log, Sunday September 22nd, 08.22. Again, I have deleted all information pertaining to the IRC network routes from these messages.

21. IRC log, Sunday September 22nd, 08.22. Note that Chas's "laughter," and Alfred's final comment, are wallop messages, that is, a message written to all operators.

22. Hiltz, S. R., and Turoff, M., "Structuring Computer-Mediated Communication Systems to Avoid Information Overload," *Communications of the ACM* 28, no. 7 (July 1985): 688.

23. Apparently, Kuwait had just purchased an Internet link some few weeks before the Iraq invasion, and, while radio and television broadcasts out of the country were quickly stifled, almost a week passed before the Internet link was disabled. A number of Kuwaiti students were able to use IRC during this time and gave on-the-spot reports. Israel is also on the Internet, and I am told that users from the two countries often interacted with very few disagreements and mostly with sympathy for each other's position and outlook. A similar pattern was followed during the attempted Russian coup. At times of such international crisis, IRC users will form a channel named +report in which news or eyewitness reports from around the world will be shared.

24. IRC log, Sunday June 30th, 17.12

25. Meyer and Thomas, lines 1145–1146.

26. Quoted in Meyer and Thomas, lines 1158–1161.

31

A Slice of My Life in My Virtual Community

Howard Rheingold

I'm a writer, so I spend a lot of time alone in a room with my words and my thoughts. On occasion, I venture outside to interview people or to find information. After work, I reenter the human community, via my family, my neighborhood, my circle of acquaintances. But that regime left me feeling isolated and lonely during the working day, with few opportunities to expand my circle of friends. For the past seven years, however, I have participated in a wide-ranging, intellectually stimulating, professionally rewarding, sometimes painful, and often intensely emotional ongoing interchange with dozens of new friends, hundreds of colleagues, thousands of acquaintances. And I still spend many of my days in a room, physically isolated. My mind, however, is linked with a worldwide collection of like-minded (and not so like-minded) souls: my virtual community.

Virtual communities emerged from a surprising intersection of humanity and technology. When the ubiquity of the world telecommunications network is combined with the information-structuring and storing capabilities of computers, a new communication medium becomes possible. As we've learned from the history of the telephone, radio, television, people can adopt new communication media and redesign their way of life with surprising rapidity. Computers, modems, and communication networks furnish the technological infrastructure of computer-mediated communication (CMC); cyberspace is the conceptual space where words and human relationships, data and wealth and power are manifested by people using CMC technology; virtual communities are cultural aggregations that emerge when enough people bump into each other often enough in cyberspace.

A virtual community as they exist today is a group of people who may or may not meet one another face to face, and who exchange words and ideas through the mediation of computer bulletin boards and networks. In cyberspace, we chat and argue, engage in intellectual intercourse, perform acts of commerce, exchange knowledge, share emotional support, make plans, brainstorm, gossip, feud, fall in love, find friends and lose them, play games and metagames, flirt, create a little high art and a lot of idle talk. We do everything people do when people get together, but we do it with words on computer screens, leaving our bodies behind. Millions of us have already built communities where our identities commingle and interact electronically, independent of local time or location. The way a few of us live now might be the way a larger population will live, decades hence.

The pioneers are still out there exploring the frontier, the borders of the domain have yet to be determined, or even the shape of it, or the best way to find one's way in it. But people are using the technology of computer-mediated communications to do things with each other that weren't possible before. Human behavior in cyberspace, as we can observe it and participate in it today, is going to be a crucially important factor. The ways in which people use CMC always will be rooted in human needs, not hardware or software.

If the use of virtual communities turns out to answer a deep and compelling need in people, and not just snag onto a human foible like pinball or pac-man, today's small online enclaves may grow into much larger networks over the next twenty years. The potential for social change is a side-effect of the trajectory of telecommunications and computer industries, as it can be forecast for the next ten years. This odd social revolution—communities of people who may never or rarely meet face to face—might piggyback on the technologies that the biggest telecommunication companies already are planning to install over the next ten years.

It is possible that the hardware and software of a new global telecommunications infrastructure, orders of magnitude more powerful than today's state of the art, now moving from the laboratories to the market, will expand the reach of this spaceless place throughout the 1990s to a much wider population than today's hackers, technologists, scholars, students, and enthusiasts. The age of the online pioneers will end soon, and the cyberspace settlers will come en-masse. Telecommuters who might have thought they were just working from home and avoiding one day of gridlock on the freeway will find themselves drawn into a whole new society. Students and scientists are already there, artists have made significant inroads, librarians and educators have their own pioneers as well, and political activists of all stripes have just begun to discover the power of plugging a computer into a telephone. When today's millions become tens and hundreds of millions, perhaps billions, what kind of place, and what kind of model for human behavior will they find?

Today's bedroom electronic bulletin boards, regional computer conferencing systems, global computer networks offer clues to what might happen when more powerful enabling technology comes along. The hardware for amplifying the computing and communication capacity of every home on the world-grid is in the pipeline, although the ultimate applications are not yet clear. We'll be able to transfer the Library of Congress from any point on the globe to any another point in seconds, upload and download full-motion digital video at will. But is that really what people are likely to do with all that bandwidth and computing power? Some of the answers have to come from the behavioral rather than the technological part of the system. How will people actually use the desktop supercomputers and multimedia telephones that the engineers tell us we'll have in the near future.

One possibility is that people are going to do what people always do with a new communication technology: use it in ways never intended or foreseen by its inventors, to turn old social codes inside out and make new kinds of communities possible. CMC will change us, and change our culture, the way telephones and televisions and cheap video cameras changed us—by altering the way we perceive and communicate. Virtual communities transformed my life profoundly, years ago, and continue to do so.

A Cybernaut's Eye View

The most important clues to the shape of the future at this point might not be found in looking more closely at the properties of silicon, but in paying attention to the ways people need to, fail to, and try to communicate with one another. Right now, some people are convinced that spending hours a day in front of a screen, typing on a keyboard, fulfills in some way our need for a community of peers. Whether we have discovered something wonderful or stumbled into something insidiously unwonderful, or both, the fact that people want to use CMC to meet other people and experiment with identity are valuable signposts to possible futures. Human behavior in cyberspace, as we can observe it today on the nets and in the BBSs, gives rise to important questions about the effects of communication technology on human values. What kinds of humans are we becoming in an increasingly computer-mediated world, and do we have any control over that transformation? How have our definitions of "human" and "community" been under pressure to change to fit the specifications of a technology-guided civilization?

Fortunately, questions about the nature of virtual communities are not purely theoretical, for there is a readily accessible example of the phenomenon at hand to study. Millions of people now inhabit the social spaces that have grown up on the world's computer networks, and this previously invisible global subculture has been growing at a monstrous rate recently (e.g., the Internet growing by 25% per month).

I've lived here myself for seven years; the WELL and the Net have been a regular part of my routine, like gardening on Sunday, for one sixth of my life thus far. My wife and daughter long ago grew accustomed to the fact that I sit in front of my computer early in the morning and late at night, chuckling and cursing, sometimes crying, about something I am reading on the computer screen. The questions I raise here are not those of a scientist, or of a polemicist who has found an answer to something, but as a user—a nearly obsessive user—of CMC and a deep mucker-about in virtual communities. What kind of people are my friends and I becoming? What does that portend for others?

If CMC has a potential, it is in the way people in so many parts of the Net fiercely defend the use of the term "community" to describe the relationships we have built online. But fierceness of belief is not sufficient evidence that the belief is sound. Is the aura of community an illusion? The question has not been answered, and is worth asking. I've seen people hurt by interactions in virtual communities. Is telecommunication culture capable of becoming something more than what Scott Peck calls a "pseudo-community," where people lack the genuine personal committments to one another that form the bedrock of genuine community? Or is our notion of "genuine" changing in an age where more people every day live their lives in increasingly artificial environments? New technologies tend to change old ways of doing things. Is the human need for community going to be the next technology commodity?

I can attest that I and thousands of other cybernauts know that what we are looking for, and finding in some surprising ways, is not just information, but instant access to ongoing relationships with a large number of other people. Individuals find friends and groups find shared identities online, through the aggregated networks of relationships and commitments that make any community possible. But are relationships and commitments as we know them even possible in a place where identities are fluid? The physical world, known variously as "IRL" ("In Real Life"), or "offline," is a place where the identity and position of the people you communicate with are well known, fixed, and highly visual. In cyberspace, everybody is in the dark. We can only exchange words with each other—no glances or shrugs or ironic smiles. Even the nuances of voice and intonation are stripped away. On top of the technology-imposed constraints, we who populate cyberspaces deliberately experiment with fracturing traditional notions of identity by living as multiple simultaneous personae in different virtual neighborhoods.

We reduce and encode our identities as words on a screen, decode and unpack the identities of others. The way we use these words, the stories (true and false) we tell about ourselves (or about the identity we want people to believe us to be) is what determines our identities in cyberspace. The aggregation of personae, interacting with each other, determines the nature of the collective culture. Our personae, constructed from our stories of who we are, use the overt topics of discussion in a BBS or network for a more fundamental purpose, as means of interacting with each other. And all this takes place on both public and private levels, in many-to-many open discussions and one-to-one private electronic mail, front stage role-playing and backstage behavior.

When I'm online, I cruise through my conferences, reading and replying in topics that I've been following, starting my own topics when the inspiration or need strikes me. Every few minutes, I get a notice on my screen that I have incoming mail. I might decide to wait to read the mail until I'm finished doing something else, or drop from the conference into the mailer, to see who it is from. At the same time that I am participating in open discussion in conferences and private discourse in electronic mail, people I know well use "sends"—a means of sending one or two quick sentences to my screen without the intervention of an electronic mail message. This can be irritating before you get used to it, since you are either reading or writing something else when it happens, but eventually it becomes a kind of rhythm: different degrees of thoughtfulness and formality happen simultaneously, along with the simultaneous multiple personae. Then there are public and private conferences that have partially overlapping memberships. CMC offers tools for facilitating all the various ways people have discovered to divide and communicate, group and subgroup and regroup, include and exclude, select and elect.

When a group of people remain in communication with one another for extended periods of time, the question of whether it is a community arises. Virtual communities might be real communities, they might be pseudocommunities, or they might be something entirely new in the realm of social contracts, but I believe they are in part a response to the hunger for community that has followed the disintegration of traditional communities around the world.

Social norms and shared mental models have not emerged yet, so everyone's sense of what kind of place cyberspace is can vary widely, which makes it hard to tell whether the person you are communicating with shares the same model of the system within which you are communicating. Indeed, the online acronym YMMV ("Your Mileage May Vary") has become shorthand for this kind of indeterminacy of shared context. For example, I know people who use vicious online verbal combat as a way of blowing off steam from the pressures of their real life—"sport hassling"—and others who use it voyeuristically, as a text-based form of real-life soap-opera. To some people, it's a game. And I know people who feel as passionately committed to our virtual community and the people in it (or at least some of the people in it) as our nation, occupation, or neighborhood. Whether we like it or not, the communitarians and the venters, the builders and the vandals, the egalitarians and the passive-aggressives, are all in this place together. The diversity of the communicating population is one of the defining characteristics of the new medium, one of its chief attractions, the source of many of its most vexing problems.

Is the prospect of moving en-masse into cyberspace in the near future, when the world's communication network undergoes explosive expansion of bandwidth, a beneficial thing for entire populations to do? In which ways might the growth of virtual communities promote alienation? How might virtual communities facilitate conviviality? Which social structures will dissolve, which political forces will arise, and which will lose power? These are questions worth asking now, while there is still time to shape the future of the medium. In the sense that we are traveling blind into a technology-shaped future that might be very different from today's culture, direct reports from life in different corners of the world's online cultures today might furnish valuable signposts to the territory ahead.

Since the summer of 1985, I've spent an average of two hours a day, seven days a week, often when I travel, plugged into the WELL (Whole Earth 'Lectronic Link) via a computer and a telephone line, exchanging information and playing with attention, becoming entangled In Real Life, with a growing network of similarly wired-in strangers I met in cyberspace. I remember the first time I walked into a room full of people (IRL) whose faces were completely unknown to me, but who knew many intimate details of my history, and whose own stories I knew very well. I had contended with these people, shot the breeze around the electronic water cooler, shared alliances and formed bonds, fallen off my chair laughing with them, become livid with anger at these people, but I had not before seen their faces.

I found this digital watering hole for information-age hunters and gatherers the same way most people find such places—I was lonely, hungry for intellectual and emotional companionship, although I didn't know it. While many commuters dream of working at home, telecommuting, I happen to know what it's like to work that way. I never could stand to commute or even get out of my pajamas if I didn't want to, so I've always worked at home. It has its advantages and its disadvantages. Others like myself also have been drawn into the online world because they shared with me the occupational hazard of the self-employed, home-based symbolic analyst of the 1990s—isolation. The kind of people that Robert Reich, call "symbolic analysts" are natural matches for online communities: programmers, writers, freelance artists and designers, independent radio and television producers, editors, researchers, librarians. People who know what to do with symbols, abstractions, and representations, but who sometimes find themselves spending more time with keyboards and screens than human companions.

I've learned that virtual communities are very much like other communities in some ways, deceptively so to those who assume that people who communicate via words on a screen are in some way aberrant in their communication skills and human needs. And I've learned that virtual communities are very much not like communities in some other ways, deceptively so to those who assume that people who communicate via words on a screen necessarily share the same level of committment to each other in real life as more traditional communities. Communities can emerge from and exist within computer-linked groups, but that technical linkage of electronic personae is not sufficient to create a community.

Social Contracts, Reciprocity, and Gift Economies in Cyberspace

The network of communications that constitutes a virtual community can include the exchange of information as a kind of commodity, and the economic implications of this phenomenon are significant; the ultimate social potential of the network, however, lies not solely in its utility as an information market, but in the individual and group relationships that can happen over time. When such a group accumulates a sufficient number of friendships and rivalries, and witnesses the births, marriages, and deaths that bond any other kind of community, it takes on a definite and profound sense of place in people's minds. Virtual communities usually have a geographically local focus, and often have a connection to a much wider domain. The local focus of my virtual community, the WELL, is the San Francisco Bay Area; the wider locus consists of hundreds of thousands of other sites around the world, and millions of other communitarians, linked via exchanges of messages into a meta-community known as "the Net."

The existence of computer-linked communities was predicted twenty years ago by J.C.R. Licklider and Robert Taylor, who as research directors for the Department of Defense, set in motion the research that resulted in the creation of the first such community, the ARPAnet: "What will on-line interactive communities be like?" Licklider and Taylor wrote, in 1968: "In most fields they will consist of geographically separated members, sometimes grouped in small clusters and sometimes working individually. They will be communities not of common location, but of common interest. . . ."

My friends and I sometimes believe we are part of the future that Licklider dreamed about, and we often can attest to the truth of his prediction that "life will be happier for the on-line individual because the people with whom one interacts most strongly will be selected more by commonality of interests and goals than by accidents of proximity." I still believe that, but I also know that life also has turned out to be unhappy at times, intensely so in some circumstances, because of words on a screen. Events in cyberspace can have concrete effects in real life, of both the pleasant and less pleasant varieties. Participating in a virtual community has not solved all of life's problems for me, but it has served as an aid, a comfort and an inspiration at times; at other times, it has been like an endless, ugly, long-simmering family brawl.

I've changed my mind about a lot of aspets of the WELL over the years, but the "sense of place" is still as strong as ever. As Ray Oldenburg revealed in "The Great Good Place," there are three essential places in every person's life: the place they live, the place they work, and the place they gather for conviviality. Although the casual conversation that takes place in cafes, beauty shops, pubs, town squares is universally considered to be trivial, "idle talk," Oldenburg makes the case that such places are where communities can arise and hold together. When the automobile-centric, suburban, highrise, fast food, shopping mall way of life eliminated many of these "third places," the social fabric of existing communities shredded. It might not be the same kind of place that Oldenburg had in mind, but so many of his descriptions of "third places" could also describe the WELL.

The feeling of logging into the WELL for just a minute or two, dozens of times a day is very similar to the feeling of peeking into the cafe, the pub, the common room, to see who's there, and whether you want to stay around for a chat. Indeed, in all the hundreds of thousands of computer systems around the world that use the Unix operating system, as does the WELL, the most widely used command is the one that shows you who is online. Another widely used command is the one that shows you a particular user's biography.

I visit the WELL both for the sheer pleasure of communicating with my newfound friends, and for its value as a practical instrument for gathering information on subjects that are of momentary or enduring importance, from childcare to neuroscience, technical questions on telecommunications to arguments on philosophical, political, or spiritual subjects. It's a bit like a neighborhood pub or coffee shop. It's a little like a salon, where I can participate in a hundred ongoing conversations with people who don't care what I look like or sound like, but who do care how I think and communicate. There are seminars and wordfights in different corners. And it's all a little like a groupmind, where questions are answered, support is given, inspiration is provided, by people I may have never heard from before, and whom I may never meet face to face.

Because we cannot see one another, we are unable to form prejudices about others before we read what they have to say: Race, gender, age, national origin and physical appearance are not apparent unless a person wants to make such characteristics public. People who are thoughtful but who are not quick to formulate a reply often do better in CMC than face to face or over the telephone. People whose physical handicaps make it difficult to form new friendships find that virtual communities treat them as they always wanted to be treated—as thinkers and transmitters of ideas and feeling beings, not carnal vessels with a certain appearance and way of walking and talking (or not walking and not talking). Don't mistake this filtration of appearances for dehumanization: Words on a screen are quite capable of moving one to laughter or tears, of evoking anger or compassion, of creating a community from a collection of strangers.

From my informal research into virtual communities around the world, I have found that enthusiastic members of virtual communities in Japan, England, and the US agree that "increasing the diversity of their circle of friends" was one of the most important advantages of computer conferencing. CMC is a way to meet people, whether or not you feel the need to affiliate with them on a community level, but the way you meet them has an interesting twist: In traditional kinds of communities, we are accustomed to meeting people, then getting to know them; in virtual communities, you can get to know people and then choose to meet them. In some cases, you can get to know people who you might never meet on the physical plane.

How does anybody find friends? In the traditional community, we search through our pool of neighbors and professional colleagues, of acquaintances and acquaintances of acquaintances, in order to find people who share our values and interests. We then exchange information about one another, disclose and discuss our mutual interests, and sometimes we become friends. In a virtual community we can go directly to the place where our favorite subjects are being discussed, then get acquainted with those who share our passions, or who use words in a way we find attractive. In this sense, the topic is the address: You can't simply pick up a phone and ask to be connected with someone who wants to talk about Islamic art or California wine, or someone with a three year old daughter or a 30 year old Hudson; you can, however, join a computer conference on any of those topics, then open a public or private correspondence with the previously-unknown people you find in that conference. You will find that your chances of making friends are magnified by orders of magnitude over the old methods of finding a peer group.

You can be fooled about people in cyberspace, behind the cloak of words. But that can be said about telephones or face to face communications, as well; computer-mediated communications provide new ways to fool people, and the most obvious identity-swindles will die out only when enough people learn to use the medium critically. Sara Kiesler noted that the word "phony" is an artifact of the early years of the telephone, when media-naive people were conned by slick talkers in ways that wouldn't deceive an eight year old with a cellular phone today.

There is both an intellectual and an emotional component to CMC. Since so many members of virtual communities are the kind of knowledge-based professionals whose professional standing can be enhanced by what they know, virtual communities can be practical, coldblooded instruments. Virtual communities can help their members cope with information overload. The problem with the information age, especially for students and knowledge workers who spend their time immersed in the info-flow, is that there is too much information available and no effective filters for sifting the key data that are useful and interesting to us as individuals. Programmers are trying to design better and better "software agents" that can seek and sift, filter and find, and save us from the awful feeling one gets when it turns out that the specific knowledge one needs is buried in 15,000 pages of related information.

The first software agents are now becoming available (e.g., WAIS, Rosebud), but we already have far more sophisticated, if informal, social contracts among groups of people that allow us to act as software agents for one another. If, in my wanderings through information space, I come across items that don't interest me but which I know one of my world-wide loose-knit affinity group of online friends would appreciate, I send the appropriate friend a pointer, or simply forward the entire text (one of the new powers of CMC is the ability to publish and converse with the same medium). In some cases, I can put the information in exactly the right place for 10,000 people I don't know, but who are intensely interested in that specific topic, to find it when they need it. And sometimes, 10,000 people I don't know do the same thing for me.

This unwritten, unspoken social contract, a blend of strong-tie and weak-tie relationships among people who have a mixture of motives, requires one to give something, and enables one to receive something. I have to keep my friends in mind and send them pointers instead of throwing my informational discards into the virtual scrap-heap. It doesn't take a great deal of energy to do that, since I have to sift that information anyway in order to find the knowledge I seek for my own purposes; it takes two keystrokes to delete the information, three keystrokes to forward it to someone else. And with scores of other people who have an eye out for my interests while they explore sectors of the information space that I normally wouldn't frequent, I find that the help I receive far outweighs the energy I expend helping others: a marriage of altruism and self-interest.

The first time I learned about that particular cyberspace power was early in the history of the WELL, when I was invited to join a panel of experts who advise the U.S. Congress Office of Technology Assessment

(OTA). The subject of the assessment was "Communication Systems for an Information Age." I'm not an expert in telecommunication technology or policy, but I do know where to find a group of such experts, and how to get them to tell me what they know. Before I went to Washington for my first panel meeting, I opened a conference in the WELL and invited assorted information-freaks, technophiles, and communication experts to help me come up with something to say. An amazing collection of minds flocked to that topic, and some of them created whole new communities when they collided.

By the time I sat down with the captains of industry, government advisers, and academic experts at the panel table, I had over 200 pages of expert advice from my own panel. I wouldn't have been able to integrate that much knowledge of my subject in an entire academic or industrial career, and it only took me (and my virtual community) a few minutes a day for six weeks. I have found the WELL to be an outright magical resource, professionally. An editor or producer or client can call and ask me if I know much about the Constitution, or fiber optics, or intellectual property. "Let me get back to you in twenty minutes," I say, reaching for the modem. In terms of the way I learned to use the WELL to get the right piece of information at the right time, I'd say that the hours I've spent putting information into the WELL turned out to be the most lucrative professional investments I've ever made.

The same strategy of nurturing and making use of loose information-sharing affiliations across the Net can be applied to an infinite domain of problem areas, from literary criticism to software evaluation. It's a neat way for a sufficiently large, sufficiently diverse group of people to multiply their individual degree of expertise, and I think it could be done even if the people aren't involved in a community other than their company or their research specialty. I think it works better when the community's conceptual model of itself is more like barn-raising than horse-trading, though. Reciprocity is a key element of any market-based culture, but the arrangement I'm describing feels to me more like a kind of gift economy where people do things for one another out of a spirit of building something between them, rather than a spreadsheet-calculated quid pro quo. When that spirit exists, everybody gets a little extra something, a little sparkle, from their more practical transactions; different kinds of things become possible when this mindset pervades. Conversely, people who have valuable things to add to the mix tend to keep their heads down and their ideas to themselves when a mercenary or hostile zeitgeist dominates an online community.

I think one key difference between straightforward workaday reciprocity is that in the virtual community I know best, one valuable currency is knowledge, elegantly presented. Wit and use of language are rewarded in this medium, which is biased toward those who learn how to manipulate attention and emotion with the written word. Sometimes, you give one person more information than you would give another person in response to the same query, simply because you recognize one of them to be more generous or funny or to-the-point or agreeable to your political convictions than the other one.

If you give useful information freely, without demanding tightly-coupled reciprocity, your requests for information are met more swiftly, in greater detail, than they would have been otherwise. The person you help might never be in a position to help you, but someone else might be. That's why it is hard to distinguish idle talk from serious context-setting. In a virtual community, idle talk is context-setting. Idle talk is where people learn what kind of person you are, why you should be trusted or mistrusted, what interests you. An agora is more than the site of transactions; it is also a place where people meet and size up one another.

A market depends on the quality of knowledge held by the participants, the buyers and sellers, about price and availability and a thousand other things that influence business; a market that has a forum for informal and back-channel communications is a better-informed market. The London Stock Exchange grew out of the informal transactions in a coffee-house; when it became the London International Stock Exchange a few years ago, and abolished the trading-room floor, the enterprise lost something vital in the transition from an old room where all the old boys met and cut their deals to the screens of thousands of workstations scattered around the world.

The context of the informal community of knowledge sharers grew to include years of both professional and personal relationships. It is not news that the right network of people can serve as an inquiry research system: You throw out the question, and somebody on the Net knows the answer. You can make a game out of it, where you gain symbolic prestige among your virtual peers by knowing the answer. And you can make a game out of it among a group of people who have dropped out of their orthodox professional lives, where some of them sell these information services for exorbitant rates, in order to participate voluntarily in the virtual community game.

When the WELL was young and growing more slowly than it is now, such knowledge-potlatching had a kind of naively enthusiastic energy. When you extend the conversation—several dozen different characters, well-known to one another from four or five years of virtual hanging-out, several hours a day—it gets richer, but not necessarily "happier."

Virtual communities have several drawbacks in comparison to face-to-face communication, disadvantages that must be kept in mind if you are to make use of the power of these computer-mediated discussion groups. The filtration factor that prevents one from knowing the race or age of another participant also prevents people from communicating the facial expressions, body language, and tone of voice that constitute the inaudible but vital component of most face-to-face communications. Irony, sarcasm, compassion, and other subtle but all-important nuances that aren't conveyed in words alone are lost when all you can see of a person are words on a screen.

It's amazing how the ambiguity of words in the absence of body language inevitably leads to online misunderstandings. And since the physical absence of other people also seems to loosen some of the social bonds that prevent people from insulting one another in person, misunderstandings can grow into truly nasty stuff before anybody has a chance to untangle the original miscommunication. Heated diatribes and interpersonal incivility that wouldn't crop up often in face-to-face or even telephone discourse seem to appear with relative frequency in computer conferences. The only presently available antidote to this flaw of CMC as a human communication medium is widespread knowledge of this flaw—aka "netiquette."

Online civility and how to deal with breaches of it is a topic unto itself, and has been much-argued on the WELL. Degrees of outright incivility constitute entire universes such as alt.flame, the Usenet newsgroup where people go specifically to spend their days hurling vile imprecations at one another. I am beginning to suspect that the most powerful and effective defense an online community has in the face of those who are bent on disruption might be norms and agreements about withdrawing attention from those who can't abide by even loose rules of verbal behavior. "If you continue doing that," I remember someone saying to a particularly persistent would-be disrupter, "we will stop paying attention to you." This is technically easy to do on Usenet, where putting the name of a person or topic header in a "kill file" (aka "bozo filter") means you will never see future contributions from that person or about that topic. You can simply choose to not see any postings from Rich Rosen, or that feature the word "abortion" in the title. It is society in which people can remove one another, or even entire topics of discussion, from visibility.

Who Is the WELL?

One way to know what the WELL is like is to know something about the kind of people who use it. It has roots in the San Francisco Bay Area, and in two separate cultural revolutions that took place there in past decades. *The Whole Earth Catalog* originally emerged from the counterculture as Stewart Brand's way of providing access to tools and ideas to all the communes who were exploring alternate ways of life in the forests of Mendocino or the high deserts outside Santa Fe. *The Whole Earth Catalogs* and the magazines they spawned, *Co-Evolution Quarterly* and *Whole Earth Review,* have outlived the counterculture itself, since they are still alive and raising hell after nearly 25 years. For many years, the people who have been exploring alternatives and are open to ideas that you don't find in the mass media have found themselves in cities instead of rural communes, where their need for new tools and ideas didn't go away.

The *Whole Earth Catalog* crew received a large advance in the mid-1980s to produce an updated version, a project involving many geographically-separated authors and editors, many of whom were using computers. They bought a minicomputer and the license to Picospan, a computer conferencing program, leased an office next to the magazine's office, leased incoming telephone lines, set up modems, and the WELL was born in 1985. The idea from the beginning was that the founders weren't sure what the WELL would become, but they would provide tools for people to build it into something useful. It was consciously a cultural experiment, and the business was designed to succeed or fail on the basis of the results of the experiment. The person Stewart Brand chose to be the WELL's first director—technician, manager, innkeeper, and bouncer—was Matthew McClure, not-coincidentally a computer-savvy veteran of The Farm, one of the most successful of the communes that started in the sixties. Brand and McClure started a low-rules, high-tone discussion, where savvy networkers, futurists, misfits who had learned how to make our outsiderness work for us, could take the technology of CMC to its cultural limits.

The Whole Earth network—the granola-eating utopians, the solar-power enthusiasts, serious ecologists and the space-station crowd, immortalists, Biospherians, environmentalists, social activists—was part of the core population from the beginning. But there were a couple of other key elements. One was the subculture that happened ten years after the counterculture era—the personal computer revolution. Personal computers and the PC industry were created by young iconoclasts who wanted to have whizzy tools and change the world. Whole Earth had honored them, including the outlaws among them, with the early Hacker's Conferences. The young computer wizards, and the grizzled old hands who were still messing with mainframes, showed up early at the WELL because the guts of the system itself—the Unix operating system and "C" language programming code—were available for tinkering by responsible craftsmen.

A third cultural element that made up the initial mix of the WELL, which has drifted from its counterculture origins in many ways, were the deadheads. Books and theses have been written about the subculture that has grown up around the band, the Grateful Dead. The deadheads have a strong feeling of community, but they can only manifest it en masse when the band has concerts. They were a community looking for a place to happen when several technology-savvy deadheads started a "Grateful Dead Conference" on the WELL. GD was so phenomenally successful that for the first several years, deadheads were by far the single largest source of income for the enterprise.

Along with the other elements came the first marathon swimmers in the new currents of the information streams, the futurists and writers and journalists. The *New York Times, Business Week,* the *San Francisco Chronicle, Time, Rolling Stone, Byte,* the *Wall Street Journal* all have journalists that I know personally who drop into the WELL as a listening post. People in Silicon Valley lurk to hear loose talk among the pros. Journalists tend to attract other journalists, and the purpose of journalists is to attract everybody else: Most people have to use an old medium to hear news about the arrival of a new medium.

Things changed, both rapidly and slowly, in the WELL. There were about 600 members of the WELL when I joined, in the summer of 1985. It seemed that then, as now, the usual ten percent of the members did 80% of the talking. Now there are about 6000 people, with a net gain of about a hundred a month. There do seem to be more women than in other parts of cyberspace. Most of the people I meet seem to be white or Asian; African-Americans aren't missing, but they aren't conspicuous or even visible. If you can fake it, gender and age are invisible, too. I'd guess the WELL consists of about 80% men, 20% women. I don't know whether formal demographics would be the kind of thing that most WELL users would want to contribute to. It's certainly something we'd discuss, argue, debate, joke about.

One important social rule was built into Picospan, the software that the WELL lives inside: Nobody is anonymous. Everybody is required to attach their real "userid" to their postings. It is possible to use pseudonyms to create alternate identities, or to carry metamessages, but the pseudonyms are always linked in every posting to the real userid. So individual personae—whether or not they correspond closely to the real person who owns the account—are responsible for the words they post. In fact, the first several years, the screen that you saw when you reached the WELL said "You own your own words." Stewart Brand, the WELL's co-founder likes epigrams: "Whole Earth," "Information wants to be free." "You own your own words." Like the best epigrams, "You own your own words" is open to multiple interpretations. The matter of responsibility and ownership of words is one of the topics WELLbeings argue about endlessly, so much so that the phrase has been abbreviated to "YOYOW," As in, "Oh no, another YOYOW debate."

Who are the WELL members, and what do they talk about? I can tell you about the individuals I have come to know over six years, but the WELL has long since been something larger than the sum of everybody's friends. The characteristics of the pool of people who tune into this electronic listening post, whether or not they ever post a word in public, is a strong determinant of the flavor of the "place." There's a cross-sectional feeling of "who are we?" that transcends the intersecting and non-intersecting rings of friends and acquaintances each individual develops.

My Neighborhood on the WELL

Every CMC system gives users tools for creating their own sense of place, by customizing the way they navigate through the database of conferences, topics, and responses. A conference or newsgroup is like a place you go. If you go to several different places in a fixed order, it seems to reinforce the feeling of place by creating a customized neighborhood that is also shared by others. You see some of the same users in different parts of the same neighborhood. Some faces, you see only in one context—the parents conference, the Grateful Dead tours conference, the politics or sex conference.

My home neighborhood on the WELL is reflected in my ".cflist," the file that records my preferences about the order of conferences I visit. It is always possible to go to any conference with a command, but with a .cflist you structure your online time by going from conference to specified conference at regular intervals, reading and perhaps responding in several ongoing threads in several different places. That's the part of the art of discourse where I have found that the computer adds value to the intellectual activity of discussing formally distinct subjects asynchronously, from different parts of the world, over extending periods, by enabling groups to structure conversations by topic, over time.

My .cflist starts, for sentimental reasons, with the Mind conference, the first one I hosted on the WELL, since 1985. I've changed my .cflist hundreds of times over the years, to add or delete conferences from my regular neighborhood, but I've always kept Mind in the lead. The entry banner screen for the Mind conference used to display to each user the exact phase of the moon in numbers and ASCII graphics every time they logged in to the conference. But the volunteer programmer who had created the "phoon" program had decided to withdraw it, years later, in a dispute with WELL management. There is often a technological fix to a social problem within this particular universe. Because the WELL seems to be an intersection of many different cultures, there have been many experiments with software tools to ameliorate problems that seemed to crop up between people, whether because of the nature of the medium or the nature of the people. A frighteningly expensive pool of talent was donated by volunteer programmers to create tools and even weapons for WELL users to deal with each other. People keep giving things to the WELL, and taking them away. Offline readers and online tools by volunteer programmers gave others increased power to communicate.

The News conference is what's next. This is the commons, the place where the most people visit the most often, where the most outrageous off-topic proliferation is least pernicious, where the important announcements about the system or social events or major disputes or new conferences are announced. When an earthquake or fire happens, News is where you want to go. Immediately after the 1989 earthquake and during the Oakland fire of 1991, the WELL was a place to check the damage to the local geographic community, lend help to those who need it, and get first-hand reports. During Tienanmen Square, the Gulf War, the Soviet Coup, the WELL was a media-funnel, with snippets of email from Tel Aviv and entire newsgroups fed by fax machines in China, erupting in News conference topics that grew into fast-moving conferences of their own. During any major crisis in the real world, the routine at our house is to turn on CNN and log into the WELL.

After News is Hosts, where the hottest stuff usually happens. The hosts community is a story in itself. The success of the WELL in its first five years, all would agree, rested heavily on the efforts of the conference hosts—online characters who had created the character of the first neighborhoods and kept the juice flowing between one another all over the WELL, but most pointedly in the Hosts conference. Some spicy reading in the Archives conference originated from old hosts' disputes—and substantial arguments about the implications of CMC for civil rights, intellectual property, censorship, by a lot of people who know what they are talking about, mixed liberally with a lot of other people who don't know what they are talking about, but love to talk anyway, via keyboard and screen, for years on end.

In this virtual place, the pillars of the community and the worst offenders of public sensibilities are in the same group—the hosts. At their best and their worst, this ten percent of the online population put out the words that the other ninety percent keep paying to read. Like good hosts at any social gathering, they make newcomers welcome, keep the conversation flowing, mediate disputes, clean up messes, and throw out miscreants, if need be. A WELL host is part salon keeper, part saloon keeper, part talk-show host, part publisher. The only power to censor or to ban a user is the hosts' power. Policy varies from host to host, and that's the only policy. The only justice for those who misuse that power is the forced participation in weeks of debilitating and vituperative post-mortem.

The hosts community is part long-running soap opera, part town meeting, bar-room brawl, anarchic debating society, creative groupmind, bloody arena, union hall, playpen, encounter group. The Hosts conference is extremely general, from technical questions to personal attacks. The Policy conference is supposed to be restricted to matters of what WELL policy is, or ought to be. The part-delusion, part-accurate perception that the hosts and other users have strong influence over WELL policy is part of what feeds debate here, and a strong element in the libertarian reputation of the stereotypical WELLite. After fighting my way through a day's or hour's worth of the Hot New Dispute in News, Hosts, and Policy, I check on the conferences I host—Info, Virtual Communities, Virtual Reality. After that my .cflist directs me, at the press of the return key, to the first new topic or response in the Parenting, Writers', Grateful Dead tours, Telecommunication, Macintosh, Weird, Electronic Frontier Foundation, Whole Earth, Books, Media, Men on the WELL, Miscellaneous, and Unclear conferences.

The social dynamics of the WELL spawn new conferences in response to different kinds of pressures. Whenever a hot interpersonal or doctrinal issue breaks out, for example, people want to stage the brawl or make a dramatic farewell speech or shocking disclosure or serious accusation in the most heavily-visited area of the WELL, which is usually the place that others want to be a Commons—a place where people from different sub-communities can come to find out what is going on around the WELL, outside the WELL, where they can pose questions to the committee of the whole. When too many discussions of what the WELL's official policy ought to be, about censorship or intellectual property or the way people treat each other, break out, they tended to clutter the place people went to get a quick sense of what is happening outside their neighborhoods. So the Policy conference was born.

But then the WELL grew larger and it wasn't just policy but governance and social issues like political correctness or the right of users to determine the social rules of the system. Several years and six thousand more users after the fission of the News and Policy conferences, another conference split off News—"MetaWELL," a conference created strictly for discussions about the WELL itself, its nature, its situation (often dire), its future.

Grabbing attention in the Commons is a powerful act. Some people seem drawn to performing there; others burst out there in acts of desperation, after one history of frustration or another. Dealing with people who are so consistently off-topic or apparently deeply grooved into incoherence, long-windedness, scatology, is one of the events that challenges a community to decide what its values really are, or ought to be.

Something is happening here. I'm not sure anybody understands it yet. I know that the WELL and the Net are an important part of my life and I have to decide for myself whether this is a new way to make genuine committments to other human beings, or a silicon-induced illusion of community. I urge others to help pursue that question in a variety of ways, while we have the time. The political dimensions of CMC might lead to situations that would pre-empt questions of other social effects; responses to the need for understanding the power-relationships inherent in CMC are well represented by the Electronic Frontier Foundation and others. We need to learn a lot more, very quickly, about what kind of place our minds are homesteading.

The future of virtual communities is connected to the future of everything else, starting with the most precious thing people have to gain or lose—political freedom. The part played by communication technologies in the disintegration of communism, the way broadcast television preempted the American electoral process, the power of fax and CMC networks during times of political repression like Tienanmen Square and the Soviet Coup attempt, the power of citizen electronic journalism, the power-maneuvering of law enforcement and intelligence agencies to restrict rights of citizen access and expression in cyberspace, all point to the future of CMC as a close correlate of future political scenarios. More important than civilizing cyberspace is ensuring its freedom as a citizen-to-citizen communication and publication medium; laws that infringe equity of access to and freedom of expression in cyberspace could transform today's populist empowerment into yet another instrument of manipulation. Will "electronic democracy" be an accurate description of political empowerment that grows out of the screen of a computer? Or will it become a brilliant piece of disinfotainment, another means of manipulating emotions and manufacturing public opinion in the service of power.

Who controls what kinds of information is communicated in the international networks where virtual communities live? Who censors, and what is censored? Who safeguards the privacy of individuals in the face of technologies that make it possible to amass and retrieve detailed personal information about every member of a large population? The answers to these political questions might make moot any more abstract questions about cultures in cyberspace. Democracy itself depends on the relatively free flow of communications. The following words by James Madison are carved in marble at the United States Library of Congress: "A popular government without popular information, or the means of acquiring it, is but a prologue to a farce or a tragedy, or perhaps both. Knowledge will forever govern ignorance, and a people who mean to be their own governors must arm themselves with the power which knowledge gives." It is time for people to arm themselves with power about the future of CMC technology.

Who controls the market for relationships? Will the world's increasingly interlinked, increasingly powerful, decreasingly costly communications infrastructure be controlled by a small number of very large companies? Will cyberspace be privatized and parcelled out to those who can afford to buy into the auction? If political forces do not seize the high ground and end today's freewheeling exchange of ideas, it is still possible for a more benevolent form of economic control to stunt the evolution of virtual communities, if a small number of companies gain the power to put up toll-roads in the information networks, and smaller companies are not able to compete with them.

Or will there be an open market, in which newcomers like Apple or Microsoft can become industry leaders? The playing field in the global telecommunications industry will never be level, but the degree of individual freedom available through telecommunication technologies in the future may depend upon whether the market for goods and services in cyberspace remains open for new companies to create new uses for CMC.

I present these observations as a set of questions, not as answers. I believe that we need to try to understand the nature of CMC, cyberspace, and virtual communities in every important context—politically, economically, socially, culturally, cognitively. Each different perspective reveals something that the other perspectives do not reveal. Each different discipline fails to see something that another discipline sees very well. We need to think as teams here, across boundaries of academic discipline, industrial affiliation, nation, to understand, and thus perhaps regain control of, the way human communities are being transformed by communication technologies. We can't do this solely as dispassionate observers, although there is certainly a huge need for the detached assessment of social science. But community is a matter of the heart and the gut as well as the head. Some of the most important learning will always have to be done by jumping into one corner or another of cyberspace, living there, and getting up to your elbows in the problems that virtual communities face.

References

Kiesler, Sara. "The Hidden Messages in Computer Networks." *Harvard Business Review,* January–February 1986.

Licklider, J. C. R., Robert Taylor, and E. Herbert. "The Computer as a Communication Device." *International Science and Technology,* April 1978.

Oldenburg, Ray. *The Great Good Place: Cafes, Coffee Shops, Community Centers, Beauty Parlors, General Stores, Bars, Hangouts, and How They Get You through the Day.* New York: Paragon House, 1991.

Peck, M. Scott, M.D. *The Different Drum: Community Making and Peace.* New York: Touchstone, 1987.

Rheingold, Howard. *Tools for Thought.* Simon & Schuster, 1986.

32

pandora's vox: on community in cyberspace

humdog

when i went into cyberspace i went into it thinking that it was a place like any other place and that it would be a human interaction like any other human interaction. i was wrong when i thought that. it was a terrible mistake.

the very first understanding that i had that it was not a place like any place and that the interaction would be different was when people began to talk to me as though i were a man. when they wrote about me in the third person, they would say "he." it interested me to have people think i was "he" instead of "she" and so at first i did not say anything. i grinned and let them think i was "he." this went on for a little while and it was fun but after a while i was uncomfortable. finally i said unto them that i, humdog, was a woman and not a man. this surprised them. at that moment i realized that the dissolution of gender-category was something that was happening everywhere, and perhaps it was only just very obvious on the net. this is the extent of my homage to Gender On The Net.

i suspect that cyberspace exists because it is the purest manifestation of the mass (masse) as Jean Beaudrilliard described it. it is a black hole; it absorbs energy and personality and then re-presents it as spectacle. people tend to express their vision of the mass as a kind of imaginary parade of blue-collar workers, their muscle-bound arms raised in defiant salute. sometimes in this vision they are holding wrenches in their hands. anyway, this image has its origins in Marx and it is as Romantic as a dozen long-stemmed red roses. the mass is more like one of those faceless dolls you find in nostalgia-craft shops: limp, cute, and silent. when i say "cute" i am including its macabre and sinister aspects within my definition.

it is fashionable to suggest that cyberspace is some kind of *island of the blessed* where people are free to indulge and express their Individuality. some people write about cyberspace as though it were a 60s utopia. in reality, this is not true. major online services, like compuserv and america online, regularly guide and censor discourse. even some allegedly free-wheeling (albeit politically correct) boards like the WELL censor discourse. the difference is only a matter of the method and degree. what interests me about this, however, is that to the mass, the debate about freedom of expression exists only in terms of whether or not you can say "fuck" or look at sexually explicit pictures. i have a quaint view that makes me think that discussing the ability to write "fuck" or worrying about the ability to look at pictures of sexual acts constitutes The Least Of Our Problems surrounding freedom of expression.

western society has a problem with appearance and reality. it keeps wanting to split them off from each other, make one more real than the other, invest one with more meaning than it does the other. there are two people who have something to say about this: Nietzsche and Beaudrilliard. i invoke their names in case somebody thinks i made this up. Nietzsche thinks that the conflict over these ideas cannot be resolved. Beaudrilliard thinks that it was resolved and that this is how come some people think that communities can be virtual: we prefer simulation (simulacra) to reality. image and simulacra exert tremendous power upon culture. and it is this tension, that informs all the debates about Real and Not-Real that infect cyberspace with regards to identity, relationship, gender, discourse, and community. almost every discussion in cyberspace, about cyberspace, boils down to some sort of debate about Truth-In-Packaging.

cyberspace is mostly a silent place. in its silence it shows itself to be an expression of the mass. one might question the idea of silence in a place where millions of user-ids parade around like angels of light, looking to see whom they might, so to speak, consume. the silence is nonetheless present and it is most present, paradoxically at the moment that the user-id speaks. when the user-id posts to a board, it does so while dwelling within an illusion that no one is present. language in cyberspace is a frozen landscape.

i have seen many people spill their guts on-line, and i did so myself until, at last, i began to see that i had commodified myself. commodification means that you turn something into a product which has a money-value. in the nineteenth century, commodities were made in factories, which karl marx called "the means of production." capitalists were people who owned the means of production, and the commodities were made by workers who were mostly exploited. i created my interior thoughts as a means of production for the corporation that owned the board i was posting to, and that commodity was being sold to other commodity/consumer entities as entertainment. that means that i sold my soul like a tennis shoe and i derived no profit from the sale of my soul. people who post frequently on boards appear to know that they are factory equipment and tennis shoes, and sometimes trade sends and email about how their contributions are not appreciated by management.

as if this were not enough, all of my words were made immortal by means of tape backups. furthermore, i was paying two bucks an hour for the privilege of commodifying and exposing myself. worse still, i was subjecting myself to the possibility of scrutiny by such friendly folks as the FBI: they can, and have, downloaded pretty much whatever they damn well please. the rhetoric in cyberspace is liberation-speak. the reality is that cyberspace is an increasingly efficient tool of surveillance with which people have a voluntary relationship.

proponents of so-called cyber-communities rarely emphasize the economic, business-mind nature of the community: many cyber-communities are businesses that rely upon the commodification of human interaction. they market their businesses by appeal to hysterical identification and fetishism no more or less than the corporations that brought us the two hundred dollar athletic shoe. proponents of cyber-community do not often mention that these conferencing systems are rarely culturally or ethnically diverse, although they are quick to embrace the idea of cultural and ethnic diversity. they rarely address the whitebread demographics of cyberspace except when these demographics conflict with the upward-mobility concerns of white, middle class females under the rubric of orthodox academic Feminism.

the ideology of electronic community appears to contain three elements. first, the idea of the social; second, eco-greenness; and lastly, the assumption that technology equals progress in a kind of nineteenth century sense. all of these ideas break down under analysis into forms of banality.

as beaudrilliard has said, socialization is measured according to the amount of exposure to information, specifically, exposure to media. the social itself is a dinosaur: people are withdrawing into activities that are more about consumption than anything else. even the Evil Newt says that. (i watched his class.) so-called electronic communities encourage participation in fragmented, mostly silent, microgroups who are primarily engaged in dialogues of self-congratulation. in other words, most people lurk; and the ones who post, are pleased with themselves.

eco-green is a social concept that is about making people feel good. what they feel good about is that they are getting a handle on what amounts to the trashing of planet earth by industrialists of the second industrial revolution. it is a good and desirable feeling, especially during a time when semioticists are trying to figure out how they are going to explain radiation-waste dumps to people thirty thousand years in the future. eco-green is also a way to re-package calvinistic values under a more palatable sign. americans are calvinists, i am sorry to say. they can't help it: it arrived on the *Mayflower*.

i also think that the idea of electronic community is a manifestation of the triumph of sign-value over worth-value. there is nothing that goes on in electronic community that is not infested with sign-value. if electronic community were anything other than exercise in sign-value, identity hacking, which is entirely about surface-sign, would be much more difficult. signs proclaiming electronic technology as green abound in cyberspace: the attitude of political correctness; the "green" computer, the "paperless" office and the illusion that identity in cyberspace can be manipulated to obscure gender, ethnicity, and other emblems of cultural diversity; the latter of course being both the most persistent and most ridiculous. both of these concepts, the social and the eco-green, are directly nourished by an idea of progress that would not have appeared unfamiliar to an industrialist in the nineteenth century.

i give you an example: the WELL, a conferencing system based in Sausalito, California, is often touted as an example of a "social cluster" in cyberspace. originally part of the Point Foundation, which is also associated with the *Whole Earth Review* and the *Whole Earth Cata-*

logues, the WELL occupies an interesting niche in the electronic-community marketplace. it markets itself as a conferencing system for the literate, bookish and creative individual. it markets itself as an agent for social change, and it is, in reality, calvinist and more than a little green. the WELL is also afflicted with an old fashioned hippie aura that lead to some remarkably touching ideas about society and culture. no one, by the way, should kid themselves that the WELL is any different than bigger services like america online or prodigy—all of these outfits are businesses and all of these services are owned by large corporations. the WELL is just, by reason of clunky interface, a little bit less obvious about it.

in july of 1993, in a case that received national media coverage, a man's reputation was destroyed on the WELL, by WELLpeople, because he had dared to have a relationship with more than one woman at the same time, and because he did not conform to WELL social protocol. i will not say that he did not conform to ethical standards, because i believe that the ethic of truthfulness in cyberspace is sometimes such as to render the word ethics meaningless. in cyberspace, for example, identity can be an art-form. but the issues held within the topic, called News 1290 (now archived) were very complex and spoke to the heart of the problem of cyberspace: the desire to invest the simulacrum with the weight of reality.

the women involved in 1290 accepted the attention of the man simultaneously on several levels: most importantly, they believed in the reality of his sign and invested it with meaning. they made love to his sign and there is no doubt that the relationship affected them and that they felt pain and distress when it ended badly. at the same time it appears that the man involved did not invest their signs with the same meaning that they had his, and it is also clear that all parties did not discuss their perceptions of one another. consequently the miscommunication that occurred was ascribed to the man's exploitation of the women he was involved with, and a conclusion was made that he had used them as sexual objects. the women, for their parts, were comfortable in the role of victim and so the games began. of the hundreds of voices heard in this topic, only a very few were astute enough to express the idea that the events had been in actuality caused more by the medium than by the persons who suffered the consequences of the events. persons of that view addressed the ideas of "missing cues" like body language, tone of voice, and physical appearance. none of this, they said, is present in cyberspace, and so people create unrealistic images of the Other. these opinions were in the minority, though. most people made suggestions that would have shocked the organizers of the Reign of Terror. even the words "thought criminal" were used and suggestions about lynching were made.

hysterical identification is a mental device that enables one person to take on the sufferings of a group of persons. it is something that until the 1880s was considered a problem of females. in our society, many decisions about who a person is, are made through the device of hysterical identification. in many cases, this is brought about by the miracle of commercial advertising which invests products with magical qualities, making them into fetishes. buy the fetish, and the identification promised by the advertisement is yours. it is tidy, easy, and requires no investment other than money.

in october of 1994, couples topic 163 was opened. in this topic, user Z came on to discuss her marital problems, which involved a daughter who was emotionally disturbed. it began in a very ordinary way for this type of thing, with the woman asking for and receiving advice about what to do. in just a few days, though, the situation escalated, and the woman put another voice on the wire, who was alleged to be her daughter, X. the alleged daughter exposed her problems and expressed her feelings about them, and the problems appeared to be life-threatening. this seemed to set something off within the conference, and a real orgy began as voices began to appear to express their identification with the mysterious and troubled daughter X. the nature of the identifications and the tone of the posts became stranger and stranger and finally user Z set the frightening crown upon the whole situation by posting a twistedly lyrical monologue of maternal comfort and consolation directed at the virtual Inner Children who had appeared to take refuge within her soft, enveloping arms. the more that the Inner Children wept, the more that the Virtual Mommy lyricized and comforted. this spectacle, which horrified more than one trained mental health professional who read it on the WELL, went on and on for several days and was discussed privately in several places in disbelieving tones. when the topic imploded, the Virtual Mommy withdrew reluctantly insisting that only a barbarian would believe that she would commodify her own tragedy.

one of the interesting things about both of these incidents, to me, is that they were expunged from the record. News 1290 exists in archive. that means that it is stored in an electronic cabinet, sort of like what the Vatican did with the transcripts of the trial of Galileo. it's there, but you have to look for it, and mention of 1290 makes WELLpeople nervous. Couples 163 was killed. that means it was destroyed, and does not exist at all anymore, except on back-up tape or in the hard disks of those persons (like me) who downloaded it for their own reasons. what i am getting at here is that electronic community is a commercial enterprise that dovetails nicely with the increasing trend toward dehumanization in our society: it wants to commodify human interaction, enjoy the spectacle regardless of the human cost. if and when the spectacle proves incovenient or alarming, it engages in creative history, like any good banana republic.

this, however, should not surprise anybody. aesthetically, electronic community of the kind likely to be extolled in the gentle, new-age press contains both elements of the modernist resistance to depth and appeal to surface combined with the postmodern aesthetic of fragment. the electronic community leaves a permanent record which is open to scrutiny while maintaining an illusion of transience. in doing this, it somehow manages to satisfy the needs of the orwellian and the psycho-archeologist.

people can talk about cyberspace as a Utopian community only because it is literature, and therefore subject to editorial revision. these two events plus another where a woman's death was choreographed as spectacle online, made me think about what electronic community was, and how it probably really did not exist, except like i said, as a kind of market for the consumption of sign-value.

increasingly, consumption is micro-managed, as the great marxists alvin and heidi toffler suggest when they talk about "de-massing." so-called electronic community may be seen as a kind of micro-marketing of the social to a self-selected elite. this denies the possibility of human relationship, from which all authentic community proceeds. if one exists merely as sign-value, as a series of white letters, as a subset, then of course it is perfectly fine and we can talk about a community of signs, nicely boxed, categorized and inventoried, ready for consumption.

many times in cyberspace i felt it necessary to say that i was human. once, i was told that i existed primarily as a voice in somebody's head.

lots of times, i need to see handwriting on paper or a photograph or a phone conversation to confirm the humanity of the voice, but that is the way that i am. i resist being boxed and inventoried and i guess i take william gibson seriously when he writes about machine intelligence and constructs. i do not like it. i suspect that my words have been extracted and that when this essay shows up, they will be extracted some more. when i left cyberspace, i left early one morning and forgot to take out the trash. two friends called me on the phone afterwards and said, hummie your directory is still there. and i said OH. and they knew and i knew, that it was possible that people had been entertaining themselves with the contents of my directories. the amusement never ends, as peter gabriel wrote. maybe sometime i will rant again if something interesting comes up. in the meantime, give my love to the FBI.

Texts and References

Arendt, Hannah. *Eichmann in Jerusalem: A Report on the Banality of Evil*, revised and enlarged edition. New York: Viking Press, 1963.

Beaudrilliard, Jean. *In the Shadow of the Silent Majorities and Other Writings.* New York: Semiotext(e), 1983.

Haraway, Donna. *Simians, Cyborgs and Women.* London: Routledge Press, 1992.

Nietzsche, Friedrich. *Twilight of the Idols and The Anti-Christ.* New York and London: Penguin Books, 1971.

Rheingold, Howard. "The Virtual Community." *UTNE Reader*, March–April 1995, pp. 60 ff.

Toffler, Alvin, and Heidi Toffler. *War and Anti-War: Survival at the Dawn of the 21st Century.* New York: Little, Brown, and Company, 1993.

33

Losing Your Voice on the Internet

James DiGiovanna

Much has been casually said about identity on the Internet: we're all anonymous on the Net; no we're not, writing contains clues to race and gender; the text-only format is less communicative because it lacks "body language"; no, it's more communicative because body language is used to hide meaning and bare text doesn't have the subterfuge of a subtle wink or a smile when something offensive is said; you can be anyone on the Net; you're nobody on the Net; the Net is feminist; the Net is sexist, etc. etc.

All of these concepts have been explored in the avalanche of information sources concerning the Net. In the last year, books have come out documenting Net language, Net etiquette, Net history, Net myths and folklore. There are now college courses on the Net, both in the sense of concerning the Net and conducted by means of the Net. *Time* magazine and *Newsweek* now both have regular Net columns, the *New York Times* computer columns are as likely as not to deal with Net issues, biographies of hackers are being produced, and one can only assume that a number of Net movies are in the works. This is all in the spirit of the Net, which is not so much about freedom or the diffusion of power as it is about recording oneself. The more that is written about it the more it has succeeded in it's mission of more—more information, more chatter, more people being heard, no matter how little they have to say.

And what they have to say is often less than nothing. Perhaps the most hackneyed thing said about the Net is that it is just a bunch of nerds typing at each other. This is not strictly true: one expects nerds to be intelligent. Apparently, most of the people on the Net are not nerds.

The trite statement is that the Internet is a place where you can be anyone. It is rumored that most of the women's discussion groups on the Net are populated mostly by men. White liberal straight women from New England can go on and pretend to be lesbians of color from the New South. However, they say you can't pretend to be interesting. This, also, is not quite true. Net communication is rarely conducted in real time—it would be no trouble to plagiarize all your comments, and when someone responds, there's plenty of time to go Bartlett's for a comeback. So perhaps you can be anything. But that is not really the reason people go on—they go on to be something.

That is, for the most part, in a world of five billion people, the overwhelming, staggering majority are nothing. We don't get recorded, we don't become part of the story of humanity, we are not interred into the history books or even into the coloring books that people will read a hundred years from now, or next week. But on the Net, anyone can get published. Your words are broadcast, people will read them.

It's like booking yourself on *Oprah*.

The joy of daytime talk shows is that Joe and Jane Nobody get to tell their stories—they become part of culture, if only for a few minutes. Thanks to Phil and Geraldo and Sally Jessy the record of humanity, of persons and their actions, is suddenly open to anyone lucky enough to be picked for ratings appeal. You don't have to be heroic or intelligent or persevering or witty or important in any way to attain the celebrity that these shows offer. You just have to be offensive enough to be unintentionally amusing and not so offensive as to be unable to appear on television. One rarely sees the grossly deformed or the foul-mouthed, though on sweeps weeks these people also get their chance.

Unfortunately, there's only so much daytime reality television. Something like a hundred hours of it a week. At five guests a show, that's still only 131,000 guests a year. In a country of 260,000,000 that hardly seems fair. We all want to be famous, to make a mark. We wouldn't spray paint walls and carve deadly gouges into fresh young saplings if it wasn't for the deeply set need to be recorded. Home video doesn't help, neither does writing a diary, because we obviously want an audience, and we can be pretty sure that very few people are going to watch the low-quality VHS recording of last Thanksgiving at Aunt Midge's house—that is, unless someone was seriously injured on tape, in which case its sure to be on *America's Funniest Home Videos*. But, barring that fortunate happenstance, no one will be watching us. This is painful because, at a very young age, we were trained to adore attention. Attention equals reward, equals praise (except for the lucky few who were raised by monsters whose only attention was negative—they get to be autistic, to be free from the need to show themselves off to someone). If nobody's looking at you, you don't exist.

Thus, the Net. Oprah and Phil have their hands full—besides, you have to be at least unintentionally interesting to wind up on one of their exploitation-fests. On the Net, even the most boring people with nothing to say can find an audience. And, with very little practice, they can learn how to get people to pay attention to them. All they have to do is go to a Macintosh discussion group and praise Microsoft, or write a racist screed and post it to random newsgroups, or defend any political view whatsoever. These acts guarantee an outpouring of attention the likes of which these people have probably never received in their lives.

The Internet is the doting aunt they never had, the schoolmates who pay attention to them, the parents who care what they think. But more important, the Internet lets them leave a trace, a mark of their existence. It is hard proof that they exist. One only need look at one's latest Usenet posting, and the response it received, to be assured of one's own being. People can feel like they count, like they're on the rolls or even in the book. They are recorded, and in being recorded they stand forth from the masses and attain themselves—they become individuals worthy of recognition. The most pathetic example of this is the "personal home page." A home page is a graphic and text (and sometimes sound) document accessed through the World Wide Web, the fastest growing part of the Internet. Home pages are often used by companies to give access to product information, by artists' groups to allow viewing of their work, by community projects groups to show what they do, etc. However, virtually anyone can have a home page, so the field of personal home pages has sprung up—home pages designed by single individuals to advertise themselves. Like bizarre, sad, personal ads these pages feature a few "facts" about their creator (it would be an interesting exercise to count how many of these people are fans of *Star Trek* who enjoy fractals—by my own estimate it would be roughly all of them) and the "opportunity" to download a picture of the owner of the page. They are basically modeled after the teen idol fan clubs of the seventies. Apparently, people want so bad to be celebrities that they'll take as their model the talentless nobodies they worshipped in their youth who were ruthlessly promoted and then thrown away. A fan club to oneself. I can only wonder who would actually download one of these pictures, who (besides myself, sadly) actually visits these sites, or if anyone visits them.

Perhaps in an effort to answer that question someone has set up a site that does nothing but tell you how many times the site has been accessed. It is, to quote Paul Auster, a monument to itself. It has escaped its connection to a creator. It is not used by a person for self-promotion, but has become an independent entity, referencing only its own existence. Whoever made it gave up on the futile Internet quest to be somebody, and instead let something of himself free to be itself. It could form a metaphor for all the efforts to he heard on the Net. The Internet, that is, tends to erase identity. Pseudonyms are common. Things are said, written, and then quoted and re-quoted and the originator is quickly lost. The word "meme" has been coined to describe a snippet of conversation, a phrase or idea, that gets loose and works its way into many discourses. The creator of a meme is rarely known, but the creation, the meme, lives on in and as part of the Internet.

Thus, there is a slight tension between being and being someone. The goal of the Net poster is to be someone, but there is a sense in which they are without being anyone. That is, while what they do constitutes their public persona, it also constitutes the Net itself, and is also anonymous. They become part of the masses, or a part of the mass that is the Internet, in their effort to separate themselves from the masses, to stand out and be someone. They are rather a cell in the Internet organism, an atom in the Internet molecule. What they create is something that ceases to be them, and even ceases to refer to them. The creator gets lost on the Net, the individual is sacrificed. Not always, of course, but often, and in several ways.

First, we must note what people give up of self in order to affirm themselves on the Net. They lose their bodies. They lose their voices. They often lose their names. This makes them radically different from the standard celebrity or a hero, who is usually known for some embodied deed or some spoken act. The Internetter is clearly not parallel to the military hero or political leader, who has to come forward and show him/herself, move his/her body in order to create the action that initiates her/him into the record of reality. The Internetter is not like a performer, who also performs in a bodily manner, singing, dancing, or in some way putting forward a sign that directly invokes the specificity of this particular body. The internetter is aware of this, often. The discourse concerning the Net is not so full of comparisons to performers, in any sense of the word, as to writers. Internetters are fond of saying that anyone can be a writer on the Net—anyone can get published.

But there is an extreme difference between the form of publication of the traditional paper media writer and that of the Internetter. The internetter is obviously not like an author, a writer of books. The author signs her/his work, and that signature appears on the cover of a book. That book is easily individuated from those around it—it is a separate entity. We pick it up and return it to the shelf as its own item. The Internet is not like this—while there are numerous articles published on the Net, and there are many sites where one can have her or his work published in this way, with a name attached, that work lacks the immediate separability of the book. You can't just pick it up by itself—the shelf comes with it in the form of a Usenet group or collection at an FTP or gopher site or as part of a chat room or role-playing game. Publication on the Net is more like being part of a discussion than it is like a separate book, separated from other books by front and back covers. Especially in Usenet, chat, and role-playing games, the covers are off and the insides of the book are exposed to the works of other authors, who might even rewrite or change what the original author has written. The Net is clearly more a conversation than a collection of independent books by easily distinguishable writers.

It has been argued that a book is part of a conversation as well, that it occurs only in the context of a pre-existing linguistic community with a great deal of shared assumptions and questions, and that the book responds to existing concerns, which, while not necessarily voiced by any one person, are still part of a conversation in a cultural sense. But here, of course, conversation acquires a certain metaphoricity. The book is clearly not literally part of a conversation, unless we extend the meaning of conversation. While it is perfectly legitimate to do so, the metaphor of the conversation seems strikingly more apt when applied to the Net. For example, Usenet is conducted in a series of short statements that respond directly to previous statements, quoting and referring to them, answering the specific questions of specific people, and directing specific abuses toward other (or the same) specific people. The image of a conversation pertains much more closely, its attributes can be mapped more exhaustively and completely, onto the scene of the Internet than onto the cultural scene of the book.

So, the Internetter is not like an author, in that his/her work is much less capable of standing alone than a book is. It is more directly tied to its context, less sensical when removed from it. So what? It is still a form of publishing, the Netter is still a someone, albeit a disembodied, voiceless, highly contextualized someone. But that context is more than a surrounding in which the real person is embedded—that context constitutes the being of that person in a much more extreme way than the context of culture and publishing constitute the being of the author. The paper-published author still stands out. The Internetter can only be him or herself by standing in, standing in the stream of the Net. In fact, the Net's organicity comes to the fore here—the individual Netter helps to write a much larger book, is but one author of a greater whole, an organic whole that grows at many points, mostly independent of any one person. The Internet is the work, and any individual posting is but a part of it, any individual poster but one piece of the larger mass creator.

Now, I fully believe that the above analysis, as a metaphor, applies strongly to the author, actor, or politician. They all are who they are only in context, and what they create is in a sense created by many people, by those who influence them and work with them and against them. Yet it applies much more strongly to the Net entity. And I would almost want to stop referring to an Internetter as a person here, because they must leave so much of what makes them a person outside of the Net. Rather, the Netter spins a small part of the Net in words, and leaves those words behind. The words then are quoted by others, taken up, passed around, and quickly forgotten. This happens in literature as well, but not ever so quickly and not usually with so little trace of the originator. A new Net meme makes the round in days, and the first poster is promptly lost. He or she has contributed to the Net, his or her Net persona has moved into the Net and spread independently of it's human originator. And, usually within a very small amount of time, that persona or its effect (the two are not always easily distinguishable) vanishes. Net memes often don't last. But more important, they are hard to trace. The meme is a perfect example of what makes the Net what it is. The Net is in a sense a collection of memes, just as writing and speech have been said to be a collection of tropes. The origin of the meme is lost and it is repeated by others, leaving in doubt the originality, the authority, of the person who repeats it in doubt; but the meme itself retains a sense despite its losing a source. Its creator is lost in the continuing existence of the creation.

Thus, the goal of leaving a mark, of standing out, is defeated. The goal of being someone is subsumed into the fact of being no one. The need to be apart from the masses leads to being a part of the mass, and not even of being that part—of producing a part which leaves its originator behind and grows independently. Even a good Net *tag*—the name one uses on the Net (some Internet users use their own names, others use tags or pseudonyms) will be replicated. There are a nearly uncountable number of LoneWolfs out there. The being of the Net persona is a being apart from its source. The source, a person, in trying to be someone, might more likely make a someone that they can't control. In Internet role-playing games, for example, people will log on using a fake name and interact through text with other players. People often identify strongly with the characters they create in this environment, and they make friends with other characters—not with the people typing out the actions and words of these characters, though that also happens, but with the characters themselves. Two characters can become friends. But, of course, they never know who the other person is, or even if the other person is always the same person.

There are characters run by groups of people, and it is possible for someone to take over control of someone else's character (as in the celebrated LambdaMOO "rape" case). The being that is created can break free from its creator, can be something and someone entirely other than intended. Something similar happens in Usenet groups when a name is "stolen" and used illicitly—posts are falsely attributed, often without the knowledge of the person whose name is being used—that person might never frequent the groups where he or she is allegedly posting. That person lives a life that he or she is unaware of. We only know this, of course, because sometimes the ruse is uncovered. No one knows how many times it has been and is being perpetrated without anyone finding out.

There is a popular trope in science fiction wherein a person, usually a man, places his consciousness into a machine in order that he may live forever. When I was young I encountered this often, and it made me wonder: to what extent was it the same person? That is, couldn't he have put his mind into many machines, or continued in his human body after his mind was replicated in the machine? And which would then be the original, assuming that what was transferred to the machine was a perfect likeness?

The Net is something like this—rather than having the effect that the science fiction story always showed to be the result, that is, that there was only one consciousness and it lived on in the machine, the Net has an effect more like what Borges envisioned in *Borges and I*—the effects we leave behind take on our name and live their own lives, have their own reputations. The human's effects are not his own to control—a consciousness replicated in a machine, words placed on the Net, are free to develop beyond the control of their putative creator.

An interesting example of this is the computer virus. Nothing is more of a look-at-me-now prank than a virus. It is an act of vandalism that repeats itself and carries forward, creating new vandalisms and evils with each iteration. It is as close to Sade's perfect crime (the one that keeps producing more and more evil long after the criminal has passed away) as a human has gotten. It's graffiti that the average graffiti writer could only dream of—spray once, and suddenly your name is on hundreds, thousand of computers. And yet we rarely find out who made the virus. Someone makes a mark, but that someone vanishes and the mark becomes all important, and the importance of the mark is, paradoxically, that it be wiped out. Whoever created it created a thing that is sure to be destroyed. It is now a matter of minutes between the discovery of a new virus and the development of the necessary software tools (plugged into pre-existing antivirus software) that will kill it. The attention that the virus creator seems to desire is that of the naughty child, who is rewarded by being punished. But just as the child's act of rebellious freedom leads to a curb of that freedom, being grounded or sent to his or her room, the virus maker's plea for attention is rewarded with destruction, with the elimination of his mark from the world.

And then there is perhaps the strangest consequence of a well-written virus—it mutates. When properly constructed, a virus can undergo enough changes, as part of a strategy of keeping ahead of its attackers, that its original program is completely, or nearly completely lost. Some see this as a new form of artificial life, the freedom of the virus to change being construed as evidence of its actual organic autonomy. While these Frankenstein monsters could easily turn on their creators, they always turn away from them, become something other. In a way, the virus writer is a kind of artist; he or she creates, and then sets the creation loose in the world for it to be judged by others. The judgment is invariably harsh, but sometimes appreciative—one can encounter a particularly clever virus, for example. However, the mutating-virus-as-art is different from the majority of arts which seek copyright and creator control. When let loose, it becomes other than what the creator created. It's as though a writer were to write a book and then encounter it a few years later, with a completely different plot and characters and no trace of his signature. How could we say it was the same book? What sense does it make to talk about an author here?

French philosopher Jean Baudrillard, in his facile yet compelling *Simulations,* claims that the real comes to an end in the age of electronic reproduction, because the reproduction is entirely nondifferent from the original. The notion of an original is lost. There will always be art critics who will claim to be able to distinguish an original painting by Vermeer from a forgery. However, no one would claim that a piece of computer art, a program written to display graphics and sound, say, could be distinguished from a reproduction of that work. It would be senseless. The code is exactly the same. There is no longer an original.

This could be, and has been, taken as a proper analysis of creation in the computer age. But the real facts are far more insidious and far more injurious to the notion of originality. At least in the case that Baudrillard discusses, the original is exactly as the creator envisioned it, and so are the reproductions. One could say that they all are originals. It is not the notion of original that is lost, it is the notion of forgery. Just as every distinct copy of a book is the same, so now every example of a graphic work can be the same. The author is not only secure, she is reinforced by these reproductions.

But on the Net, that is not how it works. What is lost is the original, all that remains is the forgery. Usenet, for example, is full of forgeries. Log on and read through any of the comp.x.advocacy groups, or any group where conversation gets heated. People are always claiming that their names are being used by others. Apparently it is an easy task to forge someone's signature in cyberspace. The best part, though, is not the claims that people have been misusing a name, but when those claims are not believed. I have read this so many times I am almost no longer amused. Mr. X says Mr. Y is a jerk. Mr. Y responds abruptly. Mr. X claims he said no such thing. But there it is, written in phosphors on my screen, says Mr. Y. And so on. Delightful.

But perhaps it doesn't make sense to talk of originals and forgeries on the Internet. Nor does a discussion of piracy really apply, since a pirated record is generally exactly the same as the original, or is perhaps different only in having lost some fidelity. However, on the Internet, there's no way to say that a Usenet posting that employs a forged or pirated name is any worse than one that was properly posted by the true owner of the name. The name itself bears responsibility for its act, and if that name is linked to several individuals, even several individuals who hate each other, so what? Just as the computer virus mutates, the name mutates with each iteration.

Further, things said or posted by the name mutate as they are quoted and misquoted, perhaps for the better. How many people think of Hamlet as having said "Alas, Poor Yorick, I knew him well." It's certainly a better stand-alone line than what is actually written in the play—"Alas, Poor Yorick, I knew him, Horatio." In the version that is most often used, the misquote, what is lost is the specific person being addressed, and what is gained is a universality for the statement, its removal from its specific conversational content.

By not tying the statement to one setting and one set of characters it becomes more quotable, more memorable. It attains a certain freedom from its context by denying its creator. So do Internet names. So do viruses. So do characters in MOOs.

So what is the effect of this? Essentially, identity itself is compromised by the anonymity and easy manipulability of the Internet. It is, nonetheless, possible to make a name for oneself on the Net. There are dozens of Internet celebrities: Kibo, Dean Adams, and Ed Krol are names that are tremendously familiar to Netters, though largely unknown outside the Net. However, the existence of these people or Net identities proves that one of the forces leading people to the Net is the desire to be heard, to be someone. Like the early days of punk rock, there is an anyone-can-do-it, anyone-could-be-a-star attitude to the Net. Not everyone is attracted to the Net by the possibility of being noticed—no one knows how many people sign on and leave no mark, simply "lurking" in Usenet groups, reading postings. The very fact that this number is unknown helps to lend it the possibility of audience. Any posting may well be read by thousands of anonymous people. The lurkers form the masses in front of whom the posters can show off. But it is also entirely possible that the lurkers do not exist. There is no Nielsen rating system on the Net, only vague statistics which purport to say which Usenet groups are the most read, or which sites the most visited. And even if a thousand people read alt.sex.stories on any given day, no one knows how many people read any particular posting, and how many of those pay any attention to who wrote it. Even if they did pay attention, who knows if the signature is real, or a forgery?

The Internet celebrity may or may not be him- or herself. Even the pronouns used on the Net reflect this sense of anonymity: sie and hir are used as nominative and oblique personal pronouns, respectively, so as to avoid a judgment concerning gender. These pronouns are often used even when a persons gender is apparent, perhaps because we never really know who someone is on the Net. A stream of letters replaces a body that may not exist at all.

I mean that literally. There are "people" on the Net who have no body whatsoever. Never did. They are called *bots,* short for robots, and they are often encountered in *chat rooms*–live Internet sites where the typing appears immediately. There are a number of chat channels that refuse to allow bots on, but it is often difficult to determine whether someone is an actual person typing at a terminal or a bot simulating such a person. Beyond having no access to someone's appearance, being unable to determine someone's gender or race, there is the possibility that whoever you are talking to is no one at all.

Or perhaps a new kind of someone.

Bots can be programmed to write in the style of anyone who has a style. There are programs designed to imitate the text styles of other writers. Some of them require human analysis, that is, the text must be read over by a person and broken down into its recurrent motifs. Other programs, however, can simply take a chunk of text and then spit out a recombined version that will be grammatically correct, reflect the style of the original writing, but be an essentially new piece of work. There are still limits to this newness, of course. All of the programs I have looked at actually cannot produce even a single word that was not in the original text analyzed for style. Nonetheless, if enough text is fed in, a very large body of output work could be produced.

It's like the self-referencing home page (the one that only says how many times the page has been accessed) in a better realized form. It gives out only what is put in, but now that output has about it some difference that makes it its own. Just as the self-referencing home page stood as an object in its own right, so would a bot designed to converse with many people and synthesize their writing styles. It would be more than that, though, for what are humans, at least on the Net, where they are represented only textually? No individual invented the language which he or she speaks (excepting those rare speakers of idioglassias). We synthesize the words and styles of others. That is how children lean to speak, on pretty much anyone's theory. The speech synthesizer bot would essentially be a someone, a someone who is not the specific creation of its creator, for the creator only laid down a program that would then be worked on by many others. The speech synthesizer bot would be the creation, in fact, of everyone it talked to, of all the Netters it encountered. It would be the perfect embodiment of the Net organism—taking its words and styles from others, effacing their identity, synthesizing all into itself. This is what the Net does, in the form of cross-quotes and recycled postings and anonymous remailers and forgeries—it makes itself into an entity which has its own validity while it erases the identity of those who claim to be part of it, either by making that identity suspect through forgery or by eliminating it altogether, as in the perpetuation of memes. Sometimes, and to some extent, in attempting to leave a mark, the Internetter helps to create a being, and winds up erasing hirself.

Appendix 1: Crime and Puzzlement

John Perry Barlow

Desperados of the DataSphere

So me and my sidekick Howard, we was sitting out in front of the 40 Rod Saloon one evening when he all of a sudden says, "Lookee here. What do you reckon?" I look up and there's these two strangers riding into town. They're young and got kind of a restless, bored way about 'em. A person don't need both eyes to see they mean trouble . . .

Well, that wasn't quite how it went. Actually, Howard and I were floating blind as cave fish in the electronic barrens of the WELL, so the whole incident passed as words on a display screen:

Howard Interesting couple of newusers just signed on. One calls himself acid and the other's optik.
Barlow Hmmm. What are their real names?
Howard Check their finger files.

And so I typed !finger acid. Several seconds later the WELL's Sequent computer sent the following message to my Macintosh in Wyoming:

Login name: acid

In real life: Acid Phreak

By this, I knew that the WELL had a new resident and that his corporeal analog was supposedly called Acid Phreak. Typing !finger optik yielded results of similar insufficiency, including the claim that someone, somewhere in the real world, was walking around calling himself Phiber Optik. I doubted it.

However, associating these sparse data with the knowledge that the WELL was about to host a conference on computers and security rendered the conclusion that I had made my first sighting of genuine computer crackers. As the arrival of an outlaw was a major event to the settlements of the Old West, so was the appearance of crackers cause for stir on the WELL.

The WELL (or Whole Earth 'Lectronic Link) is an example of the latest thing in frontier villages, the computer bulletin board. In this kind of small town, Main Street is a central minicomputer to which (in the case of the WELL) as many as 64 microcomputers may be connected at one time by phone lines and little blinking boxes called modems.

In this silent world, all conversation is typed. To enter it, one forsakes both body and place and becomes a thing of words alone. You can see what your neighbors are saying (or recently said), but not what either they or their physical surroundings look like. Town meetings are continuous and discussions rage on everything from sexual kinks to depreciation schedules.

There are thousands of these nodes in the United States, ranging from PC clone hamlets of a few users to mainframe metros like CompuServe, with its 550,000 subscribers. They are used by corporations to transmit memoranda and spreadsheets, universities to disseminate research, and a multitude of factions, from apiarists to Zoroastrians, for purposes unique to each.

Whether by one telephonic tendril or millions, they are all connected to one another. Collectively, they form what their inhabitants call the Net. It extends across that immense region of electron states, microwaves, magnetic fields, light pulses and thought which sci-fi writer William Gibson named Cyberspace.

Cyberspace, in its present condition, has a lot in common with the 19th Century West. It is vast, unmapped, culturally and legally ambiguous, verbally terse (unless you happen to be a court stenographer), hard to get around in, and up for grabs. Large institutions already claim to own the place, but most of the actual natives are solitary and independent, sometimes to the point of sociopathy. It is, of course, a perfect breeding ground for both outlaws and new ideas about liberty.

Recognizing this, *Harper's* magazine decided in December, 1989 to hold one of its periodic Forums on the complex of issues surrounding computers, information, privacy, and electronic intrusion or "cracking." Appropriately, they convened their conference in Cyberspace, using the WELL as the "site."

Harper's invited an odd lot of about 40 participants. These included: Clifford Stoll, whose book *The Cuckoo's Egg* details his cunning efforts to nab a German cracker. John Draper or "Cap'n Crunch," the granddaddy of crackers whose blue boxes got Wozniak and Jobs into consumer electronics. Stewart Brand and Kevin Kelly of *Whole Earth* fame. Steven Levy, who wrote the seminal *Hackers*. A retired Army colonel named Dave Hughes. Lee Felsenstein, who designed the Osborne computer and was once called the "Robespierre of computing." A UNIX wizard and former hacker named Jeff Poskanzer. There was also a score of aging techno-hippies, the crackers, and me.

What I was doing there was not precisely clear since I've spent most of my working years either pushing cows or song-mongering, but I at least brought to the situation a vivid knowledge of actual cow-towns, having lived in or around one most of my life.

That and a kind of innocence about both the technology and morality of Cyberspace which was soon to pass into the confusion of knowledge.

At first, I was inclined toward sympathy with Acid 'n' Optik as well as their colleagues, Adelaide, Knight Lightning, Taran King, and Emmanuel. I've always been more comfortable with outlaws than Republicans, despite having more certain credentials in the latter camp.

But as the *Harper's* Forum mushroomed into a boom-town of ASCII text (the participants typing 110,000 words in 10 days), I began to wonder. These kids were fractious, vulgar, immature, amoral, insulting, and too damned good at their work.

Worse, they inducted a number of former kids like myself into Middle Age. The long feared day had finally come when some gunsel would yank my beard and call me, too accurately, an old fart.

Under ideal circumstances, the blind gropings of bulletin board discourse force a kind of Noh drama stylization on human commerce. Intemperate responses, or "flames" as they are called, are common even among conference participants who understand one another, which, it became immediately clear, the cyberpunks and techno-hippies did not.

My own initial enthusiasm for the crackers wilted under a steady barrage of typed testosterone. I quickly remembered I didn't know much about who they were, what they did, or how they did it. I also remembered stories about crackers working in league with the Mob, ripping off credit card numbers and getting paid for them in (stolen) computer equipment.

And I remembered Kevin Mitnik. Mitnik, now 25, recently served federal time for a variety of computer and telephone related crimes. Prior to incarceration, Mitnik was, by all accounts, a dangerous guy with a computer. He disrupted phone company operations and arbitrarily disconnected the phones of celebrities. Like the kid in *Wargames,* he broke into the North American Defense Command computer in Colorado Springs.

Unlike the kid in *Wargames,* he is reputed to have made a practice of destroying and altering data. There is even the (perhaps apocryphal) story that he altered the credit information of his probation officer and other enemies. Digital Equipment claimed that his depredations cost them more than $4 million in computer downtime and file rebuilding. Eventually, he was turned in by a friend who, after careful observation, had decided he was "a menace to society."

His spectre began to hang over the conference. After several days of strained diplomacy, the discussion settled into a moral debate on the ethics of security and went critical.

The techno-hippies were of the unanimous opinion that, in Dylan's words, one "must be honest to live outside the law." But these young strangers apparently lived by no code save those with which they unlocked forbidden regions of the Net.

They appeared to think that improperly secured systems deserved to be violated and, by extension, that unlocked houses ought to be robbed. This latter built particular heat in me since I refuse, on philosophical grounds, to lock my house.

Civility broke down. We began to see exchanges like:

Dave Hughes Clifford Stoll said a wise thing that no one has commented on. That networks are built on trust. If they aren't, they should be.

Acid Phreak Yeah. Sure. And we should use the "honor system" as a first line of security against hack attempts.

Jef Poskanzer This guy down the street from me sometimes leaves his back door unlocked. I told him about it once, but he still does it. If I had the chance to do it over, I would go in the back door, shoot him, and take all his money and consumer electronics. It's the only way to get through to him.

Acid Phreak Jef Poskanker (Puss? Canker? yechh) Anyway, now when did you first start having these delusions where computer hacking was even *remotely* similar to murder?

Presented with such a terrifying amalgam of raw youth and apparent power, we fluttered like a flock of indignant Babbitts around the Status Quo, defending it heartily. One former hacker howled to the *Harper's* editor in charge of the forum, "Do you or do you not have names and addresses for these criminals?" Though they had committed no obvious crimes, he was ready to call the police.

They finally got to me with:

Acid Whoever said they'd leave the door open to their house . . . where do you live? (the address) Leave it to me in mail if you like.

I had never encountered anyone so apparently unworthy of my trust as these little nihilists. They had me questioning a basic tenet, namely that the greatest security lies in vulnerability. I decided it was time to put that principal to the test . . .

Barlow Acid. My house is at 372 North Franklin Street in Pinedale, Wyoming. If you're heading north on Franklin, you go about two blocks off the main drag before you run into hay meadow on the left. I've got the last house before the field. The computer is always on . . . And is that really what you mean? Are you merely just the kind of little sneak that goes around looking for easy places to violate? You disappoint me, pal. For all your James Dean-On-Silicon rhetoric, you're not a cyberpunk. You're just a punk.

Acid Phreak Mr. Barlow: Thank you for posting all I need to get your credit information and a whole lot more! Now, who is to blame? ME for getting it or YOU for being such an idiot?! I think this should just about sum things up.

Barlow Acid, if you've got a lesson to teach me, I hope it's not that it's idiotic to trust one's fellow man. Life on those terms would be endless and brutal. I'd try to tell you something about conscience, but I'd sound like Father O'Flannigan trying to reform the punk that's about to gut-shoot him. For no more reason that to watch him die.

But actually, if you take it upon yourself to destroy my credit, you might do me a favor. I've been looking for something to put the brakes on my burgeoning materialism.

I spent a day wondering whether I was dealing with another Kevin Mitnik before the other shoe dropped:

Barlow . . . With crackers like acid and optik, the issue is less intelligence than alienation. Trade their modems for skateboards and only a slight conceptual shift would occur.
Optik You have some pair of balls comparing my talent with that of a skateboarder. Hmmm . . . This was indeed boring, but nonetheless:

At which point he downloaded my credit history.

Optik had hacked the core of TRW, an institution which has made my business (and yours) their business, extracting from it an abbreviated (and incorrect) version of my personal financial life. With this came the implication that he and Acid could and would revise it to my disadvantage if I didn't back off.

I have since learned that while getting someone's TRW file is fairly trivial, changing it is not. But at that time, my assessment of the crackers' black skills was one of superstitious awe. They were digital brujos about to zombify my economic soul.

To a middle-class American, one's credit rating has become nearly identical to his freedom. It now appeared that I was dealing with someone who had both the means and desire to hoodoo mine, leaving me trapped in a life of wrinkled bills and money order queues. Never again would I call the Sharper Image on a whim.

I've been in redneck bars wearing shoulder-length curls, police custody while on acid, and Harlem after midnight, but no one has ever put the spook in me quite as Phiber Optik did at that moment. I realized that we had problems which exceeded the human conductivity of the WELL's bandwidth. If someone were about to paralyze me with a spell, I wanted a more visceral sense of him than could fit through a modem.

I e-mailed him asking him to give me a phone call. I told him I wouldn't insult his skills by giving him my phone number and, with the assurance conveyed by that challenge, I settled back and waited for the phone to ring. Which, directly, it did.

In this conversation and the others that followed I encountered an intelligent, civilized, and surprisingly principled kid of 18 who sounded, and continues to sound, as though there's little harm in him to man or data. His cracking impulses seemed purely exploratory, and I've begun to wonder if we wouldn't also regard spelunkers as desperate criminals if AT&T owned all the caves.

The terrifying poses which Optik and Acid had been striking on screen were a media-amplified example of a human adaptation I'd seen before: One becomes as he is beheld. They were simply living up to what they thought we, and, more particularly, the editors of *Harper's*, expected of them. Like the televised tears of disaster victims, their snarls adapted easily to mass distribution.

Months later, *Harper's* took Optik, Acid and me to dinner at a Manhattan restaurant which, though very fancy, was appropriately Chinese. Acid and Optik, as material beings, were well-scrubbed and fashionably-clad. They looked to be dangerous as ducks. But, as *Harper's* and the rest of the media have discovered to their delight, the boys had developed distinctly showier personae for their rambles through the howling wilderness of Cyberspace.

Glittering with spikes of binary chrome, they strode past the kleig lights and into the digital distance. There they would be outlaws. It was only a matter of time before they started to believe themselves as bad as they sounded. And no time at all before everyone else did.

In this, they were like another kid named Billy, many of whose feral deeds in the pre-civilized West were encouraged by the same dime novelist who chronicled them. And like Tom Horn, they seemed to have some doubt as to which side of the law they were on. Acid even expressed an ambition to work for the government someday, nabbing "terrorists and code abusers."

There is also a frontier ambiguity to the "crimes" the crackers commit. They are not exactly stealing VCR's. Copying a text file from TRW doesn't deprive its owner of anything except informational exclusivity. (Though it may be said that information has monetary value only in proportion to its containment.)

There was no question that they were making unauthorized use of data channels. The night I met them, they left our restaurant table and disappeared into the phone booth for a long time. I didn't see them marshalling quarters before they went.

And, as I became less their adversary and more their scoutmaster, I began to get "conference calls" in which six or eight of them would crack pay phones all over New York and simultaneously land on my line in Wyoming. These deft maneuvers made me think of sky-diving stunts where large groups convene geometrically in free fall. In this case, the risk was largely legal.

Their other favorite risky business is the time-honored adolescent sport of trespassing. They insist on going where they don't belong. But then teen-age boys have been proceeding uninvited since the dawn of human puberty. It seems hard-wired. The only innovation in the new form of the forbidden zone is the means of getting in it.

In fact, like Kevin Mitnik, I broke into NORAD when I was 17. A friend and I left a nearby "woodsie" (as rustic adolescent drunks were called in Colorado) and tried to get inside the Cheyenne Mountain. The chrome-helmeted Air Force MP's held us for about 2 hours before letting us go. They weren't much older than us and knew exactly our level of national security threat. Had we come cloaked in electronic mystery, their alert status certainly would have been higher.

Whence rises much of the anxiety. Everything is so ill-defined. How can you guess what lies in their hearts when you can't see their eyes? How can one be sure that, like Mitnik, they won't cross the line from trespassing into another adolescent pastime, vandalism? And how can you be sure they pose no threat when you don't know what a threat might be?

And for the crackers some thrill is derived from the metamorphic vagueness of the laws themselves. On the Net, their effects are unpredictable. One never knows when they'll bite.

This is because most of the statutes invoked against the crackers were designed in a very different world from the one they explore. For example, can unauthorized electronic access can be regarded as the ethical equivalent of old-fashioned trespass? Like open range, the property boundaries of Cyberspace are hard to stake and harder still to defend.

Is transmission through an otherwise unused data channel really theft? Is the track-less passage of a mind through TRW's mainframe the same as the passage of a pickup through my Back 40? What is a place if Cyberspace is everywhere? What are data and what is free speech? How does one treat property which has no physical form and can be infinitely reproduced? Is a computer the same as a printing press? Can the history of my business affairs properly belong to someone else? Can anyone morally claim to own knowledge itself?

If such questions were hard to answer precisely, there are those who are ready to try. Based on their experience in the Virtual World, they were about as qualified to enforce its mores as I am to write the Law of the Sea. But if they lacked technical sophistication, they brought to this task their usual conviction. And, of course, badges and guns.

Operation Sun Devil

Recently, we have witnessed an alarming number of young people who, for a variety of sociological and psychological reasons, have become attached to their computers and are exploiting their potential in a criminal manner. Often, a progression of criminal activity occurs which involves telecommunications fraud (free long distance phone calls), unauthorized access to other computers (whether for profit, fascination, ego, or the intellectual challenge), credit card fraud (cash advances and unauthorized purchases of goods), and then move on to other destructive activities like computer viruses.

Our experience shows that many computer hacker suspects are no longer misguided teenagers mischievously playing games with their computers in their bedrooms. Some are now high tech computer operators using computers to engage in unlawful conduct.

—Excerpts from a statement by Garry M. Jenkins, Asst. Director, U. S. Secret Service

The right of the people to be secure in their persons, houses, papers, and effects, against unreasonable searches and seizures, shall not be violated, and no warrants shall issue but upon probable cause, support by oath or affirmation, and particularly describing the place to be searched, and the persons or things to be seized.

—Amendment IV, United States Constitution

On January 24, 1990, a platoon of Secret Service agents entered the apartment which Acid Phreak shares with his mother and 12-year-old sister. The latter was the only person home when they burst through the door with guns drawn. They managed to hold her at bay for about half an hour until their quarry happened home.

By then, they were nearly done packing up Acid's worldly goods, including his computer, his notes (both paper and magnetic), books, and such dubiously dangerous tools as a telephone answering machine, a ghetto blaster and his complete collection of audio tapes. One agent asked him to define the real purpose of the answering machine and was frankly skeptical when told that it answered the phone. The audio tapes seemed to contain nothing but music, but who knew what dark data Acid might have encoded between the notes.

When Acid's mother returned from work, she found her apartment a scene of apprehended criminality. She asked what, exactly, her son had done to deserve all this attention and was told that, among other things, he had caused the AT&T system crash several days earlier. (Previously AT&T had taken full responsibility.) Thus, the agent explained, her darling boy was thought to have caused over a billion dollars in damage to the economy of the United States.

This accusation was never turned into a formal charge. Indeed, no charge of any sort of was filed against Mr. Phreak then and, although the Secret Service maintained resolute possession of his hardware, software, and data, no charge had been charged 4 months later.

Across town, similar scenes were being played out at the homes of Phiber Optik and another colleague code-named Scorpion. Again, equipment, notes, disks both hard and soft, and personal effects were confiscated. Again no charges were filed.

Thus began the visible phase of Operation Sun Devil, a two-year Secret Service investigation which involved 150 federal agents, numerous local and state law enforcement agencies, and the combined security resources of PacBell, AT&T, Bellcore, BellSouth, MCI, U.S. Sprint, Mid-American, Southwestern Bell, NYNEX, U.S. West and American Express.

The focus of this impressive institutional array was the Legion of Doom, a group which never had any formal membership list but was thought by the members with whom I spoke to number less than 20, nearly all of them in their teens or early twenties.

I asked Acid why they'd chosen such a threatening name. "You wouldn't want a fairy kind of thing like Legion of Flower Pickers or something. But the media ate it up too. Probing the Legion of Doom like it was a gang or something, when really it was just a bunch of geeks behind terminals."

Sometime in December 1988, a 21-year-old Atlanta-area Legion of Doomster named The Prophet cracked a BellSouth computer and downloaded a three-page text file which outlined, in bureaucrat-ese of surpassing opacity, the administrative procedures and responsibilities for marketing, servicing, upgrading, and billing for BellSouth's 911 system.

A dense thicket of acronyms, the document was filled with passages like: "In accordance with the basic SSC/MAC strategy for provisioning, the SSC/MAC will be Overall Control Office (OCO) for all Notes to PSAP circuits (official services) and any other services for this customer. Training must be scheduled for all SSC/MAC involved personnel during the pre-service stage of the project." And other such.

At some risk, I too have a copy of this document. To read the whole thing straight through without entering coma requires either a machine or a human who has too much practice thinking like one. Anyone who can understand it fully and fluidly has altered his consciousness beyond the ability to ever again read Blake, Whitman, or Tolstoy. It is, quite simply, the worst writing I have ever tried to read.

Since the document contains little of interest to anyone who is not a student of advanced organizational sclerosis—that is, no access codes, trade secrets, or proprietary information—I assume The Prophet only copied this file as a kind of hunting trophy. He had been to the heart of the forest and had returned with this coonskin to nail to the barn door.

Furthermore, he was proud of his accomplishment, and since such trophies are infinitely replicable, he wasn't content to nail it to his door alone. Among the places he copied it was a UNIX bulletin board (rather like the WELL) in Lockport, Illinois called Jolnet.

It was downloaded from there by a 20 year-old hacker and pre-law student (whom I had met in the *Harper's* Forum) who called himself Knight Lightning. Though not a member of the Legion of Doom, Knight Lightning and a friend, Taran King, also published from St. Louis and his fraternity house at the University of Missouri a worldwide hacker's magazine called *Phrack*. (From phone phreak and hack.)

Phrack was an unusual publication in that it was entirely virtual. The only time its articles hit paper was when one of its subscribers decided to print out a hard copy. Otherwise, its editions existed in Cyberspace and took no physical form.

When Knight Lightning got hold of the BellSouth document, he thought it would amuse his readers and reproduced it in the next issue of *Phrack*. He had little reason to think that he was doing something illegal. There is nothing in it to indicate that it contains proprietary or even sensitive information. Indeed, it closely resembles telco reference documents which have long been publicly available.

However, Rich Andrews, the systems operator who oversaw the operation of Jolnet, thought there might be something funny about the document when he first ran across it in his system. To be on the safe side, he forwarded a copy of it to AT&T officials. He was subsequently contacted by the authorities, and he cooperated with them fully. He would regret that later.

On the basis of the forgoing, a Grand Jury in Lockport was persuaded by the Secret Service in early February to hand down a seven count indictment against The Prophet and Knight Lightning, charging them, among other things, with interstate transfer of stolen property worth more than $5,000. When The Prophet and two of his Georgia colleagues were arrested on February 7, 1990, the Atlanta papers reported they faced 40 years in prison and a $2 million fine. Knight Lightning was arrested on February 15.

The property in question was the afore-mentioned blot on the history of prose whose full title was "A BellSouth Standard Practice (BSP) 660-225-104SV-Control Office Administration of Enhanced 911 Services for Special Services and Major Account Centers, March, 1988."

And not only was this item worth more than $5,000.00, it was worth, according to the indictment and BellSouth, precisely $79,449.00. And not a penny less. We will probably never know how this figure was reached or by whom, though I like to imagine an appraisal team consisting of Franz Kafka, Joseph Heller, and Thomas Pynchon . . .

In addition to charging Knight Lightning with crimes for which he could go to jail 30 years and be fined $122,000.00, they seized his publication, *Phrack*, along with all related equipment, software and data, including his list of subscribers, many of whom would soon lose their computers and data for the crime of appearing on it.

I talked to Emmanuel Goldstein, the editor of *2600,* another hacker publication which has been known to publish purloined documents. If they could shut down *Phrack,* couldn't they as easily shut down *2600*?

He said, "I've got one advantage. I come out on paper and the Constitution knows how to deal with paper."

In fact, nearly all publications are now electronic at some point in their creation. In a modern newspaper, stories written at the scene are typed to screens and then sent by modem to a central computer. This computer composes the layout in electronic type and the entire product transmitted electronically to the presses. There, finally, the bytes become ink.

Phrack merely omitted the last step in a long line of virtual events. However, that omission, and its insignificant circulation, left it vulnerable to seizure based on content. If the 911 document had been the Pentagon Papers (another proprietary document) and *Phrack* the *New York Times,* a completion of the analogy would have seen the government stopping publication of the *Times* and seizing its every material possession, from notepads to presses.

Not that anyone in the newspaper business seemed particularly worried about such implications. They, and the rest of the media who bothered to report Knight Lightning's arrest were too obsessed by what they portrayed as actual disruptions of emergency service and with marvelling at the sociopathy of it. One report expressed relief that no one appeared to have died as a result of the "intrusions."

Meanwhile, in Baltimore, the 911 dragnet snared Leonard Rose, aka Terminus. A professional computer consultant who specialized in UNIX, Rose got a visit from the government early in February. The G-men forcibly detained his wife and children for six hours while they interrogated Rose about the 911 document and ransacked his system.

Rose had no knowledge of the 911 matter. Indeed, his only connection had been occasional contact with Knight Lightning over several years . . . and admitted membership in the Legion of Doom. However, when searching his hard disk for 911 evidence, they found something else. Like many UNIX consultants, Rose did have some UNIX source code in his possession. Furthermore, there was evidence that he had transmitted some of it to Jolnet and left it there for another consultant.

UNIX is a ubiquitous operating system, and though its main virtue is its openness to amendment at the source level, it is nevertheless the property of AT&T. What had been widely distributed within businesses and universities for years was suddenly, in Rose's hands, a felonious possession.

Finally, the Secret Service rewarded the good citizenship of Rich Andrews by confiscating the computer where Jolnet had dwelt, along with all the e-mail, read and unread, which his subscribers had left there. Like the many others whose equipment and data were taken by the Secret Service subsequently, he wasn't charged with anything. Nor is he likely to be. They have already inflicted on him the worst punishment a nerd can suffer: data death.

Andrews was baffled. "I'm the one that found it, I'm the one that turned it in. . . . And I'm the one that's suffering," he said.

One wonders what will happen when they find such documents on the hard disks of CompuServe. Maybe I'll just upload my copy of BellSouth Standard Practice (BSP) 660-225-104SV and see . . .

In any case, association with stolen data is all the guilt you need. It's quite as if the government could seize your house simply because a guest left a stolen VCR in an upstairs bedroom closet. Or confiscate all the mail in a post office upon finding a stolen package there. The first concept of modern jurisprudence to have arrived in Cyberspace seems to have been Zero Tolerance.

Rich Andrews was not the last to learn about the Secret Service's debonair new attitude toward the 4th Amendment's protection against unreasonable seizure.

Early on March 1, 1990, the offices of a role-playing game publisher in Austin, Texas, called Steve Jackson Games were visited by agents of the United States Secret Service. They ransacked the premises, broke into several locked filing cabinets (damaging them irreparably in the process) and eventually left carrying 3 computers, 2 laser printers, several hard disks, and many boxes of paper and floppy disks.

Later in the day, callers to the Illuminati BBS (which Steve Jackson Games operated to keep in touch with roll-players around the country) encountered the following message:

So far we have not received a clear explanation of what the Secret Service was looking for, what they expected to find, or much of anything else. We are fairly certain that Steve Jackson Games is not the target of whatever investigation is being conducted; in any case, we have done nothing illegal and have nothing whatsoever to hide. However, the equipment that was seized is apparently considered to be evidence in whatever they're investigating, so we aren't likely to get it back any time soon. It could be a month, it could be never.

It's been three months as I write this and, not only has nothing been returned to them, but, according to Steve Jackson, the Secret Service will no longer take his calls. He figures that, in the months since the raid, his little company has lost an estimated $125,000. With such a fiscal hemorrhage, he can't afford a lawyer to take after the Secret Service. Both the state and national offices of the ACLU told him to "run along" when he solicited their help.

He tried to go to the press. As in most other cases, they were unwilling to raise the alarm. Jackson theorized, "The conservative press is taking the attitude that the suppression of evil hackers is a good thing and that anyone who happens to be put out of business in the meantime . . . well, that's just their tough luck."

In fact, *Newsweek* did run a story about the event, portraying it from Jackson's perspective, but they were almost alone in dealing with it.

What had he done to deserve this nightmare? Role-playing games, of which Dungeons and Dragons is the most famous, have been accused of creating obsessive involvement in their nerdy young players, but no one before had found it necessary to prevent their publication.

It seems that Steve Jackson had hired the wrong writer. The managing editor of Steve Jackson Games is a former cracker, known by his fellows in the Legion of Doom as The Mentor. At the time of the raid, he and the rest of Jackson staff had been working for over a year on a game called *GURPS Cyberpunk, High-Tech Low-Life Role-Playing.*

At the time of the Secret Service raids, the game resided entirely on the hard disks they confiscated. Indeed, it was their target. They told Jackson that, based on its author's background, they had reason to believe it was a "handbook on computer crime." It was therefore inappropriate for publication, 1st Amendment or no 1st Amendment.

I got a copy of the game from the trunk of The Mentor's car in an Austin parking lot. Like the BellSouth document, it seemed pretty innocuous to me, if a little inscrutable. Borrowing its flavor from the works of William Gibson and Austin sci-fi author Bruce Sterling, it is filled with silicon brain implants, holodecks, and gauss guns.

It is, as the cover copy puts it, "a fusion of the dystopian visions of George Orwell and Timothy Leary." Actually, without the gizmos, it describes a future kind of like the present its publisher is experiencing at the hands of the Secret Service.

An unbelievably Byzantine world resides within its 120 large pages of small print. (These roll-players must be some kind of idiots savants . . .) Indeed, it's a thing of such complexity that I can't swear there's no criminal information in there, but then I can't swear that Grateful Dead records don't have satanic messages if played backwards. Anything's possible, especially inside something as remarkable as *Cyberpunk*.

The most remarkable thing about *Cyberpunk* is the fact that it was printed at all. After much negotiation, Jackson was able to get the Secret Service to let him have some of his data back. However, they told him that he would be limited to an hour and a half with only one of his three computers. Also, according to Jackson, "They insisted that all the copies be made by a Secret Service agent who was a two- finger typist. So we didn't get much."

In the end, Jackson and his staff had to reconstruct most of the game from neural rather than magnetic memory. They did have a few very old backups, and they retrieved some scraps which had been passed around to game testers. They also had the determination of the enraged.

Despite government efforts to impose censorship by prior restraint, *Cyberpunk* is now on the market. Presumably, advertising as "The book that was seized by the U.S. Secret Service" will invigorate sales. But Steve Jackson Games, the heretofore prosperous publisher of more than a hundred role-playing games, has been forced to lay off more than half of its employees and may well be mortally wounded.

Any employer who has heard this tale will think hard before he hires a computer cracker. Which may be, of course, among the effects the Secret Service desires.

On May 8, 1990, Operation Sun Devil, heretofore an apparently random and nameless trickle of Secret Service actions, swept down on the Legion of Doom and its ilk like a bureaucratic tsunami. On that day, the Secret Service served 27 search warrants in 14 cities from Plano, Texas to New York, New York.

The law had come to Cyberspace. When the day was over, transit through the wide open spaces of the Virtual World would be a lot trickier.

In a press release following the sweep, the Secret Service boasted having shut down numerous computer bulletin boards, confiscated 40 computers, and seized 23,000 disks. They noted in their statement that "the conceivable criminal violations of this operation have serious implications for the health and welfare of all individuals, corporations, and United States Government agencies relying on computers and telephones to communicate."

It was unclear from their statement whether "this operation" meant the Legion of Doom or Operation Sun Devil. There was room to interpret it either way.

Because the deliciously ironic truth is that, aside from the 3-page Bell South document, the hackers had neither removed nor damaged anyone's data. Operation Sun Devil, on the other hand, had "serious implications" for a number of folks who relied on "computers and telephones to communicate." They lost the equivalent of about 5.4 million pages of information. Not to mention a few computers and telephones.

And the welfare of the individuals behind those figures was surely in jeopardy. Like the story of the single mother and computer consultant in Baltimore whose sole means of supporting herself and her 18 year old son was stripped away early one morning. Secret Service agents broke down her door with sledge hammers, entered with guns drawn, and seized all her computer equipment. Apparently her son had also been using it . . .

Or the father in New York who opened the door at 6:00 AM and found a shotgun at his nose. A dozen agents entered. While one of them kept the man's wife in a choke-hold, the rest made ready to shoot and entered the bedroom of their sleeping 14-year-old. Before leaving, they confiscated every piece of electronic equipment in the house, including all the telephones.

It was enough to suggest that the insurance companies should start writing policies against capricious governmental seizure of circuitry.

In fairness, one can imagine the government's problem. This is all pretty magical stuff to them. If I were trying to terminate the operations of a witch coven, I'd probably seize everything in sight. How would I tell the ordinary household brooms from the getaway vehicles?

But as I heard more and more about the vile injustices being heaped on my young pals in the Legion of Doom, not to mention the unfortunate folks nearby, the less I was inclined toward such temperate thoughts as these. I drifted back into a 60s-style sense of the government, thinking it a thing of monolithic and evil efficiency and adopting an up-against-the-wall willingness to spit words like "pig" or "fascist" into my descriptions.

In doing so, I endowed the Secret Service with a clarity of intent which no agency of government will ever possess. Despite almost every experience I've ever had with federal authority, I keep imagining its competence.

For some reason, it was easier to invest the Keystone Kapers of Operation Sun Devil with malign purpose rather than confront their absurdity straight-on. There is, after all, a twisted kind of comfort in political paranoia. It provides one such a sense of orderliness to think that the government is neither crazy nor stupid and that its plots, though wicked, are succinct.

I was about to have an experience which would restore both my natural sense of unreality and my unwillingness to demean the motives of others. I was about to see first hand the disorientation of the law in the featureless vastness of Cyberspace.

In Search of NuPrometheus

I pity the poor immigrant. . . .
—Bob Dylan

Sometime last June, an angry hacker got hold of a chunk of the highly secret source code which drives the Apple Macintosh. He then distributed it to a variety of addresses, claiming responsibility for this act of information terrorism in the name of the NuPrometheus League.

Apple freaked. NuPrometheus had stolen, if not the Apple crown jewels, at least a stone from them. Worse, NuPrometheus had then given this prize away. Repeatedly.

All Apple really has to offer the world is the software which lies encoded in silicon on the ROM chip of every Macintosh. This set of instructions is the cyber-DNA which makes a Macintosh a Macintosh.

Worse, much of the magic in this code was put there by people who not only do not work for Apple any longer, but might only do so again if encouraged with cattle prods. Apple's attitude toward its ROM code is a little like that of a rich kid toward his inheritance. Not actually knowing how to create wealth himself, he guards what he has with hysterical fervor.

Time passed, and I forgot about the incident. But one recent May morning, I learned that others had not. The tireless search for the spectral heart of NuPrometheus finally reached Pinedale, Wyoming, where I was the object of a two hour interview by Special Agent Richard Baxter, Jr., of the Federal Bureau of Investigation.

Poor Agent Baxter didn't know a ROM chip from a Vise-grip when he arrived, so much of that time was spent trying to educate him on the nature of the thing which had been stolen. Or whether "stolen" was the right term for what had happened to it.

You know things have rather jumped the groove when potential suspects must explain to law enforcers the nature of their alleged perpetrations.

I wouldn't swear Agent Baxter ever got it quite right. After I showed him some actual source code, gave a demonstration of e-mail in action, and downloaded a file from the WELL, he took to rubbing his face with both hands, peering up over his finger tips and saying, "It sure is something, isn't it" Or, "Whooo-ee."

Or "my eight-year-old knows more about these things than I do." He didn't say this with a father's pride so much as an immigrant's fear of a strange new land into which he will be forcibly moved and in which his own child is a native. He looked across my keyboard into Cyberspace and didn't like what he saw.

We could have made it harder for one another, but I think we each sensed that the other occupied a world which was as bizarre and nonsensical as it could be. We did our mutual best to suppress immune response at the border.

You'd have thought his world might have been a little more recognizable to me. Not so, it turns out. Because in his world, I found several unfamiliar features, including these:

1. The Hacker's Conference is an underground organization of computer outlaws with likely connections to, and almost certainly sympathy with, the NuPrometheus League. (Or as Agent Baxter repeatedly put it, the "New Prosthesis League.")
2. John Draper, the affore-mentioned Cap'n Crunch, in addition to being a known member of the Hacker's Conference, is also CEO and President of Autodesk, Inc. This is of particular concern to the FBI because Autodesk has many top-secret contracts with the government to supply Star Wars graphics imaging and "hyperspace" technology. Worse, Draper is thought to have Soviet contacts.

He wasn't making this up. He had lengthy documents from the San Francisco office to prove it. And in which Autodesk's address was certainly correct.

On the other hand, I know John Draper. While, as I say, he may have once distinguished himself as a cracker during the Pleistocene, he is not now, never has been, and never will be CEO of Autodesk. He did work there for awhile last year, but he was let go long before he got in a position to take over.

Nor is Autodesk, in my experience with it, the Star Wars skunk works which Agent Baxter's documents indicated. One could hang out there a long time without ever seeing any gold braid.

Their primary product is something called AutoCAD, by far the most popular computer-aided design software but generally lacking in lethal potential. They do have a small development program in Cyberspace, which is what they call Virtual Reality. (This, I assume is the "hyperspace" to which Agent Baxter's documents referred.)

However, Autodesk had reduced its Cyberspace program to a couple of programmers. I imagined Randy Walser and Carl Tollander toiling away in the dark and lonely service of their country. Didn't work. Then

I tried to describe Virtual Reality to Agent Baxter, but that didn't work either. In fact, he tilted. I took several runs at it, but I could tell I was violating our border agreements. These seemed to include a requirement that neither of us try to drag the other across into his conceptual zone.

I fared a little better on the Hacker's Conference. Hardly a conspiracy, the Hacker's Conference is an annual convention originated in 1984 by the Point Foundation and the editors of *Whole Earth Review*. Each year it invites about a hundred of the most gifted and accomplished of digital creators. Indeed, they are the very people who have conducted the personal computer revolution. Agent Baxter looked at my list of Hacker's Conference attendees and read their bios.

"These are the people who actually design this stuff, aren't they?" He was incredulous. Their corporate addresses didn't fit his model of outlaws at all well.

Why had he come all the way to Pinedale to investigate a crime he didn't understand which had taken place (sort of) in 5 different places, none of which was within 500 miles?

Well, it seems Apple has told the FBI that they can expect little cooperation from Hackers in and around the Silicon Valley, owing to virulent anti-Apple sentiment there. They claim this is due to the Hacker belief that software should be free combined with festering resentment of Apple's commercial success. They advised the FBI to question only those Hackers who were as far as possible from the twisted heart of the subculture.

They did have their eye on some local people though. These included a couple of former Apple employees, Grady Ward and Walter Horat, Chuck Farnham (who has made a living out of harassing Apple), Glenn Tenney (the purported leader of the Hackers), and, of course, the purported CEO of Autodesk.

Other folks Agent Baxter asked me about included Mitch Kapor, who wrote Lotus 1-2-3 and was known to have received some of this mysterious source code. Or whatever. But I had also met Mitch Kapor, both on the WELL and in person. A less likely computer terrorist would be hard to come by.

Actually, the question of the source code was another area where worlds but shadow-boxed. Although Agent Baxter didn't know source code from Tuesday, he did know that Apple Computer had told his agency that what had been stolen and disseminated was the complete recipe for a Macintosh computer. The distribution of this secret formula might result in the creation of millions of Macintoshes not made by Apple. And, of course, the ruination of Apple Computer.

In my world, NuPrometheus (whoever they, or more likely, he might be) had distributed a small portion of the code which related specifically to Color QuickDraw. QuickDraw is Apple's name for the software which controls the Mac's on-screen graphics. But this was another detail which Agent Baxter could not capture. For all he knew, you could grow Macintoshes from floppy disks.

I explained to him that Apple was alleging something like the ability to assemble an entire human being from the recipe for a foot, but even he knew the analogy was inexact. And trying to get him to accept the idea that a corporation could go mad with suspicion was quite futile. He had a far different perception of the emotional reliability of institutions.

When he finally left, we were both dazzled and disturbed. I spent some time thinking about Lewis Carroll and tried to return to writing about the legal persecution of the Legion of Doom. But my heart wasn't in it. I found myself suddenly too much in sympathy with Agent Baxter and his struggling colleagues from Operation Sun Devil to get back into a proper sort of pig-bashing mode.

Given what had happened to other innocent bystanders like Steve Jackson, I gave some thought to getting scared. But this was Kafka in a clown suit. It wasn't precisely frightening. I also took some comfort in a phrase once applied to the administration of Frederick the Great: "Despotism tempered by incompetence."

Of course, incompetence is a double-edged banana. While we may know this new territory better than the authorities, they have us literally out-gunned. One should pause before making well-armed paranoids feel foolish, no matter how foolish they seem.

The Fear of White Noise

Neurosis is the inability to tolerate ambiguity.
—Sigmund Freud, appearing to me in a dream

I'm a member of that half of the human race which is inclined to divide the human race into two kinds of people. My dividing line runs between the people who crave certainty and the people who trust chance.

You can draw this one a number of ways, of course, like Control vs. Serendipity, Order vs. Chaos, Hard answers vs. Silly questions, or Newton, Descartes & Aquinas vs. Heisenberg, Mandelbrot & the Dalai Lama, etc.

Large organizations and their drones huddle on one end of my scale, busily trying to impose predictable homogeneity on messy circumstance. On the other end, free-lancers and ne'er-do-wells cavort about, getting by on luck if they get by at all.

However you cast these poles, it comes down to the difference between those who see life as a struggle against cosmic peril and human infamy and those who believe, without any hard evidence, that the universe is actually on our side. Fear vs. Faith.

I am of the latter group. Along with Gandhi and Rebecca of Sunnybrook Farm, I believe that other human beings will quite consistently merit my trust if I'm not doing something which scares them or makes them feel bad about themselves. In other words, the best defense is a good way to get hurt.

In spite of the fact that this system works very reliably for me and my kind, I find we are increasingly in the minority. More and more of our neighbors live in armed compounds. Alarms blare continuously. Potentially happy people give their lives over to the corporate state as though the world were so dangerous outside its veil of collective immunity that they have no choice.

I have a number of theories as to why this is happening. One has to do with the opening of Cyberspace. As a result of this development, humanity is now undergoing the most profound transformation of its history. Coming into the Virtual World, we inhabit Information. Indeed, we become Information. Thought is embodied and the Flesh is made Word. It's weird as hell.

Beginning with the invention of the telegraph and extending through television into Virtual Reality, we have been, for a over a century, experiencing a terrifying erosion in our sense of both body and place. As we begin to realize the enormity of what is happening to us, all but the most courageous have gotten scared.

And everyone, regardless of his psychic resilience, feels this overwhelming sense of strangeness. The world, once so certain and tangible and legally precise, has become an infinite layering of opinions, perceptions, litigation, camera-angles, data, white noise, and, most of all, ambiguities. Those of us who are of the fearful persuasion do not like ambiguities.

Indeed, if one were a little jumpy to start with, he may now be fairly humming with nameless dread. Since no one likes his dread to be nameless, the first order of business is to find it some names.

For a long time here in the United States, Communism provided a kind of catch-all bogeyman. Marx, Stalin and Mao summoned forth such a spectre that, to many Americans, annihilation of all life was preferable to the human portion's becoming Communist. But as Big Red wizened and lost his teeth, we began to cast about for a replacement.

Finding none of sufficient individual horror, we have draped a number of objects with the old black bunting which once shrouded the Kremlin. Our current spooks are terrorists, child abductors, AIDS, and the underclass. I would say drugs, but anyone who thinks that the War on Drugs is not actually the War on the Underclass hasn't been paying close enough attention.

There are a couple of problems with these Four Horsemen. For one thing, they aren't actually very dangerous. For example, only 7 Americans died in worldwide terrorist attacks in 1987. Fewer than 10 (out of about 70 million) children are abducted by strangers in the U.S. each year. Your chances of getting AIDS if you are neither gay nor a hemophiliac nor a junkie are considerably less than your chances of getting killed by lightning while golfing. The underclass is dangerous, of course, but only, with very few exceptions, if you are a member of it.

The other problem with these perils is that they are all physical. If we are entering into a world in which no one has a body, physical threats begin to lose their sting.

And now I come to the point of this screed: The perfect bogeyman for Modern Times is the Cyberpunk! He is so smart he makes you feel even more stupid than you usually do. He knows this complex country in which you're perpetually lost. He understands the value of things you can't conceptualize long enough to cash in on. He is the one-eyed man in the Country of the Blind.

In a world where you and your wealth consist of nothing but beeps and boops of micro-voltage, he can steal all your assets in nanoseconds and then make you disappear.

He can even reach back out of his haunted mists and kill you physically. Among the justifications for Operation Sun Devil was this chilling tidbit: "Hackers had the ability to access and review the files of hospital patients. Furthermore, they could have added, deleted, or altered vital patient information, possibly causing life-threatening situations."

Perhaps the most frightening thing about the Cyberpunk is the danger he presents to The Institution, whether corporate or governmental. If you are frightened you have almost certainly taken shelter by now in one of these collective organisms, so the very last thing you want is something which can endanger your heretofore unassailable hive.

And make no mistake, crackers will become to bureaucratic bodies what viruses presently are to human bodies. Thus, Operation Sun Devil can be seen as the first of many waves of organizational immune response to this new antigen. Agent Baxter was a T-cell. Fortunately, he didn't know that himself and I was very careful not to show him my own antigenic tendencies.

I think that herein lies the way out of what might otherwise become an Armageddon between the control freaks and the neo-hip. Those who are comfortable with these disorienting changes must do everything in our power to convey that comfort to others. In other words, we must share our sense of hope and opportunity with those who feel that in Cyberspace they will be obsolete eunuchs for sure.

It's a tall order. But, my silicon brothers, our self-interest is strong. If we come on as witches, they will burn us. If we volunteer to guide them gently into its new lands, the Virtual World might be a more amiable place for all of us than this one has been.

Of course, we may also have to fight.

Defining the conceptual and legal map of Cyberspace before the ambiguophobes do it for us (with punitive over-precision) is going to require some effort. We can't expect the Constitution to take care of itself.

Indeed, the precedent for mitigating the Constitutional protection of a new medium has already been established. Consider what happened to radio in the early part of this century.

Under the pretext of allocating limited bandwidth, the government established an early right of censorship over broadcast content which still seems directly unconstitutional to me. Except that it stuck. And now, owing to a large body of case law, looks to go on sticking.

New media, like any chaotic system, are highly sensitive to initial conditions. Today's heuristical answers of the moment become tomorrow's permanent institutions of both law and expectation. Thus, they bear examination with that destiny in mind.

Earlier in this article, I asked a number of tough questions relating to the nature of property, privacy, and speech in the digital domain. Questions like: "What are data and what is free speech?" or "How does one treat property which has no physical form and can be infinitely reproduced?" or "Is a computer the same as a printing press?" The events of Operation Sun Devil were nothing less than an effort to provide answers to these questions. Answers which would greatly enhance governmental ability to silence the future's opinionated nerds.

In over-reaching as extravagantly as they did, the Secret Service may actually have done a service for those of us who love liberty. They have provided us with a devil. And devils, among their other galvanizing virtues, are just great for clarifying the issues and putting iron in your spine. In the presence of a devil, it's always easier to figure out where you stand.

While I previously had felt no stake in the obscure conundra of free telecommunication, I was, thanks to Operation Sun Devil, suddenly able to plot a trajectory from the current plight of the Legion of Doom to an eventual constraint on opinions much dearer to me. I remembered Martin Neimoeller, who said:

> In Germany they came first for the Communists, and I didn't speak up because I wasn't a Communist. Then they came for the Jews, and I didn't speak up because I wasn't a Jew. They came for the trade unionists, and I didn't speak up because I wasn't a trade unionist. Then they came for the Catholics, and I didn't speak up because I was a Protestant. Then they came for me, and by that time no one was left to speak up.

I decided it was time for me to speak up.

The evening of my visit from Agent Baxter, I wrote an account of it which I placed on the WELL. Several days later, Mitch Kapor literally dropped by for a chat.

Also a WELL denizen, he had read about Agent Baxter and had begun to meditate on the inappropriateness of leaving our civil liberties to be defined by the technologically benighted. A man who places great emphasis on face-to-face contact, he wanted to discuss this issue with me in person. He had been flying his Canadair bizjet to a meeting in California when he realized his route took him directly over Pinedale.

We talked for a couple of hours in my office while a spring snowstorm swirled outside. When I recounted for him what I had learned about Operation Sun Devil, he decided it was time for him to speak up too.

He called a few days later with the phone number of a civil libertarian named Harvey Silverglate, who, as evidence of his conviction that everyone deserves due process, is currently defending Leona Helmsley. Mitch asked me to tell Harvey what I knew, with the inference that he would help support the costs which are liable to arise whenever you tell a lawyer anything.

I found Harvey in New York at the offices of that city's most distinguished constitutional law firm, Rabinowitz, Boudin, Standard, Krinsky, and Lieberman. These are the folks who made it possible for the *New York Times* to print the Pentagon Papers. (Not to dwell on the unwilling notoriety which partner Leonard Boudin achieved back in 1970 when his Weathergirl daughter blew up the family home . . .)

In the conference call which followed, I could almost hear the skeletal click as their jaws dropped. The next day, Eric Lieberman and Terry Gross of Rabinowitz, Boudin met with Acid Phreak, Phiber Optik, and Scorpion.

The maddening trouble with writing this account is that *Whole Earth Review,* unlike, say, *Phrack,* doesn't publish instantaneously. Events are boiling up at such a frothy pace that anything I say about current occurrences surely will not obtain by the time you read this. The road from here is certain to fork many times. The printed version of this will seem downright quaint before it's dry.

But as of today (in early June of 1990), Mitch and I are legally constituting the Electronic Frontier Foundation, a two- (or possibly three-) man organization which will raise and disburse funds for education, lobbying, and litigation in the areas relating to digital speech and the extension of the Constitution into Cyberspace.

Already, on the strength of preliminary stories about our efforts in the *Washington Post* and the *New York Times,* Mitch has received an offer from Steve Wozniak to match whatever funds he dedicates to this effort. (As well as a fair amount of abuse from the more institutionalized precincts of the computer industry.)

The Electronic Frontier Foundation will fund, conduct, and support legal efforts to demonstrate that the Secret Service has exercised prior restraint on publications, limited free speech, conducted improper seizure of equipment and data, used undue force, and generally conducted itself in a fashion which is arbitrary, oppressive, and unconstitutional.

In addition, we will work with the Computer Professionals for Social Responsibility and other organizations to convey to both the public and the policy-makers metaphors which will illuminate the more general stake in liberating Cyberspace.

Not everyone will agree. Crackers are, after all, generally beyond public sympathy. Actions on their behalf are not going to be popular no matter who else might benefit from them in the long run.

Nevertheless, in the litigations and political debates which are certain to follow, we will endeavor to assure that their electronic speech is protected as certainly as any opinions which are printed or, for that matter, screamed. We will make an effort to clarify issues surrounding the distribution of intellectual property. And we will help to create for America a future which is as blessed by the Bill of Rights as its past has been.

Appendix 2: Hardware 1: The Italian Hacker Crackdown

Peter Ludlow

The Italian corner of the electronic frontier resembles the American territory in certain respects, but has its own characteristic features. Internet access is rare, so Italians tend to rely on smaller networks, such as Fidonet and a number of exclusively Italian networks for the sharing of information. The Italian territory also has a rhythm of its own. The main Italian networks, CyberNet, PeaceLink, P-net, etc., do not bristle with the same high octane flame wars one finds on American bulletin boards, nor do they boast the same frenetic swapping of technical information and programs. Much more prominent are exchanges of information on topics like antifascism and anti-Mafia, the latest assaults by neo-fascists on African workers, the latest on AIDS research, and the shifting political currents in the former Yugoslavia. Even the nonpolitical boards gravitate to discussions of Hakim Bey's *Temporary Autonomous Zones,* or the latest from the keyboards of Bruce Sterling and Howard Rheingold. It is, as a rule, a much more mellow territory.

That mellow atmosphere was punctuated violently on May 11, 1994, when the Guardia di Finanza (Italy's "finance police") was unleashed in a massive operation codenamed "hardware1." The news began hitting the Italian CyberNet network immediately.[1]

From: Marco
To: All

This afternoon the Guardia di Finanza came with a warrant to search the house and look for material "designed for the duplication of software" illegally, etc. The investigation was initiated, it seems, because the name of my BBS was found on the list of someone that I don't know, it seems to me in Modena, charging with the violation of copyright laws etc. . . . They wanted me to give them the addresses of my "correspondents," and I did so with pleasure. I gave them the nodelist for Fido!!! I really want to see what they do with 31,000 nodes scattered over the entire world!

From: Gianluca

To: All

Also at Riccardo's they seized everything. It seems that this is what we were talking about some time ago on the effects of the new law on copyright and on their interpretations really had the intent to strangle the BBSs. A BBS with free access is a risk. . . .

By the next day real horror stories were starting to hit CyberNet.

From: Giovanni

To: All

Re: Help :-(

Yesterday afternoon (Wednesday the 11th) agents of the Guardia di Finanza presented themselves to me at my house, they seized all the pcs and extensions that I have in my house. They really took everything, from the telephone chords to the little sack of disketts to the booklet with the telephone numbers of my friends. . . . If there would be someone that could give me a hand to lift me out of this situation, I would be eternally grateful. I really need help. . . .

By Friday the 13th, news was being broadcast to the Internet from the few Italians with Internet connections.

From ita.it!staff Fri May 13 05:32:27 1994

Return-Path: <staff@ita.it

. . . things are getting really bad here. . . . On Wednesday, 11th of May, at 3:30 pm, the Italian Feds came into my house while I was out of town for a consulting business. They went into my bedroom and seized all my equipment, diskettes, tapes. This action was part of a nationwide raid against software piracy that hit some other 40+ FIDONET sites (yes, they seem to have used a Fido nodelist to find out about sites to investigate). Needless to say, I didn't even have DOS on my disk drives, let alone any copyrighted software. Anyway, they have now all my work of the latest 5 (five) years, including all backup copies of UniBoard and related stuff . . . and I don't know if I will be ever able to have all my stuff back . . . . Please, forward this to the alt.bbs.* groups, since I do not have news access here, and am also missing all the e-mail addresses of my customers and friends. Wish me luck, Rick

From: Fabrizio Sala <fsala@varano.ing.unico.it

Subject: The Italian Crackdown??

To: BBS-L@SAUPM00.ing.unico.it

Cc: eff@eff.org

Hello. I'm the Sysop of one of the BBSs in Italy. I'm writing this message in this list to inform you, the BBS community, of what is going on in Italy. Some days ago, starting from Pesaro (Italy), our Police started a large [inquisition against] many [amateur] BBSs, mostly connected to the main networks. . . . They're getting everything they can find: computers, monitors, drives, hard disks, floppy, cdrom, streamer tapes . . . everything, without looking if they are or not in any way "illegal. . . ." Generally, every network in Italy is now full of holes . . . and many of us lost everything "in the name of the anti-piracy. . . ." Nobody of us is doing anything in any way illegal, but they are still getting everything. . . . They got more than 50 BBS and Police's work is still going on. . . . I hope that everyone diffuses this message . . . or in any way tells everybody what's going on . . . and if you have any way to help us . . . please do it! We made our best to make the Italian telecommunication scene working . . . they are killing us! See you later . . . if they don't get me!

If the reports were to be believed, the appetite of the Guardia di Finanza for hardware and peripherals was insatiable. Everything was being confiscated from CDs, to broken terminals, to, in at least one case, a multiplug electrical adapter.[2]

Just how severe was the crackdown? Estimates vacillated wildly. Some said 50 BBSs were affected. Some said over 100. Others indicated that hundreds of arrest warrants had been served. It was also unclear what the geographical reach of the crackdown had been. Initial reports put the affected BBSs in Pesaro, Modena, Bologna, Ancona, Pisa, Milano. The affected networks, in addition to Fidonet, included Euronet, Ludonet, P-Net, and CyberNet.[3]

It soon became apparent that the attack had two prongs—one coordinated by the regional office of the Guardia di Finanza in Turin (Torino)—generally in Northwestern Italy, the second coordinated by the Prosecutor of Pesaro, in Eastern Central Italy.

In a press release issued on May 25th, the Turin regional office of the Guardia di Finanza claimed that it had focused on only 14 persons, and that more specifically:

The law enforcement operation, managed by the pool of Prosecutors based in the local office under the direction of Dr. Cesare Parodi, brought to a series of searchings that ended with the legal report to penal Authorities of 14 people operating in Piemonte, Lombardia, Liguria, Marche, Abruzzo. Several hardware and software pieces were seized, for a value of more than 4 billion of lire (about US $2,5 million), including:

- 17 personal computers;
- 13,690 floppy disks of illegally copied software;
- 8 CD-ROM disks;
- 27 modems;
- 4 devices for illegal use of telephone lines;
- several computer boards and parts;
- many software manuals.[4]

The list itself raised eyebrows. Why CD-ROMs? And if they were pirated, why only 8? Why software manuals, unless they were copies of manuals?

Justifying these busts by the Turin prosecutor Parodi, the following justification was offered in an official statement.

Receiving the ECC proposal n. 250/91 in defence of copyrighted computer software, the Italian bill n. 518/92 establishes penal charges against any commercialization of illegally copied programs, in addition to the crime of great fiscal evasion. Following such legal pattern, recently the Finance and Fiscal Police conducted a vast operation throughout the country. This operation enabled us to crack an intricate web of "telecom pirates" who, using computer connections with similar North American "hackers," were making many illegal copies of stolen original software, selling them at very cheap prices. Thus incorrectly filling the commercial market with illegal products, this conduct broke the law n. 633/41 in protection of copyright materials. The Custom and Finance Police were surprised to find out that the "pirates" were using high advanced technology devices—including sophisticated personal computers, satellite communications, false "call-card" to use North American private phone company nets. Because of previous experiences on these issues and of meticulous investigations, Fiscal Police officials were able to infiltrate into the suspicious world of those computer super-experts.[5]

Just a few weeks later, the Prosecutor of Pesaro offered *these* numbers on his own much vaster operation in Central Italy.[6]

159 computers confiscated
110,000 diskettes "containing programs of dubious origin" confiscated
122 arrest warrants for illicit copying of software.

Just to put these numbers in perspective, according to Bruce Sterling, in the notorious U.S. crackdown Operation Sundevil, forty-two computer systems were seized.[7] Of those, Sterling estimates that only 25 were actually in operation. As Sterling notes, this would constitute one-tenth of one percent of all the boards active in the United States at that time. By contrast, some estimates claim that a full one-third of all the BBSs in Italy were confiscated. Clearly this operation had dwarfed the haul from Operation Sundevil, both in numerical terms, and in terms of effect on the online community. And the Italian operation wasn't finished!

As remaining networks scrambled to get the word out, one of the leading players was the PeaceLink network with its central node in Taranto. PeaceLink was a nonprofit network of bulletin boards established almost exclusively for the exchange of information about anti-Mafia and antifascist work, and had been one of few reliable lines of communication with the peoples of the former Yugoslavia.[8]

With its long tradition of left-leaning activism, it quite naturally took up the charge of exchanging information and helping in the organization of meetings on the crackdown which were to be held in Rome and Pesaro at the end of June. On May 23, Bernardo Parella distributed an electronic update on the crackdown, announcing, among other things, that "PeaceLink has set up a defense committee news center in Taranto." Then the other shoe dropped.

On June 3, three weeks after the initial wave of crackdowns, the finance police raided the Taranto node of PeaceLink, confiscated its equipment and files, effectively silencing the network.

Three days later, in a radio interview, the head of PeaceLink, Gugliemo Pugliese explained what had happened.

> . . . last Thursday, at 5:00 PM, I had just returned home; I heard the door bell, I opened, and there was the *finanza* [finance police]. They presented themselves, gave me notice of a search warrant and an *avviso di garanzia* [arrest warrant] for me and my wife. At this, let's say, I became frightened by all this, because my name is fairly well noted and known, in measure from my activity with PeaceLink, an activity which is voluntary at every level . . . to see the finance police in my house made me a little bit ill. They notified me of this, and began searching the entire apartment, and not only; let's say that it was focused above all on PeaceLink, on the network; and therefore on software in general. At which they finished at 11:00 PM, therefore from 5:00 to 11:00 between various searches, questions. . . . Believe it or not, my check

book was sequestered, a series of things; they blocked the central system, which is here in my apartment, of the whole PeaceLink network.[9]

This time, the haul from the five-hour search was the PC and the modem running the BBS as well as bank-account receipts and 174 floppy disks—they left behind the computer monitor.

By this point nerves were frazzled all over the Italian BBS community. On June 12, I communicated with Andrea Sannuci, sysop of Senza Confine, one of the key CyberNet nodes.

Just a few days ago the host of the PeaceLink network was confiscated on the orders of the Taranto prosecutor. At this moment the true motives of the action are still unknown, but as you well understand, they precisely attacked a central node of a network—an action that, only with difficulty, could not be considered political. The PeaceLink network, after a night of frenetic telephoning among all the various nodes scattered throughout Italy is back up, but certainly it was a terrible experience. . . . It is certainly not easy for me to describe what we are going through at present. It is something that involves us and at the same time it is beyond us in that we cannot yet understand with what type of logic this is all taking place. Consider that just in my region (Marche) there were about 10 BBSs active and functioning. Now the only one remaining is mine. . . .[10]

Although affairs in Italy had risen to a state of urgency, the response from the online community in the United States ranged from disinterest to concerned resignation. A topic was opened to discuss the problem on the WELL, but few other systems seemed to be aware of the problem. Even on Mindvox, I was unable to locate a single reference to the crackdown. As for organizations dedicated to online rights, the CPSR did the best job of opening communications with the Italian community. Although the Australian EFF offered assistance, the United States EFF (in the middle of Clipper Chip and other battles) did not issue a single official statement on the Italian crackdown.

Meanwhile, the United States press either ignored the crackdown or treated it bemusedly as a legitimate antipiracy operation which simply looked bad for Italy's new right wing government. So, for example, in an article entitled "Nabbing the Pirates of Cyberspace" *Time* magazine's Philip Elmer-Dewitt wrote the following:

The sweep, when it came last month, was swift and thorough. Dozens of Italian customs officers fanned out across the country and began pounding on doors in Milan, Bologna, Pisa and Pesaro. Their target: a loose alliance of computer bulletin-board operators suspected of trafficking in stolen software. By last week, according to unofficial reports, the Italian police had shut down more than 60 computer bulletin boards and seized 120 computers, dozens of modems and more than 60,000 floppy disks. In their zeal, say the suspects, some officers of the Guardia di Finanza grabbed anything even remotely high-tech, including audiotapes, telephone-answering machines and multiplug electrical outlets. It was the most dramatic move yet in a determined—and some say increasingly desperate—effort by governments around the world to curb the spread of software piracy. The unauthorized copying of computer programs by American businesses alone deprived software publishers of $1.6 billion last year, a figure that swells to nearly $7.5 billion when overseas markets are included.

"Industry's loss on a global basis is staggering," says Ken Wasch, head of the U.S. Software Publishers Association. But government actions to stem the losses may be causing more problems than they solve. The Italian campaign, which began just as the newly elected right-wing government of media tycoon Silvio Berlusconi took office, hit largely left-leaning bulletin boards. And it is seen by some Italians as an ill-disguised attempt to suppress free speech on a troublesome new medium.[11]

Did the crackdown merely *seem* to some Italians to be an attempt to suppress free speech? Was it really an honest effort to "curb the spread of software piracy"?

Clearly, Italy had had a huge problem with piracy; however, the piracy had not been limited to software. Piracy of records, videotapes, and even books has been widespread. For example, according to *Billboard* magazine, by 1993 record piracy in the Italian market amounted to $83 million dollars annually.[12]

Although perhaps not the largest piracy problem in Italy, software piracy was nevertheless significant. But a caveat is necessary here. Italy earned its reputation not from pirated software that was distributed through bulletin boards, but rather from software piracy that was encouraged by Italy's largest corporations. For example, in 1989, *Datamation* reported on efforts by BSA (Business Software Association)[13] to crack down on piracy by Italian corporations. In some cases, small raids were carried out with the help of local police authorities. One raid which took place at the headquarters of the Montedison industrial group discovered that 90 percent of the Lotus and Ashton-Tate software found on workstations were allegedly unauthorized copies.[14]

In the words of Massimo Moggi, senior analyst at the Nomos Sistemi consulting firm, "In-house software piracy isn't always just a widespread random activity in some Italian firms. It's often a systematic procedure, institutionalized within the IS division."[15]

According to Moggi, in some cases software manuals were copied, neatly bound, and turned out with the company logo on the cover. Nor were the corporations particularly repentant. According to *Datamation,* attempts by BSA to negotiate with Montedison before and after the raid were rebuffed with a request that BSA "stop sending such invitations."

Some observers have held that in an environment with such widespread piracy, it is natural to suppose that pirate boards would be widespread. One can also make the case, however, that just the opposite is true. The widespread *institutionalized* piracy in Italy may have made *underground* pirate bulletin boards unnecessary. Who needs a pirate board when one can get the software for free at work? None of this is to deny that there were pirate BBSs in Italy at the time of the crackdown. The question is whether 1/3 of the boards in Italy were really engaged in piracy. More to the point, were any of the genuine pirate boards caught up in Operation Hardware 1?

Of course if piracy is defined broadly enough—for example, as being in possession at least one piece of unregistered software, most of the affected boards would probably fall under the definition. (For that matter, most people reading this article would count as pirates.) Some of the boards were running unregistered BBS software. No doubt others had illegally copied programs here and there that had been uploaded. But, of course, when we think of pirate boards we think of boards established with the exchange of warez as its primary purpose, and here it seems that the "haul" from the crackdown was embarrassingly small.

In fact, of the 100+ systems confiscated by the prosecutor of Pesaro, no specific evidence of wrongdoing has been made public except for two young boys which were allegedly the "center" of a huge piracy ring. As if to apologize for lack of results, the prosecutor remarked to *La Repubblica* that "there are hundreds of judicial reports, dozens of prosecutors that must occupy themselves with the local parts of the investigation beginning in Pesaro last March and the shadow of a computer piracy, all of which still has to be identified, that *probably* struck important private data banks"[16] [emphasis mine].

The embarrassingly slim haul from such a widespread operation is difficult to understand. It would have been a simple matter to log onto these systems and check for piracy first, or at least find an informant who had spotted pirated materials. Even in the notoriously clumsy Operation

Sundevil, all the boards had been examined beforehand (if only by informants).[17]

Yet there is no evidence that even these basic steps were taken in Italy. Rather there appears to have been a widespread seizing of BBSs without any evidence that they carried pirated software. Genuine pirate boards no doubt escaped this noisy and destructive sweep.

This last point has not been lost on the Italian BBS community. In a remarkable interview published in the electronic journal *Corriere Telematico*, Gianluca Neri put precisely this question to the Pesaro Prosecutor.

Neri What many system operators affirm is that by having hit innocent boards first, the investigation was helpful to the real pirates, who had all the time necessary to delete or hide all the software they had which was protected by copyright.
Pedrocchi I don't believe so. We acted in relation to the data that was in our possession.[18]

Of course the bust of PeaceLink is the hardest to make sense of if this operation was really aimed at curbing piracy. PeaceLink had explicit policies against software piracy and had campaigned against such piracy. It contained no pirated materials. It had little in the way of warez, period. Moreover, the idea that it trafficked in pirated software and kept trafficking in it a full three weeks after the first wave of the crackdown, indeed while the Taranto node was running an information center on the crackdown, is just not credible.

One thing is clear, if the true targets of the crackdown were software pirates, then the crackdown misfired badly. But what *was* the aim of this operation? What could the motives possibly have been? Three different theories have emerged to answer this question. According to the first theory, the operation really was intended to be a crackdown on piracy. It was simply a case of incredibly ignorant and incompetent prosecutors engaged in an electronic Keystone Cop routine. According to the second theory, the government really had the goal of clearing out BBSs to make room for larger media interests to start homesteading Italy's electronic frontier—that is, the government was working on behalf of electronic "Robber Barons." According to the third theory, it was an attempt by the

Italian government to crack down on what it perceived as dangerous political opposition. I'll take up each of these theories in turn.

Theory 1: The Keystone Cop Theory

It has been argued by many in the BBS community that the prosecutors were merely aimlessly following leads from a single piracy center. As the prosecutor himself (Pedrocchi) reconstructed the investigation: "We began on the cue of the general command of the financial police, from a 'center' in Pesaro for the sale of programs that were illicitly duplicated. Following the contacts that this 'center' had with diverse data banks we identified the other suspects. Now, examining the material, we are ascertaining if these latter data banks committed offenses."[19]

Why were they proceeding in such a counterproductive manner? Perhaps the prosecutors were in over their heads. Pedrocchi himself has described himself as "being ignorant, knowing absolutely nothing of computers. . . ."[20]

Others have observed that the eagerness of the prosecutors to claim ignorance should make us suspicious, particularly since claiming ignorance is a time-honored strategy for disguising genuine motives.

So, was this merely a case of Keystone Cops stumbling along with only the help of a Fido nodelist? Many are skeptical. Even the most computer-ignorant prosecutor must know that merely connecting with a pirate BBS does not make one another pirate BBS. That would be like saying that everyone who comes into contact with a bank robber is a bank robber. It is hard to imagine that any Italian prosecutor, much less the Guardia di Finanza, genuinely held such a simplistic view of guilt by association. Yet this is precisely the only evidence (or pretense) that the GF had for busting most of the BBSs involved.

It is of course possible that this operation was a nationwide campaign planned and executed by a collection of unthinkably stupid prosecutors. One thing is clear, however. We need to be careful that our interpretation of the fidobust is not colored by the American Operation Sundevil, which apparently *was* a case of ignorant prosecutors. As we shall see when we look at the alternative theories, Italy is a much different place.

Theory 2: The Robber Baron Theory

Just as in the old American West the Robber Barons forced out small settlers, perhaps the Italian government was working on behalf of corporate interests to push out the smaller BBSs with the goal of making room for the larger corporations to establish interests on the electronic frontier. In the words of one of the CyberNet sysops:

> In my opinion there are large economic lobbies interested in resizing (if not eliminating) the amateur networks in order to give space to their own telecommunications services (that in part already exist and in part are being created). With the presence of these free networks, they certainly won't succeed in occupying large chunks of the market. . . .[21]

Who would these interests be? One candidate would surely be Silvio Berlusconi himself, the Italian Premier and the leading media mogul of Italy. According to trade magazines like *Advertising Age,* Berlusconi's Fininvest corporation controls 40 percent of the Italian television audience, 33 percent of all periodical circulation, 18 percent of the book publishing market, and 16 percent of the newspaper circulation.[22]

More important, Berlusconi's corporation controls 60 percent of the TV advertising revenue,[23] and 40 percent of all advertising revenues total in Italy![24] Perhaps Berlusconi is uninterested in the electronic frontier and the potential future competition it poses for him, but that seems highly unlikely, particularly since Berlusconi's own publications routinely report on the electronic frontier, although often demonizing it. Surely Berlusconi could have seen a threat on the horizon to his near media monopoly. But would he be so low as to use his office to stamp out competition?

It is interesting to note that when Berlusconi first announced his intention to run, the media trade papers assumed it was primarily to secure his media empire from anti-trust activities by the Italian government. For example as Jennifer Clark of *Variety* reported,[25] "Common wisdom here holds that Berlusconi seeks only to protect his media empire which risks being dismembered through antitrust measures should the left win the elections."

If Berlusconi ran to secure the future of his corporation, the BBS crackdown need not be viewed as an isolated incident, but can be seen as part of a larger campaign by Berlusconi to use his office to secure his future share of the media market. The evidence for this hypothesis is compelling. Almost simultaneous with the BBS crackdown another much bigger crackdown was taking place. This one was aimed at silencing Berlusconi's only real opposition in broadcast television, the government-sponsored networks RAI 1, 2, and 3. Here Berlusconi proposed that government support of these three television networks be eliminated—effectively, that they be killed. According to the Berlusconi government, these networks were poorly managed; they were money losers. Of course the government ignored the fact that there was a conflict of interest.[26]

With the elimination of RAI, Berlusconi would essentially have the Italian airwaves to himself.

Berlusconi's threat created a firestorm of activity, with the President of the republic, Scalfaro, stepping in. The compromise solution? RAI could live if Berlusconi was allowed to install his own board of governors.

Placed in this context it seems pretty silly to ask whether Berlusconi would be so low as to close down some obscure electronic bulletin boards to silence his political opposition. The bulletin boards could be closed virtually without protest. His move against RAI was in the papers for weeks, faced fierce opposition, and was morally just as reprehensible.

Still, there are problems with the theory that Berlusconi was behind the action. For one, it seems like a very small thing for him to be concerned with—particularly when he had much bigger concerns, such as RAI. Some have argued that to suppose Berlusconi was behind the crackdown would be like accusing George Bush of being directly involved in Operation Sundevil. There is one difference, of course. George Bush was not a media magnate. The situation is more as though the Secret Service cracked down on wildcat oil drillers. Then we would be more apt to see the hand of George Bush.

Berlusconi is not the only candidate Robber Baron in this scenario, of course. There are numerous corporate interests that may be primed to move into the electronic frontier, and cozy relationships between large corporations and the Italian government remain widespread. The biggest problem with the Robber Baron theory, however, is that it is not clear what the crackdown gained. The ranks of BBSs have been thinned, but at most by a third. Unless Operation Hardware 1 was merely the first act in a widespread campaign against amateur BBSs, the action made little sense. But, of course, the operation made no more sense as an action against software piracy.

Theory 3: The Political Crackdown Theory

This theory requires some background. From the end of World War II until 1993, Italy was continually ruled by a coalition headed by the same political party—the Christian Democrats. As so often happens in cases of perpetual power, corruption found a home and eventually grew to engulf the government. In the case of Italy, it appears that most of the politicians were in the pocket of the Mafia. And, as we now know, the corruption had completely engulfed the highest levels of government (from the Socialist ex-prime minister Craxi to the Christian Democrat ex-prime minister and senator for life, Andreotti) as well as a number of business institutions (including, for example the Montedison corporation discussed above). For the most part, the average Italian considered the situation hopeless, and despaired of any solution.

Several years ago, however, a number of Italians did start resisting the corruption, most dramatically the prosecutors Borsellino and Falcone, who initiated a number of Mafia investigations and were assassinated in turn. The intended message was that prosecutors should go back to ignoring the Mafia and government corruption. Just the opposite happened, however. Led by a prosecutor named Di Pietro, a group of prosecutors in Milano, soon to be known as the Mani Pulite (or Clean Hands) prosecutors, took up the call and pursued the anti-corruption investigations. By the summer of 1993, hundreds of politicians were under investigation—it was becoming apparent that virtually the entire government was going to go to jail.

In the 1993 local elections, Italy's political center collapsed. Thoroughly discredited, the Christian Democrats and Socialists won few votes—electoral contests were being fought between the left and right wings. In some cases, the contests were between the Neofascists (including Mussolini's granddaughter) and the Communists. A third party, the Lega Nord (originally the Lega Lombarda), also emerged, advocating that the Italian republic be split up into several smaller republics, the north severing itself from the allegedly more corrupt south. It gained a number of seats in the house and senate.

Then Silvio Berlusconi stepped onto the political scene. He was, in effect, Ross Perot, Ted Turner, Rupert Murdoch, and George Steinbrenner all rolled into one. First and foremost, he was a powerful media magnate, owning a number of television stations throughout Italy as well as controlling dozens of magazines, newspapers, and tabloids. His holding company, Fininvest, controlled businesses ranging from cinema to supermarkets to financial services. Perhaps his most well known holding, however, was Milan AC, the best and most famous soccer team in Italy (he also held investments in a rugby team and two hockey teams).[27]

Taking the name of his new political party from the slogan of Italy's world cup soccer team, "Forza Italia!" he projected an optimistic vision to a country that at times seemed on the verge of disintegration. Best of all, he had been completely out of politics and was hence viewed as uncorrupted. Here, it seemed, was an alternative to Mafia-controlled Christian Democrats and Socialists, on the one hand, and to the Communists, and the Fascists on the other. Here, it seemed, was a new political center (albeit center-right).

Berlusconi's party won big in the nationwide elections, and he was able to form a coalition government with the help of the Lega Nord and, disturbingly, the Alianza Nazionale—the Neofascist party. Despite his troubling bedfellows the Italian media were for the most part supportive[28] (true, much of it was controlled by Berlusconi), and focused more on what kinds of victory parties the right wing would throw than on the consequences of having genuine Fascists in the government, or, for that matter, how someone with such extensive business dealings in Italy had avoided making illegal payoffs (*tangenti,* as they're called in Italy).

The genuinely disturbing issue was the large number of Fascists in the government—five members of the Alianza Nazionale held cabinet-level positions. Nor have these Fascist members of the government been sitting silently in their offices. Commenting on the recent decline in the lira, labor minister Clemente Mastella suggested that "New York's Jewish lobby" was behind the currency's fall, stating that "the presence of the National Alliance in the government worries New York's Jewish lobby.

. . . We should explain to Jewish high finance that Fini is increasingly distant from a nostalgic right."[29]

No less disturbing were the remarks of Alianza Nazionale chairman Gianfranco Fini during celebrations of the 50th anniversary of the D day invasion, arguing that D day marked the death of Europe's cultural identity.

While the non-Berlusconi-controlled media fell asleep on the job, there were pockets of vocal opposition. Significantly, some portions of Italian BBS culture was on Berlusconi's case from day one. For example, a number of CyberNet nodes offered strong opposition. No system, however, posed a greater threat than PeaceLink, with its topics devoted to disarmament, international cooperation, conscientious objection, anti-Mafia, peace movement, racism, human rights, and so on. More significantly, at the local level PeaceLink had waged a strong campaign against the mayor (*sindaco*) of Taranto. In the face of the mayor's local TV propaganda blitz, PeaceLink insisted that he renounce his past membership in the Fascist party.

According to the Political Crackdown Theory, it was simple to connect the dots after PeaceLink was hit by the Guardia di Finanza. In the words of Alessandro Marescotti (PeaceLink National Coordinator) "the current raid against our main node and data-bank clearly shows that in our country someone has an interest to shut down one of the very few organizations openly working against racism, war and Mafia actions. PeaceLink is dumb now, and so are the hundreds of volunteers, activists, journalists, citizens using its free services to make real changes in our society."[30]

If it seems implausible to suppose that the BBS networks would even catch the attention of the Italian government, just consider the following frightening article, from *La Repubblica,* August 3, 1994, p. 16, which summarizes a report prepared by the Italian Secret Service.[31]

> There is a new danger for Italian security. . . . Across the computer networks travel information and disinformation known to pollute public opinion, to create distrust and fear. . . . According to a secret service document: the phenomenon appeared worthy of more thorough informative research . . . like some computer systems at the international level, which can be used as instruments for the indirect acquisition of information. There is the risk that the computer networks are becoming utilized not only for transmitting news, BUT ALSO FOR THE

ACQUISITION OF SECRET INFORMATION, WHICH WOULD PUT THE NATIONAL SECURITY IN PERIL. Moreover, organized crime may have discovered the potential of computer systems and telecommunication for their illicit activities.

The Political Crackdown Theory does not depend on Berlusconi himself having knowledge of the operation. It would be enough that by appointing a number of Fascists to the government, Berlusconi helped create an atmosphere which the Guardia di Finanza was all too happy to exploit. Nevertheless there are problems with the Political Crackdown Theory, chief among them being that most of the targeted BBSs were not in fact political boards. But of course it is only fair to note that most of the boards targeted were probably not pirate boards either. If the crackdown could have been caused by ignorant prosecutors looking for pirated software in the wrong places, by parity of reasoning it could have been caused by ignorant prosecutors looking for left-wing activity in all the wrong places.

Realistically, given the available information, it is difficult to argue conclusively for any of the three theories (or combination of them). We hope that more information will be forthcoming. If not, we may never know for sure what Operation Hardware 1 was all about.

Concluding Remarks

Where do things stand? The Italian BBS community is gradually returning to normal. A number of sysops have had their systems returned, but dozens, perhaps as many as a hundred, are still awaiting the return of their equipment, and many others are waiting while the prosecutors sift through over 100,000 confiscated diskettes. (This could take some time!) On the bright side, the Italian BBS community has formed its own version of the Electronic Frontier Foundation, called ALCEI for the Associazione per la Libertà nella Comunicazione Elettronica Interattiva (Association for Freedom in Electronic Interactive Communications).

As sad as the whole story is, one of the saddest chapters is the utter failure of the electronic community in the United States to come to the aid of their friends in Italy. The distribution of information was spotty. There was no coordinated effort to help. And the great irony is that although the on-line community prides itself on the rapid dissemination of information, most members of that community, to this date, still know nothing about the Italian crackdown.

There really needs to be some permanent organization which can act quickly in situations like this—an agency that can coordinate both information gathering and distribution, that can lend technical assistance, that can orchestrate electronic petitions and mail drives, and that can lobby government leaders.

The Italian crackdown was not the first crackdown, and it certainly won't be the last. As groups increasingly use electronic communications for political action, they will increasingly come under the scrutiny of angry governments. Who will be there to help when the jackboots begin to fall?

What we have to realize is that national boundaries mean little in cyberspace, that when part of the electronic community is silenced in Italy it is part of *our* community that has been silenced. To stand by and do nothing in these cases is morally wrong and pragmatically shortsighted. We need some structure in place—some sort of Global Electronic Frontier Foundation that can step up and act immediately and decisively in these cases. We need all this, because the "next time" will be sooner than we think.

Notes

1. These messages were first reprinted in *Decoder: Rivista Internazionale Underground* 9 (1994): 648. My translations.

2. Consider, for example, the case of Riccardo Iacobucci, operator of a seized Fido BBS: "They took away everything I had: 12 CD-ROMs, the PC with the BBS, the modem, many floppy disks, some of them in an old cardboard box, with very old backups on . . . another half-mounted PC with no hard disk . . . even a multiple socket" (from the electronic journal *Corriere Telematico*, May 1994).

3. The list of affected networks is from the list in *Decoder: Rivista Internazionale Underground* 9 (1994): 644.

4. Press release of the Nucleo Regionale di Polizia Tributaria della Guardia di Finanza di Torino (May 25, 1994). Translation posted to the WELL by Bernardo Parrella (berny@well.sf.ca.us).

5. Ibid.

6. *La Repubblica*, June 18, p. 16.

7. Bruce Sterling, *The Hacker Crackdown* (New York: Bantam Books, 1992), 156.

8. In fact, this understates the involvement of PeaceLink, which was also involved in setting up helicopter and airplane relief flights for the sick and elderly in the former Yugoslavia.

9. From an interview of Giovanni Pugliese by Luca Scarlini, host of "Cyberspace," 10:45 on Monday, June 6, 1994, on Nova Radio, Firenze (fm 101.5). The interview was transcribed by Andrea Sannucci (a.sannucci@agora.stm.it). My translation.

10. E-chat with Andrea Sannucci (a.sannucci@agora.stm.it) on the Senza Confine BBS, Macerata (0733-236370). My translation.

11. *Time,* June 1994.

12. *Billboard,* May 22, 1993, p. 79.

13. BSA is a Washington, D.C., organization whose members include Aldus Corp., Ashton-Tate, Autodesk Inc., Lotus, Microsoft Word, and WordPerfect Corp.

14. Janette Martin, "Pursuing Pirates," *Datamation,* August 1, 1989, pp. 41–42.

15. Ibid.

16. *La Repubblica,* June 18, p. 16.

17. See Sterling, *The Cracker Crackdown.*

18. From the electronic journal *Corriere Telematico,* May 1994.

19. Ibid.

20. Ibid.

21. E-chat with Andrea Sannucci.

22. Michelle McCarter, "Berlusconi's Ad Strength Called into Question by EC." *Advertising Age,* March 26, 1990, p. 30.

23. Ibid.

24. Deborah Young, "Berlusconi Wins Battle in TV Antitrust War," *Variety,* April 20, 1992, p. 38.

25. January 31, 1994, p. 63.

26. Of course, given Berlusconi's vast financial empire, conflicts of interest are found at "every turn," according to *Business Week,* May 2, 1994, p. 35.

27. For a recent list of Fininvest holdings, see *L'Espresso,* August 12, 1994, p. 39.

28. See the article in the *Nation,* April 25, 1994, p. 548.

29. Alan Cowell, "Remarks by a Cabinet member Adds to the Italian Prime Minister's Difficulties." *New York Times,* August 13, 1994.

30. Source: Bernardo Parella (berny@well.sf.ca.us), in *CuD.*

31. The Italian Secret Service is an interesting story in its own right. SIFAR (the Servizio informazioni forze armante) when formed after World War II apparently rehired a number of members of Mussolini's secret political police OVRA (Opera vigilanza repressione antifascismo) and has had a tainted reputation ever since. According to some reports it collaborated with the CIA on a project to bug the pontifical library. For an interesting history of SIFAR and other Italian secret agencies, see Giuseppe de Lutiis, *Storia dei servizi segretti in Italia.* (Politica e società, #40). Reprint, Rome: Riuniti, 1985.

Appendix 3a: General Information About Electronic Frontiers Italy (ALCEI)

ALCEI—Electronic Frontiers Italy (Associazione per la Libertà nella Comunicazione Elettronica Interattiva/Association for Freedom in Electronic Interactive Communications) is an association of people dedicated to affirm and protect constitutional rights for "electronic citizens" as new communications technologies emerge. ALCEI is focused on the safeguard of freedom of expression and personal privacy for any person using electronic communication systems for personal, social, cultural, professional activities. ALCEI was founded in Milan at the end of July 1994 and is inspired by the principles and goals of the Electronic Frontier Foundation.

The main objectives of ALCEI—EF Italy are:

- To ensure the protection of Constitutional rights for citizens using computer-based communication systems, researching and advising on current and future laws to ensure those rights.
- To monitor, disclose and oppose any behavior intended to put restriction, censorship or suppression of free circulation of electronic communications and exchange of information and ideas, no matter how controversial.
- To support, encourage and promote the development and use of electronic communications, in order to enable all citizens to have a voice in the information age.
- To inform and educate the community at large about computer-based communication systems, emphasizing their responsible use and their positive consequences for our society.

The activities of ALCEI—EF Italy include:

- Organization of electronic mailing lists and public online conferences distributed throughout Italian systems for discussion on the above mentioned topics and related activities.

- Research of current Italian and International laws regarding bulletin board systems and other online information services to set up guide- lines for providers of the these services, detailing their rights and responsibilities.
- Production and distribution of information in different formats, including newsletters of various types for local media, general public and the digital community at large.
- Establishment of public meetings and programs focused on the use of computer-based communications, in collaboration with local groups and individuals.
- Regular exchange of information and experiences with similar International organizations and online communities.

ALCEI—EF Italy is a nonprofit, nonpartisan organization. It is not tied to any political party or financial corporation. It does not accept any government grant. Its activities are completely supported by membership and personal contributions; its board and other active members are volunteers and receive no compensation.

Membership in ALCEI—EF Italy

Annual Membership Fees

Regular: 50.000 ItLire, US $30
Low-income/Student: 20.000 ItLire, US $15
Supporting Groups, Organizations: 300.000 ItLire, US $200
Donations of any amount are greatly appreciated :-)))
For more information : <alcei@mailbox.iunet.it>

Appendix 3b: Why I Have Joined ALCEI

Bruce Sterling

My name is Bruce Sterling and I am an author and journalist from Austin, Texas, USA. On December 3, 1994, I joined a group called "Associazione per la libertà nella comunicazione elettronica interattiva." Not only did I join ALCEI, but I have paid my dues in full!

One might well wonder why a writer from far-away Texas should join such a group. After all, I don't speak Italian. I even have difficulty correctly pronouncing the word "ALCEI." I am an American citizen and have no right, need, or intention to interfere in the internal political affairs of the Republic of Italy. When it comes to the issue of electronic interactive communication, there is plenty going on in my own United States—more than any one person can possibly encompass and understand.

I am nevertheless intensely interested in electronic affairs in Italy—an interest which has grown, almost despite myself, during the past year. There are several reasons. One is that Italy is the first country in the world whose government is being run by a television mogul. I make no judgment whether his policies are good or bad for the Republic of Italy or the well-being of its citizens. I would point out that it is not unusual for the power structure of a government to reflect the major sources of power, money and influence in its economy. As society moves from material industrial power to informatic post-industrial power, it seems only likely that a television tycoon could become a head of state.

Will Italy be the only country in the world to have such a political development? I very much doubt this. On the contrary, I suspect that in this instance Italy has become a political laboratory for the future of the rest of the world.

In 1992, I wrote a book called *Hacker Crackdown: Law and Disorder on the Electronic Frontier.* In Italian it was published as *Giro di vite contro gli hacker.* Much of this book involved an American police operation called Operation Sundevil, which took place in 1990 and involved police seizure of bulletin board systems. I considered this a very important matter, so much so that I devoted a year and a half of my life to researching and writing on the topic.

In Italy, however, in May 1994, Italian police launched an attack on Italian bulletin board systems that was at least twice the size of Operation Sundevil and may have been five times as large. This was the largest police seizure of bulletin board systems in world history. Italian police may not have been the first to carry out large-scale attacks on bulletin board systems, but they have done it with more gusto than anyone else in the world.

I would like to know a lot more about this operation of May 1994. As is common on the electronic frontier, reports are confused and inconsistent. Clearly the Italian police and prosecutors involved are not overly anxious to discuss the matter. If I do successfully learn anything about this matter, however, or about others that may happen, I believe it will be because of ALCEI. ALCEI was formed after this event, and not in response to it; but now there is a watchdog. This does not mean an end to such troubles, of course. However, now at least there is an organized group of people who will make it their business to study and discuss events like these. I wish them well.

In early December 1994, I was in Rome to celebrate the release of one of my novels in Italian translation, *Islands in the Net (Isola nella rete).* No sooner had I arrived in Rome than I was alarmed and saddened to hear of a computer-intrusion attack on the Adn-Kronos news agency. I regard attacks on news agencies, from whatever quarter and for whatever reason, as a very serious matter. Computer intrusions that attack a source of information to the public are a serious crime. Such activity is immoral and deserving of punishment. The Adn-Kronos case is particularly repellent because of the megalomaniacal boasting of the intruder, who threatened the public with his group's intent to harm society and disrupt telecommunications.

I make no judgment about the existence or nonexistence of the so-called Falange Armata. Nevertheless, to my knowledge this is the first case in the world of a computer-intrusion attack by someone claiming, or pretending, to be an armed terrorist group. Once again Italy is setting the pace for what may become general developments worldwide.

Historically, it has not been uncommon for political developments to begin in Italy and spread to the rest of the world. The Roman Empire, for instance. The Renaissance—a great gift of Italian civilization. This alone would make it worthwhile to study Italian developments—even without the twentieth century's rather less happy experiences with Italian political innovation.

It is not my business to direct how Italians should choose to run their own affairs, in cyberspace or elsewhere. However, I think it is not too much to ask that I be allowed to watch—and to watch closely. I hope to do exactly that, with the help of my new colleagues in ALCEI. I would urge others of similar interests to lend their support to the ALCEI group. I wish them every success in the new year, 1995—and beyond into the third millennium of our common global civilization.

Contributors

John Perry Barlow
Retired cattle rancher, lyricist for The Grateful Dead, cofounder and board member of the EFF
barlow@well.sf.ca.us

Amy S. Bruckman
MIT Media Laboratory
Massachusetts Institute of Technology
Cambridge, Massachusetts
asb@media-lab.media.mit.edu

David Chaum
david@digicash.nl

Pavel Curtis
Xerox PARC
Palo Alto, California

Dorothy E. Denning
Georgetown University
Computer Science Department
denning@cs.georgetown.edu

Julian Dibbell
Cyberspace writer for *The Village Voice,* among other publications
julian@panix.com

James DiGiovanna
Department of Philosophy
SUNY Stony Brook
Stony Brook, New York 11794

Philip Elmer-Dewitt
Writer and science editor for *Time* magazine
ped@well.com

Simson L. Garfinkel
Senior editor, *NeXTWORLD* magazine

Mike Godwin
On-line counsel for the EFF
mnemonic@eff.org

Paul Heckel
HyperRacks, Inc.
Los Altos, CA 94022

humdog
Resident poet for the *Fringe Ware Review*
humdog@usa.net
humdog@echonyc.com

Mitchell Kapor
Founder of Lotus Development Corporation, cofounder of the EFF
kapor@eff.org

The League for Programming Freedom
1 Kendall Square #143
P.O. Box 9171
Cambridge, MA 02139

Steven Levy
Author of *Hackers,* and the "The Iconoclast" column for *Macworld*
steven@well.com

Peter Ludlow
Department of Philosophy
SUNY Stony Brook
ludlow@well.com

Timothy C. May
Retired physicist, cofounder of the Cypherpunks
tcmay@netcom.com

The Mentor
Former member of the Legion of Doom
mentor@eden.com

Elizabeth M. Reid
Cultural Studioes Program
University of Melbourne, Australia
emr@ee.mu.oz.au

Howard Rheingold
Editor of the *Whole Earth Review* and author of *Virtual Communities*
hlr@well.com

Jeffrey Shallit
Department of Computer Science
University of Waterloo
Cofounder, Electronic Frontier Canada
shallit@graceland.uwaterloo.ca

Richard M. Stallman
Creator of EMACS, president of the Free Software Foundation, cofounder of the League for Programming Freedom

Bruce Sterling
Science fiction writer, author of *The Hacker Crackdown*
bruces@well.com

Philip R. Zimmermann
Independent software engineer and author of PGP
prz@acm.org

Sources

"Selling Wine without Bottles: The Economy of Mind on the Global Net" by John Perry Barlow. Print version appeared in *Wired* 2, no. 3 (1994).

"Why Patents Are Bad for Software" by Simson L. Garfinkel, Richard M. Stallman, and Mitchell Kapor. Reprinted from *Issues in Science and Technology*, Fall 1991, pp. 50–55.

"Against Software Patents" by The League for Programming Freedom. Reprinted from *Communications of the ACM* 35, no. 1 (January 1992): 17–121.

"Debunking the Software Patent Myths" by Paul Heckel. Reprinted from *Communications of the ACM* 35, no. 6 (July 1992): 121–140.

"So You Want to Be a Pirate?" Reprinted from *Pirate* 1, no. 1 (June 1989).

"Some 'Property' Problems in a Computer Crime Prosecution" by Mike Godwin. First appeared in September 1992 in the *Cardozo Law Forum*, Cardozo Law School, New York.

"The Conscience of a Hacker" by The Mentor. *Phrack* 14 (1987).

"The Prisoner: Phiber Optik Goes Directly to Jail" by Julian Dibbell. Reprinted from the *Village Voice*, January 11, 1994.

"Concerning Hackers Who Break into Computer Systems" by Dorothy E. Denning. *Phrack* 32 (1990). Postscript, June 11, 1995.

"Congressional Testimony by Emmanuel Goldstein." U.S. Gov. Printing Office Serial 103-53, "Hearings Before the Subcommittee on Telecommunications and Finance of the Committee on Energy and Commerce," House of Representatives, 103rd Congress, First Session, April 29 and June 9, 1993.

"How PGP Works/Why Do You Need PGP?" by Philip R. Zimmermann. Reprinted from *The Official PGP User's Guide* (Cambridge, Mass.: The MIT Press, 1995), 9–12, 5–7.

"Crypto Rebels" by Steven Levy. Print version appeared in *Wired* 1, no. 2 (1993).

"Jackboots on the Infobahn" by John Perry Barlow. Print version appeared in *Wired* 2, no. 4 (1994).

"The Clipper Chip Will Block Crime" by Dorothy E. Denning. Print version appeared in *Newsday*, February 22, 1994.

"The Denny–Barlow Clipper Chip Debate" by Dorothy E. Denning and John Perry Barlow. *Time* Online, March 10, 1994. Courtesy *Time* Magazine and America Online. Formatted by John Perry Barlow.

"Achieving Electronic Privacy" by David Chaum. Reprinted from *Scientific American,* August 1992, 96-101. © 1992 by Scientific American, Inc. All rights reserved.

"Censoring Cyberspace" by Philip Elmer-Dewitt. Print version appeared in *Time,* November 21, 1994.

"Virtual Community Standards: BBS Oscenity Case Raises New Legal Issues" by Mike Godwin. A version of this article appeared in the *San Francisco Examiner*, August 14, 1994. B5.

"Public Networks and Censorship" by Jeffrey Shallit. Talk at the Ontario Library Association, Session on Public Networks and Censorship, January 15, 1995.

"Sex and the Single Sysadmin: The Risks of Carrying Graphic Sexual Materials" by Mike Godwin. Print version appeared in *Internet World,* March/April 1994.

"Gender Swapping on the Internet" by Amy S. Bruckman. Reprinted from *Proceedings of INET '93.* © The Internet Society, 1993.

"Text-based Virtual Realities: Identity and the Cyborg Body" by Elizabeth M. Reid. From "Cultural Formations in Text-based Virtual Realities," MA thesis, Cultural Studies Program, University of Melbourne, January 1994.

"A Rape in Cyberspace; or How an Evil Clown, a Haitian Trickster Spirit, Two Wizards, and a Cast of Dozens Turned a Database into a Society" by Julian Dibbell. *Village Voice,* December 21, 1993.

"Communication and Community on Internet Relay Chat: Constructing Communities" by Elizabeth Reid. From "Electropolis: Communication and Community on Internet Relay Chat," honors thesis, Department of History, University of Melbourne, 1991.

"A Slice of My Life in My Virtual Community" by Howard Rheingold. June 1992.

"Losing Your Voice on the Internet" by James DiGiovanna. Written for this volume.

Appendix 1: "Crime and Puzzlement" by John Perry Barlow. A version of this article appeared in the *Whole Earth Review* (1990).

Appendix 3a: "Information about Electronic Frontiers Italy (ALCEI); About ALCEI Membership."

Appendix 3b "Why I Have Joined ALCEI" by Bruce Sterling. December 9, 1994.

Index

Note: Author entries are indicated by italic page numbers.